# Learn to Read Your Birth-chart in 5 Steps

*Your Astrological Roadmap for Life*

A *Making Sense of It* Workbook

## Francis O'Neill
**DFAstrolS | DMSAstrol**

Some Inspiration (Publications)

# Learn to Read Your Birth-chart in 5 Steps
## Your Astrological Roadmap for Life

Copyright © 2024 Francis O'Neill. All Rights Reserved.

ISBN: **9781919623948** (Paperback)

A catalogue record for this book is available from the British Library (UK)

No part of this publication may be reproduced, stored in any form or by any means, graphic, electronic, or mechanical, including photocopying, scanning, recording or otherwise, without prior permission, in writing, from the author, except by a reviewer, who may quote brief passages in a review.

Although every precaution has been taken in the preparation of this book, the publisher and author assume no responsibility for errors or omissions. Neither is any liability assumed for damages resulting from the use of this information contained herein.

Cover image: by author

Printed by: **Lightning Source**

**A Making Sense of It workbook**

**About the *Making Sense of It* series**
These are books, by the author, linked together by the common thread of seeking to discover and aid better understanding of spirituality and spiritual health.

Other titles in the series: **Discover Proper Astrology** books | **Life and Death: Making Sense of It**. | **Love's Story of Why We Are Here** | **Steps to Health, Wealth & Inner Peace** | **Christmas Past.** For availability and updates on these titles please visit the website.

Some Inspiration (Publications)
*SomeInspiration.com*
Cotswolds, UK

# Acknowledgements

To all the people who have encouraged and/or taught me, through their books, chats or teaching, about Western astrology. What a journey and home-coming. I wouldn't have missed it for the world.

Here are a few of those wonderful people: John Addey, Stephen Arroyo, John Astrop, Reinhold Ebertin, Michel Gauqelin, Liz Greene, Andrea Grieveson, Charles Harvey, Margaret Hone, Richard Idemon, Tad (A.T.) Mann, Jeff Mayo, Dane Rudhyar, Howard Sasportas, and Martin Schulman.

# Please leave a review of this book

As an author I really value the feedback of people reading my book/s. I need to know that my contribution is helping, or not.

If, in the course of reading this book, you have decided that you enjoy it, would you please consider leaving a thoughtful review of it; on the bookstore where you purchased it. I'd love to hear how it helped you or impacted on you. Thank you.

# Contents

Introduction

Introducing Western Astrology ................................................................................. 1

About the Course ....................................................................................................... 7

The Course ............................................................................................................... 23

Key to the Astrological Symbols ............................................................................. 24

**Step One: Learn about the Birth-chart** ............................................................... 27

    Part 1 Introducing the Birth-chart ..................................................................... 28

    Part 2 A closer look at the Birth-chart .............................................................. 32

    Part 3 A look at Mozart's birth-chart ................................................................. 35

**Step Two: Learn to Read the Signs** .................................................................... 40

    Part 1 Typical (and atypical) Sun Sign Descriptions ........................................ 41

    Part 2 The Zodiac Signs Matrix ......................................................................... 65

    Part 3 Compensatory behaviour ....................................................................... 75

    Part 4 Zodiac Themes ........................................................................................ 77

    Step 2 Quizzes ................................................................................................... 83

**Step Three: Learn to Read the Planets & Aspects** ............................................ 89

    Part 1 An Astronomical Overview ..................................................................... 91

    Part 2 Planet Rulership .................................................................................... 100

    Part 3 What each of the Planets mean ........................................................... 104

    Part 4 Reading the Aspects ............................................................................. 110

    Step 3 Quizzes ................................................................................................. 120

    Step Three Extra Practice homework ............................................................. 129

**Step Four: Learn to Read the Angles & Houses** ............................................. 133

    Part 1 Learn to read the Angles ...................................................................... 134

    Part 2 Learn to Read the Houses .................................................................... 140

    Step 4 Quizzes ................................................................................................. 149

## Step Five: Learn to Read Your Birth-chart..................157
### Opening Comments..................158
### Part 1 A Broad Reading of your Chart..................160
### Part 2 A Comprehensive Approach..................182
### Part 3 Example: Using Bill Lomas chart..................188
### Part 4 Report on Bill Lomas Example Birth-chart..................206
### Step 5 Exercises..................213

## One Step Further: The Spiritual Roadmap..................229
### Introduction..................230
### Part 1 Contemplating the Orchestra..................236
### Part 2 The Running Order of the Signs..................240
### Part 3 Self-reflection/self-development..................252
### Part 4 The Moon Nodes..................254

## The Resources..................267
### The Zodiac Signs Resource..................268
### The Planets by Sign Resource..................286
### The Planetary Aspects Resource..................305
### The Angles Resource..................334
### The Twelve Houses Resource..................343
### The Planets by House Resource..................350

## Books & Where to Next Links..................368
## Glossary of Terms..................370
## Index..................376
## Figs..................378
## About the Author..................380

# Introduction

Here's a question for you. What is the purpose of your life? Or put another way: Why are you here? What are you here to experience, to learn or to give?

In our Western culture, we're not really used to such questions, or dealing with them in any serious way. So, if you are now thinking of some glib answers to them, it would not surprise me. In my past, I've been there with the glib answers too.

However, if you have a sense that there is a greater purpose to your being alive than, say, having a good job, holidays abroad, having a nice house and a nice car – in other words being successful in obtaining the trappings of modern life (and there is nothing wrong with those goals in themselves) – then seriously contemplating these questions could well be the starting point of your own great adventure.

Let me put my cards on the table... I believe we do have a higher purpose for being here. We come here because we have something to discover, something to learn about ourselves, and something to contribute. I also believe astrology can greatly help us discover our higher purpose, to find our Self, to open doors back to our soul. That comes after 40 years of involvement with Western astrology.

My view is, that any person with the desire, and/or ability, to peer beyond the constructs, beliefs and values we have been taught to live by, will find nourishment for the soul from studying their astrological make-up.

But to achieve this, you cannot do it through the level of astrology that is provided through our media – our newspapers, magazines or our "Stars" online. With a few exceptions, that's the shallow end of what passes for astrology. You will need, instead, to learn how to read and study your own unique birth-chart, for the insight that it offers you.

And you can do this by following the five steps laid out in this workbook.

**Learn to Read Your Birth-chart in 5 Steps**, is an astrology course workbook that could prove to be more than just another course, indeed a lifelong adventure for you, if you let it.

This project is close to my heart... I really want for you to start exploring astrology from a different perspective to how it is publicly perceived – if that is where you are coming from.

You can work through this workbook as an endeavour to learn more about Western astrology. You could, indeed, treat it as a leisure interest, as a bit of fun to see whether there is anything in astrology for you. I would say, if that is all that motivates you, perhaps don't bother as you will probably find it slow going.

Or you can treat it as a serious exploration, a way, a roadmap into finding your higher Self.

Whatever motivates you, I hope you will find this book stimulating; providing you with an interesting enquiry and an exciting journey of discovery.

# Introducing Western Astrology

## A quick tour around Western astrology

One thing you need to know, from the bat, is that there are a number of versions of astrology. In ancient times astrology developed in different forms across the globe. Today the main forms are Indian (or Vedic), Chinese, and Western astrology.

In the West you could say there are two versions of astrology. There is the popular (or pop) astrology version. This is the version (already mentioned) we find in the media. It's the "stars" or "star signs" in newspapers, magazines and online.

It might surprise you to know that star signs, in newspapers, have only been around since the 1930s. It began with the Sunday Express 24th August 1930. Originally the paper provided insight into people and events, using birth-charts, but it was soon transformed into something that everyone could participate in – that is what we see today. It really doesn't take much to work out that star signs are a marketing device - for entertainment purposes only.

Unfortunately, pop astrology does also serve to misrepresent the other, authentic version; that is modern Western astrology – also known as natal astrology.

I'm sure most of us will have heard of, and most probably seen, pop astrology. And, fairly, I'd expect that quite a number of us will also tend to assume that all astrology is the same as what we see in the media. I certainly did view it that way, back in my twenties. I thought astrology wasn't worth looking into back then. But it is not the same, of course. There are huge differences. Some of which will become obvious from the discussion below – and most certainly from the course itself.

One obvious difference to mention is that, while pop astrology has been around since the 1930s, Western astrology has been around and developed over thousands of years – handed down via Greek design.

Another obvious point is that, the birth-chart (used in Western astrology) includes all the signs of the zodiac, and all planets – not just the position the Sun was in (the Star sign) when you or I were born.

# Defining Western Astrology

Astrology is an ancient holistic and symbolical system that seeks to make sense of events in time, space and place.

It can be used for all sorts of events: in business, politics, countries, the launch of a ship or rocket, the opening of a building, the answer to a question, to the planting of a tree. But, as you might guess, the events that we are mostly interested in, is ourselves, that is what astrology has to say about us.

Astrology achieves this through recording and evaluating the birth moment of such events (drawing on the date, time and place of a birth), thus providing information for unique individual events.

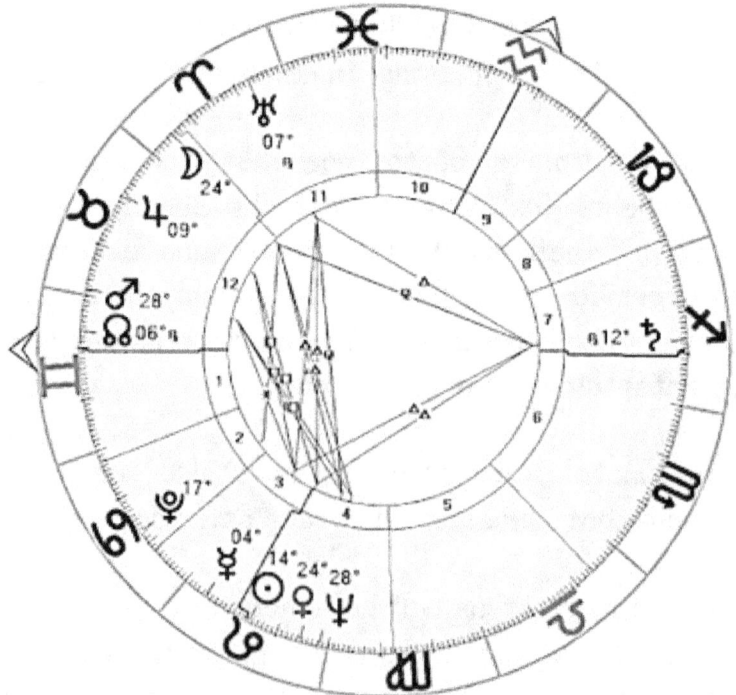

**Fig.1.** Birth-chart of the magician James Randi

The birth moment is the starting point (or projected starting point if anticipated sometime in the future) for evaluating meaningful potential and possible outcomes.

The template it uses to achieve an understanding of events, that is the birth-chart (or otherwise natal chart, or horoscope - see Fig 1), incorporates the 12 zodiac signs, the position of all the planets of our solar system, except the Earth. It is the solar system as seen from the Earth vantage point. So, think of the Earth as being in the centre of the scheme.

Stars and asteroids may also be included in the arrangement. It also includes what are known as the angles, houses and aspects. More on these in the course.

# The Zodiac

As is well-known, there are twelve signs in the zodiac. They each represent a particular theme and archetypal energy in a cyclic development that matures around the circle.

Originally the stars of the ecliptic belt became the fixed (sidereal) zodiac for the yearly calendar cycle. Later the tropical zodiac, linked to the movement of the Earth around the Sun was developed.

Because of the matrix operating behind the zodiac, the order of the signs is always the same: Aries to Taurus to Gemini to Cancer etc. The order is cyclic and begins again in Aries. The signs run in an anti-clockwise direction.

This direction of motion is respected by astrologers whether in the northern or southern hemispheres. Also, most astrologers in the Southern Hemisphere follow the Northern Hemisphere orientation for the birth-chart itself:

> In the chart for a birth south of the Equator, the Midheaven – the Sun's position at noon – is in the north instead of in the south, as it is on a Northern Hemisphere birth-chart. Technically, the Ascendant (the east) should therefore be on the right, but most southern astrologers observe the northern orientation, keeping the Ascendant on the left. The Sun enters Aries on or near March 21, but in the Southern Hemisphere this is the autumnal equinox. ... Some astrologers advocate using opposite signs

for the Southern Hemisphere so that the Sun would enter Aries on or about September 23 and correspond to the southern spring. But this solution introduces a serious dilemma for casting charts of births on or near the Equator, and, more importantly, does not seem in any way justified by the experience of astrologers working in the Southern Hemisphere.

Larousse Encyclopedia of Astrology[1]

# Two Zodiacs in Common Use

What is not so well-known, by the public at large, is that there are two zodiacs in use by astrologers.

## The Sidereal Zodiac

The sidereal zodiac involves the twelve constellations of stars around the ecliptic belt. The ecliptic is the path the Earth and planets take around the Sun. This zodiac is mostly used in Vedic astrology – but also by some Western astrologers.

By the way, although there are now 13 constellations identified along the zodiac belt (with Ophiuchus being the 13th), astrology still runs on twelve. This is because it is based upon the number 12 (and its divisions), not the constellations – and it is certainly not based upon a prime number.

## The Tropical Zodiac

This zodiac divides the tropical year into twelve 30-degree segments. The zodiac begins with Aries at the Vernal (or spring) equinox – around the 21st of March each year. Note, you'll find more on the tropical zodiac in Step One of the course.

At one time the now two zodiacs were one zodiac. The discovery of the Precession of the Equinoxes changed that into two zodiacs. It was discovered that the Vernal (or Spring) equinox is gradually moving backwards (a little each year) when measured against the star constellations. The Vernal equinox now begins towards the end of Pisces and entering Aquarius. This is where belief in the Age of Aquarius springs from.

You can read more on this in the **Bonus Pack** - see under **About the Course** section for more information.

# The Planets

The planets are the main moving markers in astrology.

In Western astrology there are ten major planets. These are the Sun, Moon, Mercury, Venus, Mars, Jupiter, Saturn, Uranus, Neptune and Pluto.

The Sun and Moon are also treated as planets (or moving bodies of light) in astrology. As is Pluto also treated as a planet - even though now relegated to a dwarf planet in astronomy.

Stars, asteroids, nodes and other components may also be brought into the equation by the astrologer's preference.

They all have meaning and that meaning is further influenced depending upon where they occur in the birth-chart (the astrological template) at the chosen moment in time.

# The Aspects

The aspects are the angular relationship between planets (essentially); and the meaning that can be derived from them.

The most common major aspects evaluated are: the Conjunction 0 degrees, Sextile 60 degrees, Square 90 degrees, Trine 120 degrees and the Opposition 180 degrees. Take a look at the chart above (Fig.1): the aspects are in the central circle.

# The Angles and Houses

The Angles are the rising sign (or Ascendant) and the sign on the Midheaven at the top of the birth-chart – see Fig 2. This is based upon the moment of birth.

Their opposite numbers – the Descendant (opposite to Ascendant) and Imum Coeli (opposite to the Midheaven) are equally important but tend to be given less emphasis in interpretation.

The houses run off the ascending point in an anti-clockwise direction.

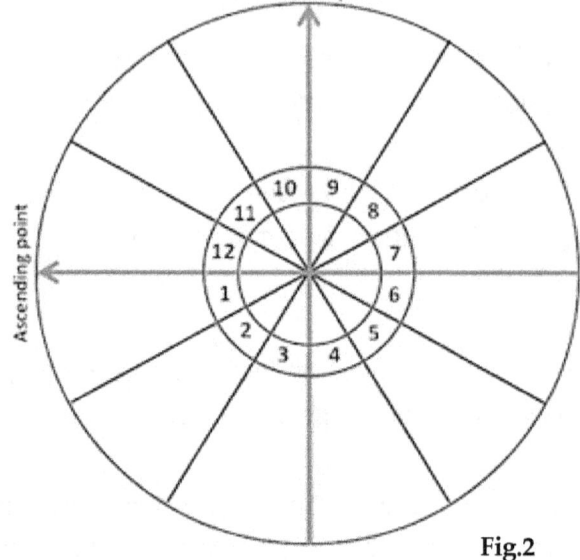

Fig.2

So that's a quick introductory tour around Western astrology. The course materials will, of course, cover all of this in much more detail.

# References

---

[1] Brau JL, Weaver H, Edmands A (1977) Larousse Encyclopedia of Astrology, P260, McGraw-Hill Book Company.

# About the Course

## The adventure you're now on...

What is publicly known of the ancient and modern art of Western astrology bears small resemblance to what, I'm sure, you will discover working through this course.

Astrology, arguably, offers one of the most profound means of capturing and interpreting a moment in Earth time and space.

In context, I happen to believe that the birth-chart, your own birth-chart, a product outcome of astrology, is one of the most important documents you can have access to, in understanding who you are - in aiding you to grasp the energy and drives behind your life.

My hope is that you will give time to learning to read your own chart for the insight and benefits, I believe, it most certainly can provide for you.

# Course Aims & Objectives

## Course aims

- To enable you to become conversant with Western natal astrology and learn how to read a Western astrological birth-chart. This could be any birth-chart but it is assumed the main focus will be your own chart.
- To offer opportunity for exploring your birth-chart as a means to provide spiritual insight – in One Step Further.

- To provide you with an excellent springboard towards your study of astrology much further should you so wish.

## What the course provides:

1. How to access or create your own Western astrological birth-chart. Software advice, plus an elementary guide to two programs is also included.
2. A full (intermediate level) introduction to all the key components of Western astrology.
3. A proven method for reading birth-charts.
4. Further help/resources for your learning journey into Western astrology.

## Schedule:

There are five Steps to work through for the main course, plus one extra. These are:

Step One: Introducing Your Birth-chart
Step Two: Learn how to read the Signs
Step Three: Learn how to read the Planets
Step Four: Learn how to read the Angles & Houses
Step Five: Learn how to read your Birth-chart
One Step Further: The Spiritual Roadmap

## What the course will do for you:

By the end of the course, you will...
- Have become familiar with key astrological components, and the workings of a modern Western astrological birth-chart.
- Be able to interpret key components of a birth-chart.
- Be able to carry out a fundamental-to-intermediate reading of your birth-chart – and indeed interpret other birth-charts as provided during the course.

- **Important**: It must be understood that developing skill at reading your birth-chart (or any chart), requires time, practice and dedication. This is not something one completes overnight.
- You will have access to valuable resources and opportunity for furthering your interest/studies.

## Resources:

Resources provided:
- Help on getting your birth-chart drawn up either through a website or some recommended software – if you wish to do it for yourself.
- The workbook contains interpretational (cookbook style) resources on each of the Signs, Planets, Angles and Houses – and more…
- The course includes quizzes and/or exercises – to help you firm up your knowledge.
- The course also provides some recommended reading and useful links to further your study of astrology.
- And there is an optional Bonus Pack…

## Optional Bonus Pack download

Getting hold of this book allows you access to the Bonus Pack that accompanies the workbook. You can download it off this link: https://someinspiration.com/bonuspack

The pack, which is FREE, includes:

- Birth-chart Resource - images of all birth-charts used on the course.
- Chart Shaping Resource – this provides a helicopter view of chart reading, not covered in the main course.
- Hemisphere Emphasis Resource – another helicopter view of the chart not covered in the main course.
- Plus, seven articles on Western astrology – including perspectives on how astrology works.
- Provided in PDF format. All items written by the author.

# You Need a Birth-chart

You will need your own birth-chart for this course!
You will be looking at a number of birth-charts (or "natal-charts" if you prefer) during the course. It is possible therefore to follow the course without your own chart to refer to. I would however press on you to have, or get hold of, your own chart.

Having your own birth-chart quite simply will make the course all the more interesting and fulfilling for you – providing insight into your own situation, and opportunity for making a comparison with others. There is nothing quite like finding your way around your own chart as a means of learning and to refer back to. Indeed, this is the only way the coursework provides true value.

Of course, if you already have your own chart at this point, that's great! You are good to go. If not, take note of these essential requirements to get it drawn up:

- Your date of birth.
- Local time of your birth – as exact as possible.
- And your place of birth – which is converted into longitude and latitude.

Getting hold of a birth-chart is easy these days. You can either get it done for you or, you can do it for yourself – with the right software...

## Getting your birth-chart done for you

You can easily get your birth-chart done for you, and for free, on the Web. Search for **Astrodienst**, which comes to mind. Also, **Café Astrology** is another. Alternatively, visit my site, **Some Inspiration** (SomeInspiration.com) and search **Need a Birth-chart?** Note, this is not an automated system and I do make a small charge for providing this service.

Your birth-chart will probably be provided in a format similar to Fig.3.

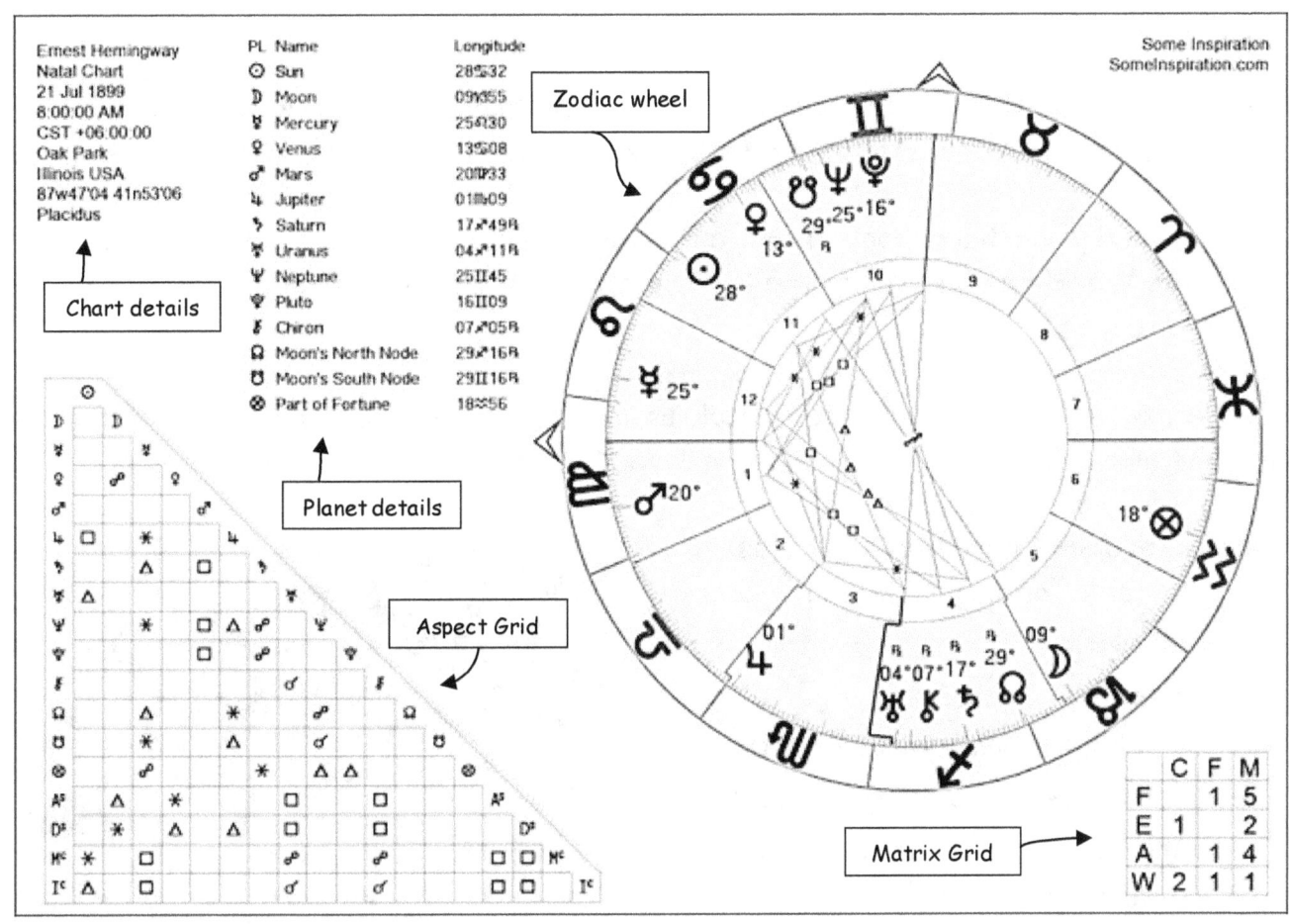

Fig.3

In this example (of the charts that I provide); as well as the ten major planets covered in the course, the chart also includes Chiron ⚷, the Moon nodes ☊☋ and the Part of Fortune ⊗. It covers all you'll need to get underway in learning how to read your chart.

Please note Chiron and the Part of Fortune are not covered in this course. The Moon nodes are covered in One Step Further.

## Make your own birth-chart – the DIY approach!

You may want to get really committed from the outset, by erecting birth-chart/s yourself rather than shopping around for one.

Learn to Read Your Birth-chart in 5 Steps  **11**

## Back in the Day...

Have a care for what it used to be like before software came along. Not so long back you would need resources, such as these, to calculate and then hand draw a birth-chart.

**One needed such hard-copy items as an ephemeris.** I still use printed versions of both the World Ephemeris for the 20$^{th}$ Century and The American Ephemeris for the 21$^{st}$ Century.

These are very useful for a quick look-up on the positions of the planets for days, months and years.

One needed such hard-copy items as:
- A table of logarithms to ease calculations
- A table of houses
- A table for noon date calculations
- Reference books for time changes
- And hard-copy birth-chart forms – usually your own.
- Plus, a handy aspect calculator, and, of course, a pen and ruler.

All these tools, and a few more were needed to create a birth-chart by hand – before software came along to do the work.

## Now with software...

It means a lot of the time-consuming work is now taken out... And a lot more time can be spent analysing and reading the resulting chart.

What follows is a look at a few suggestions for astrology programs that you can buy or even get for free. And we'll look at a very basic introduction to two of them – one you can buy and one for free.

Note, this workbook is not intended to cover the mechanics of creating birth-charts in any depth. Even so, it is useful that you know something about how they are drawn up. What follows will get you started. Help for finding your way around most programs will normally be available with them. Both software items covered do provide an introduction on how to use.

# Astrology Software

All programs mentioned here will run on Windows, but do check against the version you have. Likewise, if you want a program for your Mac or tablet do check the specs first.

For an up-to-date comprehensive list of Western astrology programs (at the time of writing) visit **astroapex.com/astro-software/**

## Software to buy

As you will soon discover, there are a number of astrological programs on the market. Examples are: **Solar Fire**, **Sirius**, **Kepler** and **Janus**. These can be easily found online.

My favourites of these are Solar Fire and Janus.

These programs provide the facility for creating professional birth-charts. Plus, they provide for a range of facilities including types of charts – e.g. Natal, Horary, Traditional, Electional and Vedic charts.

## Solar Fire

Solar Fire is the chosen software for many professional astrologers. It is probably the most expensive of all the programs. It essentially runs on Windows or tablets running Windows. But check out Solar Fire **AstroGold** for Apple computers and mobile.

## Janus

Janus is an excellent alternative to Solar Fire. It is also less expensive. See the following screenshots for basic usage of this program. Janus is listed to run on Desktop PC, Laptop PC or Notebook PC – so only Windows.

# Exampling erecting a Birth-chart in Janus

Simple instructions for building your birth-chart in Janus.

Given that you have bought a copy (via **astrology-house.com** – or check out Hank Friedman **soulhealing.com** for any deals he may be running) and installed the program.

You will also have followed instructions for setting up the location to your local area.

Next you:
1. Open the program from your computer.
2. The current chart displayed will be the "Transits" chart. Timewise, it will display for the moment you open the program. Other preloaded/saved charts will also be available on the right-hand side.
3. Go to **Chart** dropdown menu over on left top, then **New Chart**.
4. Fill in the form details for your **Name, Date and Time**.
5. Find the **Country** you were born in, under **World** dropdown, and enter **City/Town** name. This will call up your birthplace longitude and latitude – select and click **GetCity**.

6. Leave the House System at default (probably **Placidus**) and you are ready to go. Click **Cast Chart** and it will appear on the front screen – where it will be retained for you in the list on right – where you can also right-click to move it to another list that you've created.

## Janus 5 Opening screen (Fig. 4)

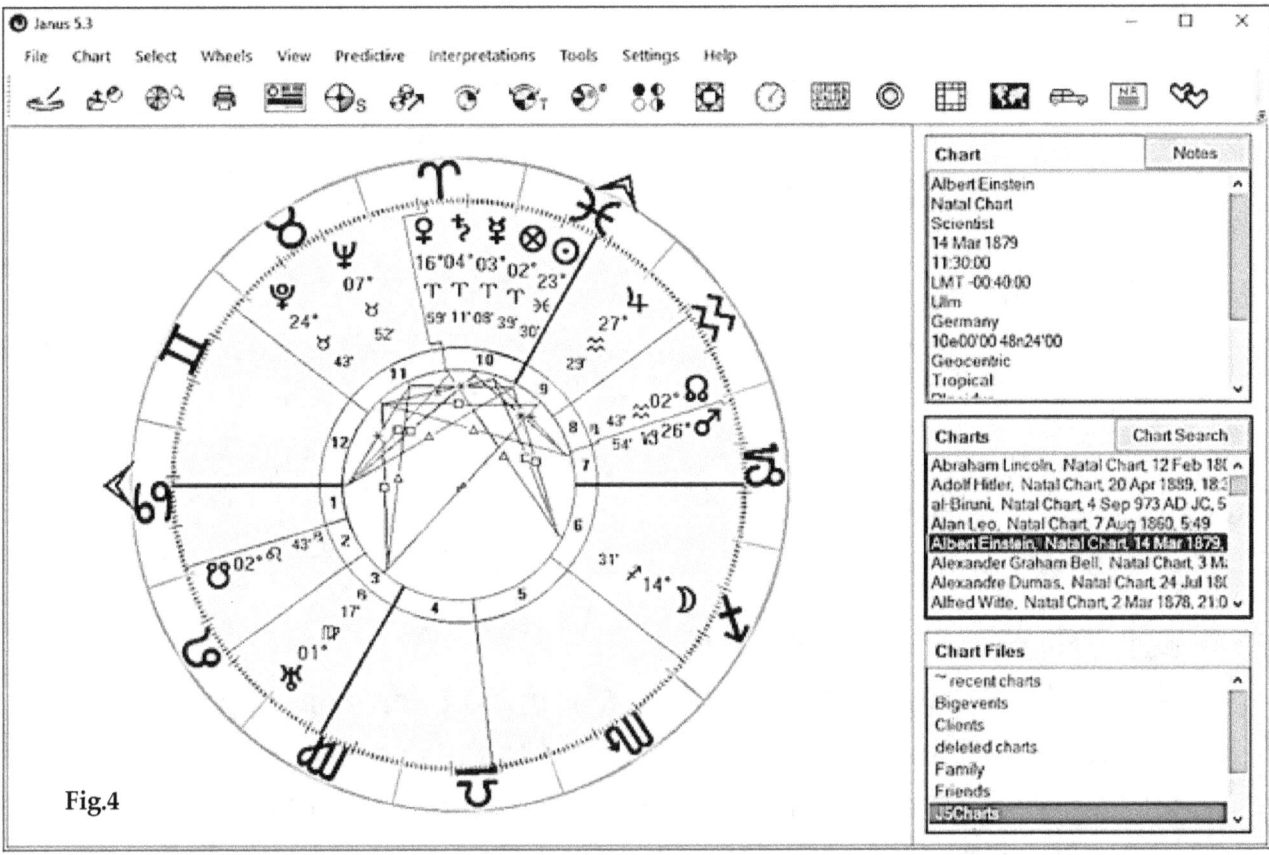

Fig.4

Note: There is more information hidden from view here, as it was screen captured at the "Restore down" setting for this illustration.

This screenshot is showing some of the menus plus the chart of Albert Einstein – which is selected from the list of birth-charts on the right-hand side. A good list of charts is already installed in the program – under J5Charts.

Learn to Read Your Birth-chart in 5 Steps   **15**

# Janus 5 Setting up a birth-chart (Fig.5)

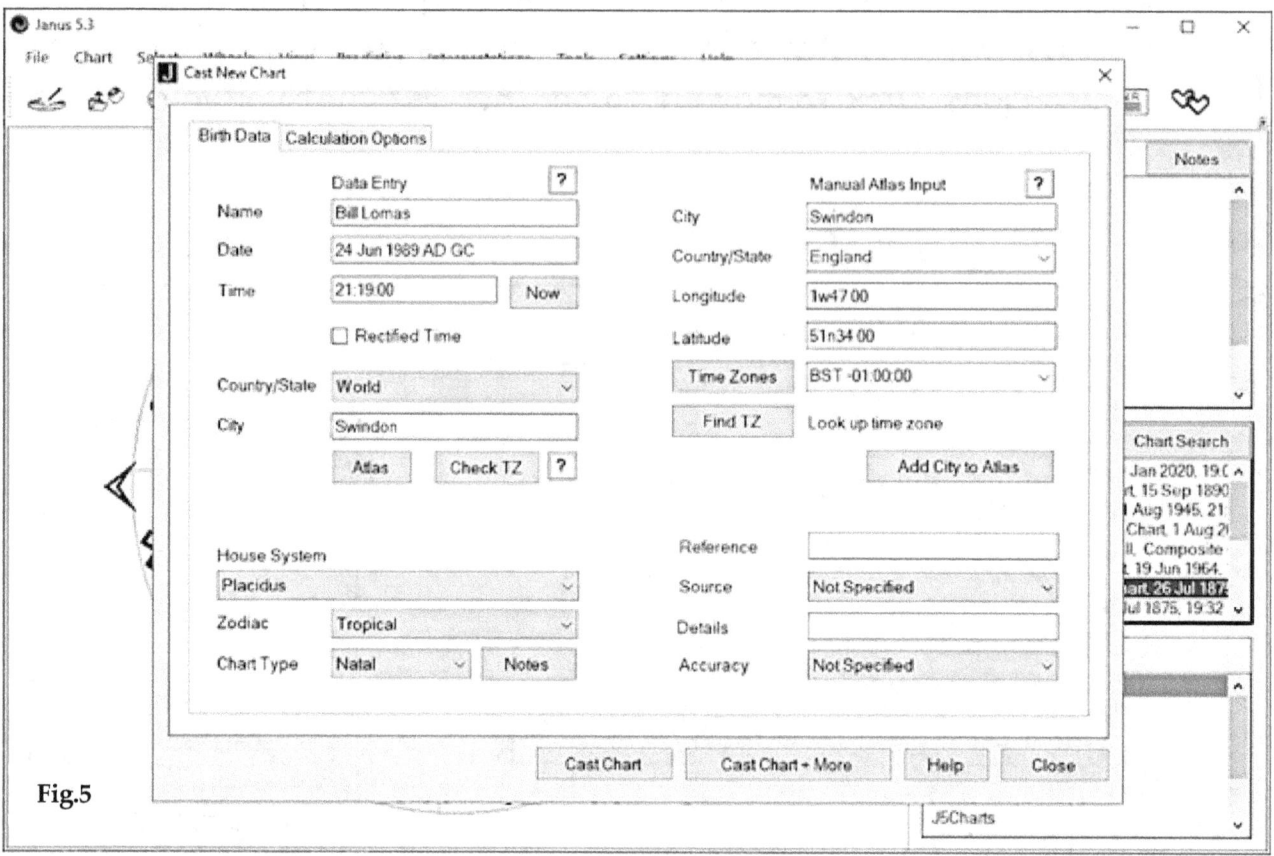

Fig.5

To erect a birth-chart in this program:
1. Go to the **Chart** menu and **New Chart** to open this form.
2. Fill in your **Name**, **Date** of birth, and local **Time** of birth – your own or as given. Be as accurate as you can be in the form.
3. Next the longitude and latitude need to be found through **Country/State** and **City** or town. The place listings are global. If not there find the nearest location. Leave as **Placidus** house system for now and hit **Cast Chart**.

# The chart is cast (Fig.6)

The birth-chart will now be up on screen - ready to be read!
It will be saved over on the right under Charts – and can be moved into a ready folder, or folder you have created later, if you so wish.

The example here is "Bill Lomas" (not his real name). It is a chart you will see a bit more of during the course. He has Sun in Cancer 7th House. In opposition to this he has Uranus, Saturn and Neptune in his 1st House – and Capricorn rising.

His Moon is in Pisces 2nd House and it is trine to Pluto at the MC in 10th House.

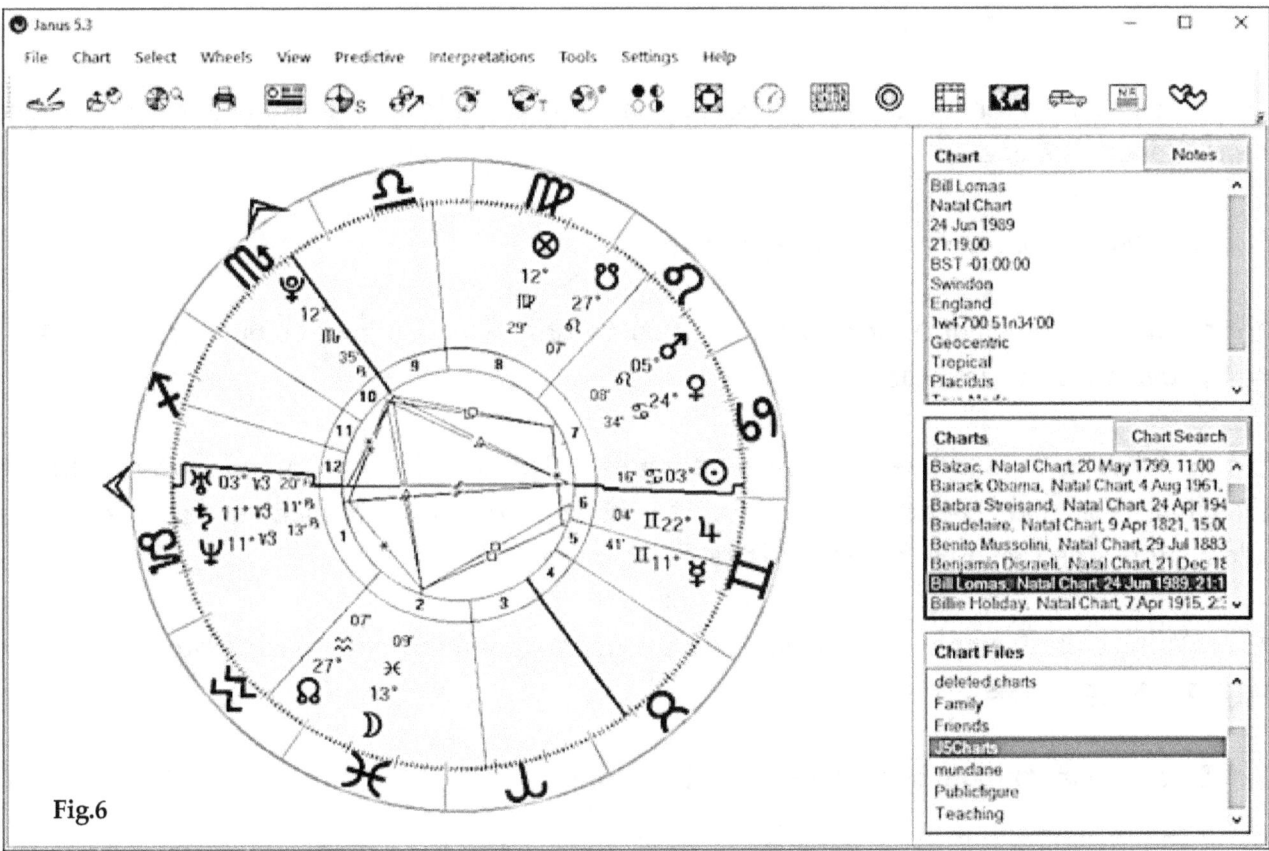

Fig.6

Note, if you right-click just outside of the chart itself (in the program) you can change the chart's appearance and also what components you see in it. The chart style that is displaying is my own – it was created in Janus.

Learn to Read Your Birth-chart in 5 Steps   **17**

If you have a printer, you can print your chart out by going to **File** > **Print Main Screen Wheel**.

To find out more on how to use Janus: In the program, go to **Help** > **Getting Started**.

I might add that Astrology House also do a lower cost, Janus Light, for all the basics needed to produce professional charts. Currently the full version is now Janus 6 – at the time of writing.

# Software for Free

There are a number of free programs that you will also find online... **Astrowin** and **Planetdance** are examples.

If choosing one, bear the following in mind:

With any free program, check that it is up to date – and provides updates. If not, it may prove to be unreliable.

Free software is less likely to be as sophisticated or as user-friendly as a paid-for program. You may need, therefore, to have some experience with astrological calculations (and also with the IT itself), to be able to use it.

AstroWin is an example of a good free program requiring one to also be fairly savvy with astrology to use it.

But I have something more user-friendly in mind...

I have road tested one or two free programs over time. Without doubt one of the best I have found, at the time of writing, is Planetdance. Search for online, download and install for free – there is a donate option to support its development. See the following screenshots for basic usage to call up your birth-chart.

# Exampling erecting a birth-chart in Planetdance

Simple instructions for Planetdance **(Runs on Windows and Android)**

Given that, at this point, you have downloaded the program (from **jcremers.com** – choose language version), then installed the program, and have opened it.

Like Janus, when you first use the program, you will need to set it up to your location. It is not difficult; just follow the cues in the software.

## Planetdance Opening screen (Fig.7)

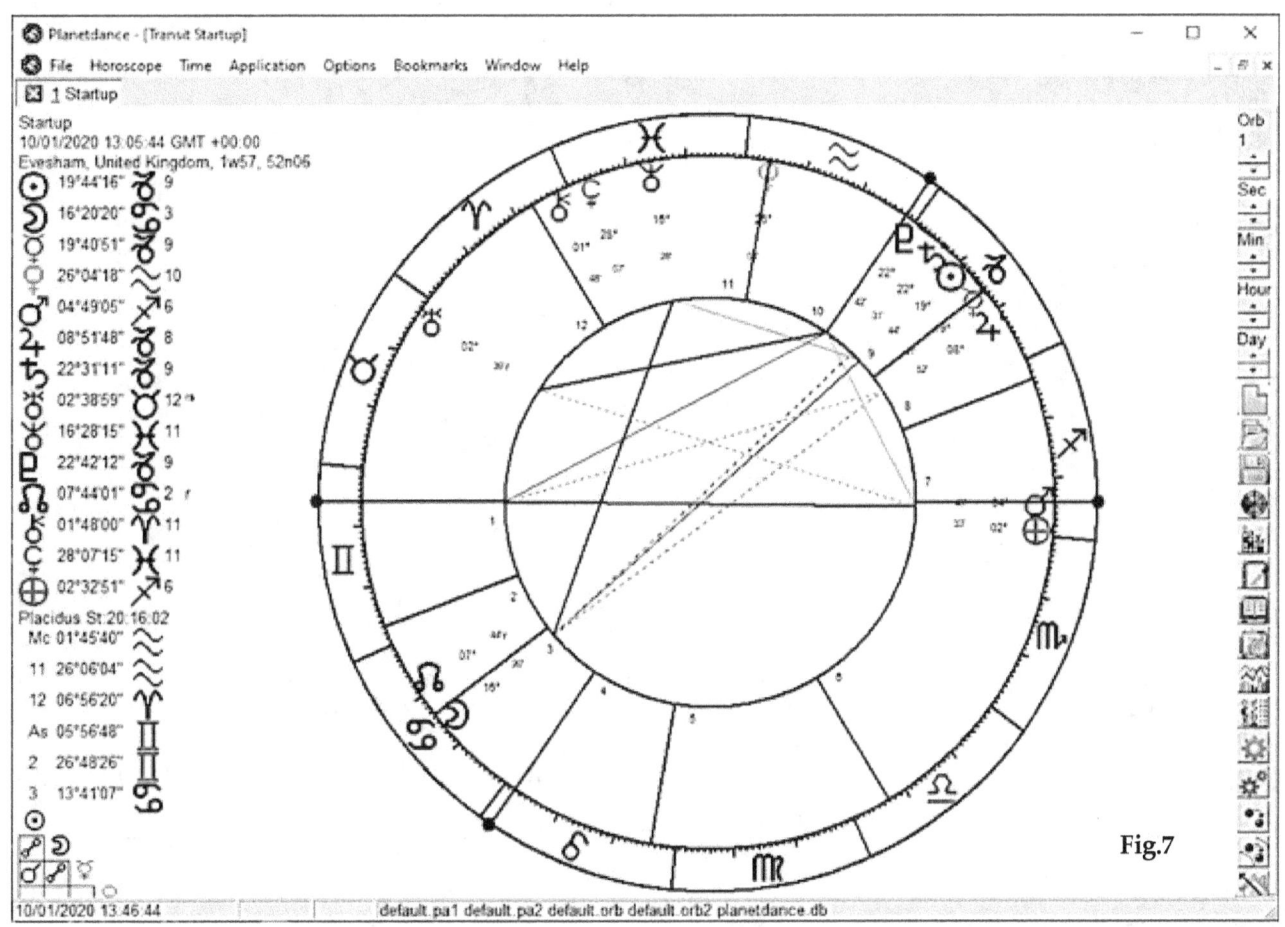

Fig.7

Note, there is more information hidden from view here, as it was screen captured at "Restore down" setting for illustration use.

Given...
1. You have opened the program.
2. You'll find the current chart displayed will be the "transits" chart – for the moment you accessed the program.
3. The chart's component values will be displayed on the left.

## Planetdance Setting up a birth-chart (Fig.8)

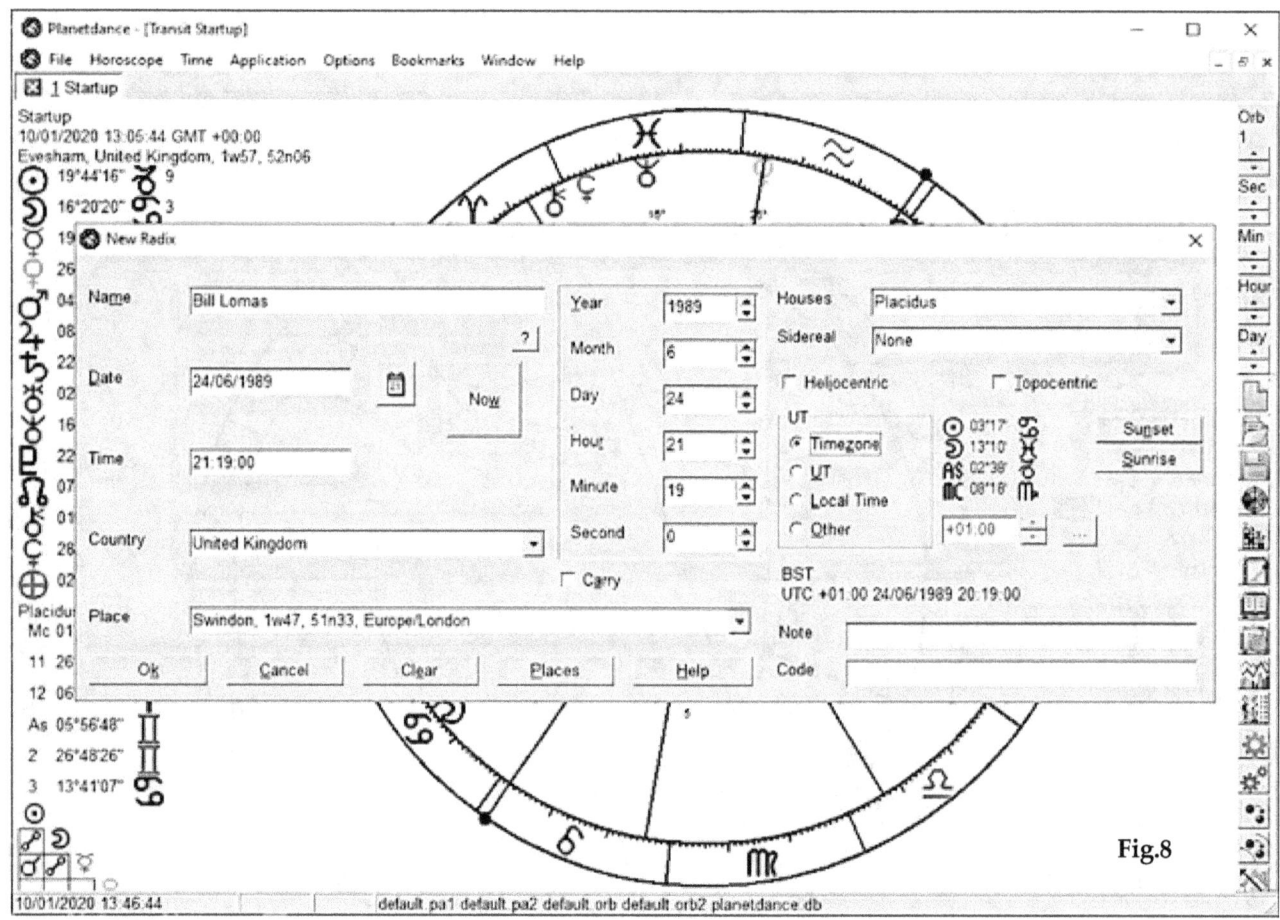

Fig.8

To set up your own birth-chart:

20  About the Course

1. Go to **File** dropdown menu, over top left, then **Radix**.
2. Change/Fill in the form details for **Name**, **Date** and local **Time**.
3. Find country under **Country** then **Place** to call up the birthplace longitude and latitude.
4. Leave Houses set to **Placidus** (for now) and you are ready to go.
5. Click **Ok** and the chart will appear on the front screen – where it will be retained for you in the top band/tab.

## PlanetDance The birth-chart of Bill Lomas is cast (Fig.9)

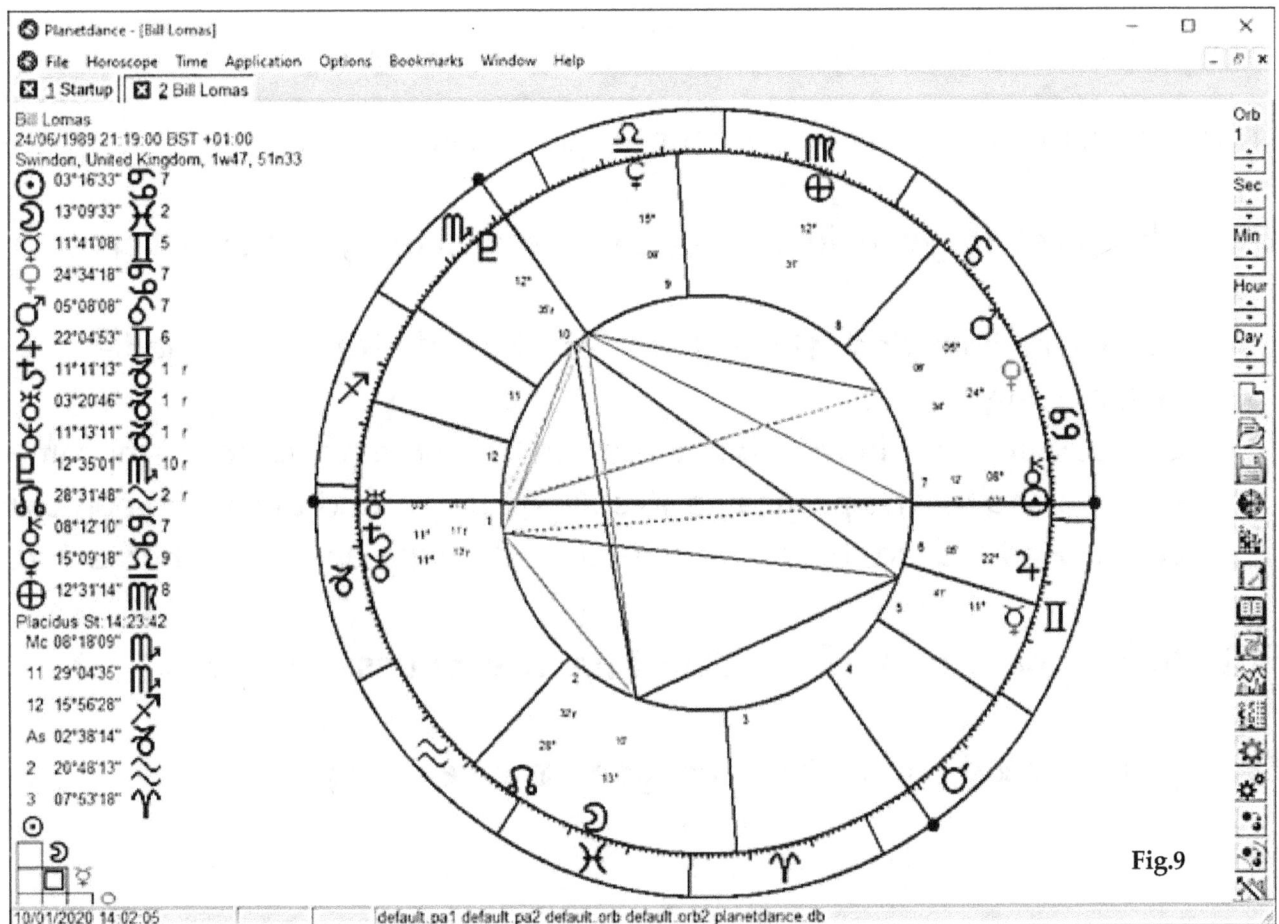

Fig.9

The chart is now saved in a tab above. As expected, Bill Lomas has the same setup here, as in Janus.

The presentation might look a little less polished than the Janus version, but all the ingredients, the planets, signs and houses are there.

This is a very useful piece of software that can be obtained for free.

To print your birth-chart, you go to **Horoscope > Print Etc**

To find out more on how to use Planetdance go to their **Help > Planetdance**.

# So, now you have options...

If you already have your birth-chart you are ready to go.

If you have yet to get hold of your own birth-chart you can either:

- Get your chart done through one of the websites mentioned – including myself.
- Or you can jump in with both feet, install an astrological program – such as one of the programs I've suggested – and draw up your own chart. And indeed, have the option of drawing up other charts too.

**But do act on this before starting the course proper.**

Once you are ready to get started, go to the next page.

# ～ The Course ～

# Learn to Read Your Birth-chart in 5 Steps
## Your astrological roadmap for life

# Key to the Astrological Symbols

This key (Fig.10) provides all the symbols you'll need while working through the main course.

| Planets | Signs | Major Aspects |
|---|---|---|
| ☉ Sun | ♈ Aries | ☌ Conjunction $0°$ (+/- $8°$) |
| ☽ Moon | ♉ Taurus | ☍ Opposition $180°$ (+/- $8°$) |
| ☿ Mercury | ♊ Gemini | △ Trine $120°$ (+/- $8°$) |
| ♀ Venus | ♋ Cancer | □ Square $90°$ (+/- $8°$) |
| ♂ Mars | ♌ Leo | ✶ Sextile $60°$ (+/- $6°$) |
| ♃ Jupiter | ♍ Virgo | ⚻ Quincunx $150°$ (+/- $2°$) |
| ♄ Saturn | ♎ Libra | |
| ♅ Uranus | ♏ Scorpio | (+/- $X°$) = Degree of orb allowed |
| ♆ Neptune | ♐ Sagittarius | |
| ♇/⯓ Pluto | ♑ Capricorn | ℞ = Retrograde planet |
| | ♒ Aquarius | |
| | ♓ Pisces | Fig.10 |

It goes without saying; getting familiar with these symbols will speed up your access and learning enormously. I'd recommend you make (write on a piece of paper or scan) and keep a copy handy while you get used to them.

## In context with this key, please take note of the following:

- For the planets, note that Pluto may be written in one of two forms. It is a personal preference on the part of the astrologer as to which they choose – or indeed which software they may be using. Only the first one is used in this workbook.
- The Moon Nodes ☊☋ (not included in the key) are treated separately in One Step Further: The Spiritual Roadmap.
- Aspects are the relationship between planets and/or angles. These are given a tolerance (known as an "orb") either side (plus or minus) of exact, usually between $2°$ & $8°$ degrees depending on the aspect – whether major or minor. Minor aspects, such as the semi-square and the semi-sextile, are not being covered in this course.
- A retrograde planet is a planet that appears, from the vantage point of the Earth, to be going backwards for a given time – before becoming stationery and going forward again. It is all relative to the Earth being faster than planets outside its orbit, or slower than planets inside its orbit – and all going around the Sun. Astrologers treat such events as symbolical and meaningful.

## Additional comment on Retrograde Planets

The planets are all going around the Sun in the same direction – anti-clockwise from the northern hemisphere viewpoint. It takes a bit of lateral thinking to figure it out but here's a simple example...

If you are walking along a footpath doing 4 miles per hour, and catching then passing someone, going in the same direction (let's say they are doing 3 miles per hour); from your vantage point the other person who was ahead of you, will appear to become stationary as you level up with them, then seemingly go backwards – or in retrograde motion – as you leave them behind; even though they will still be doing their 3 miles per hour going forward.

That works for the planets further out from the Sun than the Earth. For planets closer to the Sun than the Earth, that is Mercury and Venus, we need to add in another component to see how it could work. Returning to our scenario, you have to allow for another person to be speed walking, at say 6 miles per hour, coming up to and passing you.

This time though it helps to imagine that all three walkers are going around a traffic island. Once the faster moving person gets enough ahead of us, to be on the other side of the island away from us; they will appear to be going against our direction (retrograde), before they eventually come up behind us again, to overtake us.

Note, the Sun or Moon never go retrograde to the Earth's viewpoint – they can't.

A retrograde planet is generally associated with delays or frustration – things are getting held up or going backwards. For instance, with retrograde Mercury, delays in commerce, communications and/or journeys can be anticipated. It helps to underline astrology being based on symbolism and perception – rather than fact.

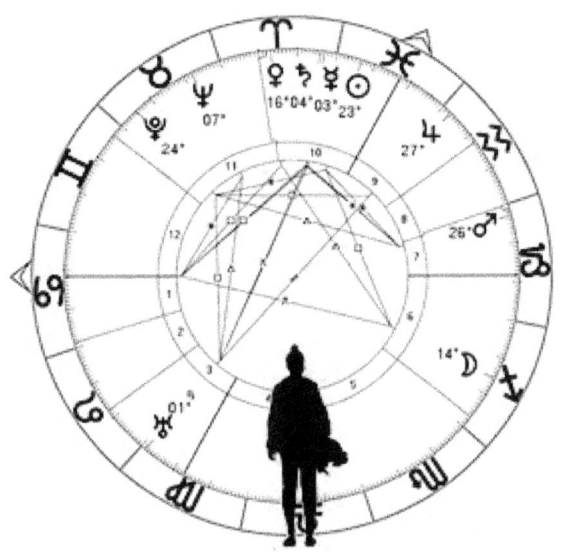

# Step One

## Learn about the Birth-chart

# Part 1
# Introducing the Birth-chart

## We know where we are!

Let me start this course proper by saying... Because we have developed an earth grid (of longitude and latitude) and the means of measuring time linked to the Earth's movement; any recorded event, happening on our planet, can be cross-referenced with an identifiable time and place.

We not only have measures for our planet but also for our solar system too. We know where we are, at any time, in our journey around the Sun. We also know where any planet in the system will be, in time and space, going around the Sun – and in relation to each other, the stars, and our planet.

Further, we also know where any planet will be, in this arrangement, if we go back a thousand years (or more) or, for that matter, forward a thousand years or more from now... We have tables (an ephemeris) that provide such information - on planets whose orbits are reliable.

In the book, **Christmas Past**, for example, I looked at the case for Jesus being born under a Jupiter-Saturn conjunction. I easily went back to that time, using an electronic ephemeris.

I might add that, give or take a few degrees, all the planets also stay within the same plane (ecliptic or zodiac belt) as the Earth, in their journeys around the Sun – and they are, of course, all going in the same circular anti-clockwise motion (northern hemisphere viewpoint).

Having this information allows us to pinpoint a moment in time, place and space that can then be given representation on an astrological grid. The grid necessarily provides a frame of reference in the signs and houses. This is what the birth-chart template represents – a 3-dimensional situation on a 2-dimensional form.

# How much data do we need?

A concern arises, in this process, as to how much data we need for this astrological grid to provide us with something useful.

## Going to one extreme

Do we, for example, just include the Sun for it to work?

Here's my Sun at 21 degrees of Libra... (Fig.11)

This is an example of the grid being used at the level of pop astrology. All it involves is my "star sign." It's one way to look at it. But with no other heavenly bodies present I think you'll agree it is not really giving you (or I) much data to go on.

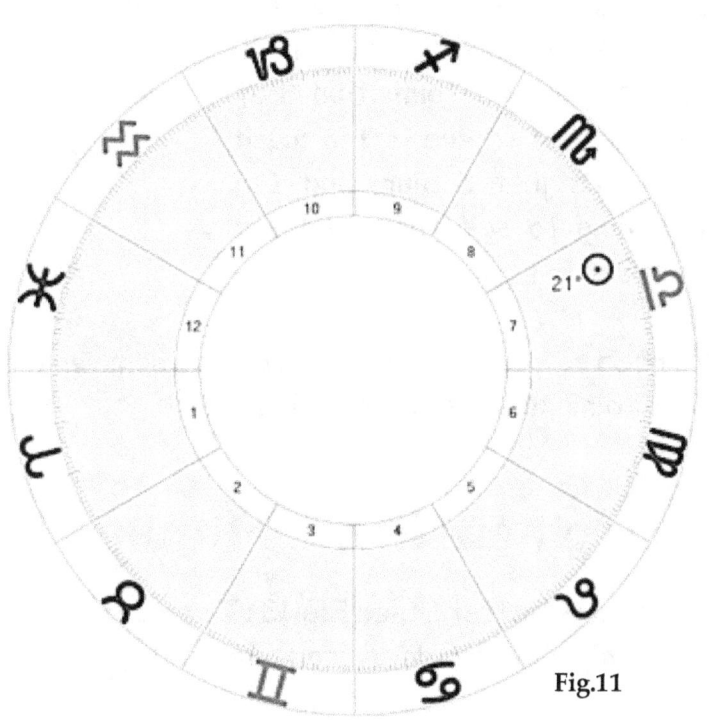

Fig.11

As useful as it may be, to know I'm a Libran (from the position of the Sun on the day I was born), it provides nothing more than general information. Information I share with all the other Librans in the world – possibly a 12th of the population.

## Going to the other extreme – too much information

I could include not just the Sun but all the planets, stars, asteroids and Arabian Parts that astrologers may bring to the table.

It is easy to do this with the software available to us.

Now (Fig.12), I have a more promising birth-chart grid, for the time and place of my birth, that is full of information. But that's just it, there is too much of it! It's just a blur, and I'm struggling to see the wood for the trees to make any sense of it.

Fig.12

We need to keep things simple and be somewhere in between these extremes, if we are going to make sense of the chart.

## Somewhere in the middle

Now this is better... (see Fig.13) I can see what's going on. Now I have the ten planets previously almost hidden from view.

30   Step One: Learn about the Birth-chart

And it's self-evident this chart is going to be more dynamic and personal than just my Sun sign.

The chart provides me with a unique document. I can immediately know that while I have Sun in Libra, I'm unlike any other Libran.

By the way I know of no astrologer who will be casting charts anywhere near approaching the complexity as shown in the second image (Fig.12) - but some will be more complex than the content of the third image (Fig.13). I think the KISS - keep it simple - principle needs to apply, to better aid our understanding.

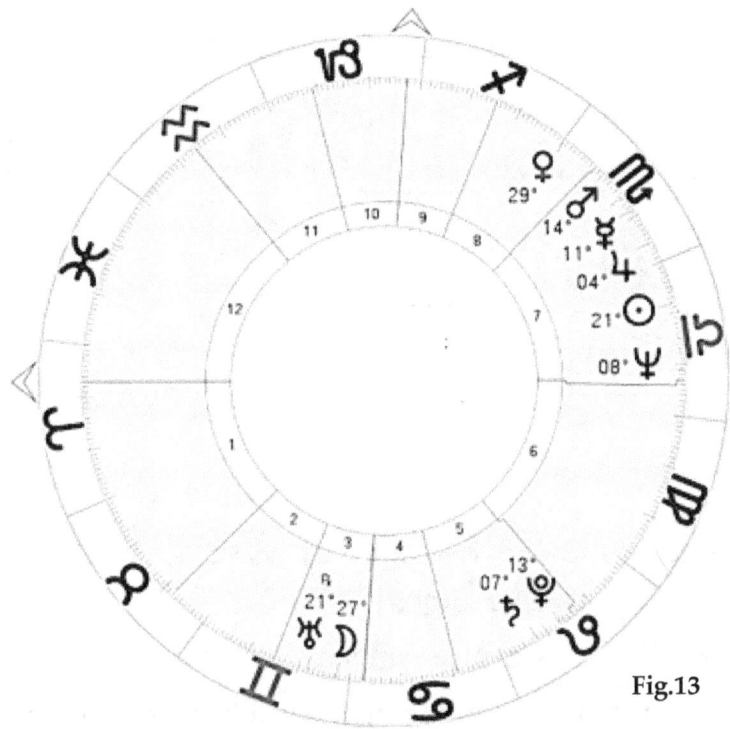

Fig.13

Once you have a good foothold on the essentials of Western astrology you can always explore further up the rockface of other components - such as Moon nodes (which are provided in One Step Further), Chiron and Part of Fortune (included in the birth-chart I provide) - and other asteroids or stars. You will find them valuable, have no doubt.

It is for this reason (i.e., keeping it simple) that this course intentionally covers the ten planets that everyone, seeking personal insight through astrology, needs to learn to understand.

Well, that's the mechanics of the astrological grid, in a nutshell. The astrological grid, or template, is based on our observation of our solar system, from an Earth vantage point. What has been left out is; once we have our grid, how do we derive meaning from it? And that is what the course will provide - and for you to decide.

But let's now take a closer look at the chart...

# Part 2

# A closer look at the Birth-chart

To recap, a birth-chart of Western astrology includes:
- The twelve Signs.
- Ten Planets – or more! Remember, Sun and Moon are counted as planets in astrology, as is Pluto, which astronomers now consider a dwarf planet.
- The Angles.
- Twelve Houses.
- And the Aspects – usually displayed in the centre of the chart.

## So, a birth-chart will incorporate...

**All twelve zodiac signs** (Fig.14): Not just the one the Sun is in!

Fig.14

32   Step One: Learn about the Birth-chart

**Ten or more planets** (Fig.15): This is where they actually were for this person at the time of their birth. Sun ☉ in Aquarius ♒ is all they would know if looking at their newspaper star signs.

**The Angles** (Fig.16): The ascending (Asc) sign (in this example it is Virgo). The descending (Dsc) sign is Pisces. The sign on

Fig.15

Fig.16

the Midheaven (Mc) is Gemini. The sign on the Imum Coeli (Ic) is Sagittarius.

**Twelve houses**: These run anticlockwise off the ascending sign. The houses can be viewed as offering twelve areas of life experience – a lot more on Angles and Houses in Step 4.

**And the aspects** (see Fig.17): Or the angular relationship between the component bodies and/or angles.

Clearly, although the Aquarius Sun sign is important in this chart it is only a part of a much bigger arrangement. Broadly this person has: Sun ☉ in Aquarius ♒ 5th House; Moon ☽ in Sagittarius ♐ 4th House; Virgo ♍ rising, and Gemini ♊ on the Midheaven. Meanwhile there are the eight other planets in their signs and houses that would need to be taken into consideration.

Learn to Read Your Birth-chart in 5 Steps    33

The birth-chart for this particular person is unique to their time, place and date of birth. Bringing it all together, like conducting an orchestra, is where this person, or any person's challenge, to become self-aware and self-integrated, lies.

All birth-chart components help to play their part in providing insight into the potential of a person.

And this is the message I really want to get across to you as you work through this course. Astrology can help you to better understand and work with your Self. It can offer enormous insight into, what I would describe as, the energy pattern (or situation) you are dealing with...

Fig.17

Meanwhile, let's take a closer look at the example birth-chart used here to see what some of these components actually mean...

# Part 3

# A look at Mozart's birth-chart

The birth-chart we've just briefly looked at (in Part 2) actually belongs to Wolfgang Amadeus Mozart – Fig.18.

Keeping in mind the orchestra analogy, already mentioned, let's take a look at some of his key components a little more closely...

## Mozart was Sun☉ in Aquarius ♒

Some keywords associated with Aquarius Sun are: original, radical, intuitive, broadminded, nonconforming, different, independent, freedom-loving, scientific, unusual, and helpful.

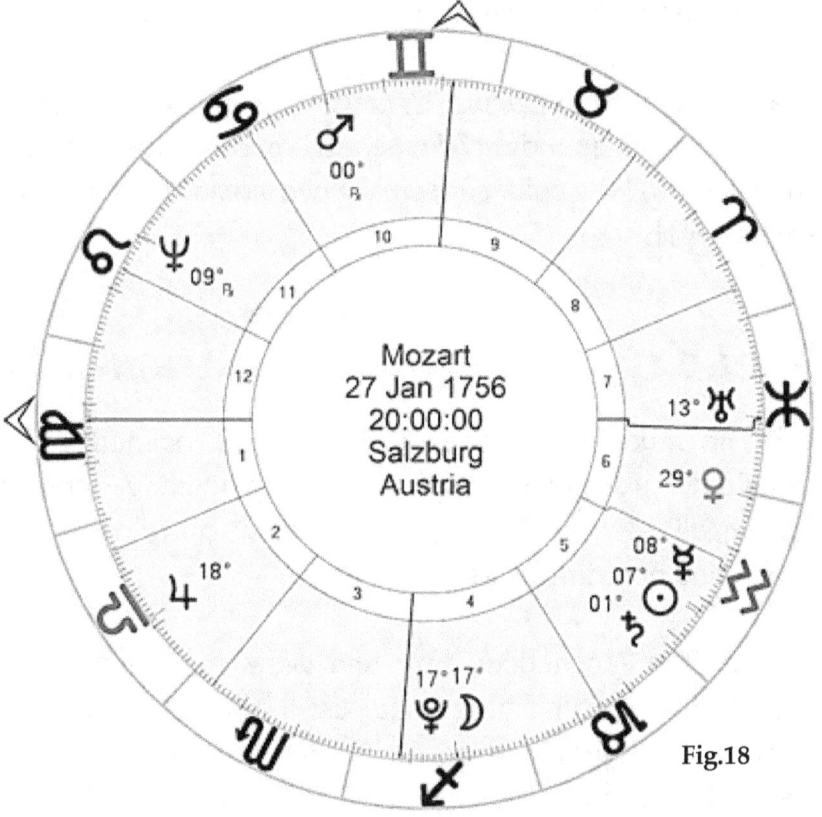

Fig.18

Learn to Read Your Birth-chart in 5 Steps   35

Here Mozart might also have been inclined to be unpredictable, tactless, rebellious, stubborn, rigid, radical, bohemian and eccentric in his behaviour. It's the other side of Aquarius.

His Sun is also in the 5th house, indicating he was inclined to be a child at heart. He would have wanted to interact and impress others around him.

Although with Sun conjunct Saturn ♄ one has to take into account there is always a serious note to anything and everything one does. It is important to be the best, and to win – losing may not be an option, and comes hard when it happens.

He was likely to have been excited about bringing new ideas (Mercury is key here), and methods, to apply to what is old, traditional and outdated. Sometimes Aquarians are simply ahead of their time, as is often said of Mozart.

Note the ruler of Aquarius, Uranus ♅, is in the 7th house suggesting Mozart would have been quite independent/detached, and probably awkward in his more intimate relationships. He could certainly have come across as a bit odd (with odd tastes), to interact with.

## He had his Moon ☽ in Sagittarius ♐

With the Moon here (see Fig.19) one is inclined to be outspoken, open, generous, enthusiastic, idealistic, inspired, and optimistic – and up for fun and adventure. And these qualities tend to attract many contacts, friends and acquaintances.

Although the Moon does wax and wane, and with Pluto ♇ involved he was also as likely to lose contacts too. His Moon conjunct Pluto in the 4th house indicates he likely had a challenging childhood and home life. Probably it was strict, sombre, not a lot of fun or love expressed openly.

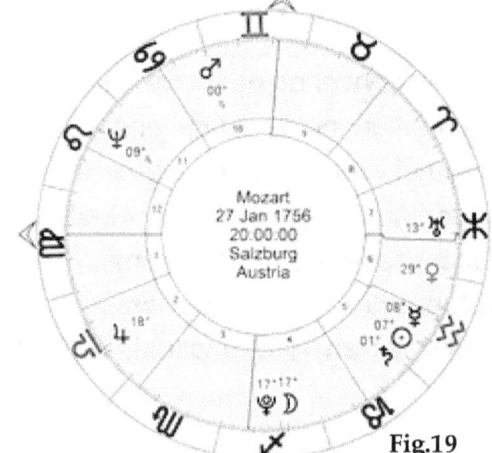

Fig.19

36    Step One: Learn about the Birth-chart

I'm also reminded that Mozart was the youngest of seven children; five of whom died in infancy. The association of Pluto with hard knocks and death is clearly not to be taken lightly here.

Generally, the Moon in Sagittarius person is likely to go through mood swings (likely, with Pluto involved, these were dark mood swings in Mozart's case), but will also tend to rise above difficulties and come out seeing the glass as half-full. He would likely have remained optimistic regarding life and his future.

It is also probable that he would have been uncomfortable with his own, or other people's, problems – and preferred to sweep them under the carpet. The Moon here indicates he would have probably wanted to avoid, or suppress feelings and powerful emotions involved. He would have preferred to keep the lid on things in other words.

Many changes of residence are also likely to have occurred with his Moon setup. One would also expect one parent to be a strong influence in the person's life. And Mozart's father did (literally) play such a role. He was his music teacher.

## He had Virgo ♍ rising

The rising sign will show how we project ourselves to the world – it's one's persona. Mozart having Virgo rising would have tended to come across as a practical, analytical and precise person.

Here was a person who could be fastidious, careful, exacting, attentive to details, methodical, quiet, unassuming, could be shy, critical, thoughtful, and somewhat self-preoccupied. It suggests an active and alert mind. Gaining knowledge and putting it to good use would have been very important to him.

With Virgo there is the tendency to strive for perfection and be quite a tough act to keep up with, or live with; a tendency to set the bar high.

### And he had Gemini ♊ on the Midheaven (Fig.20)

The midheaven angle encapsulates a theme around what we are reaching or striving for, our endeavours and goals in life. With Gemini this points to movement, knowledge, the exchange of information and communications, being an important theme in his life.

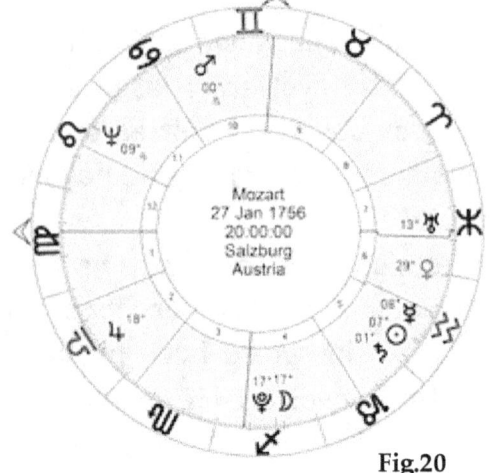
Fig.20

With Mars ♂ there, in the 10th house, success was linked to ambition, having achievable dreams and goals that could be realised – and done so with some urgency and passion.

Well, there's a quick overview of Mozart's birth-chart that I hope you will have found of interest.

## A couple more comments to make on his chart...

There are a number of important aspects in Mozart's birth-chart and there is one big one I want to mention here. It is the relationship between his Sun ☉, Mercury ☿ and Saturn ♄, in opposition to Neptune ♆.

### First a little more about Mercury ☿ (see fig.21)

If/when, you know astrology you will know that Mercury is the ruler of this chart. It is also the ruler of the Midheaven sign too. And to add, it was in a close conjunction with Mozart's Sun at the time of his birth.

Here, in Mozart, was a mercurial personality if ever there was one. Mercury is mental and nervous activity. It is quicksilver, converting experience into ideas, rapidly – and Mozart, as we know, was precocious.

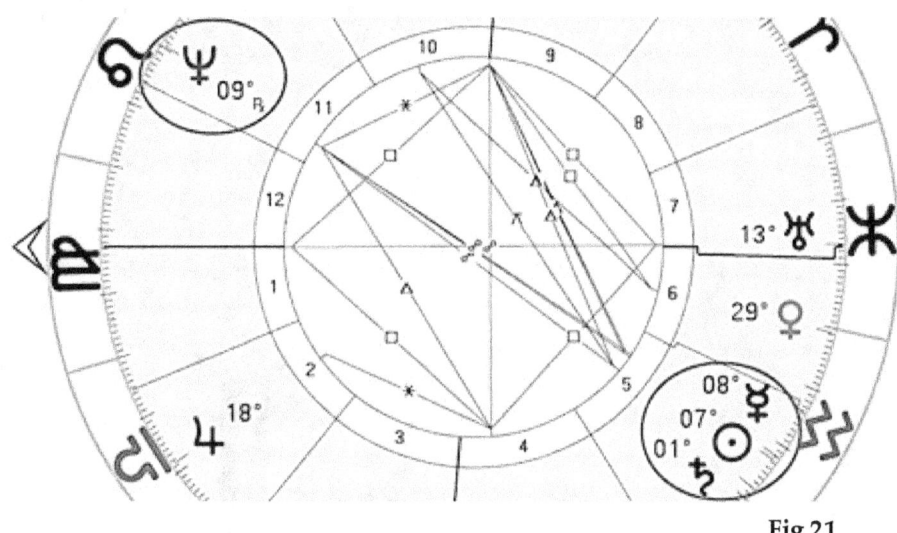

Fig.21

Mercury is the power of knowing or knowledge. Not just to know but also to inform. Mozart was essentially a "communicator." He's likely to have been a bit of a *trickster* too... and/or a bit of a *clever clogs*.

With the Sun ☉ conjunct Mercury in the 5th house, this is a very playful combination. And it could so easily have been "play" in an ordinary sense but for Saturn ♄ symbolising bringing a serious tone to the proceedings. So, in expression it was a more serious form of play that Mozart then needed to develop.

## But then we consider Neptune ♆ (Fig.21)

This is where I would suggest Mozart and his originality, being expressed through music, can be linked in his birth-chart. Study Neptune and you'll find it has a powerful link with the arts and musical composition.

So just in that dynamic of the planets in Aquarius and Neptune you have a key to where Mozart outpoured his creativity and originality. Everything in this arrangement (including the houses involved) smacks of creative tension, new music, communication and discipline.

He clearly made good use of his energy pattern – certainly in regards to his music.

Next: Onto Step Two.

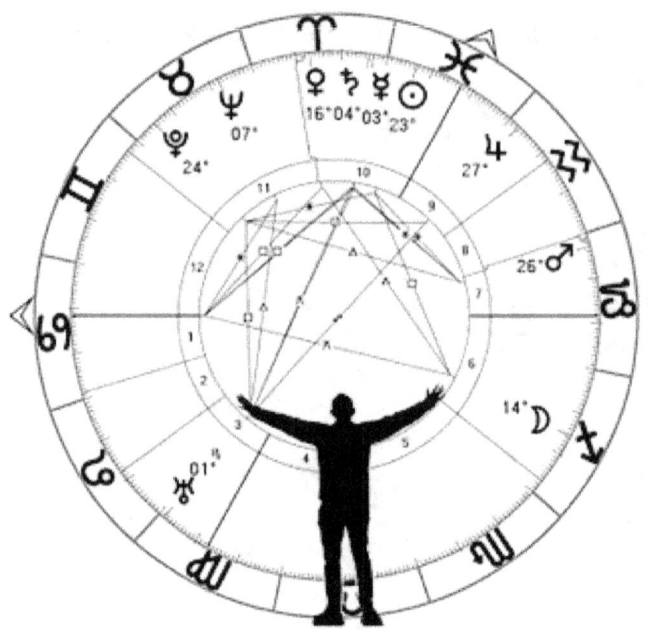

# Step Two

## Learn to Read the Signs

In context, check for the following resources, under The Resources, towards the back of the book:
- The Zodiac Signs Resource
- The Planets by Sign Resource

# Part 1

# Typical (and atypical) Sun Sign Descriptions

## Are you typical or atypical of your Sun sign?

To help ease you into studying the zodiac signs we're going to consider typical sign descriptions – with consideration for atypical signs too. So, this will be a bit more than just looking at your Sun sign. It will be a bit of a launchpad for what is to come.

Most of us will know what Sun sign (or Star sign) we are – or are supposed to be. We read a description for the sign and either go along with it (it sounds like me), or we may find we don't fit the description that much at all.

A person might say; *I'm supposed to be a Taurus from my date of birth, but I'm more like a Gemini than Taurus.*

If still interested, the person may want to pursue other descriptions for Taurus, or perhaps want to know if they were born on the cusp of the next sign (Gemini). More likely they may decide there's nothing to astrology and leave it at that.

## Born on the cusp...

Each sign has 30 degrees and you may be born with your Sun on say the 29th degree of Taurus. You will really only know by checking an ephemeris with your date of birth. This is better than relying on popular dates (Fig.22) for when the Sun moves to the next sign. It can change a little bit from year to year.

| Tropical Sign Dates | Dates can vary from year to year. |
|---|---|
| **Aries**: Mar 21 - Apr 19 | **Taurus**: Apr 20 - May 20 |
| **Gemini**: May 21 - Jun 20 | **Cancer**: Jun 21 - Jul 22 |
| **Leo**: Jul 23 - Aug 22 | **Virgo**: Aug 23 - Sep 22 |
| **Libra**: Sep 23 - Oct 22 | **Scorpio**: Oct 23 - Nov 21 |
| **Sagittarius**: Nov 22 - Dec 20 | **Capricorn**: Dec 21 - Jan 19 |
| **Aquarius**: Jan 20 - Feb 18 | **Pisces**: Feb 19 - Mar 20 |

Fig.22

If your Sun was at 29 degrees Taurus, when you were born, by the end of your first year it will (by symbolical progression) have moved into Gemini and tie in with Gemini for the next 30 years of your development and life. That suggests a strong Gemini theme overlapping your Taurean beginnings.

That said, the reason things don't fit is less likely to be about whether we are on the cusp of the next sign, or not. It is most likely to be because, relying on pop (or star sign) astrology, we are only looking at the one (Sun) sign for answers. We are not seeing the bigger picture – i.e., there is more, much more, than one sign to each of us.

If we feel closely aligned with the typical description for our Sun sign, it is highly likely to be because other (strong) components in our birth-chart support this. If we don't feel aligned with our Sun sign description, the opposite is going to be true. That is other (strong) components in our chart counter that of our Sun sign – and pull us, our sense of identity and behaviour in a different direction.

# A couple of examples

The typical-ness of a description will be more prominent where, for example, our Sun sign and rising sign are the same. Or where the Sun and Moon are in the same sign or house, or possibly in the same element (of Fire, Earth, Air or Water – more on these shortly) and are therefore talking harmoniously to each other.

# Example: A typical Cancerian

**Elisabeth Kübler-Ross** (Swiss-American psychiatrist, a pioneer in near-death studies)

Her birth-chart (Fig.23) indicates she could be described as a typical Cancerian with both her Sun and Moon in Cancer. Her Moon is also in the 4th house, plus she has another Water sign, Pisces, rising.

But then one would be advised not to overlook the other planets in her chart; notably forceful and strongly independent Mars and Uranus in her 1st house. This is a person who was able to meet challenges head-on. By the way, if looking for clues to her NDE focus of interest, then note where Saturn and Pluto fall in her birth-chart.

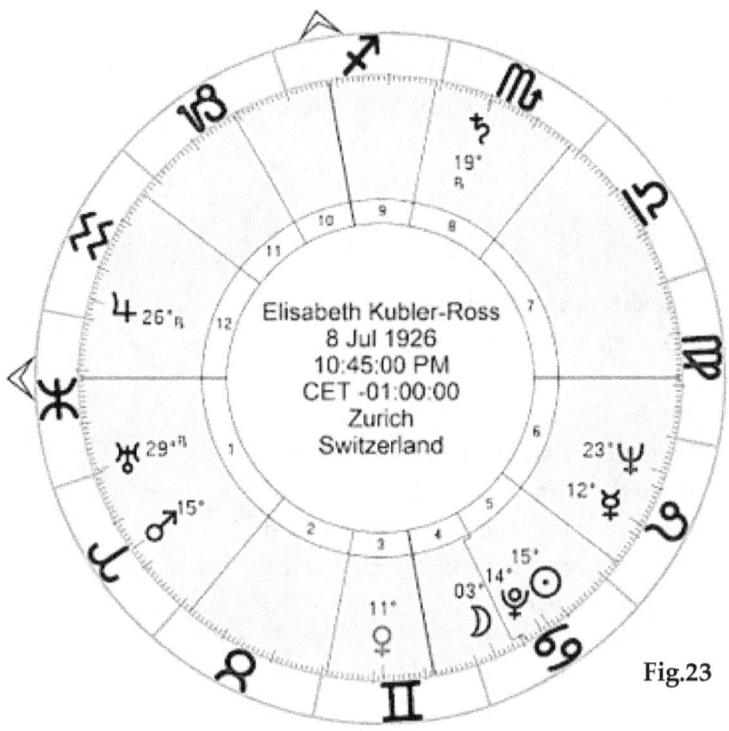

Fig.23

You might hold that thought and come back to this chart when you know more of Saturn and Pluto – and where they are in your own chart.

Where things are likely to diverge, and be a poor fit for our Sun sign description is where the Moon, for example, is in a qualitatively different sign and/or an opposing element to the Sun; or is making stronger connections to other planets than the Sun.

This would be the case if the Sun is unaspected, say in Aquarius, and the Moon is next door in Capricorn having flowing aspects to other important planets. In this scenario, the Capricorn side is more likely to shine through. It would suggest a more self-protective and careful personality, more conventional than might be expected of Aquarius.

The Aquarian side would more likely be expressed out through a need for independence, a need to go it alone, and possibly a tendency towards more scientific and inventive expression – it would tend to tease out the more scientific and inventive side of the person.

Or another possibility is where a stellium (three or more planets) is tipping the balance of energy towards a different direction.

# Example: An atypical Aries (Fig.24)

**Vincent van Gogh** (Dutch post-impressionist painter)

His birth-chart indicates that his Sagittarian Moon was likely a bigger driving force than his unaspected Sun in Aries – even though both planets were in Fire signs; and he also looked very Arian.

His Moon was (by aspect) strongly linked with Jupiter (conjunct – in the sign it rules), and with Mercury (trine), Venus, Mars and Neptune (square).

Pluto is also drawn into this pattern through Mercury/Jupiter. He also had Cancer rising to add emphasis to the Moon's strong position – as the Chart Ruler.

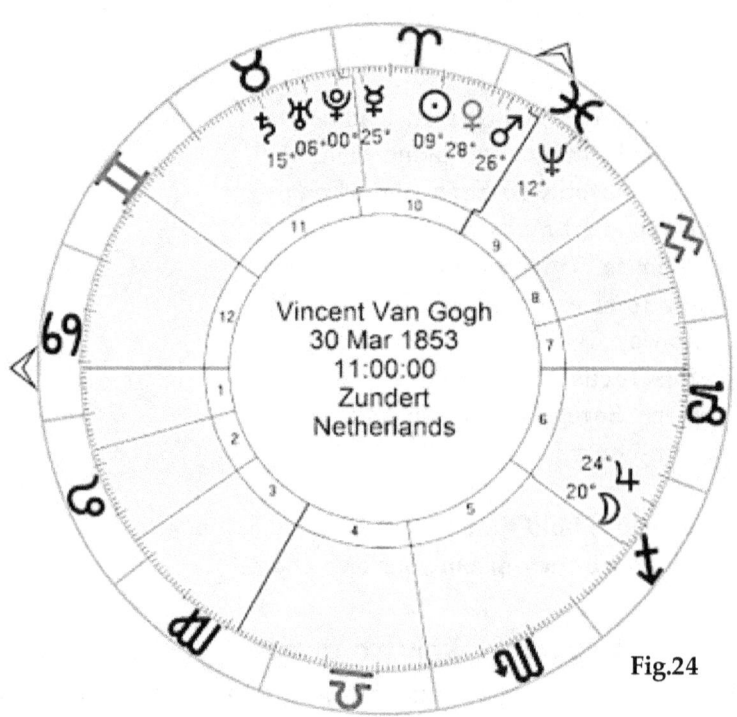

Fig.24

His Sun was a part (but unaspected) of that wonderful cluster of planets at the top of his chart where things need to blossom (reminiscent to me of his Sunflowers paintings) that found expression through his art. The clusters at the top also formed two stelliums, in Taurus and Pisces – more strong, if conflicting, voices. This was suggestive of a soul on a mission. It had to come out, and notably through Neptune (in the sign it rules) but oh the likely sense of isolation and loss, and not being entirely at-home or at peace in oneself, as reflected in this chart.

It's all out there but not in a happy way – might even be described as manic-depressive with peaks and troughs of euphoria.

# Try this exercise!

I suggest you treat what follows here as an exercise. Before you head into looking at the signs in more depth, try your hand at working through all the typical sign descriptions below. As you do, make a note of any that stand out for you – where you might say, "Oh yes I'm like that."

If possible, do this blind at first... That is, without referring back to your birth-chart. Expect surprises – especially if you are not that familiar with your chart as yet. See if you can decide which sign/s you feel more at-home with. It could provide you with unexpected insight into your Self.

At some point, do then check back with your chart, especially on your Sun, Moon, rising sign and midheaven signs.

> In my case, I have Sun in Libra but also Moon in Gemini. So, I would check both of these Air signs to see how they provide insight into my situation. Being in an Air sign, the Moon naturally backs up my Sun-sign. But I also have Aries rising, Capricorn on the Mc, and a stellium of planets in Scorpio. This means that I won't be quite a typical Libran (or for that matter a typical Gemini), as Aries, Capricorn and Scorpio will have a strong presence and be batting in there too. So even at this general level I would draw valuable insight from reading through (and attempting to synthesize) all of these signs – from the Typical Sign descriptions.

<u>Just to add</u>: what follows are broad descriptions. As you'll discover by digging further, they do not, nor are they intended to, exhaust everything that could be said about each sign, but rather to provide a useful flavour of each.

# Typical Sign descriptions

# Typical ♈ Aries

The typical Aries person will tend to be self-motivated, a self-starter, self-sufficient, spontaneous and wilful. They are inclined to be fiery and impulsive. There is a need to take action, and usually this combines with a sense of urgency, a need to get there, and often to be first in what they are doing. They will take the initiative, will be assertive and direct in nature.

It is a pioneering spirit that drives Aries. Where this involves others, they will often take a lead in matters too. This is usually for their own interests to get on with things rather than from the desire to help (or lead) others. Achieving their objectives is important. The Aries person can come across as very competitive, but often this is tinged with an endearing innocence. They tend to be optimistic and warm by nature, courageous and open to taking risks that others might shy away from.

## Relationships

The typical Aries will be friendly and most probably fun to be with, but will also seek to act independently. There is usually nothing secretive about them – they tend to be upfront with no hidden agenda. They tend to telegraph what they are feeling. They will be passionate with strong sexual feelings. They will probably not be particularly sensitive, tactful or refined in their manner.

In partnerships they will prefer to do things their way. Meanwhile, relationships that place constraints on their "go it alone" approach to life can become testing for both parties. In difficult relationships, the typical Aries will rarely carry resentment for long – "forgive and forget" will tend to be their motto – and they will soon bounce back, regaining their optimism if/when things fall apart.

## Likely vocation interests

A typical Aries will like to keep busy, to be doing. They will like quick wins off the back of clear and direct activity. Roles that involve one taking the initiative, being able to work independently, under one's own steam, are likely to be of interest. As indeed will roles where a pioneering spirit of adventure, together with a degree of competition is encouraged or expected, will be of interest. The Aries tends to also like lots of physical movement. Work outdoors, and equally in noisy industrial situations are also likely to appeal.

## Challenges

Negatively, the typical Aries will tend to be inclined to force getting their own way. There can be a tendency towards impatience, to act first and ask questions later – which can get them into trouble, and get them labelled as impulsive and naïve. It may also be a case of "more haste less speed," and finding they are having to do something again, and possibly again, because of their impatience. It would be good practice for the typical Aries to develop patience; to make a habit of checking back for any details they may have missed, and/or mistakes made as a result of their haste and trying force things through.

# Typical ♉ Taurus

The typical Taurus person will tend to be practical and down-to-earth in nature. They are inclined to be resourceful, pragmatic, industrious and conservative in their ways; as well as constructive, reliable, patient, earthy, sensual, creative and careful. They endure, and are willing to work hard for the things that make them happy. They like to keep things simple, uncomplicated. They will "call a spade a spade."

The Taurean will tend to be naturally thrifty and have a good business sense. They enjoy the pleasures of the senses, the physical world, having (or collecting) beautiful things around them. They are likely to enjoy nature, their creature comforts, rich food (can tend to over-indulge and put on weight), music and the arts in general.

## Relationships

The typical Taurean is sensual and peace-loving. They need physical contact – a lot of hugs. Most importantly the Taurus person seeks stability and comfort. Not only does that extend to material and financial security, to the things they own, but also in the way they relate to others. They are slow to change, steady, faithful and reliable; and they will seek the same in their relationships – can be overly possessive. They will tend to make friends for life, with issues around trust and constancy being very important to them.

## Likely vocation interests

The typical Taurean will like to build something, and not feel hurried while doing it either. This is so whether this build be actual material or say a business, or moving up the career ladder. A job for life would likely be attractive to the Taurean. Earthy vocations requiring a steady, constructive application of oneself, without too much risk, are likely to be of interest. Likewise, of interest are vocations where a position of trust and responsibility is required, and where practical and routine work is an expectation. Creative and hands-on work, linked with music, nature, plants or animals, is also likely to be of interest.

## Challenges

The typical Taurean is prone to being obstinate, overly-careful, resisting change, slow, sluggish and possessive. If not, careful they are inclined to become the proverbial "stick in the mud" - getting stuck plodding and ploughing their own furrows, and routinely at that. They can come across as unexciting company. Being inclined to be preoccupied with their own interests and security, the Taurean can also acquire the label of being a bit selfish or stingy. There is a need not to just receive hugs but to also give them back.

# Typical ♊ Gemini

What is most important for the typical Gemini is the "needing to find out," the "needing to know." Gemini is ever curious, collecting information and communicating this in one form or another.

The typical Gemini person will tend to be mentally quick, have enthusiasm for learning, be versatile, enjoy variety, be inquisitive, informative, adaptable, restless, talkative, changeable, sprightly and nimble. They love to share ideas and chat about the latest thing they are doing. They make a good go-between - being good at retrieving information and sharing it between two or more parties. They have an obliging manner and usually a good fun-loving sense of humour.

Gemini is optimistic, friendly, and tends to get on well with people.

## Relationships

The typical Gemini is friendly, witty and communicative - fun to be with. That said they are inclined to be light-hearted and flirtatious - a bit of a flutter-by - in their associations. They are inclined to be unemotional and cool in their affections - less about feelings and more about a mental approach to things. It can be difficult for the Gemini to form close and deepening relationships. Unless other components indicate stability, what they often need is something, or preferably someone, to help anchor them, and help keep them focused.

## Likely vocation interests

The typical Gemini will be talented at many forms of communication - such as writing, public speaking and being creative. They can usually tell a good story. Teaching, journalism, the media (all kinds - local news especially), languages, the sciences and travel may also be very attractive to them, and could be the basis for their career. They are also known to be dexterous and are likely to be attracted to light manual work or commerce involving much use of the hands - using computers for an online business would be an obvious choice, or being involved in some kind of travel and delivery service might be another.

## Challenges

The typical Gemini will tend to have "fingers in every pie" of anything that takes their interest. That said, because of their inquisitiveness, they can also tend to gossip, cut corners, skip over the surface of things (be light of touch), get easily distracted, and be inclined to spread themselves too thinly. They are inclined to be superficial in other words. They may also be accused of being a bit two-faced, or mischievous. The chattering monkey is often associated with this sign. They can tend to have an overly busy mind that can make them stressful and anxious.

# Typical ♋ Cancerian

The typical Cancerian needs to put down roots. They have a powerful need for familiarity, a sense of place, a need to feel at-home in their environment and in themselves.

Imagine for a moment the pioneers of the old Wild West. It took decisive Aries courage for people to up and venture into that wilderness. On arrival, deciding on a plot of land to settle and build a house, or farm, was a Taurean phase. Learning about the environment, resources, other settlers, neighbours, who to link up with, was the Gemini phase. Turning the land into one's homeland, or a house into a home, and starting a family, is the Cancer phase. It is that huge emotional link with where one is at – "home is where the heart is."

The typical Cancer person will tend to form strong links with their parental home, develop a strong interest in, or concern for their background, their heritage – their family tree. They can be quite nostalgic for the past. They will tend to be sensitive, impressionable, protective, caring and nurturing. They will tend to follow convention, endorsing established traditions, institutions, family and cultural codes of conduct.

That said, Cancer, which is a Water sign and ruled by the Moon, may draw on hidden depths and be sensitive to other levels of experience, hidden from most of us, but completely natural to them.

## Relationships

The typical Cancer tends to be maternal and protective of others – regardless of gender. They can be really nice and friendly to know. They may appear tough skinned, hard negotiators, but underneath can be shy and retiring, needing to be coaxed out of their shells – needing a lot of love. They want to be needed, and it is important to them to be around people who help them to feel secure and loved. They are inclined to place great importance on emotional and material security, with a strong desire for marriage or partnership and family.

## Likely vocation interests

Their care, caution and need to follow clear codes of conduct make them good business people, and professional in whatever line of work they follow. The caring professions (or caring for others at a business level, in say a family business, perhaps a shop or restaurant) will tend to have a strong appeal. The need to feel "at home" in their vocation will be a main concern and influence on their career choice/s.

## Challenges

The typical Cancerian can be over-sensitive, touchy, over-emotional, and over-protective of themselves and others. They are inclined to present a hard shell to the world but inside can be timid and avoid facing up to the challenges they need to face. They will tend to avoid straying too far from their comfort zone, what they are familiar with. So, when real change, or moving into a new situation, is called for, it can be a painful wrench that they approach with trepidation. At worst, the Cancerian can be inclined to retreat from facing life and develop feelings of inferiority. It is important for them therefore to build up a sense of an inner home, or identity, a belief in their own abilities and to value who they are.

# Typical ♌ Leo

The typical Leo is the child hero at heart. They usually exude self-confidence and a natural magnetism that attracts people to them. They carry themselves with dignity. The typical Leo has a warm and sunny disposition. They are inclined to be self-assured, optimistic, out-going, sociable and companionable. They naturally take on the role of an authority, a natural leader and organiser, a person who can make decisions. They are protective of others and generous by nature.

The typical Leo will be optimistic regarding life. They can certainly be the life and soul of the party. To them, life is as a game; they enjoy having fun, taking up challenges, taking up sports, being on an adventure, or in a drama. They can very easily see themselves as a character in a play – and the main character at that. They like to be noticed, and the centre of attention or centre stage. They usually like to have an audience.

The typical Leo will be inclined to think big. To them the glass is half full – at least. In thinking big they have a tendency not to enjoy things that require attention to detail, or are, in their opinion, too dull and unexciting. They are inclined to be laid-back, relaxed, and prefer to take their time over things. They enjoy the pleasures of life. They are creative, in the broadest sense of the word, and motivated by the urge to make their mark on the world, to gain a measure of personal recognition.

## Relationships

The typical Leo is warm, big hearted, charismatic, generous, passionate and demonstrative. They like to bring sunshine into the lives of those they befriend or love. They will enjoy making people feel special – often through magnanimous gestures. But that said, the Leo is even more likely to enjoy having attention for themselves – they need to be made to feel special themselves. This can, of course, mean that they are also inclined to overlook, or misread, the needs of others, their partners. The typical

Leo will want to take the lead in their relationships – and they will probably be at their happiest in friendships or partnerships that have an element of rivalry.

## Likely vocation interests

Leo's need some form of competition where they can measure themselves up against other people or standard. They are born leaders and quite capable of managing the concerns of others. Their sense of drama, and creative play, will tend to place them well for marketing, presenting, teaching and acting.

## Challenges

The tendency to make life a game can mean that the typical Leo may not be so inclined to take serious matters seriously. Likewise, looking for the bigger picture, they can also overlook the "small print" in life. Without maturity and adjustment, the typical Leo can develop an inclination to become arrogant, conceited, domineering, autocratic, pompous, condescending and/or susceptible to flattery – the "prima donna" comes to mind here. We all need love in our lives. The Leo child needs a lot of love and attention. Without it, it can be difficult for them to shine. Should a Leo lose their confidence, it can take a lot of love and support to help them to recover – there's nothing as sad as an unhappy lion.

# Typical ♍ Virgo

The typical Virgo will tend to be a gentle, modest, prudent and quiet person, yet also a perfectionist, seeking high standards, particularly of themselves, in their work, their health and hygiene. They are reserved, conventional, fastidious and discriminating in nature. They will tend to have an analytical and pragmatic mind – an appreciation for the workings, the order and practical approaches to things. They are known for their attention to detail, for a precise and exacting application of themselves.

The typical Virgo is diligent, careful, tidy, systematic and methodical in their approach to life. They have a concern for the "nuts and bolts," a "taking care of the small things" (the pennies) so the bigger things (the pounds) can look after themselves. They want things to run smoothly and efficiently.

## Relationships

The typical Virgo is inclined to hold back, to be shy, in social interaction. Deep down they will be friendly, generous, surprisingly intimate and giving to a fault as the next person. This is toning down the Leo need to be the centre of everything, to being on a more level playing field with others. It just takes time for them to open up with people. Because of their inclination towards seeking perfection, they are inclined to also look for this in their relationships – high expectations. Not finding this can leave them either on a mission to change people, and being accused of nagging – or to be feeling disappointed in their friends and partners.

## Likely vocation interests

The typical Virgo needs to find their place within the community. They will likely develop a strong work ethic. They will tend to enjoy working in a conventional direction of work, or environment, where routine and attention to detail is a major part of what they do. They like to work with their hands – Virgo is considered the crafts-person of the zodiac. They are probably a specialist, or expert, in matters that provide most interest or nourishment for them – health and hygiene are often of special interest. It is important for the Virgo to be of service – most probably through their work or vocation. The Virgo tendency to be modest and under-stated in their endeavours is endearing but can mean they may appear to others as unambitious; and they can get overlooked as a result. It is important, therefore, for them not to be (or become) servile in their need to serve.

## Challenges

The typical Virgo can be overly fussy, overly concerned with small matters, overly modest and, if not careful, be getting labelled as, as "dull as dishwater." They also need to control their inclination to worry. They can worry over, what others would see as, minor issues. They can be overly critical (needing to learn to be more constructive in their criticisms), pessimistic, tending to focus on what could go wrong than right – carrying the "glass is half-empty" view of themselves, and their world.

# Typical ♎ Libran

The typical Libran seeks to develop a balanced and harmonious relationship with others and their world. The Libran is communicative, an engaging, outgoing, diplomatic, tactful, sociable, kind and friendly person.

He or she will seek fair play, have a natural sense of justice and can easily (better than most) see "both sides of the coin" in a given situation. In their interaction with others, they will shine where evaluation, negotiation and co-operation are understood requirements. The Libran will often find themselves in the role of judge and/or peace-maker – reaching a conclusion that is fair, is a reason why Librans tend to make good mediators and diplomats.

It can be said that the typical Libran seeks to have "equal amounts" in their life to be happy. He or she seeks a balance between work, home-life and play, between activity and relaxation, between social interaction and spending time alone – yes, they do like to spend more time alone than is predicted of them. In their striving for balance, harmony and refinement, they will seek to live in beautiful surroundings, and having beautiful things around them too.

## Relationships

The typical Libran is romantic and will tend to begin exploring relationships, including more intimate relationships, from an early age. In truth they are looking for themselves in others – or in others to redress the imbalance in their own lives. Their charm alone can get them quickly over the hurdles of breaking the ice and making first contact. That said, they are often described as being in love with idea of love rather than the actual experience of it – in other words the reality often does not live up to the ideal, and relationships may be short lived and disappointing as a result. In context, it may be said that Libra is not necessarily the most passionate or sexually driven sign of the zodiac – by how much will be helped or determined by other chart components.

Their need for building harmonious relationships can make them vulnerable to being too accepting of unwanted circumstances, too easy-going, less demanding, buying into peace and harmony at any price. They are also inclined to become overly dependent upon their friends or partner to take the lead in decision-making.

One of the lessons for Libra is to learn about compromise and what is fair, that is to demand to be equal in their given partnership; and, at another level, to be also able to accept the less-than-ideal in their given partner. People rarely live up to another person's ideal; and the gloss can soon come off, as shown by Scorpio.

## Likely vocation interests

The typical Libran will possess artistic and creative talent, an appreciation of aesthetics, beauty, the visual arts, music and dance, and the finer things in life. They will most probably seek to work in socially harmonious and refined environments, where their talents for communications, publicity, providing information, diplomacy and sensitivity can be best appreciated. They can lead but are usually happy to let others take the lead – as long as this is done in the spirit of fairness and diplomacy.

## Challenges

The typical Libran is often accused of indecision, of "sitting on the fence." This is not always a fair representation of what is going on for them. Their indecision may stem less from being woolly about matters but from their ability to see both sides of whatever they are having to make a decision about. Even so they may miss opportunity due to wavering. They can equally be accused of being too easy-going, over-idealistic and inclined to look at life through rose-tinted glasses. Such imbalance can cause the Libran to be insecure and to lack confidence in their abilities. It is important for them to hold onto their own power and not give it away.

# Typical ♏ Scorpio

The typical Scorpio is strong-willed, emotionally intense, introspective, passionate, subtle, assertive, reserved, private, secretive, even hidden. "Still waters run deep" is a very apt description for Scorpio. The Scorpio is still and quiet on the outside, while intense within. For some a forceful torrent could be running within, for others, quiet control is the name of the game.

The Scorpio is imaginative, intuitive, analytical, able to, as it were, "see in the dark" to inspect matters and get to the "truth" of what it is they are interested in. Scorpios usually need plenty of time by themselves to think deeply about the things they feel. They are known for their ability to remain calm in stressful or adverse circumstances. They have powers of perseverance and tenacity – an ability to return from adversity. They are usually determined and decisive in their behaviour.

## Relationships

The Scorpio is inclined to be quiet, reserved and slow to get to know. But a friend one can rely on. What a Scorpio really seeks in relating is trust, honesty and authenticity. In intimate relationships the Scorpio will be a passionate partner, adding a lot of potential tension and excitement to the relationship. They are likely to have strong sexual drives.

Scorpios tend to make deep commitments. To a large extent they are governed by their intensity of feelings. They can be moody to deal with. If upset, it can take time for them to recover, to calm those waters – although they may not show it. Their need for security will tend to place demands on their relationships, and also make them vulnerable to conflict and being hurt. They can, in context, be quite possessive and controlling.

With their nature being sensitive and secretive, they won't necessarily reveal what they are really thinking, but they will be tuned in. Rightly or wrongly, they tend to rely on their instinct to know how things are in their relationships. They are usually good at picking up on vibes; and any hint of something not quite right may raise their suspicions – and a possible corresponding disquiet, even jealousy in their more intimate relationships.

## Likely vocation interests

The typical Scorpio is willing to take the lead, particularly in situations that draw on their passion, resourcefulness and dedication. They will often take a military-like approach to matters. It is not much of a leap to say that they would be in their element in activities that involve probing into matters – areas of detective work, research and application that have clear outcomes and implications.

## Challenges

When negative, the Scorpio is capable of being cold, ruthless, unforgiving, and inclined to bear resentment and vendettas. They can be quite hard and pessimistic about life. There is a duality of light and darkness operating within the typical Scorpio psyche. Arguably we all have this duality but in Scorpio it will be more noticeable, to them at least. It is like they have come up to a T junction on their road, and are deciding whether to turn left or right – towards the light or dark. The dualities of life, such as me versus others, honesty versus dishonesty, good versus evil or give versus take, and life versus death, may provide endless internal dialogue.

The typical Scorpio may indeed be tempted either way – the light side or the dark side – in their interests. Scorpio, after all, encapsulates the courage of the soldier, the covert activities of the spy, the spiritual discipline of the priest, the cold self-control of the surgeon, the probing of the psychoanalyst, or the detective with a nose for organised crime. At their best, the Scorpio seeks to see things as they really are, in the cold light of day – and will dig deep in order to get to the bottom of things, to uncover what they think or suspect is going on.

# Typical ♐ Sagittarian

The typical Sagittarian will tend to take a philosophical outlook on life. They have a strong curiosity about things. He or she will tend to be open-minded, benevolent, optimistic, versatile, adaptable, adventurous, a risk-taker, honest and direct. Unless factors suggest otherwise, the Sagittarian tends to see life as "the glass half-full" and will gamble on things getting better.

The typical Sagittarian may be full of wanderlust, seeking to broaden out their horizons, whether as a physical expansion or an expansion of their mind – or both. They will seek to accomplish this through travel, experiencing other cultures, through sports, education, reading and writing, and/or through exploring the deeper questions that life throws up – the search for meaning. They will tend to develop their own beliefs, but often these are based upon conventional structures, such as orthodox religion, the arts, sciences or philosophy. Higher education will tend to appeal to the typical Sagittarian.

## Relationships

Given they are mature and well-adjusted, in relationships the Sagittarian will tend to be passionate and conventional, be very warm, loving and considerate. Their optimism can be infectious and endearing. They will always want to see the best in others. Always, however, he or she will cherish their independence, the freedom to have fun, adventure and not feel tied down. They may have many relatively short-term relationships during their life, while finding it difficult to settle down.

## Likely vocation interests

The Sagittarian needs open doors, an opportunity to explore, be adventurous and take a risk. Any avenue that allows for speculation, versatility, travel, an enterprising and far-reaching approach to matters is likely to have appeal. As indeed are areas involving exploration, morality, the law, the sciences and religion. They like their freedom, and are at their least happy when tied down to, what they would consider, dull routine/s that hamper or limit them.

## Challenges

It has to be said that not all Sagittarians are necessarily high-brow or high rollers; they may just as easily be pleasure seekers, beach bums or gamblers, inclined to squander and be wasteful of opportunities. If not tempered, the typical Sagittarian may also be given over to having an exaggerated opinion of who they are. Being an opportunist, getting one over on others, being overly-extravagant, boastful, brash, being frank and ruthless, lacking tact with others are all possible challenging traits. They can also be inclined to take the high ground and be overly judgemental of others.

# Typical ♑ Capricorn

The typical Capricorn is a practical, cautious, often shy, patient and mature person – regardless of age. They will be hard-working, industrious, tenacious, goal-setting and ambitious. It is important for the Capricorn to be good at something and to earn recognition. They will seek to improve their status through their honest achievements. They are also inclined to be modest and/or under-stated in their achievements.

The typical Capricorn will have a constructive and responsible attitude in the world. They are usually conventional in their goals and values. They will tend to rely on trusted and tried ways, doing things by the book.

Capricorn is a business-like sign. Ruled by Saturn, it is arguably the most serious sign of the zodiac, and the typical Capricorn will certainly have a serious and introspective side to their nature. Although that doesn't preclude them having a sense of humour; and, with their oftimes dry wit, a Capricorn can be very entertaining and fun to be with.

## Relationships

The typical Capricorn is inclined to take time to get to know people. That said they will tend to make long lasting friendships. Commitments are inclined to be for life. They are cautious and conventional in forming relationships and likewise with expressing their affections – e.g., they are less likely to feel comfortable hugging people, and be more at home shaking the person's hand. In love, the Capricorn will most often seek to follow a traditional role – on-route towards possible marriage. They will tend to seek to have clear boundaries, of who does what, in the home.

## Likely vocation interests

The typical Capricorn is naturally conservative, discriminating, disciplined and authoritative. They like to know where their projected boundaries lie. Material security will be part of the package, or what drives them. They will tend to keep a cool head under pressure. They are best suited to roles that require dedication, organisation, application and responsibility, as in a teaching or management or in a leadership role. Capricorns have a mountain to climb. What that looks like and how well they can climb it will depend upon the nature of the goals they set themselves and their abilities to climb it – whether achievable or not.

## Challenges

And in context with "mountain," Capricorns can be hard on themselves, having a tendency to develop low self-esteem or be lacking in confidence. Worse-case scenario, the Capricorn is prone to feelings of isolation, is inclined to become pessimistic about life. They may be prone to depression and developing an inferiority complex about their abilities and their value, to themselves and others. A lot will depend on what else is happening in their birth-chart – and of course their upbringing giving form to that potential, regarding how easy or difficult they cope in later life.

The Capricorn is required to develop patience combined with a clear direction of travel, and a knowing (and an acceptance) of oneself and limits.

# Typical ♒ Aquarian

The typical Aquarian is intuitive, communicative, individualistic, friendly and sociable. They will be motivated by a sense of justice, fairness and freedom. They tend to have a contemporary, unconventional and progressive outlook on life, having enthusiasm for what is new, current (which could be retro in outcome), original and innovative.

There is often something eccentric or unpredictable about the Aquarian nature. It will tend to manifest in their individuality – perhaps in their style of dress, in their interests, their cultural orientation or their work.

The typical Aquarian can be highly inventive and creative and will often be found in areas where new ground in ideas is being broken. They are likely to be interested in the arts, sciences and technology, in gadgets and inventions – and really in anything that aids towards the emancipation of people at some level. Aquarians are likely to seek a cause to get behind, and will often get involved in social and political movements, concerned with freedom and justice. This is a truly humanitarian sign.

## Relationships

The typical Aquarian, in relating, will tend to be friendly and truly interested in, and accepting of people. They generally have a tolerance and understanding of other people, and are capable of perceiving what people really think and feel, no matter how they are presented or where they are from. In other respects, they can be emotionally guarded or detached. This is sometimes misunderstood as coldness or aloofness, whereas it can be that the Aquarian finds it difficult to be intimate – friendly yes, intimate not so easy. They will value their freedom, their independence, but no less value the freedom and independence for others, as for themselves. They will tend to treat others as equal to themselves.

## Likely vocation interests

At some level, the Aquarian needs to be involved in helping to bring about change and revolution - a seeking to emancipate, or ease, the lives of people. This is more probably done through social interaction, through innovation, the exchange of ideas, through use of intuitive powers. But it could equally be through the use of new technology, and both. Interests are likely to link to education, social reform, environmental matters, the sciences and technology.

## Challenges

Taken to extremes, the Aquarian nature is inclined to be over-reactive, rebellious, tactless and erratic in their behaviour. Indeed, the sign is associated with extremists and fanatics, people with an "impersonal" axe to grind. Alternatively, the Aquarian can be inclined to do things to shock, for affect, or because they want to appear different for the sake of it, to make a fashion statement let's say.

# Typical ♓ Piscean

The typical Piscean is a sensitive, emotional, impressionable, dreamy, romantic and peace-loving person. They are like an ocean in mood and will tend to feel things intensely – picking up on others' feelings as much as their own. Innately creative and imaginative, the Piscean will tend to have an appreciation of the arts, notably video/film, poetry and music. They may, alternatively, endeavour to cover up their sensitivity and seek to appear tough skinned – impervious to others needs. At heart though, the Piscean is a deeply caring, sympathetic and compassionate person. They need to be devoted to something or someone.

This person will like being out in nature, will tend to love big skies, the ocean, and wild and unspoilt places. It is important for the Piscean to be able to escape, to get away from the hustle and bustle world, either to have a favourite place to escape to, or perhaps some kind of retreat; or it might alternatively be through a practice such as meditation and yoga. There is likely to be a spiritual or religious motive, or a seeking of bodily refinement (concern for diet), behind such endeavours – "refinement" is a key theme for the typical Piscean.

## Relationships

While the typical Pisces often choose time to be on their own, in retreat, they will always want to return to be in the company of others. This is a giving sign, and the Piscean will be at their happiest when they can care for, or serve, others in some way. The Piscean is likely to be very open and friendly, easy to like. They can be very adaptable to changing circumstances, but also vulnerable to being submissive and getting let down or hurt in their relationships, in their expectations.

## Likely vocation interests

It follows that career-wise, the typical Pisces will need to feel they can be of some kind of service to humanity. They can be drawn towards the helping professions, in counselling, in nursing or equally as a home help, carer or shop assistant. That said they are highly adaptable, with a vivid imagination, and indeed their flexibility allows them to be able to play and be many characters – a quality very appropriate for acting. The movies, its fantasy and escapism can be a strong pull on the Piscean psyche. Others are likely to be attracted towards the arts, becoming writers, artists or musicians.

## Challenges

Unfortunately, sometimes the need for "escape" is found less through natural or spiritual avenues, and rather through other means, such through drugs, alcohol, fantasy, taking one's life, and at the exploitation of others. The Piscean personality tends to be changeable, and can be indecisive and vulnerable, tending to flow with the tide, and, if not watchful, in danger of drifting, like flotsam, aimlessly through life – and needing others for a steer or a rudder to lean on. The Piscean needs to develop "certainty" from within, as their external life may not always provide it for them – it will however be a mirror of where they are at on the inside, and thereby can change.

# Part 2
# The Zodiac Signs Matrix

This part will help you to better understand how the zodiac signs we use are constructed. First, though, let's remind ourselves which zodiac we are actually using here...

## The Tropical Zodiac

The zodiac that is mostly used in Western astrology is called the "tropical zodiac." It is very likely that your birth-chart will be constructed with this zodiac. The alternative is the "sidereal zodiac" (mostly used in Vedic astrology, but also by some Western astrologers) which is based upon the star constellations of the zodiac belt (of the ecliptic).

The tropical zodiac is constructed around the seasons of the Earth/Sun relationship. It is a purely symbolical arrangement. The path the Earth takes around the Sun, is divided equally into twelve 30-degree sections. Each representing a zodiac sign.

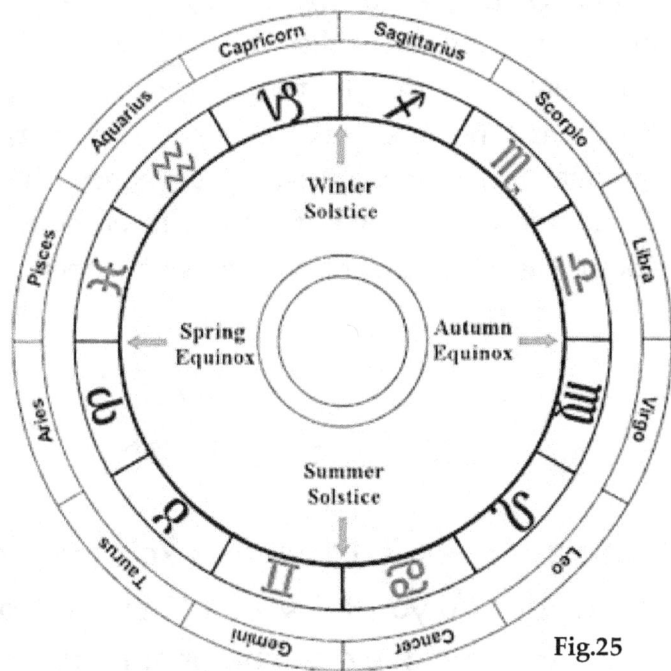

Fig.25

Learn to Read Your Birth-chart in 5 Steps  **65**

Note (Fig.25), how Aries begins at the Spring Equinox, Cancer at the Summer Solstice. Libra begins at the Autumnal Equinox and Capricorn begins at the Winter Solstice.

The tropical zodiac has probably been in use since the discovery of the Precession of the Equinoxes, from over two thousand years of observations.

Due to gravitational pull, of the Sun and Moon, the Earth wobbles, as it spins (see Fig.26). The wobble can be noticed in the cyclic motion at the poles, marking out a huge circle. This is a slow process. It takes around 26 thousand years to complete one cycle of precession.

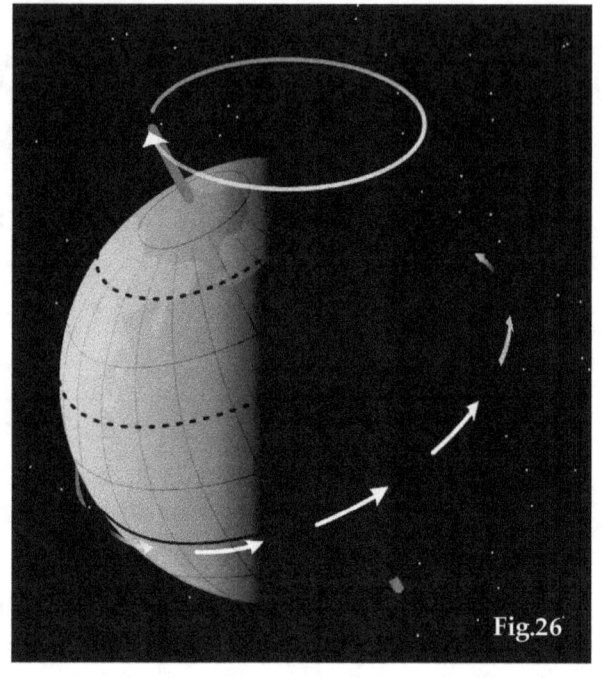

As a result, the spring equinox (the start of the tropical zodiac) occurs a little earlier each year, when measured against the background stars. It is moving backwards relative to the stars.

The spring equinox once aligned with the beginning of the constellation of Aries, but due to precession it has been moving back from Aries, through the constellation of Pisces and heading towards the constellation of Aquarius. Astrologers treat this movement as representing Ages – hence the anticipated Age of Aquarius, either here already or yet to come. Find out more about the Ages in the **Bonus Pack** - see under **About the Course** section for more information on the pack.

# The Signs Matrix

Here's a question for you. You may know there are twelve signs to the zodiac but do you know why there are only twelve? And indeed, do you know why the twelve are in the order they are in?

You're not alone if you don't know the answers to these questions. Here's a clue: The matrix of the signs is the reason...

Before going into this, let me first remind you that the signs run anti-clockwise and are always in the same order. That is, beginning at Aries the cycle goes to Taurus then Gemini; Cancer; Leo; Virgo; Libra; Scorpio; Sagittarius; Capricorn; Aquarius; and Pisces. From Pisces the cycle repeats back to Aries.

See **One Step Further: The Spiritual Roadmap** for more thoughts on this cycle.

It really helps to understand how the zodiac signs are interpreted by exploring the matrix of the signs – or, if you prefer, the building blocks of the signs.

They will help in your understanding. They will aid you in linking the keywords associated with the component signs. And help you to begin to put your own slant, thoughts and words onto the interpretation.

The matrix of the signs is built on the four elements; and on whether the sign is positive or negatively charged, and also on whether the sign is cardinal, fixed or mutable. See the illustrations below.

This gives us the big clue as to why there are only twelve signs, and in the order they are in.

# Division of Signs into Positive and Negative

The twelve signs, beginning from Aries, alternate positive and then negative around the circle (Fig.27). There are six parings altogether therefore. These are called the **Polarities.**

## Positive Signs

*Positive signs have these keywords in common: extraverted (Jungian), self-expressive, outgoing, masculine.*

## Negative Signs

*Negative signs have these keywords in common: introverted (Jungian), self-reflective, ingoing, feminine.*

Bear in mind that positive and negative do not represent value judgements on the signs, but rather their direction of focus. The focus of "positive" signs is in an external objective direction, while the focus of "negative" signs is an internal subjective direction. Rather like the positive and negative poles of a magnet/electricity they complement or oppose one another.

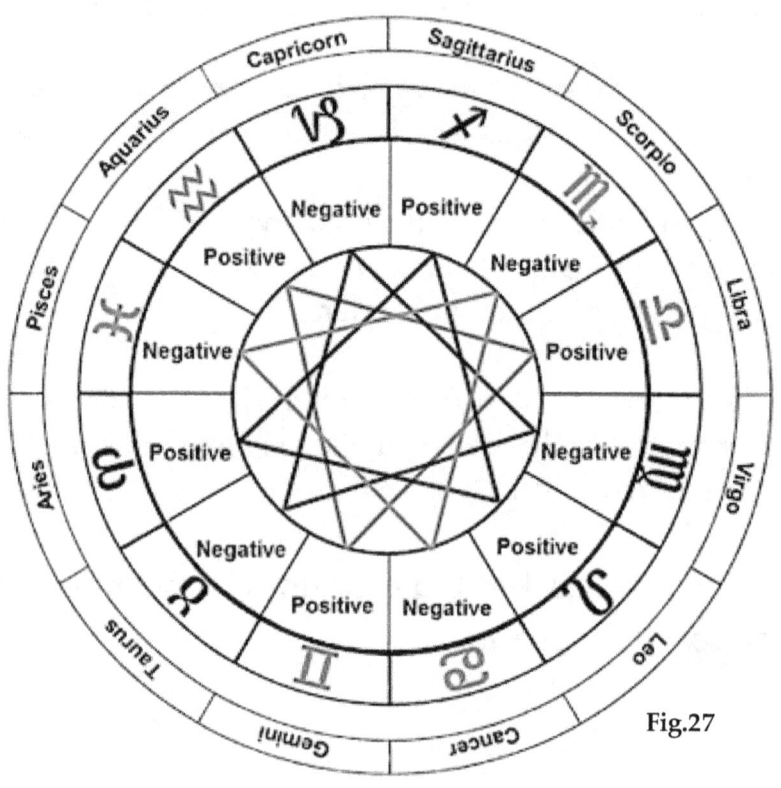

Fig.27

We all, of course, have both positive and negative signs in our birth-charts. Knowing where the emphasis is will indicate whether we tend to identify ourselves by externals (our external world, outside of ourself) or internals (our internal world of our thoughts and feelings).

Aries and Gemini, for example, are outgoing signs, more inclined to get out there and interact with the world. Whereas Taurus and Cancer are ingoing and thereby more cautious and self-reflective.

# Division of Signs into the Four Elements

The twelve signs are also divided in sequence into three groups having four signs to each group (Fig.28). These are called the **Triplicities**. You are probably already familiar with these as the four elements. Their meaning is as follows.

## Fire Signs

Keywords: ardent, keen, aspiring, etheric, leader.

## Earth Signs

Keywords: practical, cautious, solid, dependable, physical, builder.

## Air Signs

Keywords: inquisitive, intellectual, working with ideas, mental, communicator.

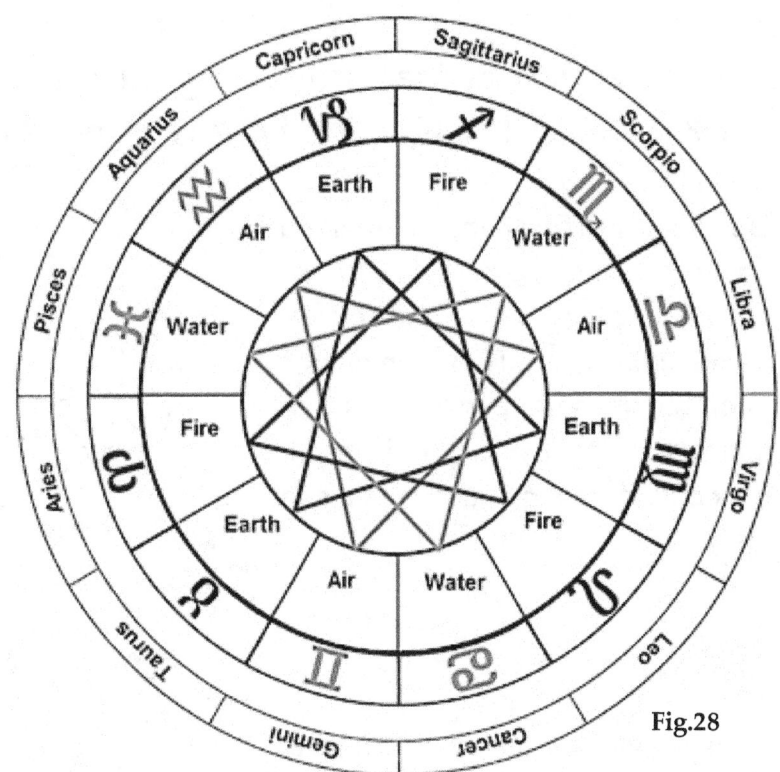

Fig.28

## Water Signs

Keywords: emotional, unstable, sensitive, fluid, nurturer.

Learn to Read Your Birth-chart in 5 Steps  **69**

## Examples

Aries, Leo and Sagittarius are all Fire signs. Their energy is positive, outgoing, spontaneous in response, and optimistic. Cancer, Scorpio and Pisces are Water signs. Their energy in negative, ingoing, cautious in response, driven by feelings – Water signs can be quite secretive too.

One can link Carl Jung's four main psychological functions with the elements. That is *thinking* (Air), *feeling* (Water), *sensation* (Earth), and *intuition* (Fire). He introduced them with having either an internally focused *introverted* (negative signs) or externally focused *extraverted* (positive signs) tendency which he called "attitudes."

# Division of Signs into Modes of Change

The signs also divide into four groups having three common signs each (Fig.29), called the **Quadruplicities (Modes or Qualities)**.

Don't worry if you get a bit mixed up with the names of these categories i.e. Triplicities, Quadruplicities. Just remember their component parts. This one concerns the cyclic rhythm, or process of **change,** and it is made up of:

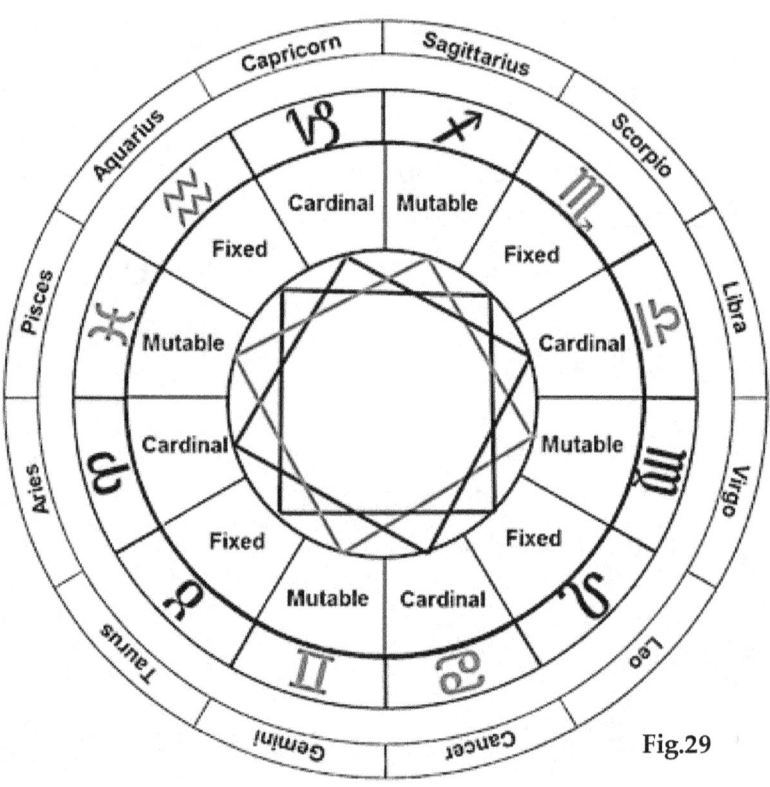

Fig.29

## Cardinal Signs

Keywords: embracing change, initiating, leading, moving on. Breathing in. The Cardinal signs are the change points in the cycle of the seasons.

## Fixed Signs

*Keywords: resistant to change, fixing, settling, stabilising, holding, inertia. Holding breath.*

## Mutable Signs

*Keywords: adapting, following, fluid, changeful, flowing and versatile. Breathing out.*

## Examples

Capricorn is Cardinal and begins on the Winter Solstice. Being an Earth sign it embraces change but in a slower more measured way than say the Cardinal sign of Aries – which tends to embrace change fast, headfirst without really thinking about it.

Aquarius meanwhile is a Fixed sign. Considering its association with invention and all things new one might ask how is it Fixed – isn't it about change? I'd say it is fixed in its stabilising of new or radical ideas, concepts and inventions that help (or might help) in one way or another to lead to change in the form of progress.

All the Fixed signs help to stabilise change in their own way – Taurus at an earthy level, Leo at fiery level, Scorpio at a watery level (think of ice) and Aquarius at an airy level.

# And all together

Taken together (Fig.30), this matrix of principles or conditions means that each sign of the twelve will also be unique, in its matrix combination. So, for example Aries is fire, cardinal and positive, while its opposite number, Libra, is air, cardinal and positive.

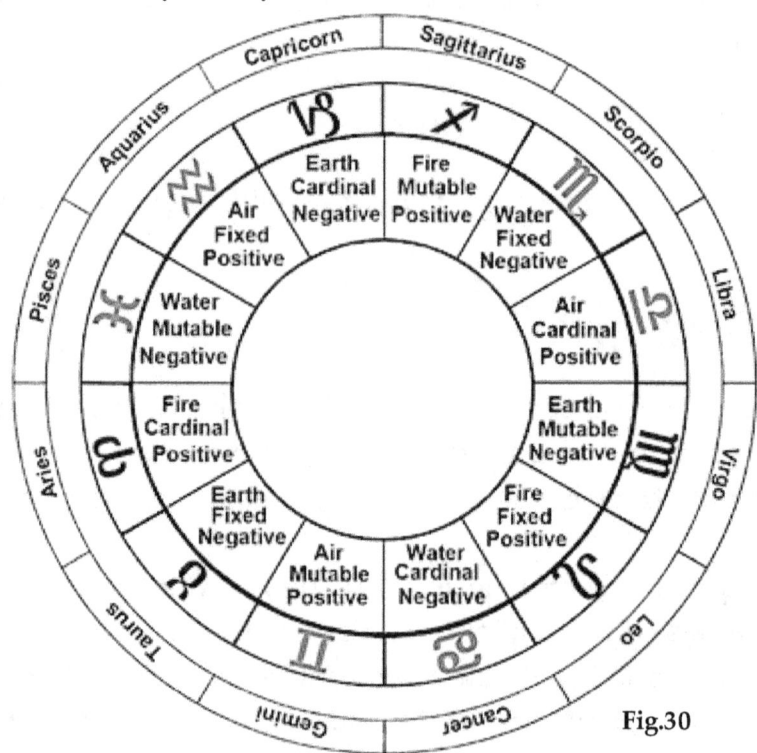
Fig.30

The simple criteria on which it is constructed means that this system depends upon having twelve signs – not more and not less. It also means, by their matrix, that the signs can only be in the order they are in.

# The Running Order of the Signs

Alongside the matrix, it helps to take into consideration that the signs are in the order we find them not just because their arrangement is beautifully cohesive but because they also form a cyclic process of development (see Fig.31).

72    Step Two: Learn to Read the Signs

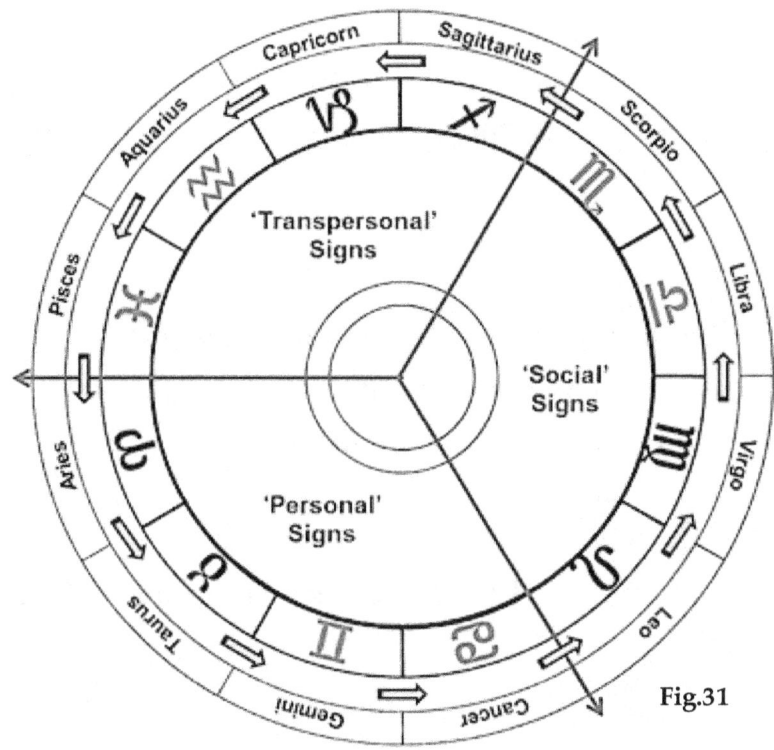

Fig.31

Broadly they fall into three categories of development: the personal, the social and the transpersonal. Within these three broad categories, lies a story of twelve steps, having a beginning and an ending, from the personal towards the transpersonal - in their highest form of expression. I discuss this further in **One Step Further: The Spiritual Roadmap**.

So, this is a cycle which begins in Aries and ends in Pisces – before returning to a new cycle. Each sign in the cycle forms part of the narrative of the cycle and thereby represents a theme, or step, in the order, process and flow of the cycle.

Just to add as a reminder here that all twelve signs in a birth-chart operate regardless of whether they are occupied by planets or not – all seek to find expression.

Planets are the players and they do emphasise, make prominent, given themes and particular directions of expression.

But also, each of the twelve signs will be linking to a house and influencing that area of life through that given house.

I hope this will become clearer as you read and work through the following...

# Personal signs

*Aries to Cancer - have a "personal" agenda – they have a "me and mine" preoccupation about them.*

## Social signs

Leo to Scorpio have a "social" agenda - or relating to others from a personal baseline. They have a "you and me" or "others and me" about them.

## Transpersonal (or global/collective) signs

Sagittarius to Pisces have a "transpersonal" (alternatively a more global/collective) agenda - or looking beyond our personal and social relationships, into a wider public, global, spiritual context. They have "the world and me" or an "us and me" (as in "all of us in this together" broader sense) about them.

Don't forget to check out Part 2 of **One Step Further** for further discussion on this topic.

# Part 3
# Compensatory behaviour

While your birth-chart contains all 12 of the signs of the zodiac not all of your signs will have a planet in them. Likewise, some of your planets may be grouped together in single signs. For example, in Anne Frank's chart (Fig.32), having Moon, Mars and Neptune in Leo.

Signs occupied by planets are going to play a more prominent role in your life. That said to understand unoccupied signs look to their ruling planet (discussed in Step 2) and the house the sign is covering.

With the Anne Frank chart (illustrated) for instance there are no planets in Virgo (detailed work/service) but it is on the 3rd house (writing, communications), while the ruling planet, Mercury, is in Gemini (again writing, communications). So, this is how you would begin to make sense of the Virgo theme in Anne Frank's chart.

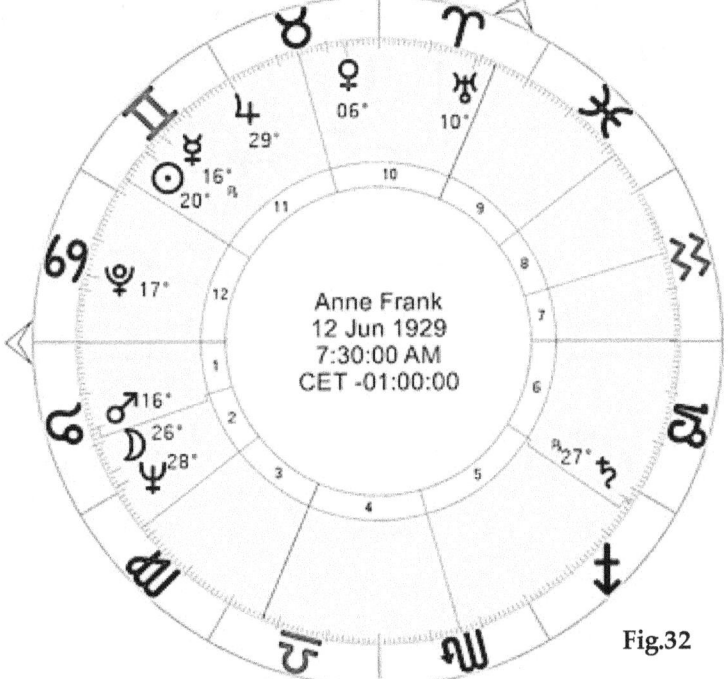

Fig.32

> Anne Frank was a victim of the Holocaust, who kept a diary (for which she is famous – published in 1947) while in hiding for two years; before being found by the Nazis.

It is worth noting that we are also inclined to compensate, turn a subconscious spotlight on, any unoccupied element or mode through our behaviour. If we lack Fire (no planets in Fire signs) for instance we can come across as fiery, overly enthusiastic, unstoppable. If we lack Earth, we may work hard to appear practical and down to earth in attitude.

> I lack Earth in my chart and spent years digging into it, as an archaeologist.

If we lack Air, we can be very chatty and all about communicating. If we lack Water, we may come across as gushing, overly sensitive and sympathetic with our feelings – or crocodile tears as some might call it.

If it's a mode we lack, then similar: For instance, no planets in Cardinal signs we can be all about getting things moving, bringing on change – or a force for change. If Fixed signs we lack then we may be preoccupied with stability and our security. If Mutable signs we lack, then we may be inclined to travel light, we're flexible, ready to move at the drop of a hat.

# Part 4

# Zodiac Themes

To further one's understanding of the signs of the zodiac it is really useful to get a grasp of, what I call, their "themes" or root ideas that they each represent and seek to express. From that, the interpretation, in terms of outcomes, can, I believe, flow and be more easily recognised.

If you have a planet in Taurus, for example, you will tend (or need) to focus the expression of that planet via a theme of "establishing structure and security." The house that is then also linked to Taurus in the birth-chart will further emphasise, or add mundane clarity to the direction of expression of the planet.

The outcome of that planet's expression could for example be carried through property, money (2$^{nd}$ or 8$^{th}$ houses), getting good qualifications (3$^{rd}$ or 9$^{th}$ houses) or a reliable and regular career (4$^{th}$, 6$^{th}$ or 10$^{th}$ houses), or it could be through earthy outdoor pursuits (2$^{nd}$ or 12$^{th}$ houses) as working with plants or in husbandry (2$^{nd}$, 4$^{th}$ or 12$^{th}$ houses), or more...

# Zodiac themes in brief

Here are the zodiac themes in brief. The full Zodiac Signs Resource will be found, under **The Resources**, towards the back of the book.

# Aries ♈ – The Ram

## Cardinal | Fire | Positive

Aries in our birth-chart is where we seek to initiate new experience objectively, urgently.

# Taurus ♉ – The Bull

## Fixed | Earth | Negative

Taurus in our birth-chart is where we seek to structure and stabilise experience - be productive, be secure and enduring.

# Gemini ♊ – The Twins

## Mutable | Air | Positive

Gemini in our birth-chart is where we seek to "know" and share through direct experience or acquired information.

# Cancer ♋ – The Crab

## Cardinal | Water | Negative

Cancer in our birth-chart is where we seek to familiarise and be "at-home" within our experience.

# Leo ♌ – The Lion

Fixed | Fire | Positive

Leo in our birth-chart is where we seek to express ourself powerfully within and through life experience.

# Virgo ♍ – The Virgin

Mutable | Earth | Negative

Virgo in our birth-chart is where, or how, we seek to prepare and participate within our community.

# Libra ♎ – The Scales

Cardinal | Air | Positive

Libra in our birth-chart is where we communicate through attraction towards our world, others and ourselves; where we seek to establish balance and harmony in relation to others and our world.

# Scorpio ♏ – The Scorpion & the Eagle

Fixed | Water | Negative

Scorpio in our birth-chart is where we experience and face up to hidden realities behind the gloss. We face some truths about life – such as everything ages and passes away, such as nothing and no one prepared us for this... Life is darker and deeper than the bed of roses of Libra. Here we are dealing with powerful emotions, that can be dark.

# Sagittarius ♐ – The Centaur/Archer

### Mutable | Fire | Positive

Sagittarius in our birth-chart is where we seek to expand experience and rediscover our enthusiasm for life – in context with knowing more, and after facing the (maybe harsh) realities of Scorpio. Where we seek to express and renew our faith in the bounty of life.

# Capricorn ♑ – The (Sea) Goat

### Cardinal | Earth | Negative

Capricorn in our birth-chart is where we face our mountain and achieve self-acceptance. Where we are challenged and experience resistance (particularly bounded by time) in gaining success in our world; in gaining our wisdom, freedom and maturity.

# Aquarius ♒ – The Water Bearer

### Fixed | Air | Positive

Aquarius in our birth-chart is where coming down off the mountain we have gained wisdom and a new sense of freedom. We seek something new, emancipating, innovative, that helps move us on from convention, tradition, old habits where they are outworn methods of operating and hindering progress. The focus now is also on helping others move on in some way. We seek to share our knowledge with the young at heart.

# Pisces ♓ – The Fishes

## Mutable | Water | Negative

Pisces in our birth-chart is where we refine, where we seek or express unconditional love and compassion, where we seek perfection; where we need to let go of our human indoctrination, preconceived notions, constructs and conditioning; and even our physical form.

# Check Your Chart

Check out how many planets you have in Positive and Negative signs.
Check out how many planets you have in Cardinal, Fixed and Mutable signs.
Check out how many planets you have in Fire, Earth, Air and Water signs.

Where is your chart balanced (even spread), top heavy (a lot of planets in say Negative signs or Air signs) or bottom heavy (no planets in say Cardinal signs, or perhaps only one in Water signs)?

Make a note of it. When we come to look at reading the chart, we'll look at a counting system that will add further weight to some of your planets.

Have a look at some of the example charts in the book (or from the **Bonus Pack**), to see how they compare.

And take a look at **The Zodiac Signs Resource** (under The Resources) for the sign your Moon is in.

Take a look at the Chart Shaping Resource and Hemisphere Emphasis in the Bonus Pack, and see if your chart fits with one of the patterns described. See under **About the Course** section for more on the Bonus Pack.

# Step 2 Quizzes

Try the following quizzes, and check with the answers further in. You'll probably need a piece of paper to jot your answers onto.

## Quiz 1 The Zodiac Signs - True or False

Decide if these statements are true or false. Check your answers with the quiz answers below.

1. The zodiac that most Western astrologers use is the Sidereal Zodiac.
2. The Tropical Zodiac relies heavily on the constellations in the ecliptic belt.
3. Virgo is a positive sign.
4. A water sign always follows a fire sign.
5. The air signs are all positive signs.
6. Each sign is unique in its matrix combination.
7. Cardinal signs help to instigate change.
8. Gemini is a transpersonal sign, while Aquarius is a personal sign.
9. Negative signs are to be avoided.
10. Libra follows Scorpio, and Virgo follows Libra.

## Quiz 2 The Personal Signs (Aries to Cancer) - True or False

1. Gemini is an earth sign that enjoys gardening.
2. Cancer is ruled by the Moon and can be secretive.
3. Taurus is a sign of communications. It likes nothing more than having a good chat.

4. Gemini is often linked to short journeys, and having knowledge of one's local area.
5. Aries will take the bull by the horns and go for its objectives.
6. Cancer is likely to make a hasty retreat in confrontation.
7. Aries is always seeking to protect its home and family.
8. Taurus likes the simple life where it can build something long lasting.

# Quiz 3 Identify the symbols

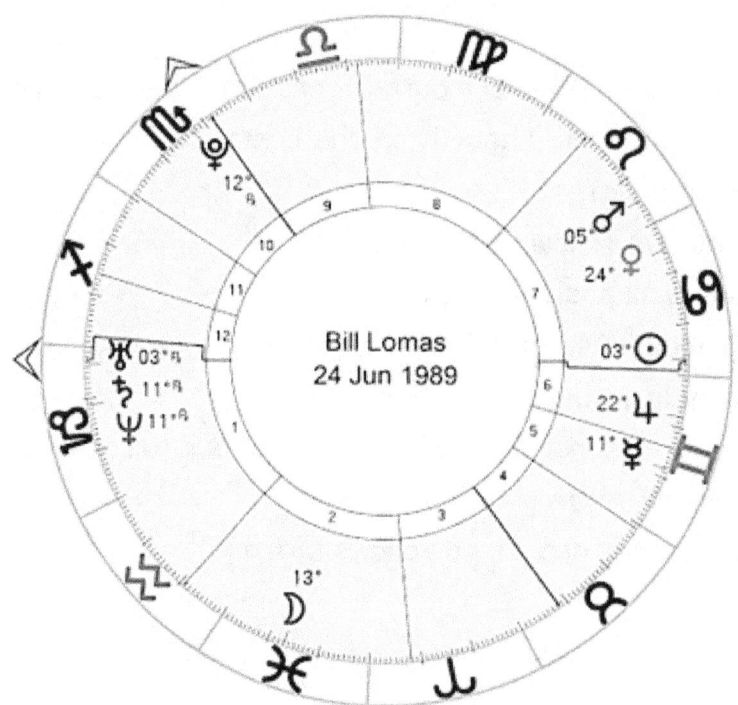

Take a look at this birth-chart, and using the key to the symbols (found directly under the opening page of The Course), see if you can identify what planets are where, all the way out to Pluto. Example: This person has Sun in Cancer 7th House; Moon is in… …House; Mercury is in … … House; Venus is in … … House; Mars is in … … House; Jupiter is in … … House; Saturn is in … … House; Uranus is in … … House; Neptune is in … … House; Pluto is in … … House.

Step Two: Learn to Read the Signs

# Quiz 4 The Social Signs (Leo to Scorpio) - True or False

1. Leo is often associated with work, being reserved and duty bound.
2. Libra is an ingoing or negative sign, often accused of being unfriendly and guarded.
3. If one sign could be ascribed to the paranormal, and things that go bump in the night, it's Scorpio.
4. Virgo may be found working in a laboratory, carrying out detailed analysis.
5. Leo enjoys competition, playing and being the centre of attention.
6. Scorpio is often noted for its diplomacy and seeking peace and harmony in negotiations.
7. Libra is often associated with fair play and justice.
8. Virgo is known for its intense moods and resentments.

# Quiz 5 The Transpersonal Signs (Sagittarius to Pisces) - True or False

1. Sagittarius is a negative sign, associated with dreams and being impressionable.
2. Aquarius is a positive sign that on one hand follows convention but also takes risks.
3. Pisces is likely to be interested in the arts and particularly music.
4. Sagittarius has links with foreign cultures and languages.
5. Capricorn is noted as a rebellious sign, change for change's sake.
6. Aquarius likes to break with convention and try something new or different.
7. Capricorn is a negative sign having links with mountains and dry wit.
8. Pisces is a practical and decisive sign that prefers to follow earthy interests.

# Answers to Quizzes

Quiz 1 Answers
1. False. It's the Tropical Zodiac most Western astrologers use.
2. False. The Tropical Zodiac doesn't rely on the stars – except the Sun.
3. False. Virgo is a "negative" feminine, ingoing sign.
4. False – it's actually the other way around.
5. True. Fire and Air signs are always "positive." Water and Earth signs are always "negative."
6. True. Each sign is unique in its combination of polarity, element and quality. Beautifully elegant. One of the reasons why the number 12 is important.
7. True. Cardinal signs provide the spark for change.
8. False – it's actually the other way around.
9. False. "Negative" in this respect is like the positive and negative poles in electricity – negative signs compliment positive signs.
10. False – wrong direction. Signs run anti-clockwise.

Quiz 2 Answers
1. False. This description better fits Taurus.
2. True.
3. False. This description better fits Gemini.
4. True.
5. True.
6. True. Cancer generally does not like confrontation – but this will depend upon what else is going in the birthchart. Will defend what is theirs
7. False. This description better fits Cancer.
8. True. Very Taurean.

Quiz 3 Answers
> Sun is in Cancer in 7th House
> Moon is in Pisces in 2nd House
> Mercury is in Gemini in 5th House
> Venus is in Cancer 7th House
> Mars is in Leo in 7th House
> Jupiter is in Gemini in 6th House
> Saturn is in Capricorn in 1st House
> Uranus is in Capricorn in 1st House
> Neptune is in Capricorn in 1st House
> Pluto is in Scorpio in 10th House.

Quiz 4 Answers
1. False. This description is more associated with Virgo. Leo wants to play, be adventurous in what they do.
2. False. This one more associated with Scorpio. Libra, in the ideal, is outgoing and friendly.
3. True. But note, this doesn't mean that every person with a strong Scorpio will be interested in, or believe in the paranormal. It always comes down to having an open or closed mind.
4. True.
5. True. But let me tell you, I have met some shy people with Sun in Leo too.
6. False. This description is more associated with Libra.
7. True. Inclined towards taking a balanced view of things.
8. False. This description is more associated with Scorpio.

Quiz 5 Answers
1. False. This description is more appropriate to Pisces. There is a possible association with Sagittarius for making dreams come true however.
2. False – but part of it is true. It's a better description for Sagittarius.
3. True. It might be visual, painting and body movement arts too though.
4. True. Amongst other adventurous aspects.
5. False. This more appropriate as a negative description of Aquarius.

6. True. In my experience the "new" can be retro too.
7. True. Very true.
8. False. This is a better description for Capricorn.

**Next: Onto Step Three.**

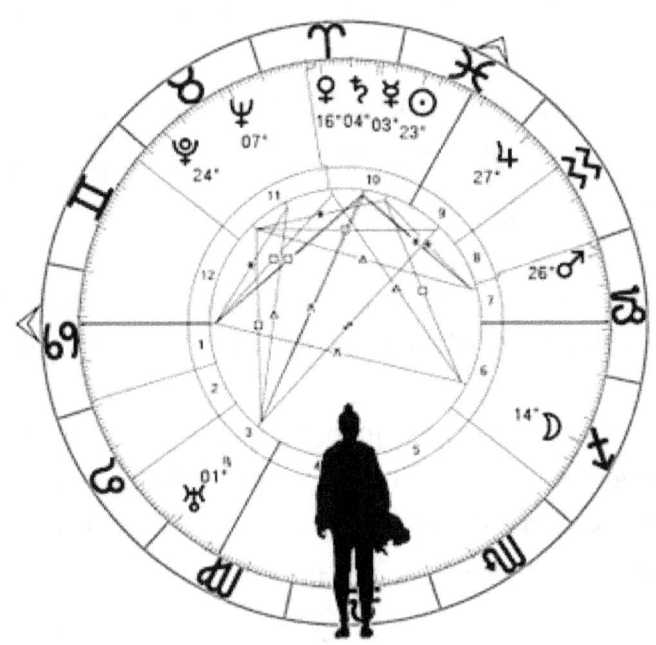

# Step Three

## Learn to Read the Planets & Aspects

In context, check for the following resources, under The Resources, towards the back of the book:
    The Planets by Sign Resource
    The Planets by Aspect Resource

This Step covers the ten main planets used is Western astrology.

From my perspective life is complicated enough without adding more complication to it. The ten planets really are enough to get hugely valuable insight into oneself, through the lens of astrology.

That said, as I've mentioned before, Western astrologers may regularly also include other components, such as asteroids, and more, into the birth-charts they produce.

What I would suggest to you is to get grounded first, in the ten planets, and explore some of the other components – such as Chiron, Lilith, Moon nodes (see One Step Further: The Spiritual Roadmap) and the Part of Fortune – later, when you are comfortable in your current knowledge.

# Part 1

# An Astronomical Overview

Image: Courtesy Wikimedia (with adaptions)

Before easing into interpretation and aspects, we begin this Step by covering some the basic nuts and bolts, but important data, with regards to the Sun, Moon and planets of our Solar System.

One scientist's criticism of astrology, that I heard recently, was that astrologers never look up at the skies, at the planets and stars. They do it in front of their computers. I'm not sure I entirely agree with him – certainly it is not true for me – but it is true that astrology can be carried out without any direct reference to the skies. If we are not using a computer we can just as easily glean the information needed from relevant hard copy tables.

And so, it follows that one could simply miss out on knowing anything about the astronomy of our solar system – where we actually live. We could carry on not knowing how far the Earth is from the Sun for instance. Or how many Earth years it takes Mars or Jupiter to get around the Sun.

We don't need to become amateur astronomers but part of learning astrology is about knowing, and being conversant with, at least some of the basic facts of our solar system.

It is really important to know we are a part of a huge system and to have knowledge as to the shape of it and where planets are in relation to each other - as well as in relation to the Earth.

And to look up at least occasionally, at the wonderment we are a part of!

And with that...let's take a look at the Solar System and some essential data.

# Solar System - some essential data

The grid below (Fig.33) provides the order of planets beginning with the Sun. In reading the grid, note the following:

- The mean (or average) distance takes into account that planets move in an elliptical orbit around the Sun.
- The sidereal period is how long (in Earth days or years) a planet takes to get around the Sun - note Pluto takes 248 Earth years (or around three to four human lifetimes end to end) to make the journey once.
- Earth Diameters is how many times bigger or smaller a body is than the Earth. The Earth is 12,742 km in diameter.
- The Ecliptic is the path the Earth takes around the Sun. Give or take a degree of orbital inclination (Pluto is at the steepest angle), all the planets also move around the Sun in the same ecliptic plane as the Earth - and in the same direction.
- As mentioned, the Sun and Moon are treated as "planets" in astrology - as indeed is Pluto, although now officially a dwarf planet, that behaves more like a comet.

| Name | Symbol | Mean distance from Sun (Millions Miles) | Sidereal Period (in Earth days/years) | Earth Diams | Orbital inclination to Ecliptic |
|---|---|---|---|---|---|
| Sun | ☉ | 0.0 | 0.0 | 109.00 | 0 deg. 0 min. |
| Mercury | ☿ | 36.00 | 87.97d | 0.39 | 7 deg. 0 min. |
| Venus | ♀ | 67.2 | 224.7d | 0.97 | 3 deg. 24 min. |
| Earth | ⊕ | 92.9 | 365.26d | 1.0 | 0 deg. 0 min. |
| Moon | ☽ | 92.9 | 27.32d | 0.27 | 5 deg. 18 min. |
| Mars | ♂ | 141.5 | 687.0d | 0.53 | 1 deg. 51 min. |
| Jupiter | ♃ | 483.3 | 11.86y | 10.97 | 1 deg. 18 min. |
| Saturn | ♄ | 886.1 | 29.46y | 9.03 | 2 deg. 29 min. |
| Uranus | ♅ | 1783 | 84.02y | 4.0 | 0 deg. 46 min. |
| Neptune | ♆ | 2797 | 164.79y | 3.90 | 1 deg. 47 min. |
| Pluto Dwarf planet | ♇ | 3670 | 248.4y | 0.46? | 17 deg. 19 min. |

Fig.33

In context, note:
- These are the ten main bodies used in Western astrology today.
- Some astrologers may include asteroids, from within the asteroid belt – such as Ceres, Vesta, and Juno. The belt lies between Mars and Jupiter.
- Chiron (an asteroid lying between Saturn and Uranus) is now more commonly being included, since its discovery in 1977.
- Astrologers may also include one to any number of the more prominent stars (other than the Sun). These are considered fixed in their position/s.

# The Ephemeris

To find exact positions of the planets, astrologers use an ephemeris (already mentioned). Here's an example of a page. The following illustration (Fig.34) is taken from The American Ephemeris for the 21st Century.[1] It is showing the exact planetary positions for September and October 2046.

An ephemeris provides tables for the positions of the planets, by Tropical Zodiac sign, as commonly used in astrology. Their positions are therefore geocentric, or as viewed from the movement of the Earth.

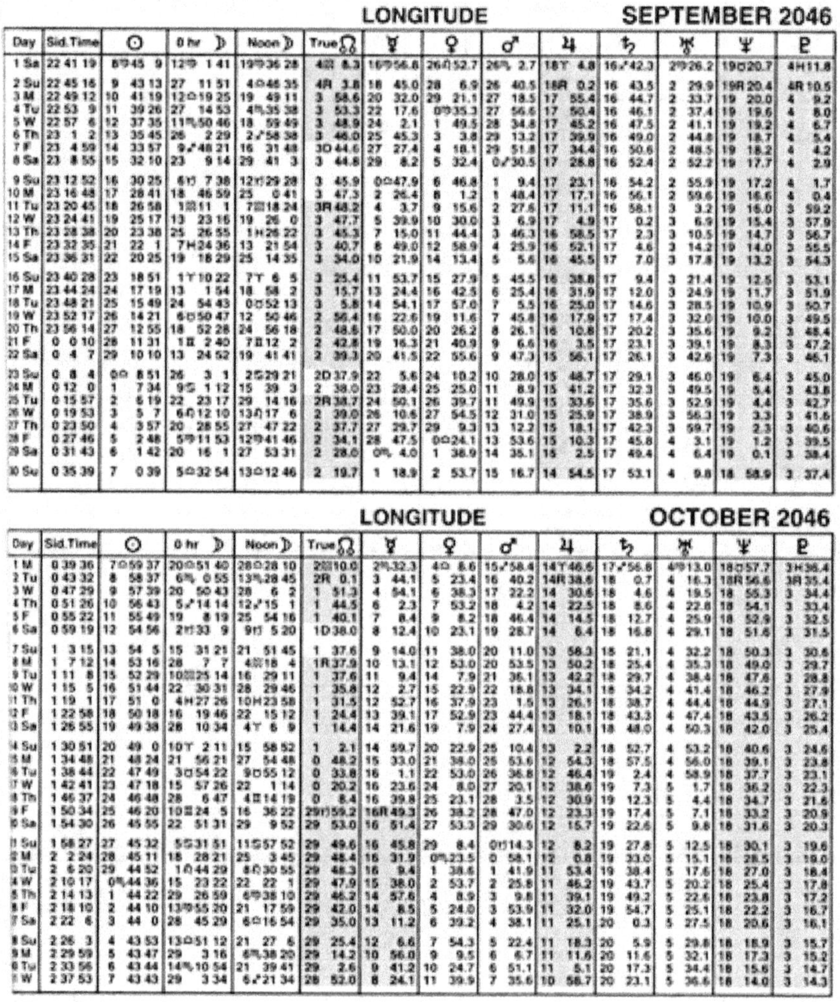

Note the highlighted areas represent retrograde movement. Observe that Jupiter, Neptune and Pluto are retrograde throughout the two-month period. Mercury goes retrograde on Friday the 19th October 2046.

Note also, as this example demonstrates, the exact position of the planets can be listed for years ahead.

Fig.34

For anyone drawing up birth-charts by hand, or looking at trends, a hard-copy ephemeris is essential.

94     Step Three: Learn to Read the Planets & Aspects

But even when using software, having a hard-copy ephemeris comes into its own when looking for quick reference of the planets' positions on future dates and times. And I suspect astrologers generally find the hard-copy version easier to work with for this purpose than any electronic or online version.

# Comment on Astrological Trends

Astrological trends are not being covered in this workbook. While discussing the ephemeris it is an apt point to comment on this – as astrological trends do make full use of the ephemeris, electronically or otherwise.

The number of different approaches and interpretations would easily take up a book by itself – and indeed there are good books (e.g., by Jeff Mayo, A.T.Mann, Howard Sasportas, Stephen Arroyo etc.) available, and one or two websites (e.g., Astrodienst and Café Astrology) that cover the matter when/if you want to begin looking into them.

It should be noted that being able to interpret trends comes with not only reading and practice but through experience too. It can be a complex matter to deal with – particularly where more than one theme is operating, as is often the case.

But the bigger part of my not including trends is because it really is secondary to learning to read, and become familiar with your birth-chart. This in itself is a lot to be going on with. The old adage, *don't run before you can walk* seems appropriate here. So, if it does interest you to explore, consider looking into trends once you have read your chart under your belt.

## But what do we mean by "trends?"

Well think on them as "forecasts" and/or (old school) "predictions." It's a given that everything is ever moving and changing. In simple terms your birth-chart is seen as the symbolical starting and reference point for you going forward with your life.

The planets, of course, keep moving and their relationship with your chart changes accordingly. The view is that this, as everything else in astrology, has meaning and can provide insight into current and future trends (or I may use the term, "themes") as represented in your chart.

Over the centuries astrologers have observed and developed a variety of techniques for gathering intel on what the movement of planets means. Notably they look for aspects formed by transiting, or progressed planets, to the positions of the natal planets of the birth-chart. These are the same aspects that you will become familiar with through the course. That is conjunctions, sextiles, squares, quincunxes, trines and oppositions. These are all common to look out for. Astrologers also take in the movement of the planets across the Angles and through the houses too.

## Two popular techniques used in anticipating trends

The astrological means for establishing trends broadly splits into two techniques: Transiting planets and Progressions.

## Transiting planets

Transiting planets are where they actually are (were or will be) in the sky, at a given date and time, and seen in relation to the birth-chart. The slower moving outer planets offer particularly valuable insight using this technique.

Using transits, if you wanted to, for example, look at where the planets will be for your 30$^{th}$ year (or were – if you have passed that point), you would look in the ephemeris and check out their positions in your 30$^{th}$ year.

Commonly the slower moving planets, Jupiter out to Pluto are considered most useful for anticipating trends/outcomes. These offer trends, that with forward and retrograde movement, may last for a year or more.

In Fig.35 the inner dial is the birth-chart of George Michael, while the outer dial shows the transiting planets for the 25th December 2016, at a guesstimate time of 3:00 AM. The transiting planets in the 6th house are particularly important here.

## Progressed planets

Progressed planets, and note there is more than one approach to this, is where the planets are symbolically moved forward (or indeed backward) in relation to the birth-chart.

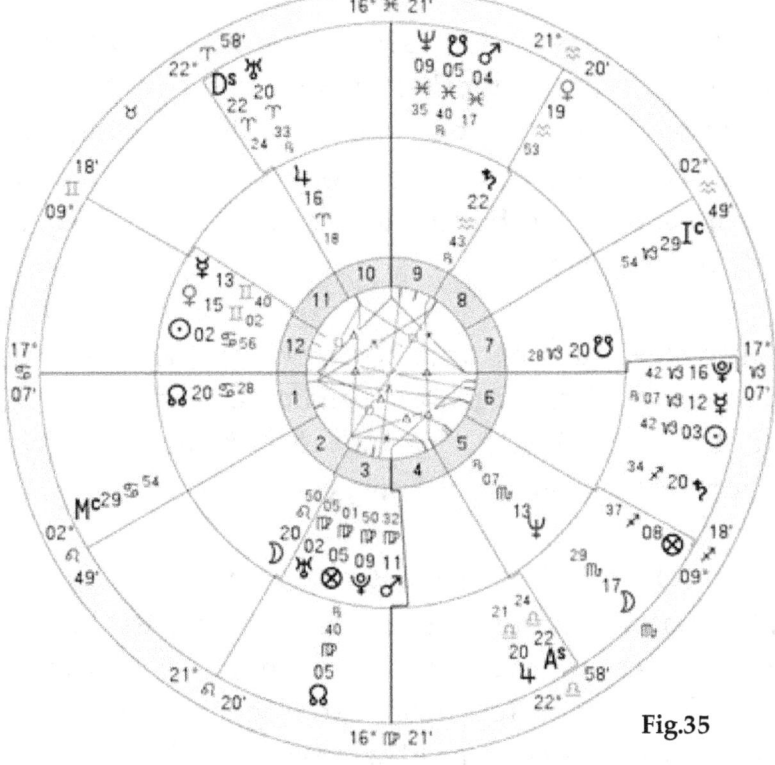

Fig.35

This technique is useful for slowing down the inner planets and looking at their trends – the progressed Moon by this method can be particularly helpful.

If using the popular, *secondary-progressions*, you would check out the movement of the planets in one day being equal to a year of life. So, if you wanted to look at the secondary-progressions for your 30th year, you would look, again in the ephemeris, for the planet's positions 30 days on from the date you were born – and how they relate to your natal chart.

So, here commonly, the faster moving planets, Sun out to Mars, are relied upon for trends. The slower planets movement, in this case, will be less noticeable over any given period of days.

# Predictions aren't what they used to be

It is fair to say that Western natal astrology (certainly less so mundane astrology) has moved on from predicting black and white outcomes to trends. It's no longer about the astrologer having to be right and telling a client *what will happen to them* at a future time. Astrology has moved away from treating people as flotsam and jetsam being moved around by the tide of life. That's the fairground fatalistic level of astrology – it works for some.

Since the turn of the 20th century, Western astrology has been taking a more psychological approach to trend outcomes – with the aim to be able to better equip a person to deal with, and indeed get the best from a given trend for themselves – whether hard and challenging or soft and flowing. *Forewarned is forearmed!*

Let's take a look at a transit as an example. Look into Step Three's Part 3 below for what Saturn represents. If Saturn by transit had come to oppose (that is 180 degrees, with an orb of 1 degree either side of exact) your natal Venus (also check Venus out below) I might (as your astrologer) anticipate a testing time for you in your relationships – close or otherwise.

Instead of saying an important relationship will come to an end (which it still might) I'd advise you of the possibilities and encourage you to be patient with people, which is one opportunity that may arise from it.

It may prove to be a frustrating period for you, with people generally. It may not be a good moment to take a holiday, indeed any pleasurable event planned may need a rethink. But it also may play out in testing how you feel about yourself – your appearance for example – and your tastes and values, how much you like yourself. You could be low in energy through this period. You might indeed feel older than your age through the phase.

It might alternatively help you to see things more realistically than ideally. If you are a creative person, it could benefit you in ways of practical application to your art. And, I might add that whatever opportunity arises, it will also pass, so try to make the most of it while it is happening.

And so, what comes out of this is not a focus on events that could happen but rather how you deal with this theme of Saturn coming into your life – if at a given time ahead – and what you might learn about yourself (perhaps greater self-acceptance) from the experience.

Bear all of this in mind if you decide to pursue looking at your trends...

# Part 2

# Planet Rulership

The planets each rule (or are "at home" in) one or more of the signs. In other words, the ruler has an affinity with the sign/s it rules.

In the illustration (Fig.36) you can see that the Sun rules Leo; the Moon rules Cancer; Mercury rules Gemini and Virgo; Venus rules Taurus and Libra.

Mars rules Aries and is also the old ruler of Scorpio; but now shares this rulership with Pluto - considered to be the new primary ruler.

Jupiter rules Sagittarius and is the old ruler of Pisces. Pisces is now ruled by Neptune. Saturn rules Capricorn and is the old ruler of Aquarius. Aquarius is now ruled by Uranus.

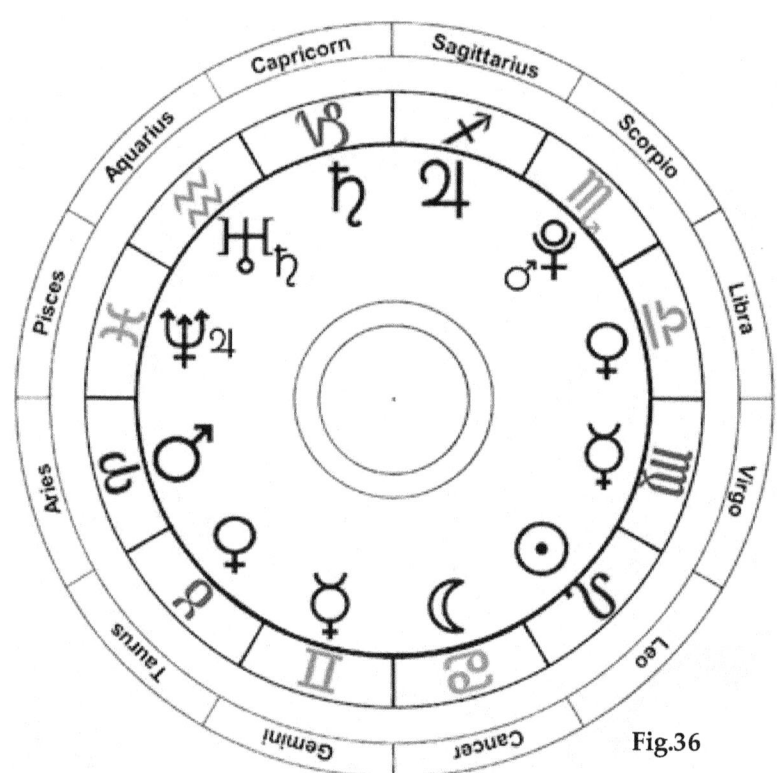

Fig.36

The planet and sign (and indeed their associated house) can tend to overlap somewhat in their interpretation. This will become clearer as you move through the course and practice with astrology.

# The Chart Ruler

There is also a "Chart Ruler." This is the planet that rules the ascending sign. If Leo is rising, for example, that would mean the Sun is the chart ruler. If Virgo is rising then Mercury would be the chart ruler.

Planets in the signs they rule, or in position of being chart ruler, gives them a greater emphasis in interpretation.

# Other (traditional) Conditions or Dignities

There are (Fig.37) other conditions (drawn from traditional astrology) said to prevail for planets in certain signs. Planets may be said to be "exalted," in "detriment" or "fall" depending upon the sign they are in.

For example, a planet that is opposite the sign it rules (or its "domicile"), is said to be in "detriment" – operating at a disadvantage.

| Sign | Domicile | Detriment | Exaltation | Fall |
|---|---|---|---|---|
| Aries | Mars | Venus | Sun | Saturn |
| Taurus | Venus | Mars | Moon | None |
| Gemini | Mercury | Jupiter | None | None |
| Cancer | Moon | Saturn | Jupiter | Mars |
| Leo | Sun | Saturn | None | None |
| Virgo | Mercury | Jupiter | Mercury | Venus |
| Libra | Venus | Mars | Saturn | Sun |
| Scorpio | Mars | Venus | None | Moon |
| Sagittarius | Jupiter | Mercury | None | None |
| Capricorn | Saturn | Moon | Mars | Jupiter |
| Aquarius | Saturn | Sun | None | None |
| Pisces | Jupiter | Mercury | Venus | Mercury |

Fig.37

So, Mars in Libra would be opposite Aries, the sign it rules (or opposite its domicile) and therefore in detriment.

You might want to explore these for yourself to see if they are helpful to your reading your birth-chart. Note, that only the original seven planets are included in this arrangement.

Like a number of modern astrologers, I have not found this traditional application to be all that helpful in natal astrology. However, it will arguably be found to be helpful in predictive forms of astrology.

## Rulership and a couple of example charts

### Billie Holiday, singer (Fig.38)

With Aquarius rising (off the time given), the chart ruler will be Uranus. Uranus is also in its own sign of Aquarius, and in the 1st house, so doubles up on the importance of Uranus in this chart.

Note, Jupiter is in Pisces and is the old ruler of Pisces – so this planet is also in its own sign.

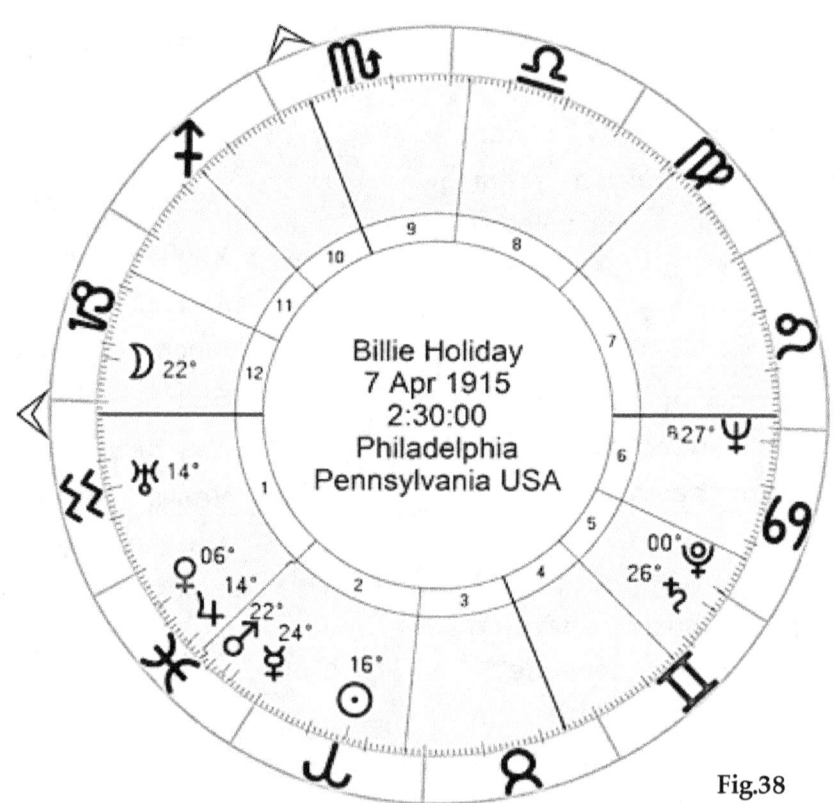

Fig.38

102   Step Three: Learn to Read the Planets & Aspects

# Coco Chanel fashion designer (Fig.39)

Chart ruler: Jupiter (or Saturn). Time given may be inaccurate, and so could either sign and planet be out.

What do you think. Did she come across as Sagittarian or Capricornian in persona?

The Sun is in its own sign – in Leo, the sign it rules. Mercury is also in its own sign – Virgo.

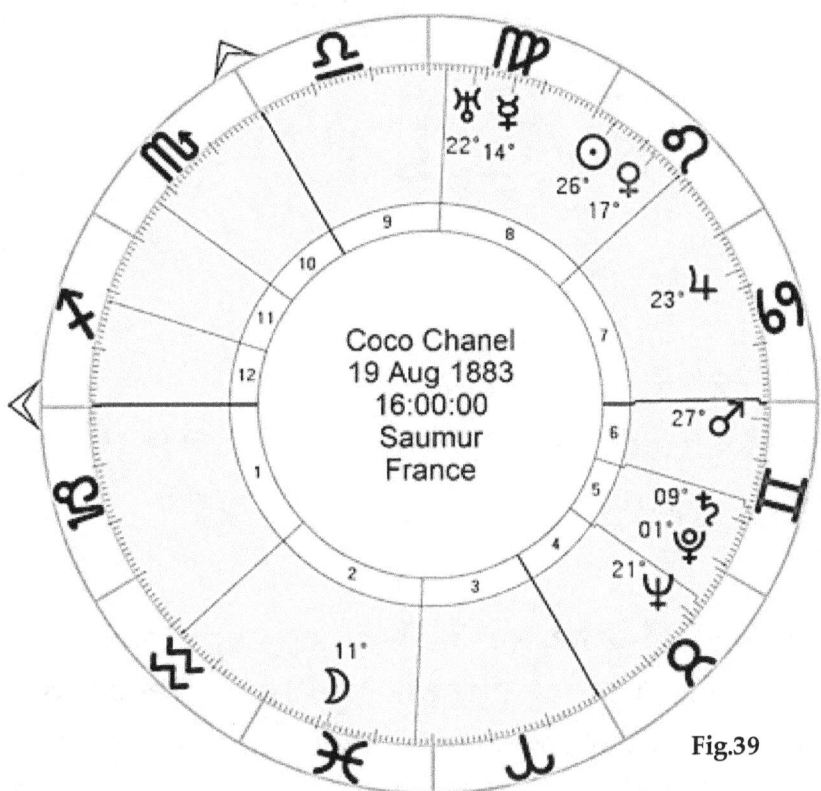

Fig.39

This has been a quick tour around rulership. I'm sure you will soon pick up on the chart ruler of your own chart. Also, you'll soon work out which planets, if any, are in signs they rule in your chart. Bear in mind none of them <u>have</u> to be in signs they rule...

# Part 3
# What each of the Planets mean

## Comment on the Personal, Intermediate and Transpersonal Planets

If you study the work of other astrologers, you will probably find that they divide the ten planets into two categories, the Inner Personal Planets (the Sun, Moon, Mercury, Venus and Mars) and the Outer Transpersonal Planets (Jupiter, Saturn, Uranus, Neptune and Pluto).

To my mind however Jupiter and Saturn are borderline planets in their meaning. Unlike, with the division of the signs, the term "social" doesn't really fit with what they symbolise, so hence here I'm calling them Intermediate Planets. They lie between the Personal and the Transpersonal and are really concerned with our relations with the physical world around us, or the world we are involved in.

Consider that before the time of telescopes the furthest planet that could be seen with the naked eye was Saturn. Looking at things symbolically, what we can take from this is that Saturn symbolises a natural boundary of what we are encapsulated in. And what we are encapsulated in converts to TIME – Saturn is Old Father Time.

# The Inner Personal Planets

The personal planets will be closer to how you perceive yourself to be. They link to your physical form; your name, your personality and self-image.

## ☉ Sun – Rules Leo

The power of self-integration; self-expression; one's essence, will and vitality; one's creative centre; the heart; the point from where one gives out and shines; where the light of the soul is focused; where one will tend to radiate from; the power source for this life.

## ☽ Moon – Rules Cancer

Maternal/feminine impulse; the Moon's position indicates instinctual and emotional responses; natural (body) rhythms, receptivity, reflectivity; one's habit patterns and conditional responses; gut behaviour; one's moods – where we wax and wane; links with the subconscious; also, a sense of belongingness, family, familiarity, security; association with the past, with memories.

## ☿ Mercury – Rules Gemini and Virgo

Alertness of mind; mental and nervous activity; the urge to know and inform; communications, linking, contacting, co-ordinating information; the power of knowledge; converting experience into ideas; knowledge of self and environment; indicates how one will tend to gain knowledge, form ideas and communicate ideas.

## ♀ Venus – Rules Taurus and Libra

The urge to relate and unify with others through sympathy, feelings and evaluation; the urge to be attractive or to the attraction of others; sensual, social and artistic pleasures; the mores and the arts; earthy idealism, earthy love, feminine attraction; the interdependence of spirit and nature; the urge towards harmony in relating to self, others and environment; indicates how/where one will tend to place one's values and appreciation for what one has in life.

## ♂ Mars – Rules Aries and (shares) Scorpio

Physical activity, drive, force, directness, aggression, decisiveness; heat and activation; emotional charge; masculine energy; combat with the forces of nature and/or the resistance of matter, urgent action, do or die; penetration, regeneration, one's sexual power/prowess/impulse; indicates how/where we tend to aggress, assert and project ourself onto our environment, our world and direct ourself forward in life.

# The Intermediate Planets

Jupiter and Saturn lie at the borderline between the inner personal world of "I" as a human being, and the outer transpersonal world of "I" as a spiritual being; and the doorway to part of a bigger life and bigger journey.

We come to identify with our physical lives, as represented by the personal planets.

In Jupiter we are seeking to develop an understanding of our situation, something bigger that gives us confidence to carry us through the dark times as well as the good times. In Saturn we are reminded of the conditions and boundaries we are held in, by Time – and the challenges we face in order to pass through it.

## ♃ Jupiter – Rules Sagittarius and shares Pisces

Expansion, growth, new horizons to aim for; "can do" optimism and natural belief in self; the urge to self-improvement and a deepening of one's participation in life; the urge to find joy and meaning to one's life; opening to a higher power, a higher good; setting moral standards; embracing a broadening world view and beliefs; travel to distant lands in experience and learning; developing belief and philosophical perspectives; Jupiter's position indicates how one will tend to broaden out and make sense of life.

## ♄ Saturn – Rules Capricorn and shares Aquarius

Awareness of limits or where one feels limited, restricted; the urge to control, condition and organise one's life; the urge towards self-acceptance, having position, status, responsibility, maturity, seriousness, discipline, perseverance, patience and humility; awareness of time, the ageing process; tests and trials; becoming wise through experience; the ring-pass-not of matter; Saturn's position indicates our relationship with time; how one will tend to deal with boundaries, limitations, obstacles and tests for this life.

# The Outer Transpersonal Planets

And finally, to the outer transpersonal planets...

The outer transpersonal planets – planets beyond Saturn – on one level are associated with generations or collectives of people. This is because they move so slowly that whole groups of us will share these planets in the same sign as each other – and the slower they are the more people share them. For instance, except for a short period in 2023, anyone born between January 2008 and January 2024 will have Pluto in Capricorn. These planets will tend to represent an unconscious link, a common thread we have with others born around the same broad period of time as us.

Where these planets will jut out more noticeably into our conscious awareness, is where they are, by house or by aspect, to other planets, noticeably the inner planets. Then their sign position can also come into play, in the individual, in sharp relief.

The outer transpersonal planets remind us that there is a deeper level to our lives, our situation is temporary and our true home is elsewhere. I'm talking from a spiritual perspective of course - you don't have to agree with my view on this. They often remind us of the gifts we individually can bring forth for the benefit or ourselves and others, but also provide reasons for why we shouldn't get too comfortable living on the Earth.

## ⛢ Uranus – Rules Aquarius

The urge to freedom and detachment beyond established conventions, limitations, boundaries of self or environment; the urge to radically alter imposed constructs; the emancipation of one's community; the emancipation of humanity; the urge towards invention, innovation, originality, revolution, break-through, crisis, revelation, awakening, higher (transpersonal) forms of communication, intuitive awareness; shocking, electric, vivid, the unexpected, the surprising, the explosive, change for change sake; Uranus' position indicates how one will tend to transcend limitations and boundaries, enter new pathways, open new doorways, be original and creative.

## ♆ Neptune – Rules Pisces

The power of the imagination; seeking the ideal; developing an emotional sense of unity with all life; selfless compassion and sacrifice; atonement; unconditional love; the urge to let go; the urge to dissolve the material and transcend to finer energies/realms/spiritual existence; the place of dreams; the ocean; merging with the intangible, the utterly beautiful; all things nebulous; the arts, notably music and composition; Neptune's position indicates how well we will tend to see through illusion and deception, how well we can transform, become more refined, become at one with our higher self or soul.

# ♇ Pluto (or ♇) – Rules Scorpio

Purification; removing that which contaminates and holds us back; return, rebirth, endings; the urge to bring to light what is hidden; renewal, regeneration, transformation through eradication; trial by fire; meeting the repressed parts of the self; destruction of inner darkness, compulsions and desires; Pluto's position indicates how one will tend to eradicate baggage, cleanse oneself of one's past, heal woundings and clear the path to one's soul – or fail to do so, or attempt to avoid doing so.

# Part 4

# Reading the Aspects

The aspects of a birth-chart are primarily the angular relationships between planets. It could also be other components. Other components could be the Ascendant and Midheaven points for example.

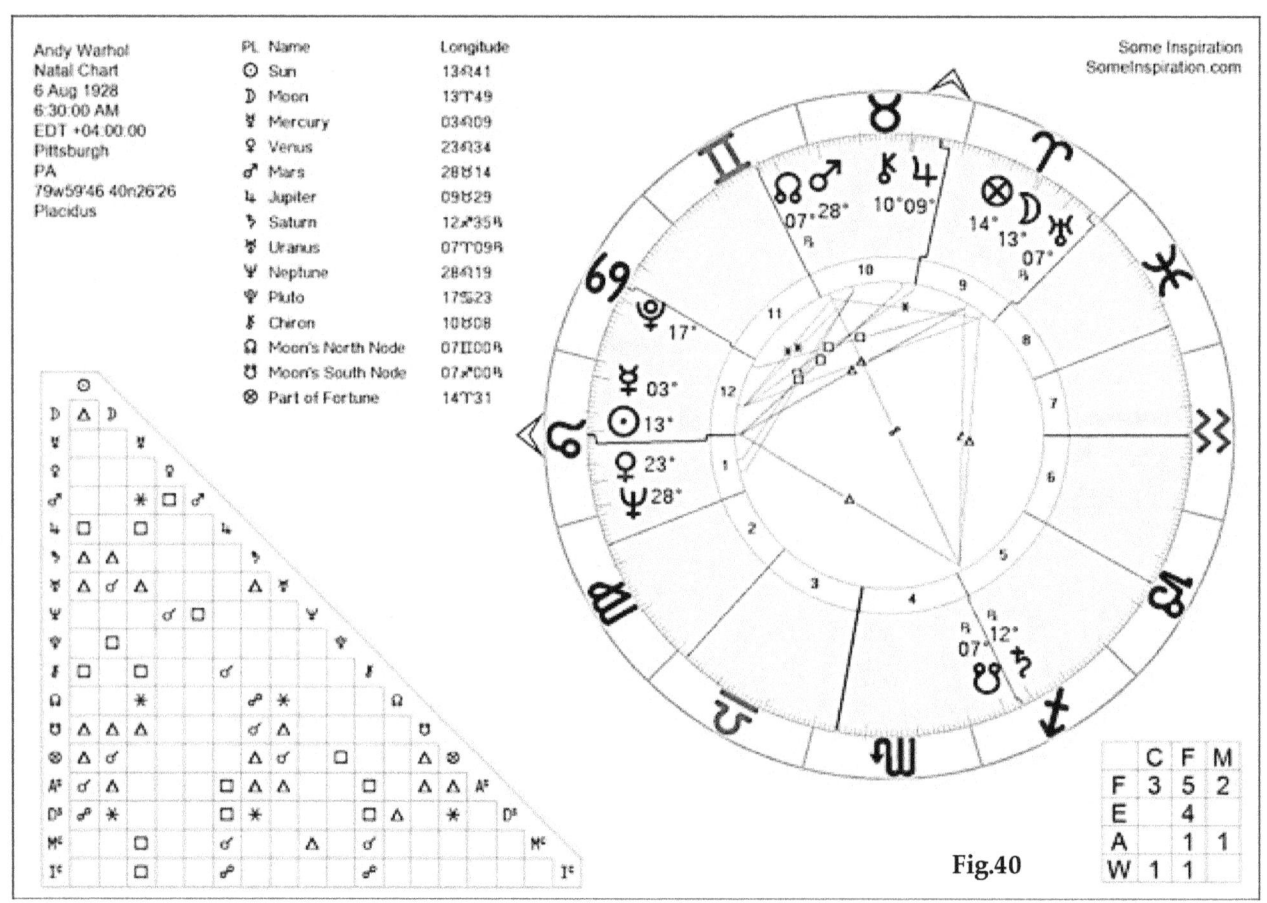

Fig.40

If your birth-chart is anything like the one above (Fig.40), in layout, you'll see the aspects in the central dial, and also in the aspect grid, possibly bottom left.

What an aspect does is bring together the principles or energies of two (or more) planets.

Regardless of the type of aspect (whether a flowing trine, or challenging square) what the person, who owns the chart, needs to be able to do is to give the planets involved an equal status – to bring them together. And sometimes this entails conscious work. This way they become most powerful, productive and constructive in their expression. This is not always as easy as it might seem...

With challenging aspects, such as squares, oppositions, quincunxes, it usually requires effort and discipline – and this is an area where conscious work on expression of energies can pay off – bringing the usefulness of the astrological birth-chart into its own.

The birth-chart helps to pinpoint what work is needed from us, and where.

That said, while individual aspects can be powerful and provide a great deal of insight into your chart, and you as a person, their characteristics and behaviour, they must needs be read in context with the rest of the chart pattern – not in isolation in other words.

## Comment on orbs

Each aspect has an orb of tolerance wherein it is considered, from years of trial and error, equally powerful as if exact. Commonly this is 8° either side of exact in the major aspects. The sextile is usually 6° of tolerance and the quincunx (or minor aspects) 1 to 2°. Astrologers may vary a little in their allowance of orbs and sometimes further allowances may be made for the planets involved.

# The Major Aspects

The aspects listed here are the major aspects used in astrology. There are minor aspects, such as the semi-sextile (30⁰), the semi-square (45⁰) and the sesquiquadrate (135⁰). Their value is in their label; being labelled as "minor." Although astrologers may also differ in opinion on their actual value, particular when one encounters a number of them in a given chart.

The accompanying illustrations here use the Sun (as a fixed point), Moon, Jupiter and/or Saturn to example the main aspects. Bear in mind that any planet can be involved in these aspects and that they can also occur in any of the signs.

## ☌ Conjunction 0° (8° orb) (Fig.41)

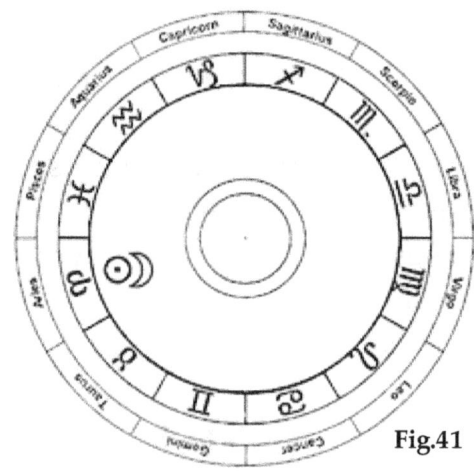

Fig.41

When two or more planets are in the same degree of celestial longitude – or within the orb allowed – they are in conjunction and likely (but not always) to be in the same sign and the same house. This is a powerful aspect – a focal point in the chart, a case of planets pulling together, or being forced to pull together. Depending on whether they get on with each other or not, their principles will react to stimulus together, and/or on each other.

Note, for obvious reasons, you won't normally see the symbol displayed in the aspect lines of the chart wheel.

## □ Square 90° (8° orb) (Fig.42)

Here two or more planets are set at a quarter of the circle apart (note, in the example the Moon could just as easily have been in Cancer instead of Capricorn), therefore square to each other. They are likely to occur in signs belonging to the same cardinal, fixed or mutable group, with a different element group and the opposite polarity.

This is a powerful aspect indicative of tension, frustration, inner conflict and potential discord arising from it. The person is likely to experience obstacles on their path associated with what the involved planets, signs and houses represent.

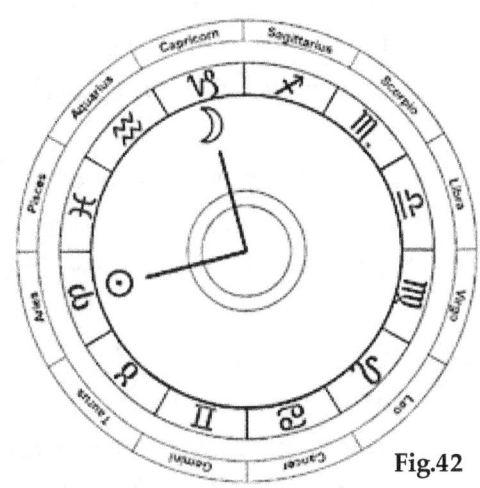
Fig.42

This aspect may be said to work best when the energy of the planets involved is applied equally, conscientiously and constructively. You might say it's a no pain, no gain aspect. When the person is determined to overcome and work with any associated weaknesses or inadequacies it then becomes a true character-building aspect.

## ✶ Sextile 60° (6° orb) (Fig.43)

When two or more planets are at a sixth of the circle apart, they are in sextile to each other. This is not as strong as the trine aspect. Even so, it is considered to be fairly strong – a harmonious learning aspect.

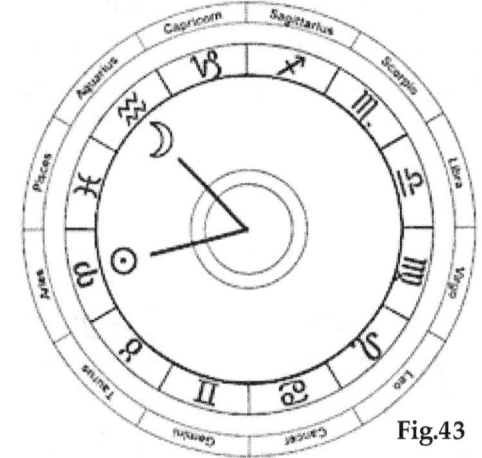
Fig.43

It is an aspect of opportunity. It is considered "harmonious" because it likely unites signs having the same polarity – either negative or positive. And it is considered a "learning" aspect because it unites different elements that tend to complement each other in their exchange – as in Earth with Water or Fire with Air.

## △ Trine 120° (8° orb) (Fig.44)

When you have two or more planets at a third of the circle apart, they are in trine to each other. They are likely to occur in signs of the same element – Fire with Fire, Water

Learn to Read Your Birth-chart in 5 Steps

with Water – and also thereby in the same polarity. This is a powerfully harmonious aspect. It represents inner harmony. Energy flows more easily and naturally between the planets and signs involved.

Given the characteristics of the planets are equally developed and exercised; this aspect provides ease of attraction, an ease of expression.

It is important to consider that a birth-chart having a mix of challenging aspects with flowing aspects will show where energy is tense and/or where it moves freely. It can help to have both, as it helps to keep us on our toes and succeed in life. Those of us who have a predominance of trines may get things too easy in life in other words. "Easy come, easy go"

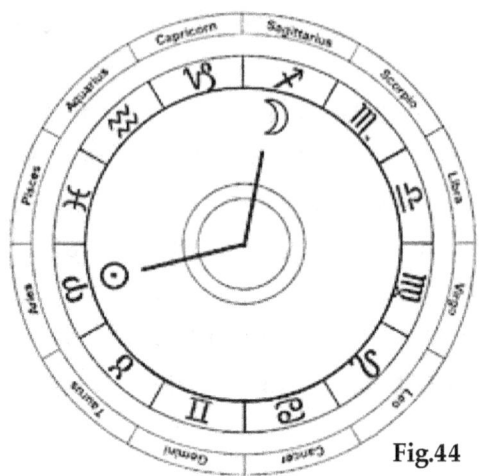
Fig.44

comes to mind. We could be inclined to get a little too relaxed and mess-up or miss opportunities.

Consider too that if a planet is involved in both a square (or opposition) and a trine, the trine might point to ways of resolving tensions invoked by the square, and thereby help one to integrate things better.

# ⚻ Quincunx 150° (2° orb) (Fig.45)

When planets are 150 degrees, or five signs apart, they are in quincunx to each other. They are likely to be in different cardinal, fixed or mutable signs, in opposing elements and opposites in polarity. Depending on one's viewpoint this is considered either a weak or fairly powerful aspect – I'm inclined to the view that it is powerful. This aspect suggests a strong, compulsive yet potentially discordant pattern, needing a conscientious handling of the planets involved. It really depends upon which planets

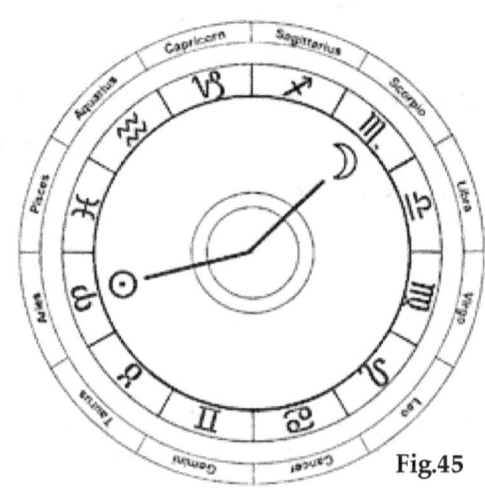
Fig.45

114    Step Three: Learn to Read the Planets & Aspects

and signs are involved as they can tend to cancel each other out - thus giving the impression of being a weak aspect - but it is more helpful to view as an energy charge or, alternatively, an energy drain.

Note there is an obvious similarity between the quincunx and the semi-sextile - which relates to signs next door to each other (not easy bedfellows) and having a recipe of similar differences and tensions.

## ☍ Opposition 180° (8° orb) (Fig.46)

When you have planets at 180 degrees apart, they are in opposition to each other. The aspect is likely to occur in signs belonging in the same cardinal, fixed or mutable group. They will have the same polarity and complementary, but different, elements.

Fig.46

Similar to the square, this is a powerful, tense and dynamic aspect. Literally it means opposition. The planets are symbolically eyeballing each other, and the corresponding need is for the planets to work together, or be brought together. Or, if not, there is a tendency towards them working separately, or pulling against each other, with one possibly working at the expense of the other.

Although the planets involved may complement one another, it often requires conscientious handling to get the two sides to communicate and work constructively in the same direction. Here again is a real need to give equal expression to both planets otherwise this will be a likely stress point in the chart.

Handled correctly, the opposition, like the square, can be an enormously powerful and positive force in the process of self-development and awakening.

⊻ Semi-sextile   ∠ Semi-square   ⚼ Sesquiquadrate

The minor aspects (and there are one or two not included here) are treated as being of less importance in the overall scheme of things. So, they tend to be given less prominence in birth-chart interpretation - somewhat subsumed by the major aspects. Should they be numerous in a chart however, then their importance will also be raised somewhat.

# Unaspected planets

Should a given planet not form any obvious angular relationship, with any component, this does not mean it will thereby be less active or less important than any other component. It will still represent an operating theme in one's life.

The difference is that it is likely to require a conscious handling at integration with the rest of one's energy pattern. Using the orchestra analogy, this is a player that has no obvious or natural link with other players and the piece being played.

In other words, it is inclined to represent a part of oneself that is less integrated. What doesn't want to be happening is that it is ignored, sidelined, and working away at a subconscious level only - being a bit of a loose cannon.

# Some common aspect combinations

## Grand Trine (8° orb) (Fig.47)

A Grand Trine occurs when three or more planets form a triangle of 120 degrees on each side around the circle. This further emphasises the trine aspect and is indicative of a very harmonious, creative and flowing energy pattern. The planets involved will tend to support each other and indicate the attraction of beneficial outcomes - with regard to what they represent and the houses they are in – without necessarily too much effort.

It suggests a person who will be at ease with the areas of life represented. Note of caution however that (as mentioned for the Trine) it could be a pattern of easy come and easy go – an opportunity that slips away. Or a person too laid back to appreciate or handle what it represents productively, or they are less able to deal with things constructively when/if things go pear-shaped.

Fig.47

# T Square (8° orb) (Fig.48)

The T Square occurs where two planets are in opposition to each other, and each is also square to a third – in the form of a "T." The pattern combines the energy of both the opposition and squares. This steps up a gear the tensions invoked by the two patterns combined.

Experienced as likely tensions, blocks and obstacles in one's path, it indicates a tendency to find life challenging in the areas indicated by the planets, signs and houses involved – and with it the need to resolve such tensions. It is often dramatic and can go either way regarding encouragement or discouragement. This can be a real maker of character if dealt with successfully.

Fig.48

# Grand Cross (8° orb) (Fig.49)

A Grand Cross occurs where four, or more, planets are both in opposition and square to each other – in the form of a cross around the circle, within the orbs allowed. The

Learn to Read Your Birth-chart in 5 Steps  **117**

Grand Cross is a make-or-break pattern of extremes for the planets, signs and houses involved. It requires a watchful and wakeful approach in order to succeed.

The dynamism is double that of the square or the opposition. It does depend on which planets are involved but in general it requires careful conscious handling to make the best of it. Where outer planets are included, there is greater emphasis on a transformational/spiritual driver to the pattern.

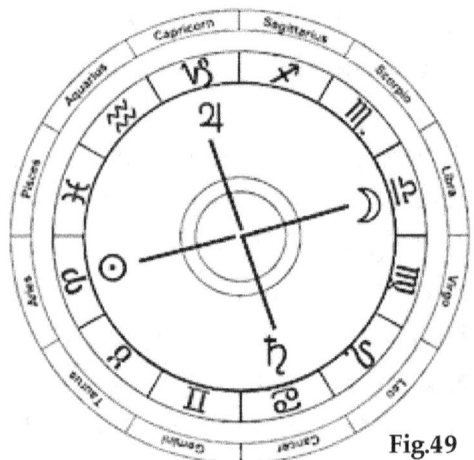
Fig.49

This pattern will certainly attract an eventful life that can either be inside or outside of one's control; or again the means by which one develops real strength of character.

# Finger of God or Yod, or double-quincunx (2° orb)
(Fig.50)

A Yod or Finger of God occurs where three or more planets are involved in a triangle involving two sides being 150 degrees (quincunxes), and the third side being 60 degrees (sextile). The planet/s on the apex (the Sun in example), from where the two quincunxes emanate, is considered a stressed focal point for energy to be poured through from the other two points.

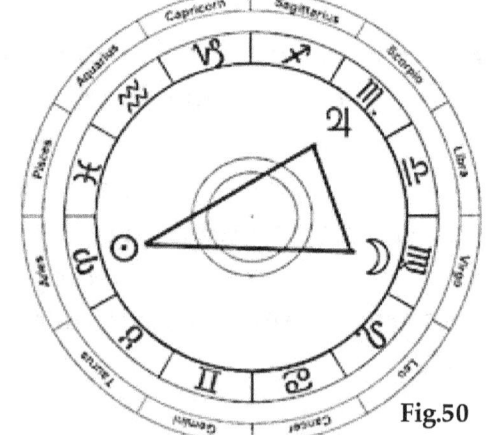
Fig.50

With this pattern something has to be done to relieve the tension. It links to powerful intention being applied – the person with it may feel strongly (a compulsion) they have a special task or mission that has to be carried through. Certainly, they won't be able to ignore its impulse.

# Check Your Chart

Where is your Jupiter, what sign is it in? What kind of aspect/s does it have with other planets?

What about Saturn. What sign is it in? What kind of aspect/s does it have with other planets?

Take a look at The Planets Resource under The Resources towards the back of the book and begin to build up a picture of what your chart is telling you.

# References

[1] Michelson, Neil F. (2001) The American Ephemeris for the 21st Century, ACS Publications.

# Step 3 Quizzes

Try the following quizzes and check with the answers further down. Jot your answers onto a piece of paper.

## Quiz 1. True/False

1. Jupiter is the largest planet in our solar system.
2. Venus' mean distance from the Sun is 94 million miles.
3. Pluto takes 9 years to complete one orbit of the Sun.
4. A retrograde planet is a planet going backwards on its orbit of the Sun.
5. Uranus' orbital inclination to the Ecliptic is 0 degrees 46 minutes.
6. Mars is the old ruler of Libra.
7. Pluto has been relegated to a dwarf planet.
8. Jupiter is the ruler of Sagittarius and the old ruler of Pisces.
9. Mercury is likely to be mentally quick in the Air sign of Libra.
10. Saturn in Scorpio suggests self-confidence and warmth in a person.
11. The opposition aspect suggests planets involved will get on with each other.
12. Saturn is the new ruler of Cancer.
13. Five of the planets are/were rulers of two signs each.
14. The Sun represents self-expression, one's vitality and creativity.
15. The Moon is at home in Cancer.
16. Neptune in Taurus suggests one who is practical and industrious.
17. Venus represents the urge to relate to others.
18. Uranus represents limitation and restriction, the urge to control.
19. Mars wants to get things going, take action.
20. The trine aspect between planets suggests harmonious flowing energy.

# Quiz 2. Jane Austen birth-chart

Jane Austen was born at 23:55 on the 16th December 1775 in Steventon, England.

***Jane Austen*** *(16 December 1775 – 18 July 1817) was an English novelist known primarily for her six major novels, which interpret, critique and comment upon the British landed gentry at the end of the 18th century.*

Extract from Wikipedia

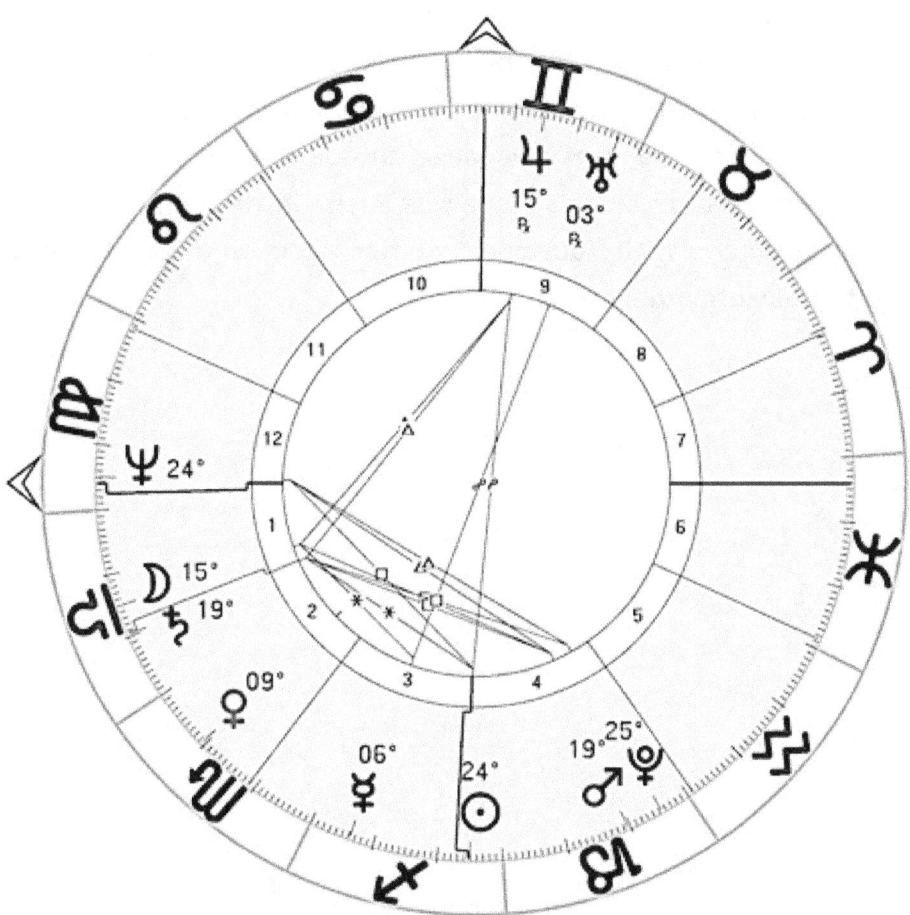

Take a look at her birth-chart and see if you can answer the following:

1. Her Sun is in Sagittarius in 4th house.
2. The Moon is in ... in ... house.

Learn to Read Your Birth-chart in 5 Steps  **121**

3. Her Venus is in ... in ... house.
4. Her Mars is in ... in ... house.
5. The planet that rules her chart is ... in ... in ... house.
6. The relationship between her Moon and Jupiter is a ... aspect.
7. The relationship between her Moon and Mars is ... aspect.
8. Briefly, what might the relationship between her Mercury and Uranus tell you about her as a person and writer? This is a multiple-choice question.
    a. She would have had a radical and independent streak about her.
    b. She was, or wanted to be, her own person.
    c. She didn't like to rock the boat.
    d. She was a bit uncertain about herself.
    e. She broke with convention in her communications.
    f. She held very conventional views and beliefs.
    g. She believed a woman's place was in the in the home.
9. Neptune is in Virgo and 12th house next to her Ascendant. Briefly, what might this indicate in the direction her writing took?

# Quiz 3. Birth-chart of "Bill Lomas"

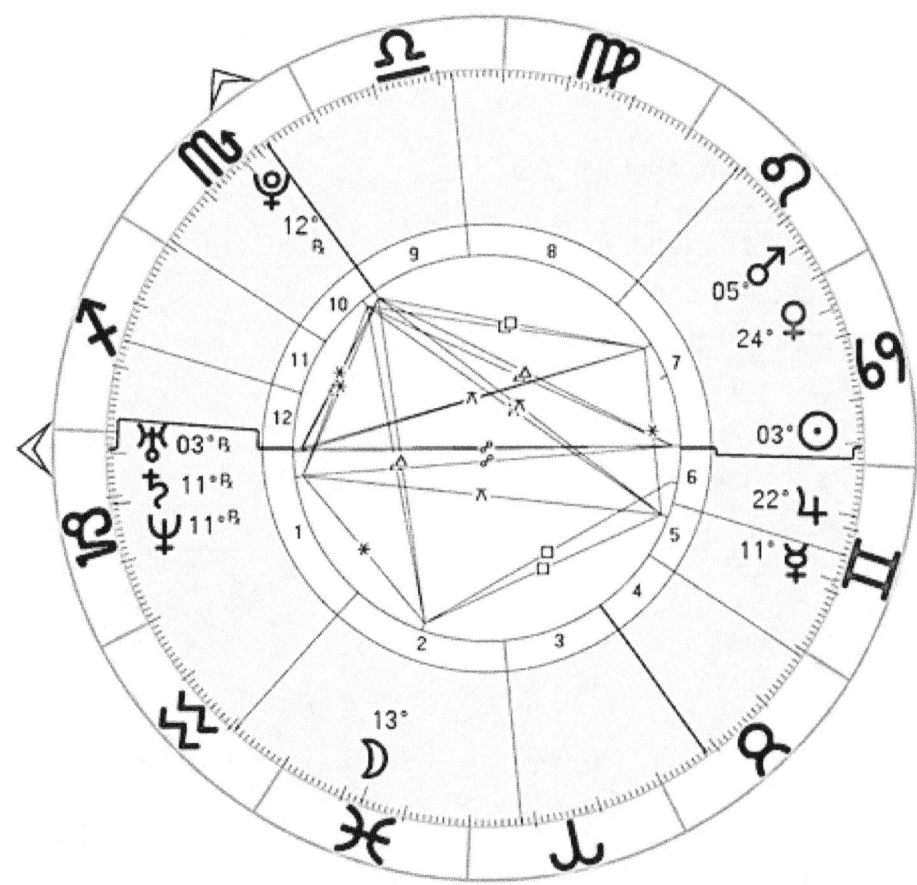

This is the birth-chart of "Bill Lomas" who has featured before. It will help to get familiar with it, as it is the chart used for the example analysis in Step Five. See if you can answer the following questions on him at this point:

1. Name the planets in challenging aspects to his Sun?
2. Name the planets in flowing aspects to his Moon?
3. One planet is unaspected in this setup. This is ...
4. There is a Yod in the arrangement. The planet that is the focus point of it, is ...
5. The aspect relationship between Saturn, Uranus and Neptune in this chart is that they are ...
6. In the energies they represent, how do you think these first house planets might get along? Really well; No obvious issues; With difficulty and challenges.

Learn to Read Your Birth-chart in 5 Steps

# Quiz 4 Marilyn Monroe Birth-chart

Marilyn Monroe was born at 9:30am (PST) on 1 June 1926 in Los Angeles, California, USA.

According to the time given, Marilyn had:
- Leo rising (her Ascendant)
- Sun (and Mercury) in Gemini 10th House
- A Taurus Midheaven
- Moon (and Jupiter) in Aquarius 7th House

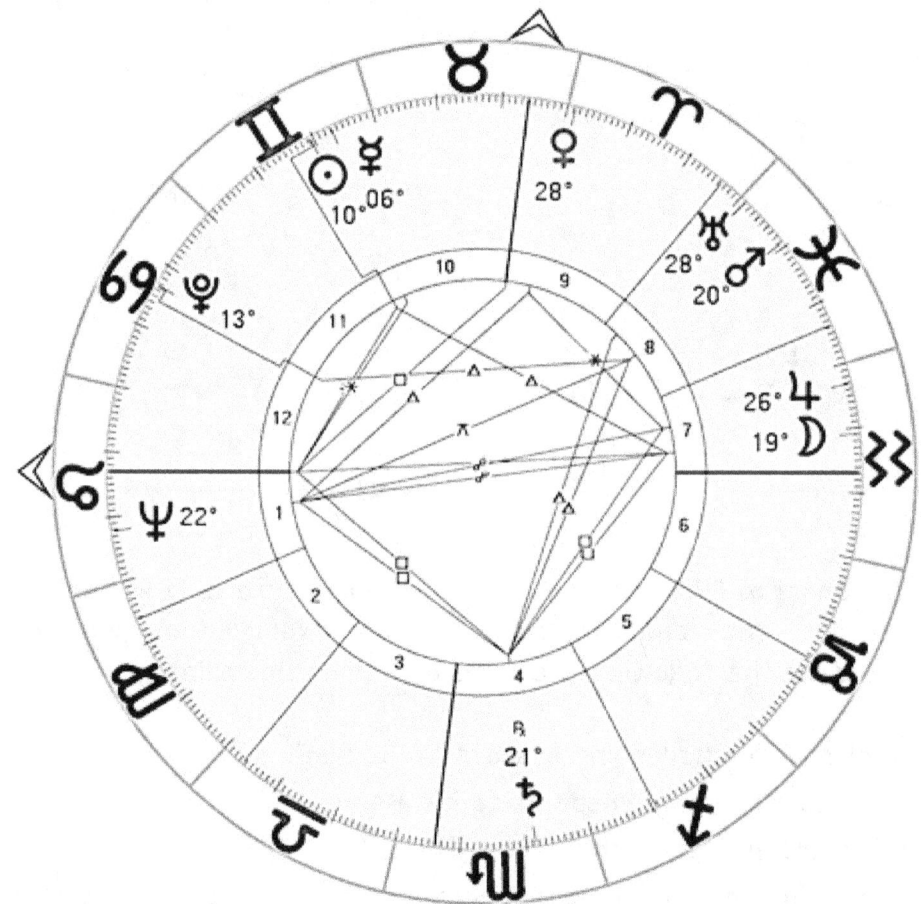

1. What about the planets not yet mentioned. What's the position of the following by sign and house? Fill in the signs and houses of these planets:

124    Step Three: Learn to Read the Planets & Aspects

Venus in ... in ... house; Mars in ... in ... house; Saturn in ... in ... house; Uranus in ... in ... house; Neptune in ... in ... house; Pluto in ... in ... house;

2. There are some pretty dynamic themes going on in this chart. See if you can spot a "T square" and the planets involved. This pattern says a lot about the screen image she projected; her powers of attraction – and indeed her vulnerability too. Enter the planets in their natural order when answering the question.

The planets are: ..., ..., ... and ....

3. There is also a "Grand Trine" in this chart. This may be a bit difficult to spot as it is broad in aspect on one side and a tiny bit outside the orb normally allowed – so that one of the aspect lines is not visible.

Enter the planets in their natural order when answering the question.

The planets are: ..., ... and ....

# Answers

## Quiz 1 True/False

1. TRUE. Jupiter is the largest planet in our solar system.
2. FALSE. Venus' mean distance from the Sun is 94 million miles. No, it's actually 67.2 million miles. 94 million miles is the distance of the Earth from the Sun.
3. FALSE. Pluto takes 9 years to complete one orbit of the Sun. No, 248.4 years is correct.
4. FALSE. A retrograde planet is a planet going backwards on its orbit of the Sun. No, a retrograde planet only appears to be going backwards. This is in relation to the Earth.
5. TRUE. Uranus' orbital inclination to the Ecliptic is 0 degrees 46 minutes.
6. FALSE. Mars is the old ruler of Libra. No, it's the older ruler of Scorpio.
7. TRUE. Pluto has been relegated to a dwarf planet in astronomy.
8. TRUE. Jupiter is the ruler of Sagittarius and the old ruler of Pisces.
9. TRUE. Mercury is likely to be mentally quick in the Air sign of Libra.
10. FALSE. Saturn in Scorpio suggests self-confidence and warmth in a person. No, it is more inclined to be cold and cautious.
11. FALSE. The opposition aspect suggests planets involved will get on with each other. No, it will depend upon the planets involved but the opposition is a challenging aspect.
12. FALSE. Saturn is the new ruler of Cancer. No, Saturn rules Capricorn and is the old ruler of Aquarius.
13. TRUE Five of the planets are/were rulers of two signs each. If you count old rulers in too.
14. TRUE. The Sun represents self-expression, one's vitality and creativity.
15. TRUE. The Moon is at home in Cancer.
16. FALSE. Neptune in Taurus suggests one who is practical and industrious. No, this is a better description for Mars. Neptune will be more inclined to be impractical and in need of inspiration to be industrious.
17. TRUE. Venus represents the urge to relate to others.
18. FALSE. Uranus represents limitation and restriction, the urge to control. No, this is a better description for Saturn.
19. TRUE. Mars wants to get things going, take action.
20. TRUE. The trine aspect between planets suggests harmonious flowing energy.

## Quiz 2. Jane Austen birth-chart
1. Her Sun is in Sagittarius in the 4th House.
2. Her Moon is in Libra in the 1st House.
3. Her Venus is in Scorpio 2nd House.
4. And her Mars is in Capricorn, 4th House.
5. Her ruling planet is Mercury.
6. They are trine to each other.
7. The Moon is square to Mars and Pluto too.
8. This Mercury opposition Uranus indicates Jane Austen would have had a radical and independent streak about her, a strong sense of irony that she expressed through her communications, at possibly all levels, not just in her writing. She was her own person. She broke with convention of the time that a woman's place was as a wife or mother; not as a writer. Her books were published as written "by a lady" rather than have her name revealed on the front cover. It was only after her death that her brother Henry Austen acknowledged publicly that it was Jane behind her works. I'd suggest it was her Libra Moon that steered her away from completely challenging convention of the time – this was her need to be a nice person, accepted and valued; and not rock the boat too much.
9. Neptune, so close to her Ascendant, gives us a clue as to why she was driven more to tell stories and write novels in preference to other kinds of writing.

## Quiz 3. Bill Lomas birth-chart
1. His Sun is in a powerful opposition to Saturn, Neptune and Uranus.
2. His Moon is in flowing aspects to Saturn, Neptune and Pluto. There is also a trine aspect to the Mc.
3. Venus is unaspected. Symbolising, in this instance, a tendency to be overlooked, and in need of friends and affection.
4. It is between Mercury, Saturn, Neptune and Pluto. Mercury is the focus for it.
5. In conjunction. All three are conjunct with each other. They also form a stellium in his 1st House.
6. With difficulty. Think about this: Saturn is seriously looking for structure and stability; Uranus will test any structure put up by Saturn and break it if it becomes too rigid; Neptune will tend to dissolve any structure.

## Quiz 4. Marilyn Monroe birth-chart

Answer 1.
- Venus in Aries 9th house
- Mars in Pisces 8th house
- Saturn in Scorpio 4th house
- Uranus in Pisces 8th house
- Neptune in Leo 1st house
- Pluto in Cancer 11th house

Answer 2.
The T square involves Moon, Jupiter, Saturn and Neptune. This is a very attractive and seductive arrangement – but vulnerable.

Answer 3.
The Grand Trine involves Mars, Saturn and Pluto. Saturn is a lynchpin here between the T square and the Grand Trine. Saturn in the 4th house suggests something tough about childhood. Monroe never had a family home as a child, rather she spent it "in 14 foster-homes and an orphanage" – see Wikipedia on Marilyn Monroe. This is something to think about.

I trust you got these questions right. Go back over them again if unsure.

# Step Three Extra

# Practice homework

## Get into the habit of interpreting charts...

Staying with Step 3. You have access to the keywords resource for all the planets, signs and aspects – in The Resources.

From what you have read and know so far, have a go at interpretating some of the main features of the charts from the Step 3 Quiz.

Write (or even record an MP3 to yourself if you'd prefer) in your own words (say 400 or 500 words) about the Sun, Moon, Ascendant and Midheaven - and any other components that grab your attention. For example, look for the "chart ruler" or a prominent aspect or a stellium – what would you say about the stellium in Bill Lomas' 1st house for example?

Save your work somewhere so that you can look back at it as your skills develop. And do, of course, always refer back to what is going on in your own birth-chart.

**Meanwhile here's a helping hand with three (of four) of the main components for you to look at...**

| Jane Austen | Bill Lomas | Marilyn Monroe |
|---|---|---|
| **Sun = Sagittarius 4th House**<br>○ Sagittarius: Free ranging, optimistic, pushes back boundaries, enlarges the picture, deepens experience; enjoys interaction and adventure; or can be inclined to be extravagant and rebellious in nature.<br>○ 04: Home and family important interest; love of houses; ties with the past; could indicate late development; reclusive tendencies.<br><br>**Moon = Libra 1st House**<br>○ Libra: Responsive and sensitive in love; needs harmonious, sociable (and often attractive, idealistic) environs to function well in; strong need | **Sun = Cancer 7th House**<br>○ Cancer: Resourceful, contemplative, protective and sensitive; inclined to be reserved, territorial and traditional; open to mood swings; strong ties to the past; or can be inclined to be over-sensitive, overly-protective, shy and retiring.<br>○ 07: Interest in other people, need for partner, need of audience; focus on building relationships; marriage; expression of power through others.<br><br>**Moon = Pisces 2nd House**<br>○ Pisces: Easy going, imaginative and adaptable; but also | **Sun (and Chart Ruler) = Gemini 10th House**<br>○ Gemini: Detached, adaptable, versatile and communicative; seeks easily digestible information and ideas; hunter/gatherer and sharer; or can be inclined to spread oneself too thinly, be shallow, superficial, inconstant.<br>○ 10: Achieving fame or recognition in chosen vocation or profession; the architect of one's own worldly success; leadership roles; corporate person; dealing with authority; political power, ambition.<br><br>**Moon = Aquarius 7th House**<br>○ Aquarius: Socially open, emancipating, living in unconventional environs; naturally |

Step Three: Learn to Read the Planets & Aspects

to be liked and comfortable with people; or can be elusive and fickle in feelings.

- 01: Strongly receptive, changeable, seen to act on impulse; needs personal involvement; expresses powers of imagination; good appetite; identification with mother, emotionally charged.

## Ascendant = Virgo

- Projects a gentle, modest, reserved, prudent, intelligent and quiet persona; inclined to be diligent, careful, tidy, systematic, methodical and analytical in their approach to life; inclined to be helpful to others, especially animals and those who are ill or vulnerable; inclined to be a perfectionist, seeking high

very sensitive to atmospheres and people – psychic abilities likely; seeks refinement in environment and in one's self; or can be indecisive, restless, vulnerable and inclined towards escapism.

- 02: Seeks security based on having financial and material resources in place, and being well-nourished; changeable or unstable finances, resources; artistic ability; business interests; need to feel earthed in peaceful, solid, reliable, steady and productive circumstances.

## Ascendant = Capricorn

- Projects a practical, cautious, often shy, patient, self-controlled and mature persona; inclined to be serious (but can have a dry sense of humour

inclined towards circumstances that break with traditions, are new or shocking; or equally can be unpredictable or erratic in behaviour.

- 07: Need for relationships (with women) for own security; easily forms emotional attachments to people; vulnerable to changes in partnerships; seeks a beautiful, harmonious home.

## Ascendant = Leo

- Projects a warm, sunny, self-assured, optimistic, outgoing, sociable and self-confident persona; will be the life and soul of the party, will want to be seen and appreciated; inclined to be protective of others and generous by nature; will enjoy having fun, taking up challenges, taking up sports, being on an

| | | |
|---|---|---|
| standards, particularly in their work, their health and hygiene.<br>○ Can otherwise be over-critical, fussy, inclined to find fault and to nag. | with it), industrious, tenacious, goal-setting and ambitious; seeks to improve status and material success through honest achievements; inclined to hold one's looks into old age.<br>○ Can otherwise be too controlled, lack spontaneity and be hard on oneself and dreams. | adventure, or in a drama.<br>○ Can otherwise have a sensitive ego, a lot of pride and inclined to be somewhat arrogant and stubborn. |

Next: Onto Step Four.

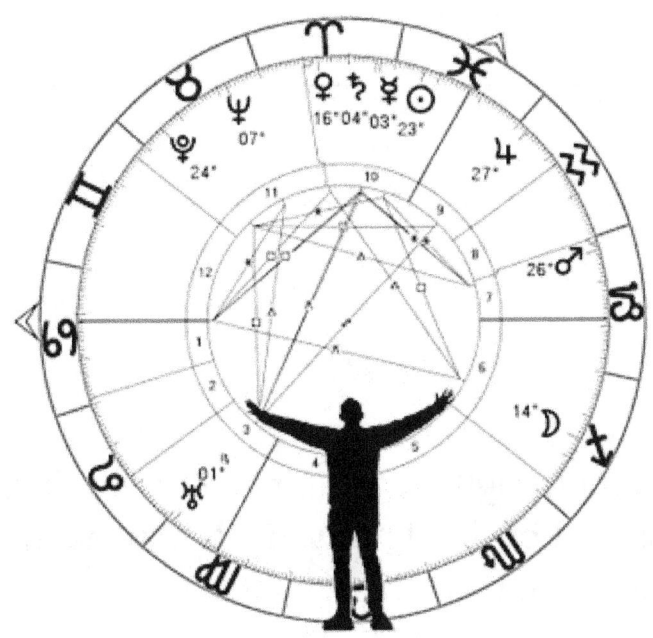

# Step Four

## Learn to Read the Angles & Houses

In context, check for the following resources, under The Resources, towards the back of the book:
  The Angles Resource
  The Twelve Houses Resource
  The Planets by House Resource

# Part 1
# Learn to read the Angles

As well as twelve zodiac signs, your birth-chart will also contain twelve houses. The houses can be best viewed as a mundane zodiac with each representing a compartment of life.

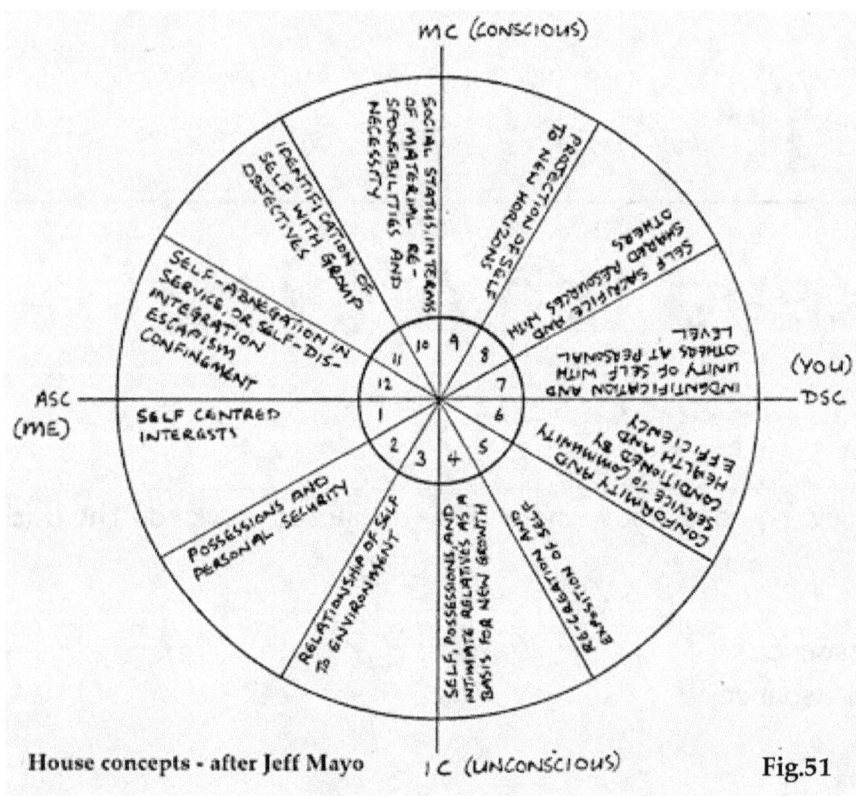

House concepts - after Jeff Mayo    Fig.51

Note: The image here (Fig.51) is a hand-drawn dial taken from my notes of some years back. They follow ideas of astrologer Jeff Mayo.

It needs mentioning that there is more than one house system used in Western astrology - see more about this below.

Your birth-chart, like all the example charts on this course, was probably built using the Placidus (proportional) House system - it is one of the popular systems. At a later time, you may want to look into other house systems for how they may/may not affect

134   Step Four: Learn to Read the Angles & Houses

the configuration of your chart. In context take a look at Part 2 of Step 4 for more on house systems.

Meanwhile, I would suggest you stick with one system you like, or the one you were given. If you are running astrological software you could experiment with different house systems to find which suits you best, but hold fire until you are familiar with the houses.

What most house systems start from is the ascending point – also called the Ascendant or rising sign. This is one of four angles of your chart – which brings us to taking a closer look at these important parts...

# The Angles of your birth-chart

The "Angles" (see Fig.52) are the ascending (Asc) sign (east), and the descending (Dsc) sign (west) on the horizontal (True Horizon) axis, together with the Midheaven (Medium Coeli - Mc) sign (south) and the IC (Imum Coeli) sign (north) on the on the vertical (meridian) axis.

These points are determined by the time and place of your birth.

The signs on the Asc and Mc are generally regarded as more important than the signs on the Dsc and Ic.

It is not difficult to see why this has come about...

The Asc represents what is rising, beginning or coming into view. It also marks off the cusp of the first house (in most house systems) so that the corresponding houses are directly keyed into the Asc -

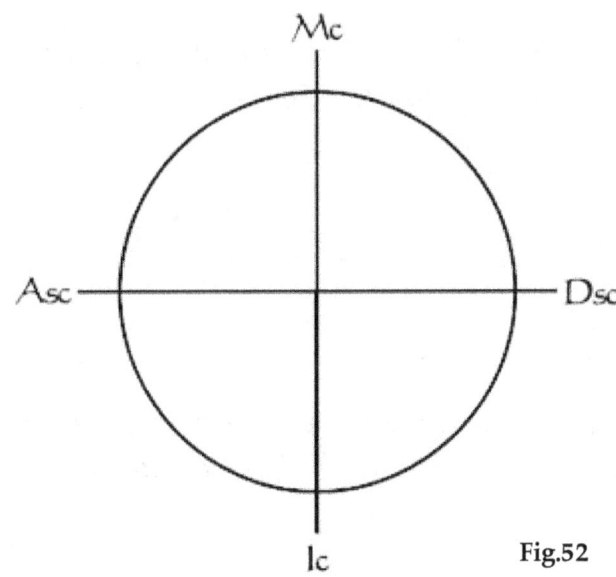

Fig.52

Ascendant. The Mc, on the other hand, represents what is culminating, reaching its climax, zenith, completely in view.

Considering the Dsc: this is the sign that is descending, coming to an end, going out of view, or setting. And the sign on the Ic is reaching its lowest point, completely out of view, behind the scenes, in the dark or background.

I have come to observe, however, that all four signs on the Angles need to be considered as important – especially in respect of the following ideas:

# Asc (Ascendant or rising sign)

## Key ideas

It represents "Me" what is very personal to me. It's my persona; my personal contact with the environment, how we are different from others around me.

It is what I want to become, and what I need to become as a person/personality

It is connected with (physical) appearance, how one appears to – and meets with – the outside world.

Consider the sign on the Asc as one's shop window for the world – how others will tend to see us. And importantly, it's the filter through which we tend to see them.

# Dsc (Descendant)

## Key ideas

This is "me and others" what others show me of myself. In what way I'm inclined to relate to others, and depend upon others – possibly for direction.

It is what I need, or attract, in others, in my relationships, and what they are likely to bring to me. Connected then with feedback and decision making through others.

The sign on the Dsc will indicate what I need from others in my development. And importantly what I may bring to them. The Dsc is connected then with the kind of feedback and links or relationships we form with other people.

It may also indicate a blind spot which we fail to deal with, effectively, in our lives and that can only be resolved through other people.

# Asc/Dsc together

The Asc/Dsc axis is like a social tightrope, a point of balance, tension between oneself and others. It is "Me" in context with "You," the externalised individual.

# Mc (Medium Coeli or Midheaven)

## Key ideas

It represents one's personal aims, goals and objectives in life; one's ambitions, where we are likely to direct our personal strivings and establish ourselves in the world; so, what one wishes to make for oneself.

It's the striving for self-fulfilment; the lens through which the outer, external world becomes a part of oneself.

The sign (and house) on the Mc may be said to energise (or qualify) the objectives and goals one tends to work towards in life, or in what way one seeks to "become" to flower, to be successful.

This may be translated into external (career status, public standing) or internal goals (consciousness, work around spiritual awareness) or better still, both.

# Ic (Imum Coeli)

## Key ideas

It is where one is coming from; how one connects with one's roots, foundations, background, unconscious motivations, physical-racial-cultural-family-genetic connections, domestic inclinations.

It is the inner private person, inner home, inner world.

The sign (and house) on the Ic represents the roots from which one blossoms, the energy (and conditions) one is (or needs to be) rooted in – to be emotionally secure and "at home" in oneself.

Along with the Moon and the sign of Cancer, it has bearing on the influences in childhood life. Often the outcome of this will be working in the background, subconscious, an inner voice, seeking to be heard or running the show.

# Mc/Ic together

The Mc/Ic axis is vertical, an internal process oriented toward inner awareness, the unconscious becoming conscious, links with mother/father and the child (Ic) becoming adult (Mc) fully mature.

Personality-wise, an occupation with one's standing in the world, and the way one wishes to be seen in public. It is concerned with inner maturity. It all links with growth. Consider it like a tree, the roots in the IC and the crown branches in the MC.

# All Angles together

The Angles (Fig.53) give us a simple if also profound hint of how to get from A to B in our journey of self-integration/self-discovery. We need firm roots (Ic) and direction (Mc) for healthy growth. If this hasn't been achieved through our early beginnings as children, we must find a way to create them. We need to be rooted in something that allows us to blossom as the best we can be.

Our environment must be balanced to support our beginnings (Ic) growth and endurance. No one is an island (Asc) and we depend upon others (Dsc) to lead happy lives and achieve our goals (Mc).

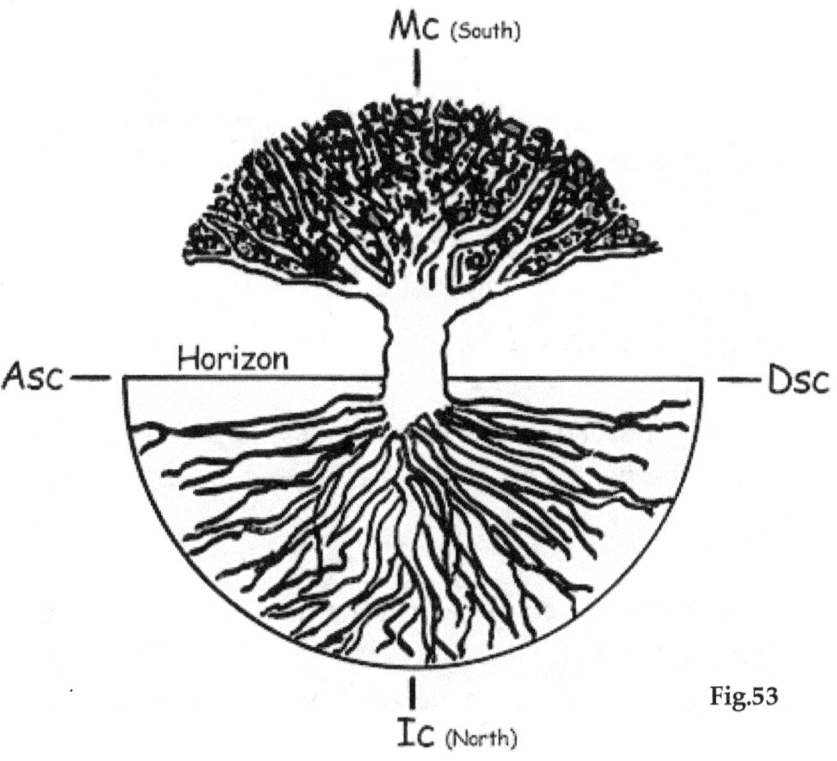

Fig.53

# Part 2

# Learn to Read the Houses

The first time the astrological houses were used in a horoscope is thought to have been as early as 4 BC.[1]

Over two thousand years later we have a plethora of house systems to choose from. In doing a little research I've noted there are at least sixteen different approaches and counting...

Astrologers tend to settle on what house system is deemed to work, or works for them. Or, perhaps more likely, their choice of house system is the one which they were taught to use from the beginning, and they have carried on using it ever since.

What all, or most astrologers, tend to agree on is the interpretation of the houses.

Houses are often treated like a "down to earth" representation of the signs. But there can be overlap, of signs having affinity with houses and planets. For instance, the 4th house is associated with home, while Cancer and the Moon likewise link to "home." The difference is likely that our 4th house is more directly linked to our "experience" of home – the bricks and mortar of our childhood home.

## How they look...

The first house begins in the East off the ascending point and runs anti-clockwise.

The grid here (Fig.54) shows the houses as they would be in their ideal spacing, or if using the Equal House System (but even in Equal House the Midheaven will actually be a floating point that can fall between the 8th to the 11th House).

Mostly, depending on the system used, the segment size of each of the houses will be proportional and thereby vary from the neat 30 degrees displayed here.

Note that, in traditional astrology, the houses are divided into angular (1,4,7 and 10), succedent (2, 5, 8 and 11) and cadent (3, 6, 9 and 12) houses. You'll notice that this follows the same principle as the mode of the signs i.e., *angular* relates to cardinal; *succedent* relates to fixed; *cadent* relates to mutable.

In their natural order (with Aries in the east rising position) the signs and houses (of equal house) would all line up with each other. By that I mean that each sign and house would be 30° in length and the 1st house would line up with Aries.

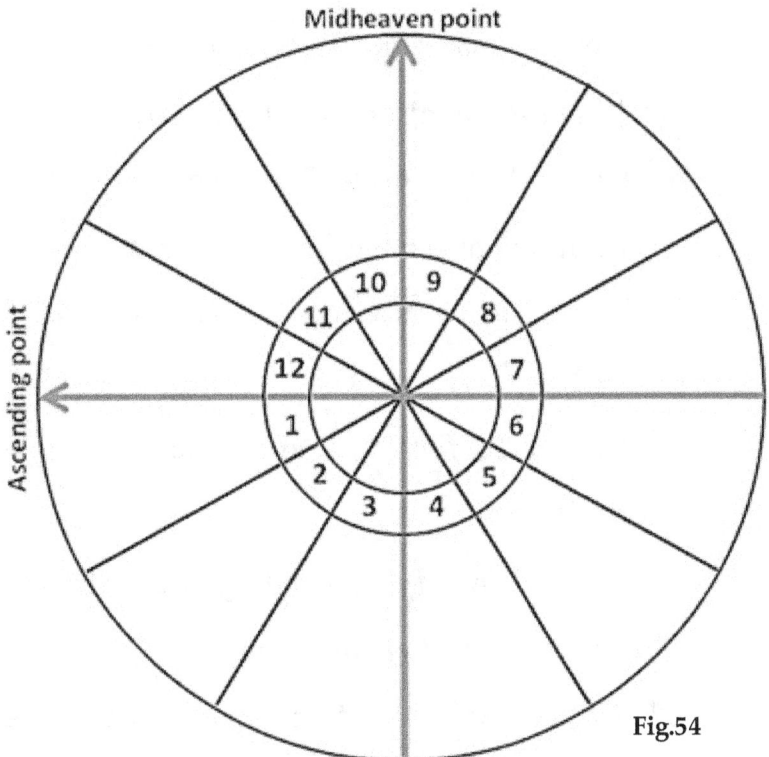

Fig.54

Learn to Read Your Birth-chart in 5 Steps

# Handy House reference

Here's a quick short-hand reference for what each of the houses stands for...

1st House: Personal matters, self-centred interests.

2nd House: Having money, possessions, resources, personal security.

3rd House: Knowledge, learning, finding out, communications, interests, local journeys. Relationship of one self to the immediate environment.

4th House: Home, home life, relatives, links to the past, one's roots. Intimate relatives as a basis for new growth.

5th House: Recreation, creativity, adventure, competition, sports. Exposition of self.

6th House: Conformity and service within one's community. Health, work and efficiency.

7th House: Identifying, relating and unifying with others. Finding partners, love matches, making agreements.

8th House: Self-sacrifice, shared resources, legal matters, undercurrents, taboos. Issues and agendas that are hidden.

9th House: Travel external and internal. Travel abroad and explorations, the bigger picture, expanding to new horizons.

10th House: Social status, management, position, power, responsibilities, necessities.

11th House: Groups, social activities, social networks. Group or collective objectives.

12th House: Self-abnegation, service for others; love of nature; escapism, confinement.

You'll find a lot more in The Twelve Houses Resource in The Resources towards the back of the workbook.

# A bit of the theory and issues with House Systems

But before moving on it could help you to know a bit more about houses – and why there is more than one system in use. To do this it will help to look, however briefly, at how they are constructed.

What I am talking about are methods of arriving at twelve houses in any given birth-chart. They vary from the simple to the complex in how they are calculated and formed. And with this in mind it is not the intention here to explore their various astronomical constructions in any depth, but rather to give a general overview of them – and example one or two. The reasons for this will, I hope, become clearer as we proceed.

It is probably fair to say that most astrologers will be unfamiliar with the nuts and bolts of how the house system, they are using, is calculated – or it might be said that they were familiar with it at one time but have since forgotten. This is not really that surprising given the complexity of it on one hand, and the ease of access to using it on the other.

Before software came along one needed to know how to use tables to calculate the house system that one preferred. With modern software doing the calculations, it is easy – a simple matter of choosing the house system at the time of constructing the birth-chart. Deciding which system to go for becomes the only complicated part of the process.

Astrologers tend to settle on what house system is deemed to work, or works for them. Or, perhaps more likely, their choice of house system is the one which they were taught to use from the beginning, and they have carried on using it ever since.

Amongst the most popular house systems are the Equal House and Placidus, plus the Regiomontanus and the Koch house systems (see Fig.56 for comparison). Bear in mind that some of these systems have been around for a long time (and often named after their originator – as in three of these listed here). Of this particular group the Koch House system is the youngest, stemming from the 1930s.[2]

Charts, as mentioned, on this course are drawn up using the Placidus House system – which is very popular. In my practice I may use Placidus, Equal House, Koch or perhaps Porphyry. More recently I've been trying out the Whole Sign house system too.

# Why so many?

Why there are so many all depends on the approach taken. Western house systems essentially divide the ecliptic (the path the Earth takes around the Sun) into twelve divisions. This can be done either directly dividing the ecliptic, or by one of the Earth's great (imaginary) circles such as the prime vertical (a great circle in the celestial sphere passing through the zenith and the east and west points of the horizon), the equator or a diurnal circle that then cuts through the ecliptic. See the following illustration (Fig.55) to get an idea.

Depending on which circle is chosen the house system can be arrived at. The Equal House system, for example, simply divides the plane of the ecliptic into twelve 30° parts, starting from the ascending point. This system follows the same principle to how the tropical zodiac signs are arrived at; but using the ascending diurnal point (as the start), instead of the Spring Equinox. The ascending point by the way will move through all the signs (360 degrees) during the 24-hour rotation of the Earth.

# The Celestial Sphere

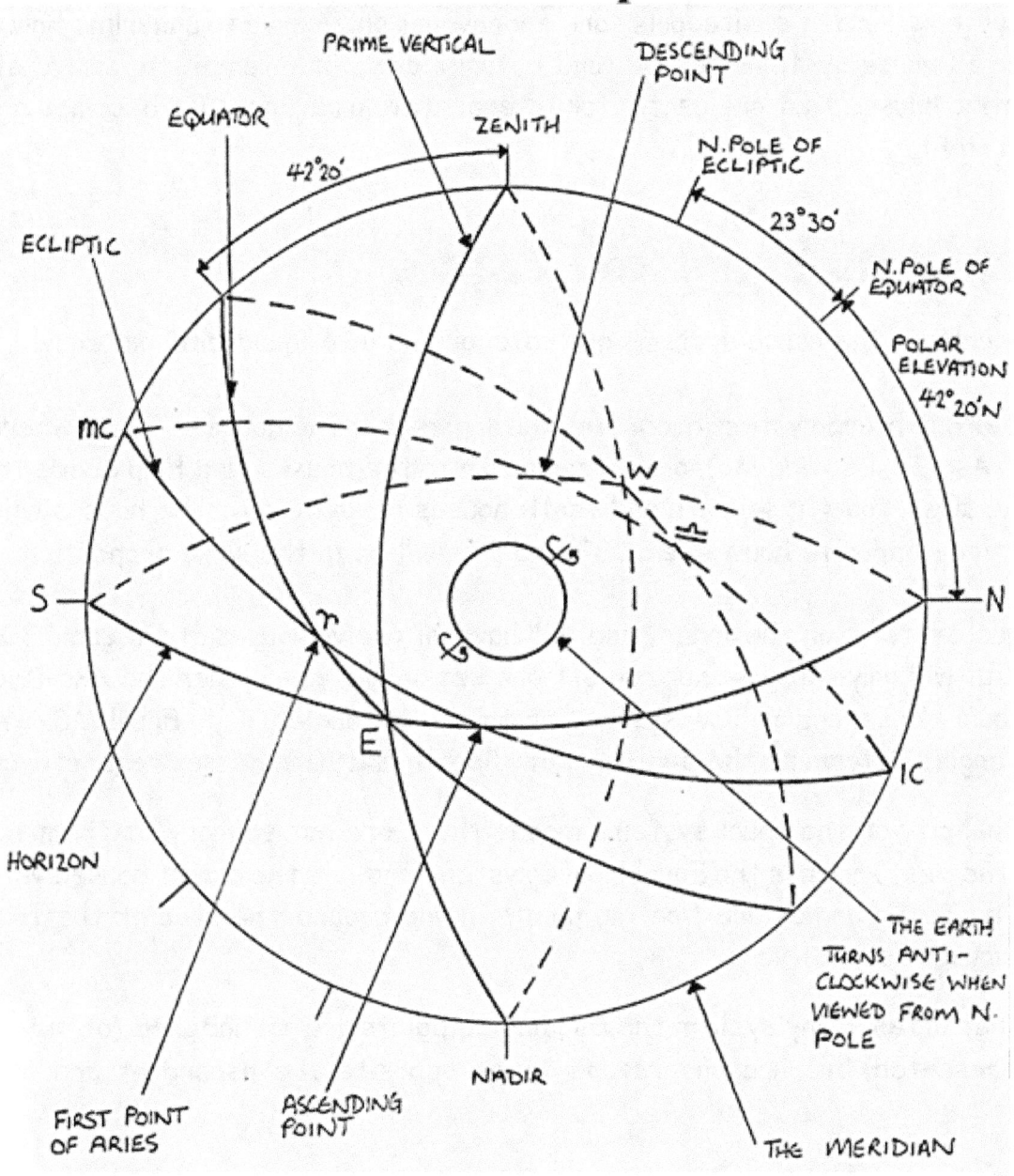

**Fig.55**     Hand-drawn by author from a Jeff Mayo illustration (with adaptions)

The image (Fig.54) shows the great circles projected around the Earth. These circles, the Ecliptic, the Prime Vertical, and the Equator are used in the calculation of various House systems. This image is set for the Polar Elevation 42°20' North – the same as Boston USA, which it was being used for at the time.

In his book, *The Elements of House Division*,[3] Ralph William Holden explores this matter much further. He divides house design into three types; Ecliptic, Space, and Time systems. Holden's categories and endeavours only serve to underline how complex and varied house systems can be (and actually are), in attempts to arrive at twelve geocentric houses that are useful for interpretation purposes. It becomes a study in its own right.

## Quadrant or Equal House systems

In general use, the house systems get categorised into "quadrant" or "equal."

The quadrant house system integrates the angles into the houses. This is where all the angles (Asc, Ic, Dsc and Mc), are integrated into the houses, and help divide the circle into the first, fourth, seventh and tenth houses respectively. The houses will vary in proportion – opposite houses (e.g., 3rd and 9th) will be in the same proportion.

The equal systems, on the other hand, will have all twelve houses at the same 30-degree width but will only integrate or run off one set of angles - either the Asc-Dsc angles, as in Equal House, and Vehlow system[4] or the Ic-Mc angles, as in Equal MC (where the Ic-Mc angles determine the beginning of the 4th and 10th houses respectively).

The simplicity of the equal systems means there are not so many of them to choose from. The best known is the Equal House system (and it's the oldest house system too). Here the Ic-Mc angles are floating points in and around the area of the fourth and tenth houses respectively.

Note that often in any system the Dsc and Ic points are not labelled (or may not even be represented) but are understood to be opposite the ascendant and midheaven angles.

## How House Systems can change interpretation

To highlight how house systems can change the interpretation, take a look at this illustration (Examples of four House Systems Fig.56) showing three quadrant and one equal being used on the same birth-chart. Note how the choice of system can affect the width of house segments and where planets occur within them (or not) as a result.

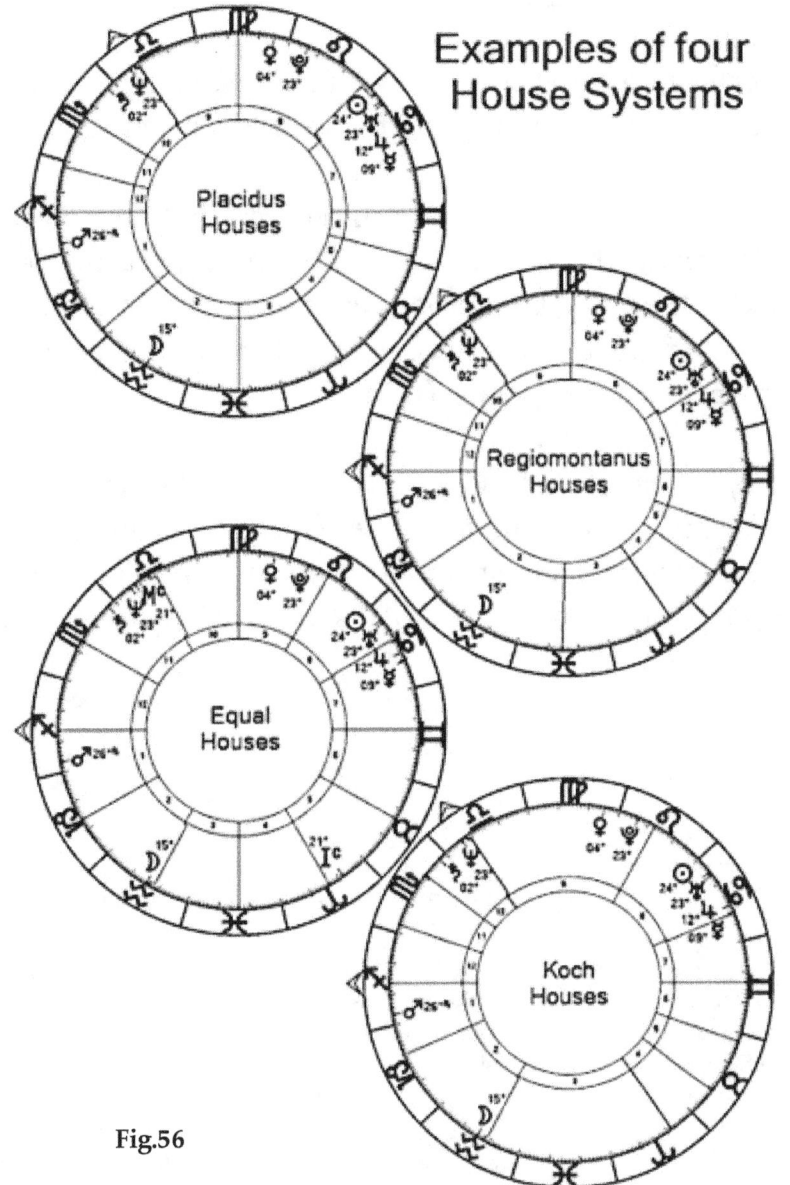

Fig.56

This shifting of house cusps of course will affect the interpretation of a given planet that is moved from one house to another. As an example, note that in the Placidus system there is a stellium of planets occurring in the 7th house; but in the other three systems this stellium is broken over two houses – the 7th and 8th. Indeed, in the Koch version there is now only one planet (Mercury) in the 7th house. This can have huge implications for the interpretation one places on the planets involved.

Learn to Read Your Birth-chart in 5 Steps

# Shelve it for later...

At this point let me say, don't worry about the plethora of house systems, and their complications. Indeed, don't worry if none of this makes much sense to you at this point.

As I said above, go with the house system you have at this time. It will probably be one of the more popular ones. Choosing which house system you prefer is something you may want to pursue further as you develop your understanding of your chart – especially if you have your own software where you can easily test things. But my advice is, if it ain't broke (i.e., it works for you) don't fix it...

For more on house systems take a look at Holden's book, discussed above. Alternatively, get hold of the *Larousse Encylopedia of Astrology*[5] – which discusses the House problem in depth and carries some great illustrations. Or take a look at AstroWiki[6] on Astro.com where you'll find some useful FAQs on House systems too.

# References

[1] Saunders, H. (1998) Article: A Brief Overview of the History of Western Astrology https://www.astrology-house.com [Accessed 15/10/2019]

[2] Although where the Koch House System is concerned the claimed originator, Walter Koch, is contested. And the accuracy of the Koch system is also disputed. See Koch House System on AstroWiki https://www.astro.com/astrowiki/en/Koch_House_System [Accessed 13/04/2021].

[3] Holden, R W (1977) The Elements of House Division. LN Fowler & Co Ltd.

[4] Note that in the Vehlow system the ascending degree gives rise to the first house not at the beginning but from the middle of it.

[5] Brau, J.L., Weaver, H., and Edmunds, A. (1980) Larousse Encyclopedia of Astrology, McGraw-Hill Book Company (PP 137-148).

[6] AstroWiki, https://www.astro.com/faq/fq_fh_owhouse_e.htm [Accessed 13/04/2021]

# Step 4 Quizzes

See how you get on with the following quizzes...

## Quiz 1. True/False

1. Equal House and Placidus are two of the most popular house systems.

2. The best house system is Placidus.

3. Most house systems divide up the ecliptic into 12 segments.

4. It doesn't matter which house system one uses as the planets will always be found in the same respective houses.

5. The Descendant angle represents me as others are likely to see me.

6. The Midheaven represents where we reach our zenith.

7. The 5th house links to possessions, resources we have or need, and security.

8. Aries rising suggests a homely, domesticated and sensitive person.

9. Aquarius on the midheaven suggests a person who aspires to independence for themselves and others in some way.

10. The third house links to communications and knowing one's locality.

11. In a quadrant house system, all four angles of the birth-chart are integrated into the houses.

12. The Ascendant represents what is ending.

13. Planets in 6$^{th}$ house have some work to do to become more efficient.

14. Sun in the 9th house is likely to love travelling, whereas Saturn in the 9th house probably only wants to travel when it's necessary.

15. Uranus in the 1st house suggests a conventional personality.

16. Neptune in the 3rd house suggests a person may have developed mediumistic skills.

17. Mercury in the 12th house suggests a person may have developed mediumistic skills.

18. A person with Pluto in the 8th house is likely to be intense.

19. Jupiter in the 10th house suggests difficulty gaining success in one's chosen profession.

20. A person who fights for a cause could have their Mars in the 11th house.

# Quiz 2. Elisabeth Kübler-Ross Birth-chart

### Reminder of who Elisabeth Kübler-Ross is/was:

*Elisabeth Kübler-Ross (July 8, 1926 - August 24, 2004) was a Swiss-American psychiatrist, a pioneer in near-death studies, and author of the internationally best-selling book, On Death and Dying (1969), where she first discussed her theory of the five stages of grief, also known as the "Kübler-Ross model." Kübler-Ross was a 2007 inductee into the National Women's Hall of Fame, was named by Time as one of the "100 Most Important Thinkers" of the 20th Century and was the recipient of nineteen honorary degrees. By July 1982, Kübler-Ross taught 125,000 students in death and dying courses in colleges, seminaries, medical schools, hospitals, and social-work institutions.*

Wikipedia[1]

*Elisabeth Kubler Ross "Life, Death and Life After Death"*
*https://www.youtube.com/watch?v=dnxHdJWSls4*

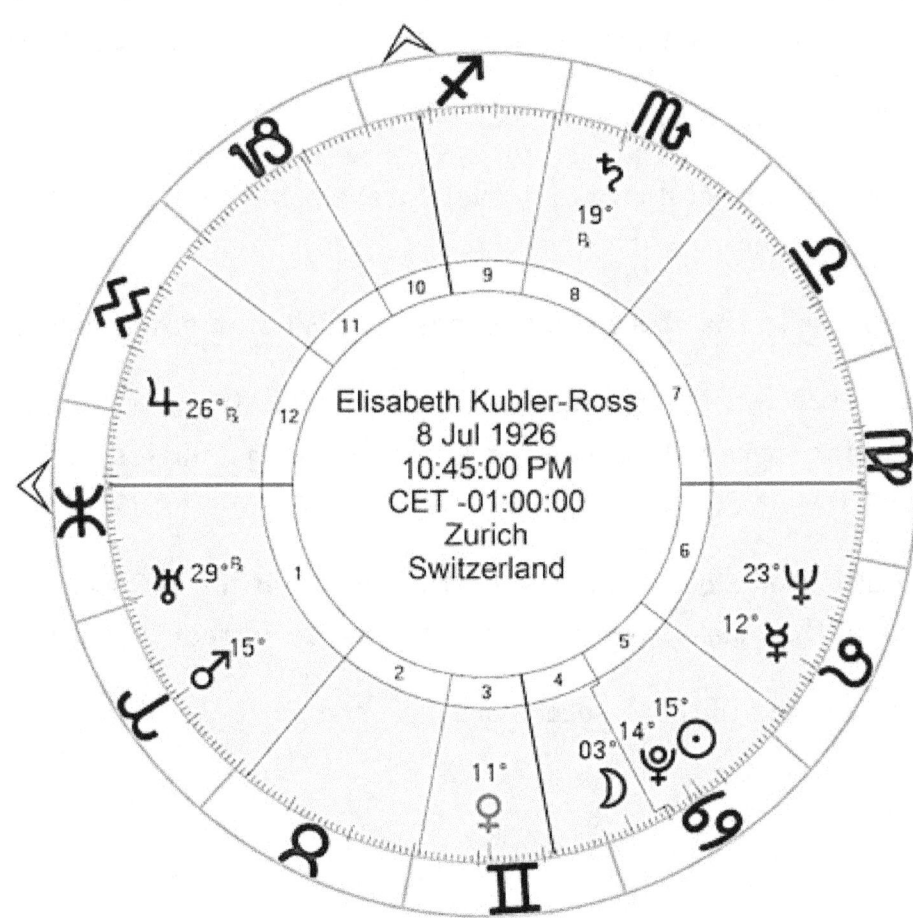

Learn to Read Your Birth-chart in 5 Steps  **151**

Answer the following **multiple-choice** questions

1. Mars and Uranus in the 1st House would imply she was:

    A soft touch; strongly independent; indecisive; conventional, a pioneer; airy-fairy; self-motivated.

2. What can be deduced from the house that the Sun and Pluto occupy? She was:

    Obsessional; competitive; powerful; strong sense of purpose; fearless; dedicated; confident.

3. The position of Saturn could suggest:

    Interest in research; Happy go lucky person; Possible phobias around death; Endures hardship; Loves meeting people; Interest in life and death matters.

4. The house position of the Moon indicates:

    Strong maternal instincts; love of travel; interest in the past; unstable finances; enjoys reading.

5. Jupiter and Neptune in the chart are in opposition. What might this mean:

    Dedication to service; Psychic/spiritual experiences; Interest in architecture; Love of big open spaces; A manager of people; Healing abilities; Inclined to be a bit narcissistic.

6. (This is not a multi-choice question) The birth-chart also has a T square. See if you can spot it and fill in the blanks for the planets involved – in their natural order.

    The planets involved in the T square are …, … and ….

# Answers to Quizzes

## 1. True/False

1. True.

2. False. It is one of the most popular but not necessarily the best. It is all a matter of opinion at this juncture.

3. True.

4. False. This is the crux of the problem when choosing a house system. Different systems can cause planets to appear in different houses. See the **Examples of Four House Systems** illustration (on P9). It would be great if the planet did stay in the same houses across the house systems available.

5. False. This description is more appropriate of the Ascendant. The Descendant links to how we are inclined to be attracted to others. What we need from others to make our lives whole.

6. True. It symbolizes where we are inclined to flower.

7. False. This is more appropriate for the 2nd house.

8. False. More appropriate for Cancer rising.

9. True.

10. True.

11. True.

12. False - the Ascendant represents what is beginning or coming into view.

13. Could be true. Planets in the 6th house could also be said to be naturally inclined to be more efficient.

14. True.

15. False. More inclined to be eccentric - so unconventional personality.

16. True.

17. True.

18. True.

19. False. The opposite is more likely to be true.

20. True.

# 2. Elisabeth Kubler-Ross birth-chart

1.
Mars in 1st House: Pioneering; independent action; displays urgency combined with energy, enterprise, courage and self-motivation; physical strength, action, aggression; good at starting own enterprise.

Uranus in 1st House: Projects conspicuous individuality; eccentric, clever, original; strong need for freedom/independence; love of change; unusual appearance or mannerisms; interests in science and technology.

**Comment**: If anything showed her pioneering spirit it is these planets in the 1st house. This is a person who would hitch her wagon to her own star.

2.
Sun in 5th House: Creative expression; games, sports and adventures; avenues for building self-confidence and expressing one's power; love of pleasure; theatre, and children.

Pluto in 5th House: Powerful need to make an impression on others/world; air of authority/leader; compulsion to create, powerful bonds with children, intense sexuality, great capacity for pleasure; extraordinary achievements likely or uncompromising and dictatorial in position of power.

Consider also Sun conjunct Pluto in this. The following notes from *The Planets Suite* book:

An intense, very confident, powerful, magnetic and dynamic personality; has a strong will combined with a wealth of creative power and energy; will have a presence about them; one who feels driven by a deep, inner sense of destiny, great faith and trust in own abilities, and who can accomplish what he or she sets their mind to; will expect to conquer any obstacle, problem or setback; a strong desire to achieve personal goals and gain personal recognition; will want to be the world's best at something – and that idea spurs on efforts; will possess natural leadership qualities, organisational qualities and executive skills; has the wherewithal to persuade others to follow their lead; will be inclined to be secretive and to love working behind the scenes; indicates an ability to transform circumstances and to re-invent oneself where necessary.

**Comment**: The notes above say it all. This was a driven and powerful person, a person seeking her own adventure, her own destiny. This is someone who could make a real contribution to the world – and she did.

3.
Saturn in 8th House: Remains cool and a strength in a crisis; endures hardships; takes responsibilities

for other people's money or resources; legal-eagle; hard-nosed; sexually repressed; can have morbid fear of death; inclined to be cynical about life.

**Comment**: Saturn will tend to flag up a lack or a tendency to over-compensate on matters of the house it occupies.

It is probable that with Saturn in the 8th house that she did develop a real concern or fear of death (which she wouldn't necessarily share with people, other than those close to her) and this is what drove her to also look into death and dying in the way that she did. Certainly, from an early life she had close encounters with death, as her life journey will testify, and this had a profound effect on her desire to help and heal others facing similar.

Note her Saturn was also in a T square. It was square to Jupiter in 12th house and Neptune (with Mercury) in the 6$^{th}$ house. These houses together are linked with health, mental health, with healing and transformation, and also (especially 12$^{th}$) linked with death. It suggests a dialogue between optimism and pessimism around the matter that caught so much of her interest and passion. Meanwhile her Sun and Pluto (a planet associated with death) were trine to Saturn. I'd suggest there was a lot of energy being poured into to a better understanding of death, the process of it, what it might lead to, and our accepting it as an essential part of our lives.

4.
Moon in 4th House: Strong interest in home, family and mother or motherhood; rich inner life; possible interest in roots, ancestry and borders; reclusive tendencies; many changes of residence likely.

**Comment**: Whether we would find such information on what is written about her or not, her Moon here suggests she had a real emotional need for family, home and a sense of being rooted. It would have given her security and strength. Home is where her heart was, and she probably would have been most comfortable when at home.

5.
Jupiter in 12th House: Charity or social worker; success with matters of the sea, success with businesses linked to gas and oil, to the arts, music and dance; activity behind the scenes; interest in metaphysical/spiritual matters; inclined towards psychic/spiritual experiences.

Neptune in 6th House: Desire to serve humanity; vocation in holistic health; likelihood of healing abilities; lack of ego gratification in work; uncertainty over one's vocation and community value; mysterious and undiagnosable health problems.

**Comment**: Desire to serve humanity on the level of metaphysical/spiritual matters is certainly one way that she expressed this opposition. These planets in the T square with Saturn and Mercury suggests this is the pattern that most readily symbolises her work, her writing and where she majored in her teaching, on death and dying.

6. Saturn, Jupiter and Neptune. Mercury is also drawn into this via being square with Saturn. See answers 3 & 5 for comment.

# References

[1] Elisabeth Kubler-Ross on Wikipedia https://en.wikipedia.org/wiki/Elisabeth_K%C3%BCbler-Ross [Accessed 24/04/2021]

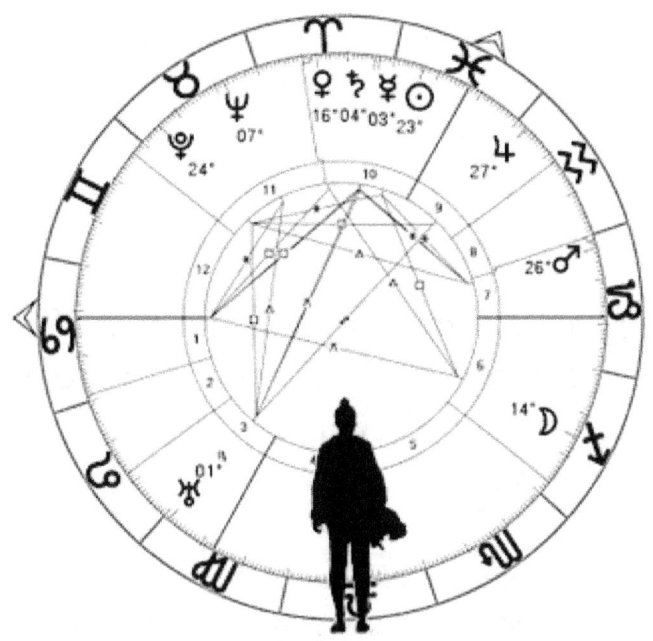

# Step Five

## Learn to Read Your Birth-chart

Step Five will draw on all the resources (in Resources) that you'll find towards the back of the book.

# Opening Comments

If you are following through and getting the best from this course, I'm trusting you will have already made a start on reading your birth-chart. That is by collecting useful information on the signs, planets, aspects, angles and houses relating to you.

You will, at very least, have already deduced that a birth-chart, your birth-chart, is a dynamic map brim full of information and potential. And, with so much information available, reading it can feel like a daunting prospect...

Well, if that is true for you, you're not alone in this – probably everyone goes through it.

If we look at the birth-chart of Jimi Hendrix (Fig.57) for instance, it doesn't take much imagination to conclude that reading his chart from cold could be quite a challenge.

Practised astrologers will intuitively pick up on notable themes in a given birth-chart. Quite often it will be notable aspects that they see first. It may be the shaping of the overall chart (see the Bonus Pack for more on shaping). It may be a stellium of planets or something else that immediately pops out at them.

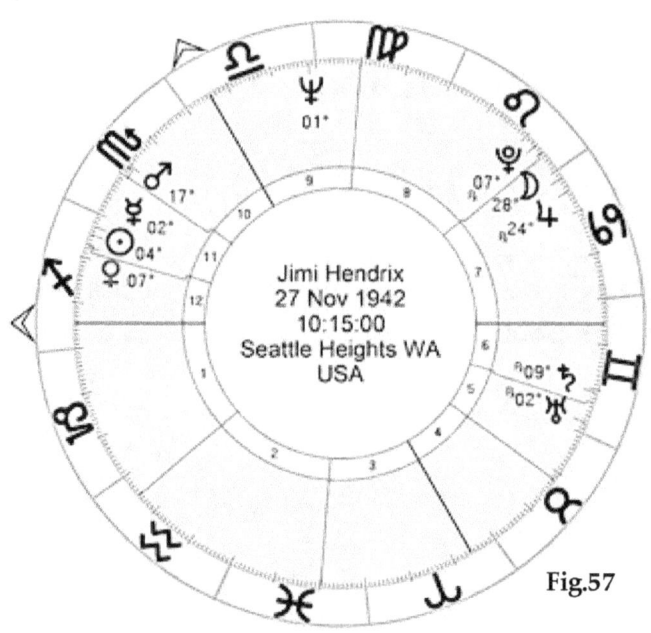

Fig.57

If you take a look at the Bill Lomas chart for instance, the first thing that drew my attention to it was the rising sign, and the three planets in his first house. Then the major aspects that were shouting out. It's one of the reasons I chose this chart as an example. We'll be looking at it in more detail below.

This is before the astrologer takes a deeper look – at the small print let's say.

This is why, short of leaving it just to one's intuition (not a good idea), Step 5 is divided up into two constructive levels of approach and evaluation...

It is also worth saying that you don't have to know everything from the get-go. You just need to build up your understanding at your own pace.

Astrologers can spend a lot of time learning astrology and improving their skill at it - via practice. Indeed, they (we) never really stop learning as each birth-chart is, by its essential nature, different, unique – familiar components but in a different arrangement.

So here we'll be looking at going from a broad reading of the main components to a more thorough and detailed approach later...

## Component descriptions

When drawing down the descriptions of each of the components in your chart, rather than copy everything down, I suggest you gather the salient keywords/points that register with you.

## Okay, onto taking a broad reading of your chart.

# Part 1

# A Broad Reading of your Chart

**Keeping it simple: by drawing on four main components and Chart Ruler**

When you want to get a starter handle, or overview, on your birth-chart (or the chart of another person), a good place to begin is with what I might call the "big four." That is the Sun, the Moon, together with the Ascendant and Midheaven angles.

And I would also add in your Chart Ruler, by sign and house; and any other prominent feature, such as a stellium of planets and/or a major aspect configuration – such as a grand cross or grand trine.

Given your birth time is reliable,[1] no matter whatever else is going on, these main four components will provide obvious points to pick up on. They will give you a very useful overview of the more prominent personal themes you are dealing with.

Of course, the position and relationships between these and the other chart components all play an important part in the matrix of understanding how we tick and the situation we are in.

But to begin with, let's remind ourselves of what these four components indicate:

## The Sun

Just as the Sun is at the centre of our solar system, so the Sun, in astrology, is the centre of who we are. It will shine through. It is the theme, or leading character (as in a play) we are most likely to identify with in our lives. In my view the Sun represents the window through which the soul can shine. It is the direct link with our essence or soul's life intention. It is our constant light source. It is the masculine or paternal principle. By sign, house and aspect it represents what is most steady and reliable in our makeup – even when, for some people (e.g., Vincent van Gogh) it may not be the most prominent theme in their birth-chart.

## The Moon

The Moon represents how we are inclined (or have learned) to respond to life. Some describe it as the bigger part of our ego and/or our subconscious. It shows the potential for our behaviour, our habits, instinctual responses, where and how we feel comfortable in our skin – or not as the case may be. By sign and house, it will reflect our early life experiencing and conditioning. As the Moon waxes and wanes so the symbolical Moon reflects the natural rhythm of our lives. As the Moon shines at night, so the Moon represents our "behind the scenes" inner life, associated with the workings of the body, with genetics, with blood line relationships, with our roots, with the past. The Moon is the feminine or maternal principle.

## The Ascendant

The sign on the Ascendant represents what is arising in our lives, what is beginning and requiring our attention, what we need to express. It is our shop window onto the world – and acts as a filter for our perspective on the world too. It will powerfully indicate how we want other people to see us – and how they may see us. It is what we project out, our persona in other words. And here's a thought: when our shop window is displaying what is also inside the shop (linking with our Descendant), we are getting the balance right – we are being our authentic self. The sign on the Ascendant will show us how we are to achieve such integration.

The sign on the Descendant will indicate what others may bring into our lives, or what we need from others to achieve integration.

## The Midheaven

The Midheaven indicates what is culminating (or seeking to culminate) in our lives, what our life experience is directed towards, seeking to achieve, to fulfil on a worldly basis. It relates to our goals, values, ambitions and endeavours – whether conscious or subconscious. The sign on the Midheaven clues us into how we may go about achieving our goals and fulfilling our lives.

## The Chart Ruler

The Chart Ruler will also be a prominent component or theme. Which planet it is will depend upon which sign is rising in your chart.

## A Stellium of Planets

A stellium is made up of a group of three or more planets in one sign – they must be in one sign. It could be the stellium is in the same sign as one of your four main players. Equally it could be in a different sign to the four. And equally you may not have a stellium in your birth-chart. So, this is a pattern that may or may not occur, depending on when you were born.

If you have one, the likelihood is that the sign it is in, is going to have prominence – whichever planets are involved. It will give greater emphasis to any of your four main players, or to be considered as a fifth player if in a different sign.

If you haven't got a stellium that is, of course, okay. You will still have the same number of planets as anyone else, they were simply spread-out differently when you were born.

# Four Birth-chart Examples

Readings of four chart examples of well-known figures – including Elizabeth Taylor, Albert Einstein and Mary Baker Eddy.

Here we will be looking at the Sun and Moon in houses, and chart ruler in a set of charts, plus three charts that have a stellium. And I will be breaking away from the four main components a little bit too.

As we began this discussion with Jimi Hendrix, let's go back to his birth-chart to start with...

# Jimi Hendrix

*James Marshall "Jimi" Hendrix (born November 27, 1942 - September 18, 1970) was an American rock guitarist, singer, and songwriter. Although his mainstream career lasted only four years, he is widely regarded as one of the most influential guitarists in history and one of the most celebrated musicians of the 20th century. The Rock and Roll Hall of Fame describes him as "the greatest instrumentalist in the history of rock music."* [2]

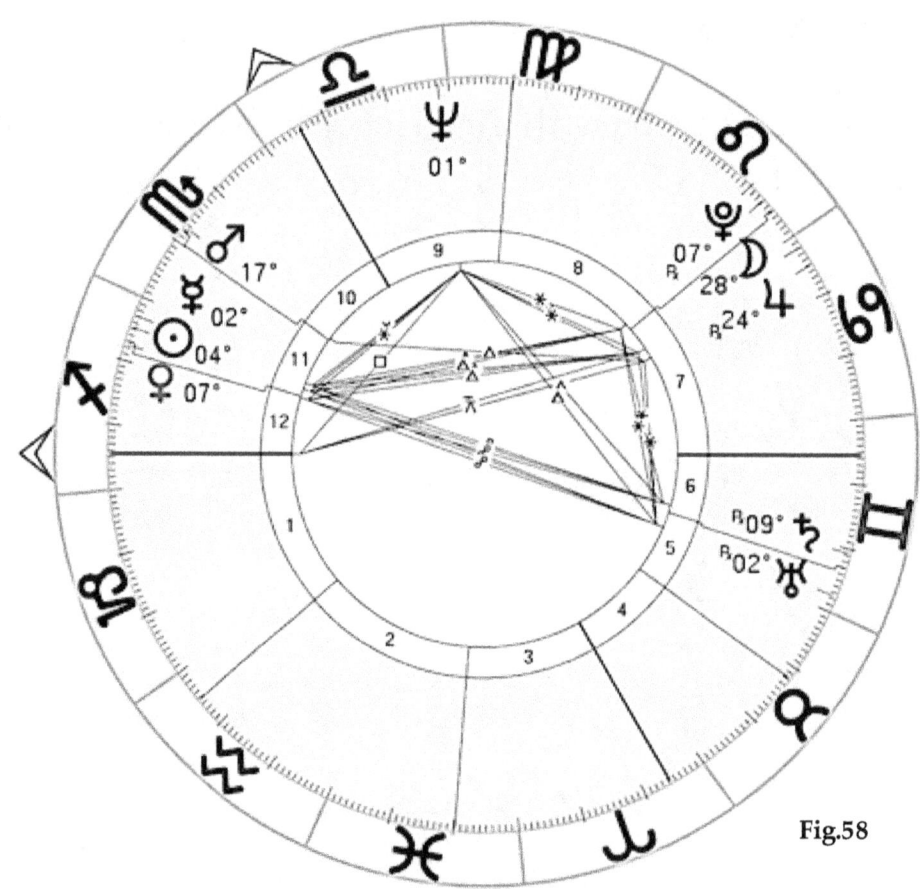

Fig.58

In his chart (Fig.58), Hendrix had:

Sun in Sagittarius 11th House
Moon in Cancer 7th House
Ascendant is in Sagittarius
Midheaven is in Libra

**164** Step Five: Learn to Read Your Birth-chart

The chart ruler is Jupiter
A stellium in Sagittarius

If we take stock of the keyword notes, from the resources provided on these components, we arrive at the following:

## Sun in Sagittarius 11th House:

**Sun in Sagittarius**: Free ranging, optimistic, pushes back boundaries, enlarges the picture, deepens experience; enjoys interaction and adventure; or can be inclined to be extravagant and rebellious in nature.

**Sun in 11th House**: Creative thinker; leader in group activities; many friends in societies or on social media; links with people in high places; likely interest in causes, the future, in technology, environmental matters.

## Comment

The Sun being in the 11th house suggests a strong identification with groups, social activities, social networks, collective objectives, innovations, inventions that help to emancipate free or release others. This house, opposite to the 5th house, has much to do with the means by which we become part of something bigger, a team, a group or movement can be bigger than the sum of its parts. This is the house of social objectives, humanity, of unions, all for one and one for all. The competition of the 5th House gives way to the appreciation and recognition of the contribution of others, and, at best, from whichever side they are on.

## Sagittarius rising/Jupiter chart ruler:

Hendrix had a double Sagittarius with this placement – i.e., Sun and his ascending sign.

**Sagittarius rising**: Projects an open-minded, philosophical, benevolent, optimistic, versatile, adaptable, adventurous and a risk-taker persona; inclined to be honest and direct in exchanges; will seek to broaden horizons and belief likely through travel and forms of further or higher education; inclined to love nature and enjoy outdoor activities; will likely be searching for meaning to life.

**Jupiter in Cancer**: Forms strong attachments to home/family; enjoys a secure and comfortable home; charitable; educational, moral and religious outlooks established in early life; good business sense; or can be overly-touchy, impressionable.

**Jupiter in 7th House**: Outgoing personality; attracts many friends and connections; good business or professional associates; attracts fortunate relationships/marriage; strong appreciation for the arts.

**Note: A stellium of planets further emphasises Sagittarius**
The Sagittarius theme of this chart is further emphasised by Hendrix having a stellium in the sign. This is made up of the Sun, Mercury and Venus.

## *Comment*

What we can say about Jimi Hendrix from his ascending sign, Sun sign, chart ruler and house, is that he was a person who was seeking to expand his experience of life. We could describe him as a joyful optimist, free-ranging, an adventurer, a nice rebel – who easily made friends. He sought to have freedom of expression in what he did. Certainly, he opened up new boundaries with his music and his stage presence. Importantly he played a leading part in the hippy (and drugs) movement that sought to emancipate people to a different way of viewing life and each other.

## Moon in Cancer in 7th House:

**Moon in Cancer**: Works off gut feelings; sensitive and receptive; needs to feel "at home" protected – happiness depends upon it; domesticated, family oriented; or can alternatively be moody, emotionally unstable.

**Moon in 7th House**: Relating, others, partners, love matches, agreements, marriage, the trappings of attraction or attracting partners, harmonious environments. This house links to all things to do with relating and relationships. Being in opposition to the 1st house which is about "me," very personal, this house is about the "other" or "us."

## Comment

Not only was his chart ruler in Cancer but also his Moon. This is a person who was instinctual in expression. Feeling at home and secure in himself was hugely important to his self-confidence. Without it he would be given to being moody and insecure. Relationships/love affairs would have been one of the avenues in which he would have sought to find that emotional security he really needed.

## Libra Midheaven:

Life goals or aspirations likely to include: achieving harmony in one's work and home-life balance, between activity and relaxation, between social interaction and spending time alone; having harmonious relations with people and environment; living in beautiful surroundings; being surrounded by art, music and the finer things in life; helping others achieve same.

## Comment

Libra in our birth-chart is where we experience attraction and seek to establish harmony in relation to others and our world. We want our world to appreciate us. At the midheaven it becomes associated with idealism, aims and goals. It has artistic and musical connections.

The Libra midheaven in Jimi Hendrix birth-chart is indicative of the peace, love, harmony and the idealism that he and the whole hippy movement were tied into. It was an idealism that for Hendrix, at least, couldn't last.

---

I hope you can see how these four components can offer valuable insight into a given chart. There is of course a lot more that could be said of Jimi Hendrix's birth-chart.

He was more radical than we glean from the main components above. To build a more intimate picture you have to take into consideration that he has a Saturn/Uranus conjunction, in opposition to his stellium in Sagittarius.

He was a hugely charismatic personality who was, at times, dealing with wildly restless up and down moods – which he expressed out through his performance and music (5th House).

Although his death was considered to be a drug related accident, I suspect he also found it difficult to live with his energy and was seeking a way to express it that would carry him to a state of Nirvana, or a way out. Now what makes me say this is the most important planet in this chart – and that is Neptune in Libra and 9th House.

Every other planet, apart from Mars, has a flowing aspect to Neptune. Its association with music is well-known and its association with spiritual refinement and retreat is also well-known.

# Elizabeth Taylor

Let's take a look at this well-known figure and her birth-chart. I must say that I chose these names on a random basis. You might notice some interesting overlaps/links between their charts. It wasn't planned. A bit of synchronicity, moments have their meaning let's say...

*Dame Elizabeth Rosemond Taylor DBE (February 27, 1932 – March 23, 2011) was a British-American actress, businesswoman, and humanitarian. She began her career as a child actress in the early 1940s, and was one of the most popular stars of classical Hollywood cinema in the 1950s. She continued her career successfully into the 1960s, and remained a well-known public figure for the rest of her life. In 1999, the American Film Institute named her the seventh-greatest female screen legend.*[3]

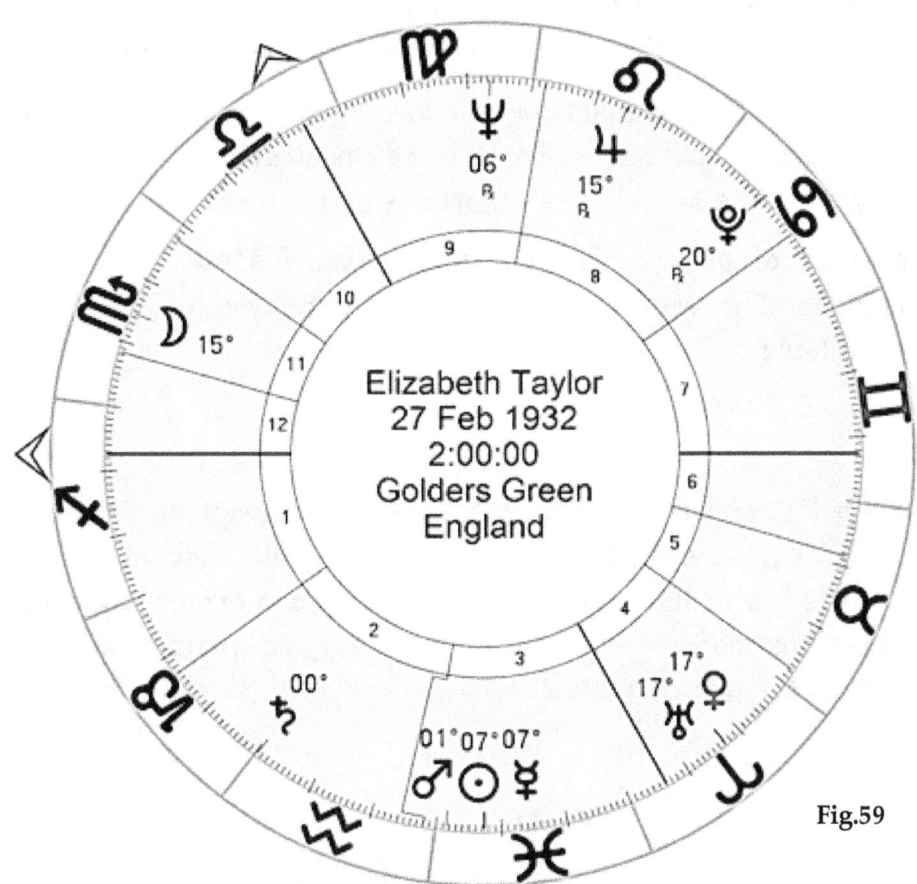

Fig.59

Learn to Read Your Birth-chart in 5 Steps  **169**

In Taylor's chart (Fig.59) she had:

Sun in Pisces 3rd House
Moon in Scorpio 11th House
Ascendant is in Sagittarius
Midheaven is in Libra
The chart ruler is Jupiter
A stellium in Pisces

## Sun in Pisces 3rd House

**Sun in Pisces**: Impressionable, reserved and receptive, but also highly adaptable, changeable and artistic; seeks perfection for self and others; seeks to inspire, and be inspired; or inclined to be impractical, insecure, uncertain about life.

**Sun in 3rd House**: Self-expression through mental pursuits, study, acquiring information; a good student; interest in communications, writing or teaching; connections with one's neighbours; brothers and sisters; being a go-between.

**Note: A stellium of planets further emphasises Pisces**
Taylor's chart has Sun, Mercury and Mars in Pisces which adds emphasis to the Piscean theme here.

## Comment

She has her Sun in Pisces with Mercury and Mars conjunct in the 3rd house of communications. This is a person who was idealistic, highly adaptable, energetic and dramatic. This is a person who, having a sense of theatre and drama, could combine that with good communications skills – good speaking voice, good projection. Here charisma and strength of character are combined.

## Moon in Scorpio 11th House

**Moon in Scorpio**: Attracted to emotionally charged circumstances; likes atmosphere of intrigue and controversy, an element of danger; passions and mood can run high; or can be resentful, controlling, moody, spiteful.

**Moon in 11th House:** Lives in an unconventional environ; breaks with tradition; enjoys going retro; enjoys radical and independent thinkers; turnover of friends; emotional need to be part of groups or societies; attraction to technology and the means of bringing about change.

## Comment

...But it doesn't end there because her Moon is in Scorpio in the 11th house and adding to the drama. The Moon has an easy-flow trine relationship with the Sun (and Mercury – also Pluto) so there was internal harmony of mind body and soul in this arrangement that could flow into a powerful expression of herself. The Moon position also indicates she was a person who would fight for humanitarian causes – such as her AIDs work (strong link with Pluto). It suggests she sought to be catalyst for making some kind of positive change in people's lives, not just on the level of acting.

## Sagittarius Ascendant

**Sagittarius Ascendant:** Projects an open-minded, philosophical, benevolent, optimistic, versatile, adaptable, adventurous and a risk-taker persona; inclined to be honest and direct in exchanges; will seek to broaden horizons and belief likely through travel and forms of further or higher education; inclined to love nature and enjoy outdoor activities; will likely be searching for meaning to life.

## Comment

Taylor had Sagittarius rising indicating a person who is a gambler, an optimist, and can we say it, an "actor" – well certainly there is no shortage of drama in the chart and mostly in a big glamourous way. This is a person who saw the glass as being half-full – or at least she wanted the world to know her that way – and no pushover.

## Jupiter chart ruler in Leo 8th House

**Jupiter in Leo:** Confident, expressive and dramatic; leadership qualities; big hearted, speculative, inspirational; strong need to impress, do things on a grand style; likes having an audience; or can tend to exaggerate, be arrogant and extravagant.

**Jupiter in 8th House**: Intensive emotional life; critical experiences; strong and passionate sexual activity, conscious of death; benefits received through others such legacies; likely interest in the paranormal.

## Comment

Taylor was "No pushover" indeed. This is passionate - and indicative of sexual prowess, a force to reckon with.

## Libra Midheaven

**Libra Midheaven**: Life goals or aspirations likely to include: achieving harmony in one's work and home-life balance, between activity and relaxation, between social interaction and spending time alone; having harmonious relations with people and environment; living in beautiful surroundings; being surrounded by art, music and the finer things in life; helping others achieve same.

## Comment

Having Libra on the Midheaven put emphasis on her relationships, seeking harmony, balance and friendship with the world – she needed people to be friends with her, to love her. This was her ideal. Relationships up close, less ideal but real were not so easy for her to work with. This is indicated by the exact Venus and Uranus conjunction in 4th house squaring Pluto. She was strongly independent – a new woman – and things could get fraught, even shocking in intimate circumstances.

Note also, all three planets in Pisces are in opposition to Neptune in Virgo 9th house. This suggests a seeking of an ideal or fantasy and a tendency to identify with the image (and projection) of one's creation. I'd suggest this is a driving force towards her desire for stardom – to be adored and recognised – a public media figure. It also suggests an addictive personality; a person who looked for escapes from reality – which she found in theatre and film, and unfortunately also in drugs and alcohol.

# Albert Einstein

*"Any intelligent fool can make things bigger and more complex... It takes a touch of genius - and a lot of courage - to move in the opposite direction."*

*Albert Einstein (14 March 1879 – 18 April 1955) was a German-born theoretical physicist who developed the theory of relativity, one of the two pillars of modern physics (alongside quantum mechanics). His work is also known for its influence on the philosophy of science. He is best known to the general public for his mass–energy equivalence formula $E = mc^2$, which has been dubbed "the world's most famous equation." He received the 1921 Nobel Prize in Physics "for his services to theoretical physics, and especially for his discovery of the law of the photoelectric effect," a pivotal step in the development of quantum theory.*[4]

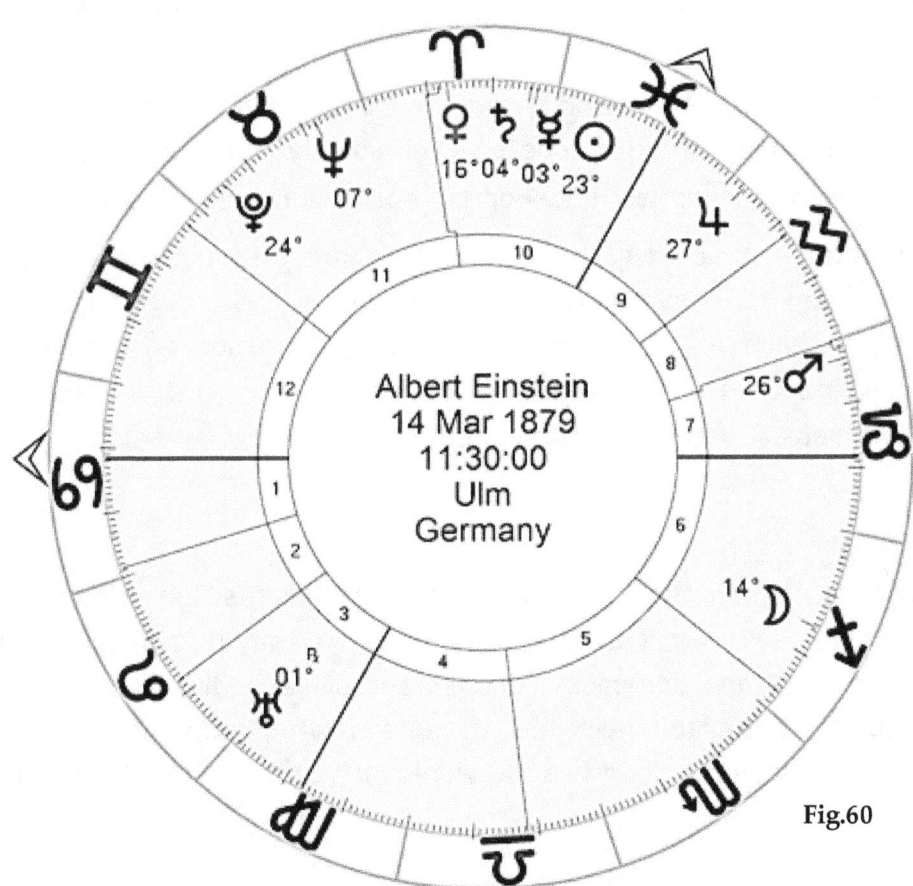

Fig.60

In Einstein's chart (Fig.60) he had:

Sun in Pisces 10th House

Moon in Sagittarius 6th House
Ascendant is in Cancer
Midheaven is in Pisces
The Moon is also the chart ruler
A stellium in Aries

## Sun and Midheaven in Pisces

**Sun in Pisces:** Impressionable, reserved and receptive, but also highly adaptable, changeable and artistic; seeks perfection for self and others; seeks to inspire, and be inspired; or inclined to be impractical, insecure, uncertain about life.

**Sun in 10th House:** Achieving fame or recognition in chosen vocation or profession; the architect of one's own worldly success; leadership roles; corporate person; dealing with authority; political power, ambition.

**Pisces Midheaven:** Life goals or aspirations likely to include: mind, body and spiritual refinement; developing one's intuition and receptiveness; being a practitioner in holistic or healing arts; being a person of service such as a medium, a nurse or a nun; going on escapes or retreats; visiting wild places; journeys overseas; caring for other creatures, a career in music.

## Comment

If we look at Einstein's birth-chart we can see that he has his Sun in Pisces 10th house, and also his Midheaven is Pisces. Though I'm reluctant to say it, this is the chart of an artist and dreamer first and foremost, and scientist secondly. Further, this is the chart of a composer, a person inspired, a person who drew heavily on his vivid imagination – and might well have viewed his work, or science, as a form of art.

## Moon in Sagittarius with Cancer Ascendant

**Cancer Ascendant:** Projects a homely (or home-builder), domesticated, sensitive, impressionable, caring and nurturing persona; inclined to be receptive to the needs and care of others; family oriented; will tend to follow established conventions, traditions, institutions, family and cultural codes of conduct.

**Moon in Sagittarius**: Optimistic, speculative, philosophical and frank; will enjoy travel and broadening horizons; inclined to like exotic learning environments, and other cultures; or can be inclined to be restless, thoughtless, overly extravagant.

**Moon in 6th House**: Concerns with health and diet, weight-watching; frequent changes of employment; protective environments; professional carer, emotional need to help others, to serve.

## Comment

Einstein's Moon is in Sagittarius 6th House. It is also the chart ruler. This suggests Einstein was quite a religious man, a philosopher, a pacifist at heart – which he was. He was most at home in some form of service to his community than war or violence. With Cancer rising he would also have identified with, and projected an air of, being homely, caring, a thoughtful and an approachable person – a person who aged gracefully and became more fatherly looking as he got older.

## The stellium in Aries and 10th House

What brought the focus of using his skills towards maths and physics, and lecturing in those subjects, is arguably Saturn, also in the 10th house and in close cahoots with Mercury. This is a person who played with numbers as one might play a musical instrument. Also note that Uranus, associated with insights, breakthroughs, innovation and the sciences, is in the 3rd house of communications; and opposes expansive Jupiter in Aquarius 9th house. Such a dialogue would have served towards a fertile and creative mind – to talk, communicate and write about maths and physics in a revolutionary and scientific manner.

The stellium, at the top of the chart, includes Mercury, Venus and Saturn in Aries (the sign of action) – while, with the Sun, there are four planets in the 10th house. This makes it a powerful focal point, a goal of expression. It is tempting to consider that Einstein's Theory of Relativity was driven by needing to give voice to Venus, into closer communion with Mercury and Saturn. Mars in Capricorn 7th house arguably lends some support to this suggestion.

# Jupiter, Uranus and Pluto T Square

A T-square in a birth-chart indicates lines of tension. What planets are forming it cannot be overlooked or ignored; they must be handled with care, worked with consciously and responsibly. This is especially so when dealing with "big hitters" as these three planets are. This arrangement is potentially creative, explosive and destructive. Einstein's involvement with helping the Americans develop the atomic bomb was his big regret - and particularly as (I'd expect) he would also have had a great love and regard for nature (Neptune in Taurus).

# Mary Baker Eddy

*Mary Baker Eddy (July 16, 1821 – December 3, 1910) was an American writer and religious leader who established the Church of Christ, Scientist, as a Christian denomination and worldwide movement of spiritual healers. She wrote and published the movement's textbook, Science and Health with Key to the Scriptures and 15 other books. She started several weekly and monthly magazines—the Christian Science Sentinel, The Christian Science Journal, and The Herald of Christian Science—that feature articles on Christian Science practice and verified testimonies of healing. In 1908, at the age of 87, she founded The Christian Science Monitor, a global newspaper that has won seven Pulitzer Prizes. Eddy's book Science and Health with Key to the Scriptures has been a best seller for decades, and was selected as one of the "75 Books by Women Whose Words Have Changed the World", by the Women's National Book Association. In 1995 Eddy was inducted into the National Women's Hall of Fame. In 2002, The Mary Baker Eddy Library opened its doors, giving the public access to one of the largest collections about an American woman.*[5]

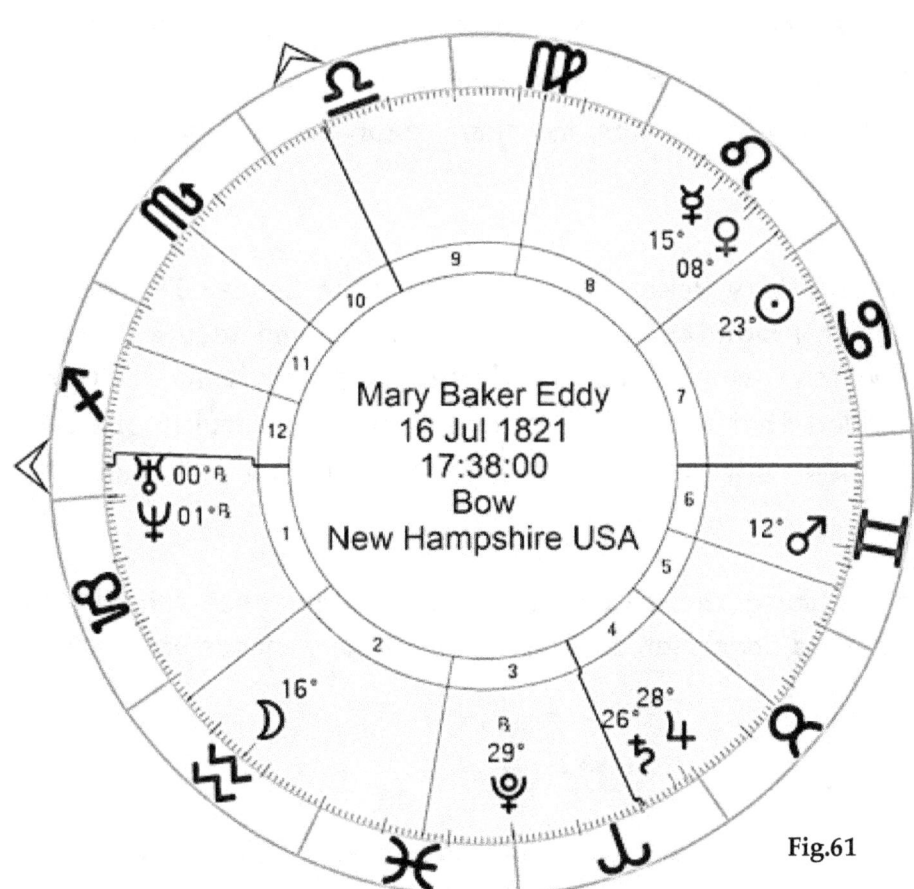

Fig.61

In Eddy's birth-chart (Fig.61) she had:

Sun in Cancer 7th House
Moon in Aquarius 2nd House
Ascendant is in Sagittarius
Midheaven is in Libra
The chart ruler is Jupiter

## Sun in Cancer 7th House

**Sun in Cancer**: Resourceful, contemplative, protective and sensitive; inclined to be reserved, territorial and traditional; open to mood swings; strong ties to the past; or can be inclined to be over-sensitive, overly-protective, shy and retiring.

**Sun in 7th House**: Interest in other people, need for partner, need of audience; focus on building relationships; marriage; expression of power through others.

## *Comment*

In the birth-chart of Mary Baker Eddy, the Sun is in Cancer 7th house. Cancer is a cautious feminine water sign that seeks the traditional and secure. It primarily needs to protect itself, which it will through family and links with home, heritage, roots, the past. It may be added that Cancerians can be very successful in the world, through their careful and cautious approach to their endeavours. They often make good business people.

With Sun in the 7th house there was the need to experience friendly support from others – a need to build Cancerian security through harmonious relationships.

## Moon in Aquarius 2nd House

**Moon in Aquarius**: Socially open, emancipating, enjoys living in unconventional environs; naturally inclined towards circumstances that break with traditions, are new or shocking; or equally can be unpredictable or erratic in behaviour.

> **Moon in 2nd House**: Seeks security based on having financial and material resources in place, and being well-nourished; changeable or unstable finances, resources; artistic ability; business interests; need to feel earthed in peaceful, solid, reliable, steady and productive circumstances.

## Comment

That said (from Comment above), the ruler of Cancer is Eddy's Moon, which is in Aquarius. This indicates a strongly independent person. It is a revolutionary position calling on the need to, in some way, break through, or break with, convention, and to do it on a structured basis – being in the 2nd house.

Much of the dialogue of this chart zones in on the balance between maintaining tradition and breaking with it – and arguably it is linked here with Eddy's concern with female emancipation (because of the feminine theme here in the chart, that is through the Sun and Moon positions). In this respect she was quite a radical thinker, a feminist.

# Libra Midheaven

> **Libra Midheaven**: Life goals or aspirations likely to include: achieving harmony in one's work and home-life balance, between activity and relaxation, between social interaction and spending time alone; having harmonious relations with people and environment; living in beautiful surroundings; being surrounded by art, music and the finer things in life; helping others achieve same.

## Comment

The Libra Midheaven of her chart implied that her goals in life linked to seeking of refinement, seeking the ideal, achieving balance and peaceful harmony, good and important relationships.

# Sagittarius Ascendant/Jupiter chart ruler

**Sagittarius Ascendant**: Projects an open-minded, philosophical, benevolent, optimistic, versatile, adaptable, adventurous and a risk-taker persona; inclined to be honest and direct in exchanges; will seek to broaden horizons and belief likely through travel and forms of further or higher education; inclined to love nature and enjoy outdoor activities; will likely be searching for meaning to life.

**Jupiter in Aries**: Self-sufficient; generosity of spirit; has honesty; takes life head on; leadership qualities; pioneering spirit; seeks new horizons; or lacks balance, has a tendency to be overly-optimistic, impulsive and have inflated self-importance.

**Jupiter in 4$^{th}$ House**: Good relations with parents; secure and comfortable home; happy home-life; good business sense; optimistic moral and religious upbringing.

# Comment

This seeking of peace (reference to her Libra Midheaven) and good relations with parents (Jupiter in 4$^{th}$ House) was likely not always easy however as it was influenced/driven by wavering states of optimism and pessimism (or that being the kind of challenging feedback she gets back from the world). This is indicated by Jupiter (the chart ruler) and Saturn in the 4$^{th}$ house (in close conjunction), which suggests a likely complex/difficult childhood with probably one parent acting as a restrictive influence – a dampener on her life's ambitions – and the other, providing encouragement in her life's ambitions. She could well have had a very straight-lace paternalistic upbringing that provided the springboard to strike out for womanhood later.

Where the chart gets really interesting is in the dynamics of Sagittarius rising, with Uranus and Neptune in Capricorn 1$^{st}$ house. Through Sagittarius, Eddy would be seen as an optimist, a person who is seeking to broaden the scope of things, is concerned with moral welfare. Sagittarius is also associated with publishing. Here we can see both a religious and philosophical fervour (Sagittarius) mixed with inspiration and selfless compassion (Neptune) in conjunction with innovation, interest in giving birth to a new science (Uranus) – "Christian Science."

But this is a person who is also highly sensitive, receptive, has intuitive qualities – is a natural healer. She might alternatively have used her skills as a psychic or a medium, if taking a different route.

## Do take a look at your own birth-chart...

I hope you've found the above excursions into a few charts of interest and helpful. What I hope this exercise might also demonstrate to you is not to take the keywords of the resources too literally. They have to be seen in context with the whole chart in each case – where interpretation is likely to alter somewhat.

If you have yet to do it, it is now time to get out your own birth-chart and check out the four main components that you are dealing with – and include your chart ruler.

## References

[1] Comment on birthtime. If you were uncertain about the time of your birth you may not be able to rely on the ascending and culminating points in your chart. If the timing was known to be out by up to 20 minutes you may be, broadly speaking, on fairly safe ground to calculate the angles into your chart. Any longer than that then your chart should be calculated without including the ascending sign, the houses or culminating sign. Such a chart is normally calculated for midday of the birthdate, and will have Aries to the east (left side of chart – the natural position for the sign of Aries) with just the planets included in the zodiac wheel – no houses.

[2] Jimi Hendrix description taken from https://en.wikipedia.org/wiki/Jimi_Hendrix [Accessed 15/06/2020]

[3] Elizabeth Taylor description taken from https://en.wikipedia.org/wiki/Elizabeth_Taylor [Accessed 15/06/2020]

[4] Albert Einstein description taken from https://en.wikipedia.org/wiki/Albert_Einstein [Accessed 15/06/2020]

[5] Mary Baker Eddy description taken from https://en.wikipedia.org/wiki/Mary_Baker_Eddy [Accessed 15/06/2020]

# Part 2

# A Comprehensive Approach

What follows is a more comprehensive or inclusive approach to reading your chart.

Much of it will involve weighting the planets according to where they are in the chart. This will provide you with insight into their value in the overall scheme. It'll become more obvious as you work through it and begin to get familiar with it.

We'll also be using an example chart, Bill Lomas or BL (not this person's real name) to aid exampling this approach for much of it.

Following on from the general but valuable overview of Part 1, the order we'll be looking at here includes the components already covered, plus so much more to consider.

I would suggest you work with these at your own pace – and in your own order if you so wish. I consider it a logical approach but it is not written in stone. You will have all the resources you need to be able to respond to any part of this list.

# Weighting the planets

It stands to reason that if you have more planets, let's say, in one element than another, that element is likely to be more pronounced in your situation, personality or character. If for instance you have more planets in positive signs than negative signs, you will have a greater tendency to be extraverted than introverted.

When I first began studying astrology, if I were registering (for instance) how many planets there were in Fire signs, Earth signs, Air and Water signs, in a birth-chart, I'd simply count how many there were in each element.

> And note: Most astrology programs will display this basic counting in the birth-charts they produce. You'll need to adjust the figures yourself if following the weighting system here.

So, for instance, with my Sun and Neptune in Libra and my Moon in Gemini with Uranus, I'd register that as 4 planets in Air signs, with a count of 4 – and I'd follow the same approach with the other elements.

Because of their prominence, I soon began adding more for the position of the Sun and Moon in a chart – giving them a count of 2 each. I suspect many astrologers will do this. But it was not until some years later, when doing a workshop, with the American astrologer Richard Idemon, that I got the idea of _really_ weighting the result. Basically, weighting means giving planets that are more prominent in a given chart a higher value than just a count of 1 each. The more noticeable the role of a planet, the bigger the value one attributes to it. It really helps to bring prominent chart features out.

Hence, the following counting system I've used (and adjusted) for many years! It will help you to identify the prominence and/or importance of planets in signs, depending on their position in your chart – or other charts you may be looking into.

# The counting system I use...

- To begin, you simply count 1 for each planet – a total of 10 with the planets we are using.

- Then you add an extra 1 each for the Sun and Moon – so they equal 2 each in whatever sign they are in.
- You add an extra 1 for the chart ruler.
- You add an extra 1 to any rising planet – that is any planet conjunct the Ascendant (within 8° degrees).
- You add an extra 1 to any other angular planet – that is, any planet conjunct (within 8° degrees) of any of the other three angles in the chart.
- You add an extra 1 for any planet that is in the sign it rules – its own sign.
- And you add an extra 1 for a stellium of three or more planets in a sign.

# The Running Order

And here's the running order I suggest you follow to obtain a more comprehensive understanding of the dynamics going on in your chart:

1. Work out the weighting of the planets within the signs' matrix
2. Add in planets within signs/angles & houses
3. Note major aspects or aspect patterns

You'll be building up a more detailed profile of your astrological potential.

# 1. First the planets in the signs – as per their matrix

**Check for:**
- Positive/Negative Signs (Polarities) that are occupied
- Elements – Fire/Earth/Air/Water (Triplicities) that are occupied
- Cardinal/Fixed/Mutable (Quadruplicities) that are occupied

# 2. Secondly the planets in signs/angles & houses

**Check for:**
- Sun, Moon, Ascendant, Midheaven
- Ruling Planet sign & house - can be as strong as Sun or Moon
- Rising Planet - if any. Again, likely to be another strong component
- Any further angular planets
- Planet/s in their own sign. Always stronger in their home sign
- Any stellium of 3 or more planets in any sign (or house). The sign/house will be powerful
- Other remaining planets in signs & houses

# 3. Not forgetting major aspects and/or aspect patterns

Mostly you will be taking stock of the aspects while covering the planets but do also consider any major aspect patterns in the chart – like a T square or Grand trine. Such a pattern will represent a powerful flowing or challenging dialogue (or both) in the chart. Although placed here at No 3 such a pattern will usually stand out and be one of the first things that you would notice in your chart, or anyone else's chart, as you gain experience.

You'll get the idea of how this works from the Part 3 example coming up... plus the example report in Part 4. There are also some practice exercises.

# Dealing with the information you discover

This is the challenging part of course. Extracting information from your birth-chart, through notetaking, is one thing. How you deal with the information you extract is another. It is really a personal matter – and to a greater or lesser degree will tie in, or be referenced to, what you already believe about your life, your constructs, your values, and how you see your part in it.

I'm going to suggest the obvious here, that you work through the running order as laid out in this Part. As you do so, make appropriate notes on each salient point, from the resources provided in the course. Read and reread, and/or copy down any keyword or comment that strikes a chord in you.

You are probably going to find themes in your chart that you immediately recognise, and probably themes that (at this point) you don't recognise or easily accept – or that seemingly conflict with what you know of yourself. Or they conflict with other themes in your chart. It's a good place to look for where work needs to be done on yourself.

What will become obvious is that this is not a 10-minute job of note-taking and evaluation. It is something that you'll find you need to sip at and come back to. Your birth-chart (I believe) provides you with an authentic mirror of yourself – and will display more than you, as a person with a name, and the story of yourself, that you may be currently familiar with.

It potentially opens doors to what Carl Jung called the process of Individuation:

> Jung saw [Individuation] as the process of self-realisation, the discovery and experience of meaning and purpose in life; the means by which one finds oneself and becomes who one really is.[1]

What I would suggest is that you begin with the broad reading of your chart (covered in Part 1 of Step Five), and then go onto cover Part 2, to capture all the details.

Keep in mind that all the personal planets, out to Mars, will be easier for you to identify with. Jupiter and Saturn will be borderline but powerful in your personal life – drivers for optimism and broadening experience, or for pessimism and putting the brakes on - being cautious.

What can be most powerful, if possibly difficult to get one's head around, are the planets, beyond Saturn. The houses they occupy and any notable relationship (aspect) they have, particularly with your Sun, Moon, Ascendant, Midheaven or ruling planet, will help you to gain insight into them.

But, of course, if I've missed making a point of it; learn from your life experience too. This is a two-way street. Your chart can provide useful insight into what you already know of yourself. It may also provide insight into what you don't know of yourself - or not so well. See the reflection in your chart of your work, your family, your friends, your environment, your interests and beliefs. If anyone pays you a few "home truths;" whether you accept them or not, these are something they see in you. So, look to your chart as to where such issues may be reflected/symbolised – and see if you can work differently with any such theme uncovered.

And, by the way, if you are linked up with other contacts who are studying astrology, get to do exchanges of reading each other's charts. It can be very revealing and helpful – to both of you.

# References

---

[1] The Society of Analytical Psychology. https://www.thesap.org.uk/articles-on-jungian-psychology-2/about-analysis-and-therapy/individuation/ [Accessed 15/10/2022]

# Part 3

# Example: Using "Bill Lomas" chart

## 1. Weighting the planets in signs – as per their matrix

**Checking for:**
a. Positive/Negative Signs (Polarities) that are occupied
b. Elements – Fire, Earth, Air, Water (Triplicities) that are occupied
c. Cardinal, Fixed and Mutable (Quadruplicities) that are occupied

Note: The Bill Lomas chart (Fig.62) is being repeated through Part 3.

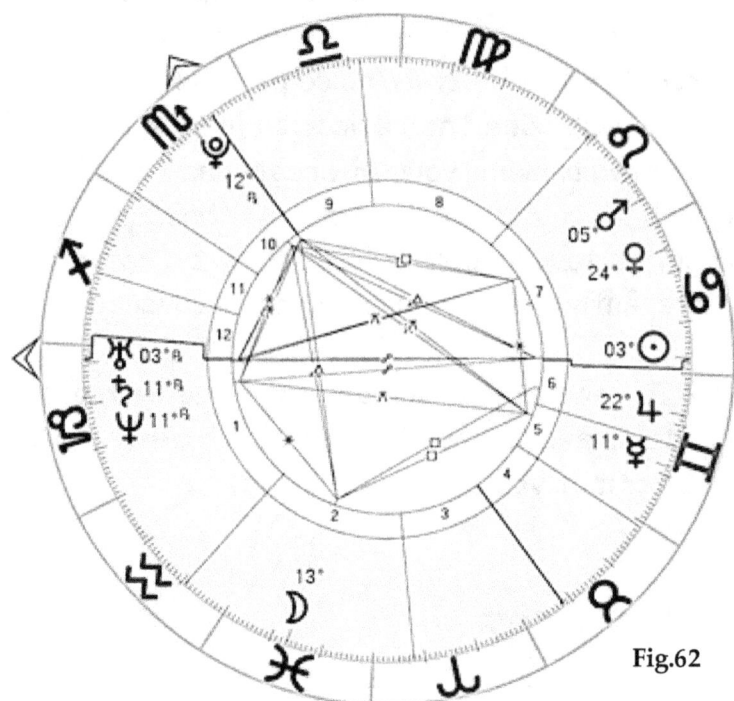

Fig.62

# a. Polarities - Positive/Negative signs emphasis

Counting the positive and negative signs (Fig.63) we find that Bill Lomas (BL) has 3 planets in positive signs – these are Mercury, Mars and Jupiter. Mercury is also in the sign it rules so we count an extra 1 for Mercury. Total positive weighting equals 4.

| Positive | 3 | + 1 (Mercury in own sign) | = 4 |
|---|---|---|---|
| Negative | 7 | + 3 (Sun + angular planet + Moon) + 2 (Saturn chart ruler & own sign) + 2 (Pluto own sign & angular) + 3 (Uranus, Saturn & Neptune rising) + 1 (stellium) | = 18 |

Fig.63

We do the same for the negative signs. There are 7 planets in negative signs. Then we add an extra 1 for each of the Sun and Moon – making 9. The Sun is also an angular planet (on the Descendant) so it gets a further 1 (now 10). Saturn gets a further 2 counts for being the chart ruler and also in Capricorn that it rules (now 12). We add an extra 2 for Pluto being an angular planet and in its own sign (now 14). Then we add an extra 3 for Uranus, Saturn and Neptune all linked to the Ascendant (now 17). And finally, we add an extra 1 for these same three planets forming a stellium. Total negative weighting equals 18.

### From the resource description:
**Predominantly Negative**: Keywords are: introverted, self-reflective, ingoing, feminine.

## Comment

*BL is inclined to be a strong ingoing person, an introvert, likely to be sensitive and in touch with his feelings or feminine side.*

At this point, while it is fresh in your mind, I suggest you check out the planetary Positive/Negative distribution in your own chart.

## b. Element emphasis

Counting the situation of BL's chart with elements (Fig.64) we arrive at the following: He has one planet in Fire signs and that's Mars, and it gets a count of 1.

He has 3 planets in Earth signs, Saturn, Uranus and Neptune, so 3 to begin with. Saturn then gets an extra 2 as chart ruler and in the sign it rules, so 5. Then Saturn, Uranus and Neptune get an extra 3 for being rising planets, so 8. Then the same three get an extra 1 for being a stellium in Earth. And that equals 9.

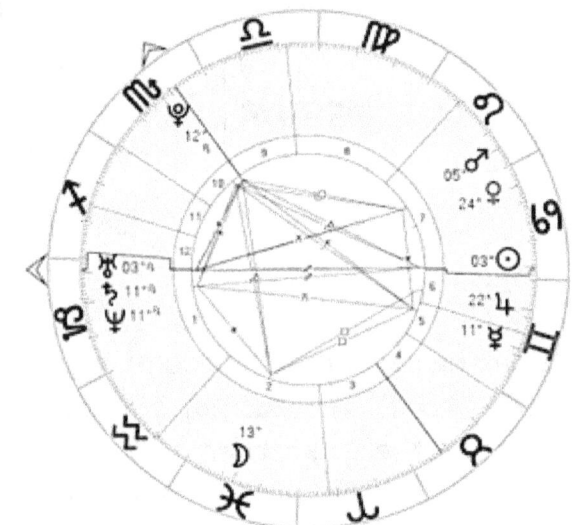

| Fire | 1 | (Mars only) | = 1 |
|---|---|---|---|
| Earth | 3 | + 2 (Saturn chart ruler & own sign) + 3 (Uranus, Saturn & Neptune rising) + 1 (stellium) | = 9 |
| Air | 2 | + 1 (Mercury in own sign) | = 3 |
| Water | 4 | + 3 (Sun + angular planet + Moon) + 2 (Pluto own sign & angular) | = 9 |

Fig.64

Looking at Air signs, BL has two planets (Mercury and Jupiter) in Air, so 2. Mercury is in the sign it rules so it gets an extra point. A total of 3.

In Water, he has four planets, so count 4. We then allow an extra 3 for the Sun and Moon being in Water and the Sun being an angular planet; so, 7. We add a further 2 points to Water as Pluto is in the sign it rules and is also angular. That totals 9.

**From the resource descriptions:**
Predominantly Earth & Water:
    **Earth Signs**: practical, cautious, solid, dependable, physical, builder.
    **Water Signs**: emotional, unstable, sensitive, fluid, nurturer.

## Comment

*BL will be inclined to be a practical, dependable and nurturing person, a giver. But also note that Mars is the only planet in Fire (Leo). This suggests a strong compensatory need to express himself in his own way, a need to do his own thing. The rising planets also suggest an unease with just accepting an entirely conventional way of being.*

**Time to check out the planetary distribution of the elements within your own birth-chart.**

# c. Mode (Cardinal/Fixed/Mutable) emphasis

BL's predominant mode is Cardinal. We arrive at this by his having five planets in Cardinal signs (Fig.65). These being his Sun and Venus in Cancer, with Saturn, Uranus and Neptune in Capricorn. So, 5 to begin with. We add an extra 2 for his Sun and also it being an angular planet. That's 7. We add an extra 2 for Saturn being the chart ruler and in the sign it rules. So that's 9. We add a further 3 for Saturn, Uranus and Neptune being rising planets – that equals 12. And finally, an extra 1 for those three planets being a stellium. A total of 13.

| Cardinal | 5 | + 2 (Sun + angular planet) + 2 (Saturn chart ruler & own sign) + 3 (Uranus, Saturn & Neptune rising) + 1 (stellium) | = 13 |
|---|---|---|---|
| Fixed | 2 | + 2 (Pluto own sign & angular) | = 4 |
| Mutable | 3 | + 1 (Moon) + 1 (Mercury in own sign) | = 5 |

Fig.65

In the Fixed signs it is Mars and Pluto making 2. But Pluto is also in its own sign and is on the Mc angle. So, 2 more are added making a total of 4.

There are three planets in Mutable signs. These are the Moon, Mercury and Jupiter. So, 3 to begin with. The Moon gets an extra point for being the Moon – now 4. And Mercury gets an extra point for being in the sign it rules, giving us a total of 5.

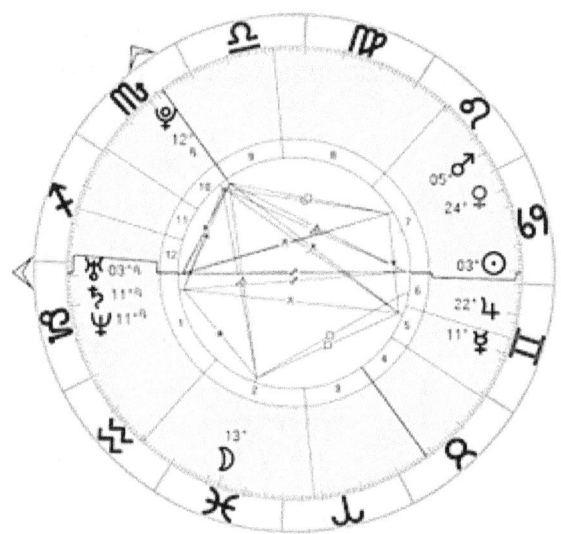

### From the resource description:

> Predominantly Cardinal
> Embracing change, initiating, leading, moving on.

## Comment

*Predominantly BL will like change. He'll make decisions and initiate change, get things going. He has a natural ability to lead on matters – on proviso his confidence is strong (for which he depends on others). He's weaker at stabilising or rooting what he generates.*

Find out what the prominent mode is in your own birth-chart.

## 2. The Planets, Angles & Houses

**Check for:**
a. Sun, Moon, Ascendant, Midheaven
b. Ruling Planet & House - can be as strong as Sun/Moon
c. Rising Planet - if any. Again, likely to be another strong component
d. Planet/s in their own sign. Always stronger in their home sign
e. Any further angular planets
f. Any stellium of 3 or more planets in any sign or house. The sign/house will be powerful
g. Other planets in signs & houses

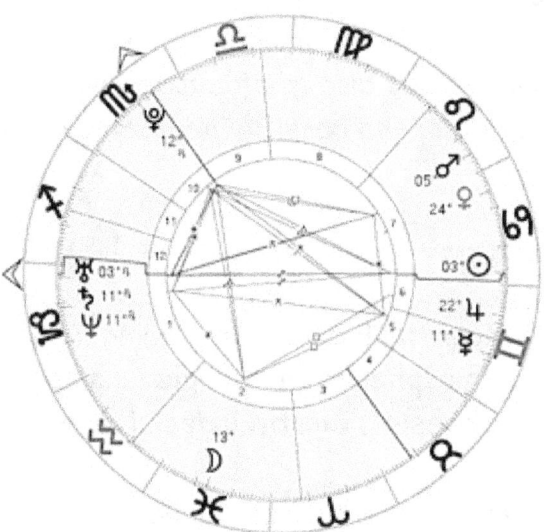

Having worked through the planets in the Signs matrix we have already built up quite a profile on the themes or drivers that Bill Lomas would find helpful to know about.

Here we are of course visiting the planets and signs again. But this time looking at their placement meaning rather than their weighting in the scheme of things.

# a. Sun, Moon, Ascendant, Midheaven

## Sun in Cancer 7th House

**Sun in Cancer**: resourceful, contemplative, protective and sensitive. Will inclined to be reserved, territorial and traditional in behaviour. Open to mood swings. Strong ties to past. Inclined to be over-sensitive, overly-protective, shy and retiring.

**Sun in 7th House**: relating, others, partners, love matches, agreements, marriage, the trappings of attraction or attracting partners, harmonious environments.

## Comment

BL is a sensitive person who cares for, and depends upon, other people. It is important for him to feel "at home" and safe. Relationships with family and friends are likely to be very important to his sense of wellbeing. They not only provide him with a security blanket but also his identity will be tied up with other people, people he knows, loves and likes, and possibly people he is not so fond of and avoids.

## Moon in Pisces 2nd House

**Moon in Pisces**: Easy going, imaginative and adaptable. But also, very sensitive to atmospheres and people – has psychic ability. Seeks refinement in environment and in oneself. Can be indecisive, restless, vulnerable and inclined towards escapism.

**Moon in 2nd House**: Possessions, resources and personal security. The focus here is largely on acquisition, having things, essential things (or what we consider essential) like a house, and money in order to be secure in ourselves – being 'earthed.' It is also about being nourished – having enough of anything and everything. Has affinity with Taurus and Venus.

## Comment

BL's Moon placement further emphasises his sensitivity and need for security. This time with the things he places around himself. It indicates he is an adaptable person able to be flexible and to adjust to the needs of other people. Having said how much of a focus there is towards other people, it is noticeable that Moon in Pisces is also inclined towards some form of escapism – a getting away from, or to going off by himself. It could be a hobby and in this case it is. What is also noticeable here is his openness and receptiveness to feelings and the ambience of places. Not much gets past him regards what is going on in other people's lives. He is able to tune in. He has a strong potential here for psychic ability too.

On the downside we can anticipate that his life, thus far, has not been a bed of roses. His moon position suggests he has waxed and waned with regards to his finances and probably the things he has owned and loved. There has been disappointment for sure.

## Capricorn Asc

**Capricorn Asc**: serious, constructive, realistic and reliable; self-disciplined and controlled, but can also be controlling, a bit too cool and lacking in spontaneity; seeks material security and structure; will come across as earthy, ambitious and determined.

## Scorpio Mc

**Scorpio Mc**: would make a good detective; enjoys research looking into things, getting to the bottom of issues; having inner knowledge is important; enjoys danger; private person; risk-taker.

## Comment

When we look at BL's ascending sign, Capricorn, we can see that he is likely to present himself to the world as a serious and trustworthy person, a person who is controlling and organised, and who probably doesn't stand any messing. It is opposite his Sun sign of Cancer the crab which is known for its hard shell. People may not see his sensitivity unless they get past that Capricorn persona.

With Scorpio on the midheaven point he will value looking into things, rooting out issues. It will be important to him that he is known for his ability to get to the source of issues – if anyone can sort it, let's get Bill in.

# b. Ruling Planet & House

See C. Rising Planet/s

# c. Rising Planet/s

## Opening comment

Saturn is not only the ruling planet but it is also in its own sign and rising. This makes it a very powerful component in this chart.

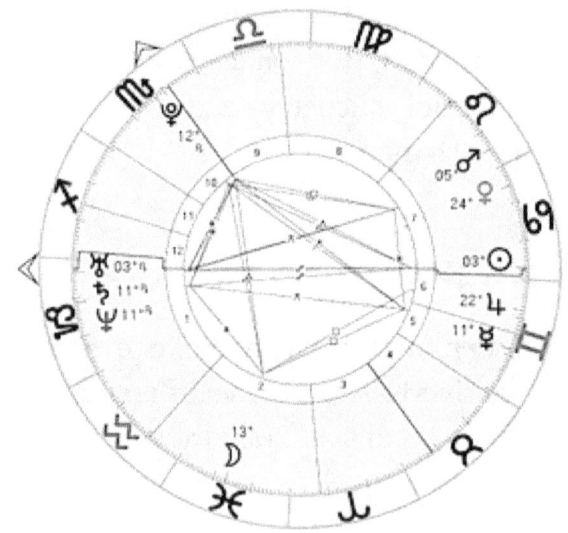

But before we go any further, just look at Saturn's bedfellows in this arrangement – Uranus and Neptune! I suggest you read up on these two.

It so happens that between them, these three planets fulfil a number of pointers in our running order. These are the ruling planet, the rising planets, a stellium of planets, and planet in its own sign. There are however two further planets each in their own sign. See if you can spot them?

Let's collect some keyword information on these factors and build up a sense of what this all means:

# Saturn in Capricorn 1st House

**Saturn in Capricorn:** Self-contained, responsible, methodical, disciplined, industrious and ambitious with strong will to achieve personal status and goals; having the patience of a saint. Or self-critical, controlling, cold-hearted, pessimistic.

**Saturn in 1st House:** Seriousness, responsibility, authority, sense of limitation, effort, obstacles, delays, pessimism.

# Uranus in Capricorn 1st House

**Uranus in Capricorn:** Scientific interests; an innovative use of one's resources; urge to change established order; extraordinary aims in life with wilfulness to achieve. Or fanatical regarding one's status and achieving certain goals.

**Uranus in 1st House:** Conspicuous individuality, eccentricity, need for freedom, love of change, unusual appearance or mannerisms.

# Neptune in Capricorn 1st House

**Neptune in Capricorn:** Idealistic or unusual views on worldly success/achievement; dream brought into reality; living a meditative ascetic life. Or lacking a sense of reality. A dreamer lacking confidence to succeed. Achievement through deception.

**Neptune in 1st House:** Extreme impressionability, charm, glamour, charisma, acting ability, musical or mathematical talent, inspiration, idealism, otherworldliness, confusion, disorientation, poor sense of time.

# Comment

*One could probably write a book on the potential of these three planets combined like this.*

Here's a person who is a charismatic individual but who is also going to be seen as a little bit odd – and certainly reserved. He likes to be in control of his circumstances.

For the most part he may come across as a conventional person but one who can also be surprising and off the wall. He will have many guises in other words and people may not know which way to take him. He will be an authority in what he knows and does. Some people may in fact see him as a genius. He will certainly have hidden depths and a highly inventive mind. If I didn't know better, I might anticipate he was a professor or an inventor – a go-to expert in his field.

These three planets have to somehow rub along together but not easily. Saturn and Uranus are not the best of bedfellows. Saturn is serious, wants to follow conventional wisdom and progress slowly. Uranus on the other hand wants to break with convention, get all excited about something new, and start afresh. Together they remind me of the slip/stick situation of tectonic plate movement. BL will tend to hold and control his behaviour, his life and goals for a time, then comes a point where he needs to make a shift. This could also so easily affect his moods – and mood swings are likely. The possible common ground between Saturn and Uranus is an interest in using scientific method, or to do things from a methodical basis to achieve new outcomes.

With Saturn and Neptune, the former is pragmatic, earthy, constructive, while the latter is idealistic and a dreamer. The astrologer can't help but ask, how does one deal with it?

Saturn, the chart ruler is literally caught in the middle here between the two outer planets. It is either very exciting or a tough gig coping with the situation. If I had Bill in front of me, I would be asking him how he handles it. Well, I did have the person who owns this chart for a reading, and I'll tell you soon enough how he has learnt to deal with it, that is at the point in his life when I saw him.

But let's move on. Well, before we do move on did you notice that BL has his Sun in opposition to the three planets in his first house? This is dramatic and individualistic. He would probably make a good actor. It could suggest further difficulty in working with, and befriending people. He might well prefer his own company but could also end up short of friends and uncertain about himself.

# d. Planet/s in their own sign

Did you spot them? Mercury, Saturn and Pluto are all in their own sign. Comments have been made about Saturn so we need to take a look at Mercury and Pluto.

## Mercury in Gemini 5th House

**Mercury in Gemini**: A quick, inquisitive and agile mind; versatile in thought and communications; knowledgeable across a wide range of subjects; or can skip over the surface of things, gathering superficial or trivial knowledge; a bit of a trickster/hustler.

**Mercury in 5th House**: Story teller; abilities in drama and theatre; competitive writer or talker; good communication with children; speculative investments; academic mixed with social pleasures.

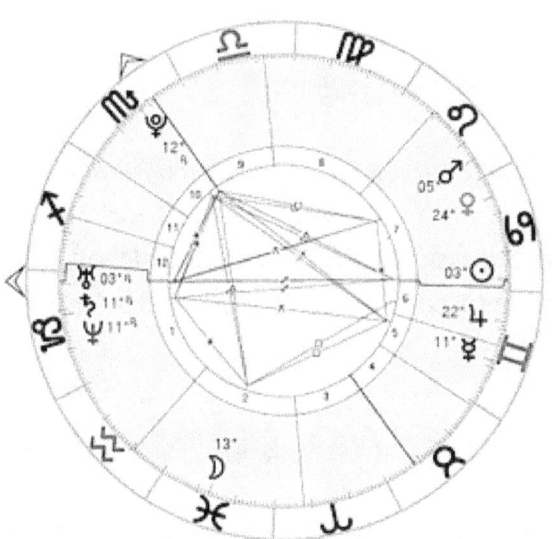

## Comment

The Mercury placement indicates that whatever privacy, control or possible inhibitions going on in BL's life, he is a communicator. He will be inclined to be chatty but also want to get across serious information. There will certainly be a sense of drama that he will draw from in his communications. He'll probably have a dry sense of humour.

## Pluto in Scorpio 10th House

**Pluto in Scorpio**: Emotionally intense and charismatic; secretive, hidden, undercover; powerful influence on others; achievement through tenacity and

Learn to Read Your Birth-chart in 5 Steps

endurance; deep-seated passion and sexual drive; or prone to power struggles, fanaticism, dark moods, paranoia.

**Pluto in 10th House**: Strong public image, charismatic and ambitious; successful realisation of business, economic or political goals; power of persuasion/determination; urge to transform established structures/poor working practices; dominating father; crisis in career and/or spectacular comebacks; authoritarian tendencies; tendency towards depression and isolation.

## Comment

*BL is inclined to be powerful in his ambitions and abilities, even though in other respects he is also inclined to hide his light under a bushel – possibly he could be even a little scared of what he is capable of. Success comes through speaking one's mind, being honest and authentic. He might also expect serious challenges with this placement.*

## e. Any further angular planets

Along with the three planets in the first house, BL also has the Sun and Pluto on the angles of the chart. Their descriptions have already been covered so there is nothing to add for this part.

## f. Stellium of Planets

The Capricorn 1st house stellium of planets – Saturn, Uranus and Neptune – has already been covered.

# g. Other planets in signs and houses

## Venus in Cancer 7th House

**Venus in Cancer**: Deep and sincere feelings of love; caring and protective towards loved ones. Romantic, needs to feel loved and secure, have affection demonstrated. Home is the focal point for social activities. Can be over-sensitive, easily hurt.

**Venus in 7th House**: happy marriage, successful relationships, popularity, social skills, social butterfly.

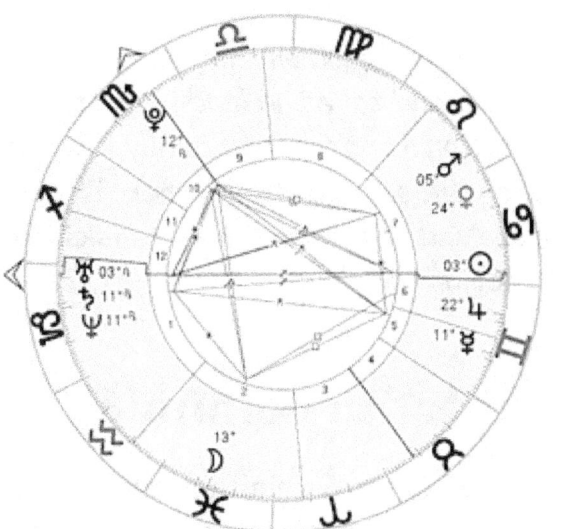

Note: Venus is unaspected. There are no obvious links from Venus to other components. This symbolises a disconnect to the planet that also most symbolises relationships and one's values.

## Comment

*Along with his Sun, this is actually a lovely position to have Venus in. It suggests a happy and secure home life, wholesome relations with others, and a sense of belonging and rootedness. But other components stretch this and cause difficulties. With the disconnect he has to consciously generate this Venusian situation. It is like it is waiting on him to initiate it. This is part of his struggle I'd suggest.*

## Mars in Leo 7th House

**Mars in Leo**: Competitive with gamesmanship and leadership qualities. Self-assurance and self-confidence. Demonstrative, dramatic, pioneering. Inclined to assume authority. Can be melodramatic and domineering towards others.

**Mars in 7th House**: Much energy devoted to relationships, active partner, quarrels with partners, possibility of lawsuits.

Note: This is the only planet in Fire signs. It has challenging aspects to Uranus and Pluto.

# Comment

*A likely theme from his Mars position is that it further emphasises his need to be in control and take the lead in matters. We could expect that in the home he will follow a traditional approach to family life. He will see himself as the bread-winner and probably rarely be seen in the kitchen. The aspects to this planet might suggest he is accident prone and or inclined to take risks. He'll enjoy an element of danger and have a tendency to act on impulse.*

# Jupiter in Gemini 6th House

**Jupiter in Gemini**: Broad-minded, versatile, inquisitive and philosophical; a strong urge to explore and to gather facts and information; likely talents in communications/marketing. Or is crafty, insincere, inclined towards superficiality.

**Jupiter in 6th House**: strong desire for service, possibility of over-work, medical or charitable work.

# Comment

*BL's Jupiter placement again emphasises communications and a love for gaining information and discussing his ideas and beliefs. Also indicates a need to be of service to others in some way.*

# 3. Major Aspect patterns

Next the major aspect patterns in the Bill Lomas birth-chart, if any...

## Notable aspect shape

There are noticeable squares or lines of tension between a number of planets in this chart. Particularly the Moon, Mercury-Jupiter, and between Mars and Pluto; and especially between the Sun and Saturn, Uranus, and Neptune.

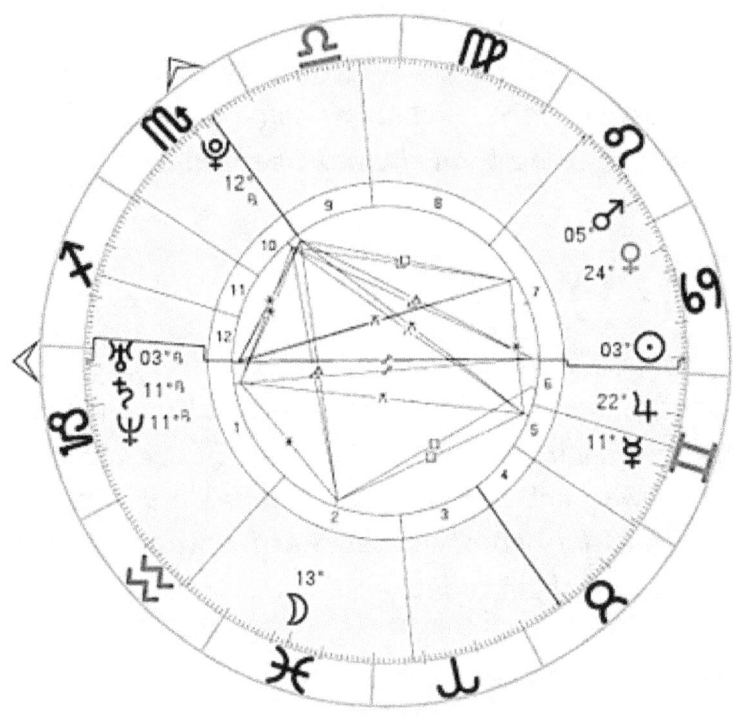

## Comment

*This is a challenging setup. BL is inclined to be a troubled person. He is inclined towards mood changes that can be dramatic, and likely he can be cutting in his communications. He may well be friendly but awkward in his interactions. People can get the wrong end of the stick with him. The Mars to Pluto square suggests a tendency to be guarded, not easily relaxed with people.*

## Finger of God

You may have noticed that BL also has a Finger of God or Yod pattern. This is a quincunx between Pluto and Mercury, and between Saturn/Neptune and Mercury. Houses involved are the 1st, 10th and 5th. The focus of this pattern is Mercury.

Learn to Read Your Birth-chart in 5 Steps

# Description of the Yod – or Finger of God

With this pattern something has to be done to relieve the tension. It links to powerful intention being applied – the person with it may feel strongly they have a special task or mission that has to be carried through. Certainly, they won't be able to ignore its impulse.

# Comment

An emphasis here on finding out, and on communications, as if one's life depended upon it. We discover that a critical concern for BL touches upon finding out and sharing information. He is probably a mind of information and a person who competes to be better informed than the next person.

# Wide Grand Trine

Sometimes, if it appears fitting, one has to step outside of the usual orbs allowed for aspects. This is a case in point... As well as challenging aspects, there are also some nice aspects running off Pluto. This is between Pluto and his Sun; and Pluto and his Moon. The allowed orb is 8 degrees. There's a $9^0$ orb between the Sun and Pluto; and there's an even wider orb of 10 degrees between the Sun and Moon. But their placement will tend to pull them together.

A reminder of these components:

**Sun in Cancer**: resourceful, contemplative, protective and sensitive. Will inclined to be reserved, territorial and traditional in behaviour. Open to mood swings. Strong ties to past. Inclined to be over-sensitive, overly-protective, shy and retiring.

7$^{th}$ House: relating, others, partners, love matches, agreements, marriage, the trappings of attraction or attracting partners, harmonious environments.

**Moon in Pisces**: Easy going, imaginative and adaptable. But also, very sensitive to atmospheres and people – has psychic ability. Seeks refinement in environment and in oneself. Can be indecisive, restless, vulnerable and inclined towards escapism.

**Moon in 2nd House**: Possessions, resources and personal security. The focus here is largely on acquisition, having things, essential things (or what we consider essential) like a house, and money in order to be secure in ourselves – being 'earthed.' It is also about being nourished – having enough of anything and everything. Has affinity with Taurus and Venus.

**Pluto in Scorpio**: Emotionally intense and charismatic; secretive, hidden, undercover; powerful influence on others; achievement through tenacity and endurance; deep-seated passion and sexual drive; or prone to power struggles, fanaticism, dark moods, paranoia.

**Pluto in 10th House**: Strong public image, charismatic and ambitious; successful realisation of business, economic or political goals; power of persuasion/determination; urge to transform established structures/poor working practices; dominating father; crisis in career and/or spectacular comebacks; authoritarian tendencies; tendency towards depression and isolation.

## Comment

*These planets are all in Water signs. One thinks of a Grand Trine as easy flowing energy. In Water, this is easy flowing water. Feelings and emotions will be powerful – could be torrential at times. I think when you read about some of the work that Bill does you will be a lot clearer as to what this configuration can mean – or how it is conducted by him.*

---

I hope you are finding the above helpful. I'm in danger of repeating myself, but what I want to say here is that BL's birth-chart is complex. Your chart is complex. As is mine. It takes time to get to grips with each of the players. It is a reason why, having a chart reading by a professional astrologer can be extremely helpful. But to be familiar with the dynamics of your chart takes more than a single reading, and not a little self-study. What works well, what is challenging, what needs adjusting – and the big questions that follow: Why do I have this astrological situation? What do I learn from this? What doors can I open? What doors can I close, or are closed, on my journey? All, grist to the mill.

# Part 4

# Report on Bill Lomas Example Birth-chart

This report is written in the 3rd person.

## Personality

As a Cancerian, Bill Lomas will be resourceful, contemplative and emotional. He will have needed to put down roots, and will have a powerful need for familiarity and routine, a sense of place, a need to feel at-home in his environment and within himself.

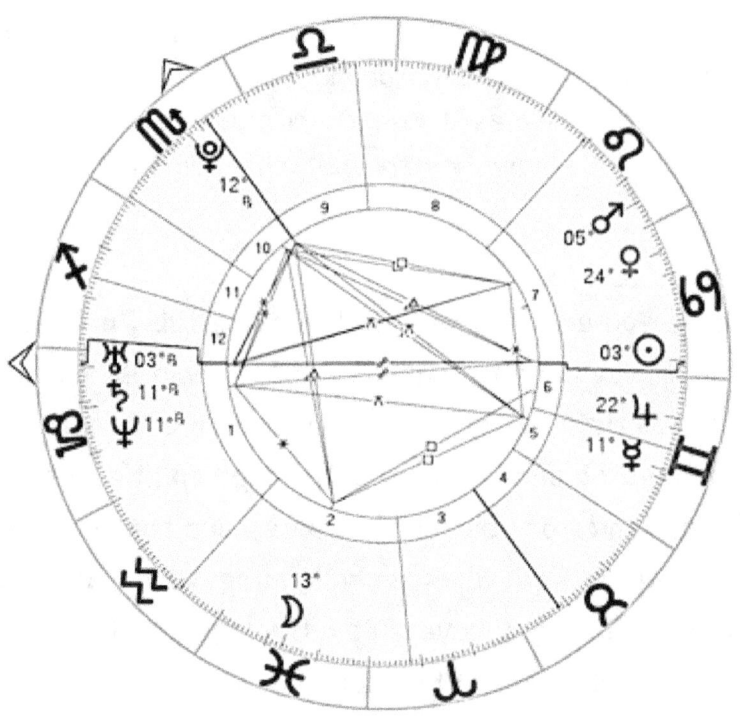

The Cancer person tends to form strong links with their parental home, develop a strong interest in, or concern for their background, their heritage – often they will get interested in their family history or family tree. They can be quite nostalgic for the past. They will tend to be sensitive, impressionable, protective, caring and nurturing. They will tend to be reserved, territorial and traditional, and to follow convention, endorsing established traditions, institutions, family and cultural codes of conduct.

The Moon rules Cancer. It is in the sign of Pisces, another water sign. It suggests this person is imaginative, adaptable and extra sensitive to atmospheres and people. It suggests psychic ability. The Moon also waxes and wanes and therefore the likelihood of changes in mood is noticeable. The Moon in this position can also make for indecision and a tendency to be restless.

With Capricorn rising, this person is likely to present himself to the world as a serious and trustworthy person, a person who is disciplined, likes to be in control of matters. People, other than who he is intimately acquainted with, are less likely to see his sensitive, vulnerable and caring nature – more likely they will meet the hard shell of the crab, the more business-like side of him that is associated with Cancer.

This is further emphasised by his Saturn in Capricorn, which also indicates a person who is self-contained, responsible, methodical, industrious and ambitious with a strong will to achieve personal status and goals. This also implies a tendency for him to be seen by others as a bit cold-hearted, with a dry sense of humour, and possibly a bit pessimistic.

Here is a person who has a certain charisma but who is also likely to be thought of as eccentric in some way. For the most part he may come across as a conventional person but he is a person who can also be surprising (Saturn/Uranus in 1st House), shocking and off the wall at times – and vague at other times (Neptune in 1st House). He may have many guises and people may not always know which way to take him. He is likely to be misunderstood regarding his intentions and may often be challenged over what he believes.

He will be a recognised authority (Saturn in Capricorn 1st House opposite Sun) in what he knows and does – and he'll no doubt be respected for his experience and knowledge in some quarters more than others. Some people may in fact see him as a kind of genius

(Saturn/Uranus). He is likely to have hidden depths and a highly inventive mind. Probably nothing will spark him more than something that is a new and fresh experience, or something that he has discovered and can make use of.

With this energy pattern one is inclined to be restless, or not entirely at peace with oneself. One minute needing a calming sense of order (Saturn), and conventional routine, the next needing some kind of excitement, something unusual as a stimulus (Uranus). In Bill's case this is likely to be driven by his mood swings, what he feels (Neptune and Moon in Pisces), which (with the Sun involved) forms a big part of his energy pattern. There is the potential for a kind of slip/stick pattern (Saturn/Uranus) in the way this happens – and it comes back to how he handles the dialogue between these four planets.

One way in which he might calm this energy pattern is through his work, applying an interest in using an inventive approach, or the scientific method, or to do things from a methodical basis to achieve outcomes and to hold the balance. He needs his feet firmly on the ground, whatever is going on.

# Relationships

The typical Cancer tends to be maternal and protective of others – regardless of gender. They can be really nice and friendly to know. They may appear tough skinned, hard negotiators, but underneath can be shy and retiring, needing to be coaxed out of their shells – needing a lot of love too, a lot of hugs. They want to be needed, and it is important to them to be around people who help them to feel secure and loved. They are inclined to place great importance on emotional and material security, with a strong desire for marriage or partnership and family.

In this respect, Bill Lomas is a sensitive person who cares for, and depends upon, other people. Relationships with family and friends are likely to be hugely important to his sense of wellbeing. They not only provide him with a security blanket but also seriously help give meaning to his life. His identity will be tied up with other people, people he knows, loves and likes, even people he dislikes and does not rub along with. Along with his Sun, this is a loving position to have Venus in. It suggests the potential for a happy and secure home life, wholesome relations with others, and a sense of belonging and rootedness.

We could expect that in the home he will follow a traditional approach to family life. He will see himself as the main bread-winner and probably rarely be seen cooking in the kitchen – except on surprise occasions possibly.

Bill's chart is also telling us that he can be dramatic and individualistic. He is inclined to want to do things his own way. His Mars position tends to further emphasise his need to be in control and take the lead in matters. It does suggest some difficulty at least in working with, and befriending people. And let's not forget that, as a Cancerian, he is predominantly a feeling, private and introverted person, probably a shy person too. He is more likely to be friendly once he gets to know you. Even so, he's no wallflower. He won't be afraid to speak his mind.

Bill Lomas is something of a paradox (his Sun opposite planets in Capricorn and Moon in Pisces) and because of it he is likely to make a distinct division between his home-life and everything, or everywhere else – he will tend to set clear boundaries in other words. Home is his very private world.

# Vocation/interests

Cancerians with their care, caution and need to follow clear codes of conduct can make them good business people, and professional in whatever line of work they follow. The caring professions (or caring for others at a business level, in say a family business, perhaps a shop or restaurant) will tend to have a strong appeal. The need to feel "at home" in their vocation will be a main concern and influence on their career choice/s.

There is a likely need (Jupiter in Gemini 6th House, Moon and Neptune) to be "of service" in some way to others.

With Scorpio (and Pluto) on the midheaven point, Bill Lomas would make a good detective. He probably enjoys researching into things, fault finding, getting to the bottom of issues. Having inner/insider knowledge is important to him. He probably also enjoys an element of danger.

There is also an emphasis here ("Finger of God" planets) on finding out, and on communications, as if one's life depended upon it. We discover that a critical concern for Bill touches upon a need to discover and share information. He is probably a mind of information and a person who competes to be better informed than the next person. It is part of what helps him to feel secure.

It is noticeable that Moon in Pisces is also inclined towards some form of escapism – a getting away from, or to going off somewhere by himself. Pisces tend to like big open vistas, visiting nature and enjoying being by the ocean or water.

What is also noticeable here is his openness and receptiveness to feelings and the ambience of places. Not much gets past him regards what is going on in other people's lives. He is highly intuitive, able to tune in. He has a strong potential here for psychic ability too.

# Money

As a Cancerian with Capricorn rising, he naturally seeks material security. Even so as indicated by having his Moon in Pisces and 2nd House, fortunes are likely to move with the tide. We can anticipate that his life, at least thus far, has not been a bed of roses. His Moon position suggests he has waxed and waned with regards to his finances and probably the things he has owned and loved. There has been disappointment for sure. Also benefits derived through, or from, others (Venus and Mars). How he has dealt with this general theme around material security will have been one of his greatest challenges.

# Challenges

The Cancerian can be over-sensitive, touchy, over-emotional, and over-protective of themselves and others. They are inclined to present a hard shell to the world but inside can feel vulnerable, a bit timid and tend to avoid facing up to the challenges they need to face up to. At worst, the Cancerian can be inclined to develop feelings of inferiority, and, in this case (Moon in Pisces), even want to retreat from life altogether.

That said this is also a person who is idealistic and dreams big. He is inclined to be powerful in his ambitions and abilities, even though in other respects he is also inclined to hide his light under a bushel – possibly he could even be a little scared of what he is capable of, or in some way carries fears of reprisals (Sun/Uranus and Neptune, Pluto in Scorpio 10th House) if he is too demonstrative or outspoken.

Saturn, the chart ruler is literally caught in the middle here between the other two outer planets. It is either very exciting or at times a tough gig coping with the situation.

Whether he can bring his dreams to fruition really depends upon the more realistic side of himself (Saturn in Capricorn 1st House) which can be inclined to be pessimistic and throw a spanner in the works. Or, if he is mature about it, he can be sober and realistic, and consider how something could be planned out and achieved. Success comes through his organising his ideas, speaking his mind, being honest and authentic.

With Moon in Pisces and Neptune in his 1st House, he could do a lot worse than to practice some form of meditation, or relaxation using music, to bring about an inner calm, that inner sense of "home" that he actually so desperately needs in his life.

# Comment on how Bill Lomas has expressed his energy in real life – thus far

The person who owns this interesting birth-chart is (to the best of my knowledge at the time of writing) still a happily married family man living in the UK.

He is an electrical engineer (or was when I met him – his job is certainly one way of expressing his Saturn/Uranus rising). He runs his own business. There is nothing he enjoys more than spending time with his family – and his hobby of going fishing. The latter gets him away into the peace and quiet of the countryside. He described his fishing as a kind of meditation.

He enjoys giving talks on his main hobby, and on conservation. He is very knowledgeable in both (Mercury/Finger of God).

What a lot of people wouldn't know, or even suspect of him, is that he is also a medium, and he works in front of audiences (Neptune rising/Mercury). He believes in the afterlife. But that said he is ever looking for evidence (Saturn rising/Pluto 10th house) that it exists or in what form it exists. He firmly believes that those who come through him are real enough.

He turned to astrology (came for a reading) at the time to gain insight into the internal dialogue and struggle he has with himself (mainly the three planets rising opposite his Sun).

He did say that he found astrology was a great help in better understanding what he is working with, and pointing a way forward. It has taught him to be both gentler on himself and on others. He said he was inclined to be heavy-handed on himself (Saturn/Pluto positions) and ever likely to develop an undermining inner dialogue with himself which has led to a poor self-image – requiring conscious effort to correct.

# Step 5 Exercises

Included below, the birth-charts of three well-known figures. People who died young, in what might be described as unusual circumstances.

Using the tables (below) and technique/s discussed through Part 2 of Step Five, try your hand at:

1. Completing the missing information in the tables. Jot it down on paper or, if you have access to MS Word, you could recreate the tables. You will find my weighting below the three examples.
2. Carry through the rest of the evaluation – collecting data from the charts. Use the various resources to build up a profile.
3. Try your hand at reading at least one of the birth-charts, either on a broad basis or in more detail. See if you can discover something about them not shared in their Wikipedia descriptions.

# Amelia Earhart - 24/07/1897 11:30 PM, Atchison Kansas USA

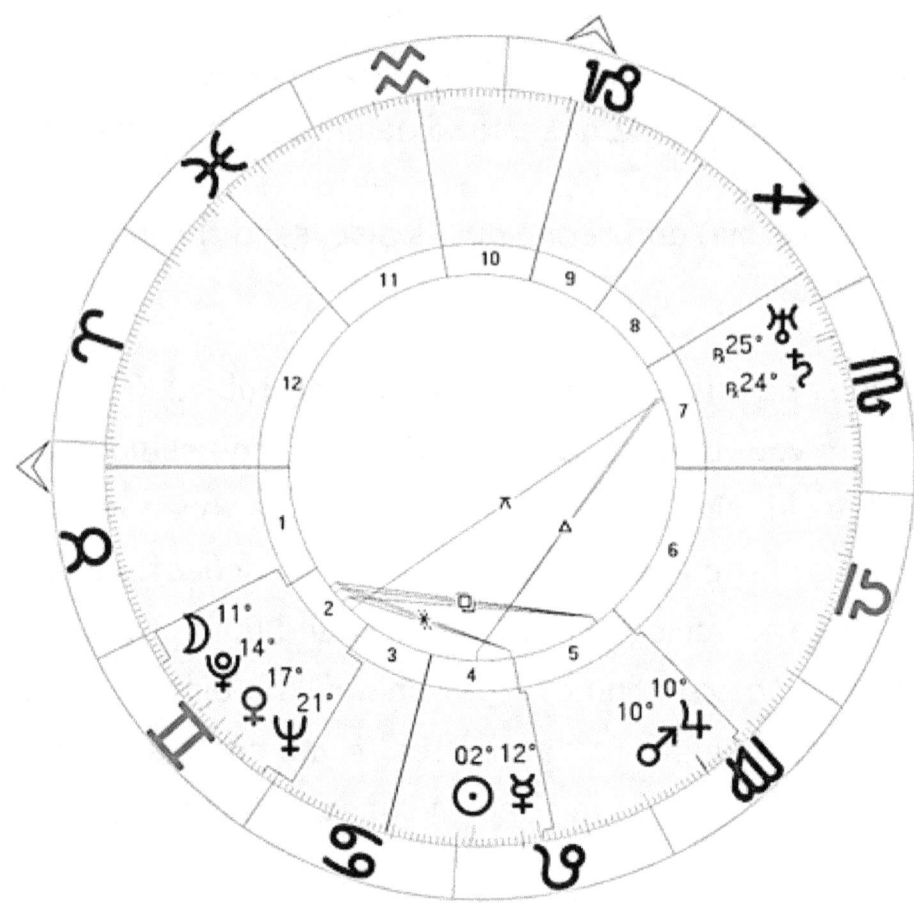

Amelia Mary Earhart was an American aviation pioneer and author. She was the first female aviator to fly solo across the Atlantic Ocean. She also set many other records, wrote best-selling books about her flying experiences, and was instrumental in the formation of The Ninety-Nines, an organization for female pilots.

During an attempt at becoming the first woman to complete a circumnavigational flight of the globe in 1937 in a Purdue-funded Lockheed Model 10-E Electra, Earhart and navigator Fred Noonan disappeared over the central Pacific Ocean near Howland Island. The two were last seen in Lae, New Guinea, on July 2, 1937, on the last land stop before Howland Island and one of their final legs of the flight. She presumably died in the Pacific during the circumnavigation, just three weeks prior to her fortieth birthday.

She was declared dead January 5, 1939.

You can find out more about Amelia Earhart off this link: https://en.wikipedia.org/wiki/Amelia_Earhart

There is another take on the ending of this story in a documentary film called; **Amelia Earhart: The Lost Evidence** (2017 on History channel). It argues that she crash-landed her plane on Mili Atoll, in the Marshall Islands. She was taken prisoner by the Japanese and later executed as an American spy.

Comment: Something I note, from looking at the tables, is that Amelia Earhart had no planets in Cardinal signs, and yet she was a brave pioneer. She did have what I would consider a dynamic trine between her Sun and Saturn/Uranus – a break for independence and freedom. But look at that Mars/Jupiter conjunction in the 5th house.

Bruce Lee had a similar gap in Cardinal signs. If anyone pioneered a new martial art, it was Lee.

Empty spaces, or singletons, can be as powerful as high numbers. Think compensation!

# 1. First the planets in signs – as per their matrix

## Polarities (Positive/Negative) emphasis:

| Positive | 6 | | = 11 |
|---|---|---|---|
| Negative | 4 | | = 4 |

Totals 15

## Element emphasis:

| Fire | 2 | | = 4 |
|---|---|---|---|
| Earth | 2 | | = 2 |
| Air | 4 | | = 7 |
| Water | 2 | | = 2 |

Totals 15

## Mode (Cardinal/Fixed/Mutable) emphasis

| Cardinal | 0 | | = 0 |
|---|---|---|---|
| Fixed | 4 | | = 6 |
| Mutable | 6 | | = 9 |

Totals 15

## 2. Secondly the planets, angles & houses

- Sun:
- Moon:
- Ascendant is:
- Midheaven is:
- Ruling Planet:
- Rising Planet - if any:
- Further angular planets:
- Planet/s in own sign:
- Stellium/s:
- Any remaining planets:

## 3. Third, any major aspects and/or aspect patterns?

# Bruce Lee - 27/11/1940 7:12 AM, San Francisco California USA

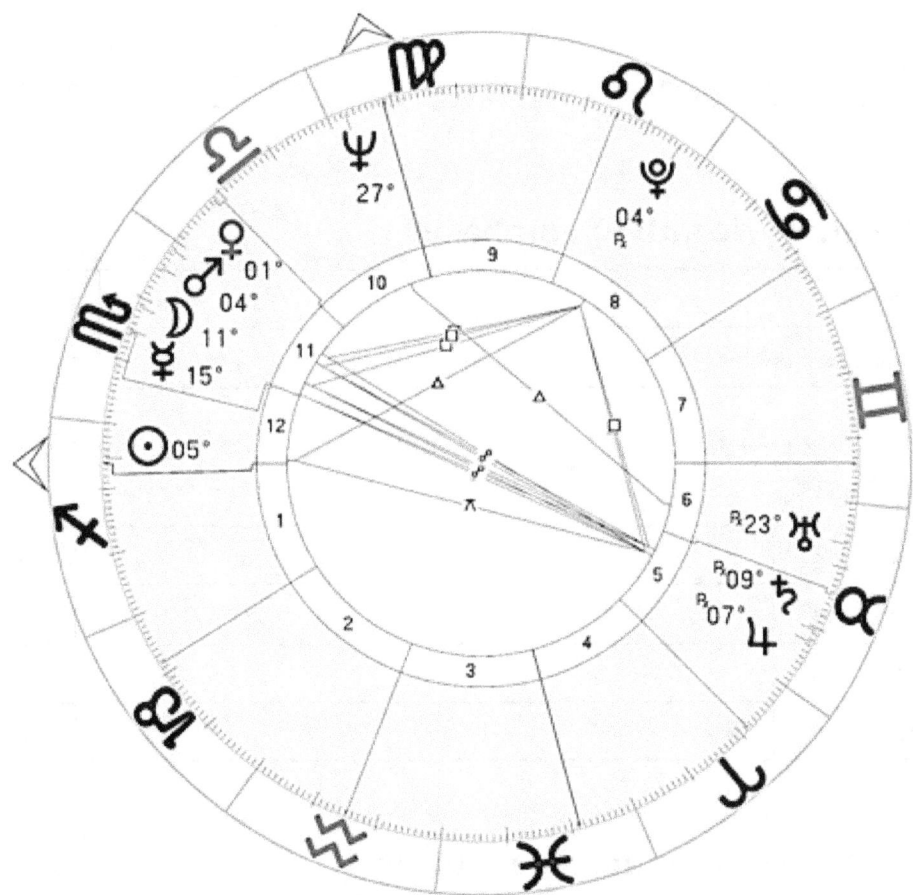

Bruce Lee was a Chinese American martial artist, actor, director, martial arts instructor and philosopher. He was the founder of Jeet Kune Do, a hybrid martial arts philosophy drawing from different combat disciplines that is often credited with paving the way for modern mixed martial arts. He is considered by commentators, critics, media, and other martial artists to be the most influential martial artist of all time and a pop culture icon of the 20th century, who bridged the gap between East and West.

On May 10, 1973, Lee collapsed during an automated dialogue replacement session for Enter the Dragon at Golden Harvest in Hong Kong. Suffering from seizures and headaches, he was immediately rushed to Hong Kong Baptist Hospital, where doctors diagnosed cerebral edema. They were able to reduce the swelling through the administration of mannitol. The headache and cerebral edema that occurred in his first collapse were later repeated on the day of his death – 20th July 1973.

This is the orthodox version of his death. There is some suspicion that Lee was murdered.

Learn to Read Your Birth-chart in 5 Steps

You can find out more about Bruce Lee off this link:
https://en.wikipedia.org/wiki/Bruce_Lee

## 1. First the planets in signs – as per their matrix

### Polarities (Positive/Negative) emphasis

| Positive | 2 | = 4 |
| Negative | 8 | = 14 |

Totals 18

### Element emphasis

| Fire | 2 | = 4 |
| Earth | 4 | = 7 |
| Air | 0 | = 0 |
| Water | 4 | = 7 |

Totals 18

### Mode (Cardinal/Fixed/Mutable) emphasis

| Cardinal | 0 | = 0 |
| Fixed | 8 | = 14 |
| Mutable | 2 | = 4 |

Totals 18

## 2. Secondly the planets, angles & houses

- Sun:
- Moon:
- Ascendant is:
- Midheaven is:

- Ruling Planet:
- Rising Planet - if any:
- Further angular planets:
- Planet/s in own sign:
- Stellium/s:
- Any remaining planets:

## 3. Major aspects and/or aspect patterns?

# Amy Winehouse - 14/09/1983 10:25 PM, Enfield, England

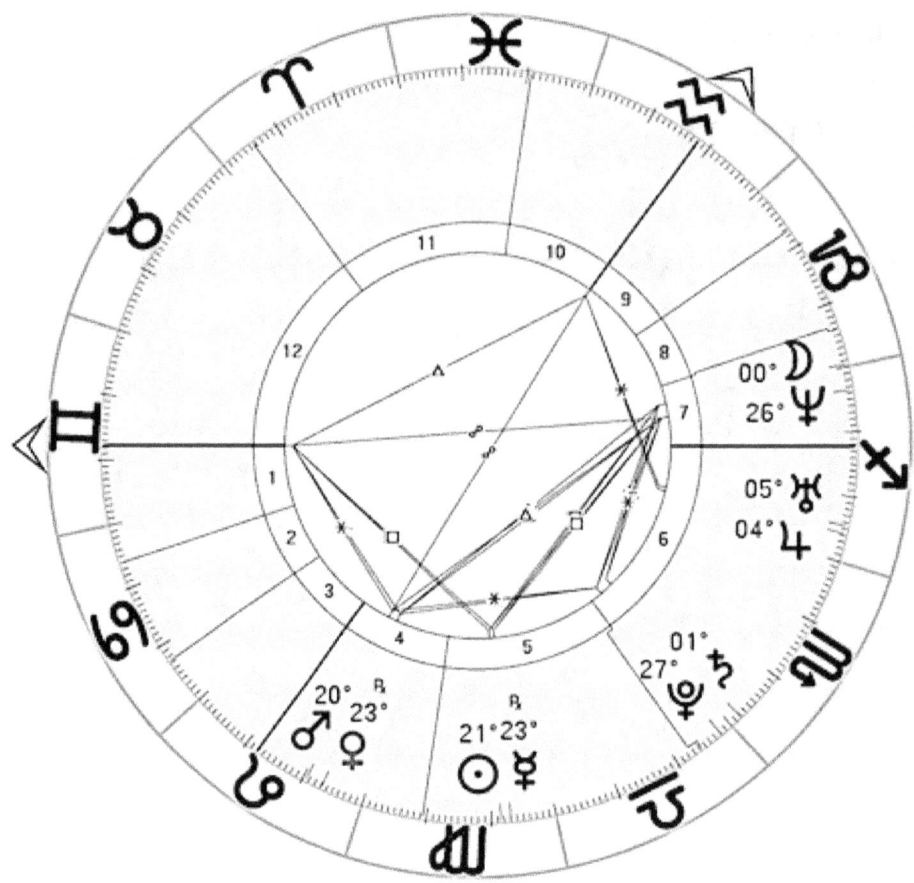

Amy Jade Winehouse was a very successful English singer and songwriter known for her deep, expressive contralto vocals and her eclectic mix of musical genres, including soul, rhythm and blues and jazz.

Death: Winehouse's bodyguard said that he had arrived at her residence three days before her death and felt she had been somewhat intoxicated. He observed moderate drinking over the next few days, and said she had been "laughing, listening to music and watching TV at 2 a.m. the day of her death." At 10 a.m. BST on 23 July 2011, he observed her lying on her bed and tried unsuccessfully to rouse her. This did not raise much suspicion because she usually slept late after a night out.

According to the bodyguard, shortly after 3 p.m., he checked on her again and observed her lying in the same position as before, leading to a further check, in which he concluded that she was not breathing and had no pulse; he said he called emergency services. At 3:54 p.m., two ambulances were called to Winehouse's home in Camden, London. Winehouse was pronounced dead at the scene. Shortly afterwards, the Metropolitan Police confirmed that she had died.

You can find out more about Amy Winehouse off this link:
https://en.wikipedia.org/wiki/Amy_Winehouse

# 1. First the planets in signs – as per their matrix

## Polarities (Positive/Negative) emphasis

| Positive | 6 | | = 7 |
|---|---|---|---|
| Negative | 4 | | = 9 |

Totals 16

## Element emphasis

| Fire | 5 | | = 7 |
|---|---|---|---|
| Earth | 3 | | = 7 |
| Air | 1 | | = 1 |
| Water | 1 | | = 1 |

Totals 16

## Cardinal/Fixed/Mutable emphasis

| Cardinal | 2 | | = 3 |
|---|---|---|---|
| Fixed | 3 | | = 3 |
| Mutable | 5 | | = 10 |

Totals 16

# 2. Secondly the planets, angles & houses

- Sun:
- Moon:
- Ascendant is:
- Midheaven is:
- Ruling Planet:

Learn to Read Your Birth-chart in 5 Steps

- Rising Planet - if any:
- Further angular planets:
- Planet/s in own sign:
- Stellium/s:
- Any remaining planets:

## 3. Major aspects and/or aspect patterns?

# Answers

## Amelia Earhart

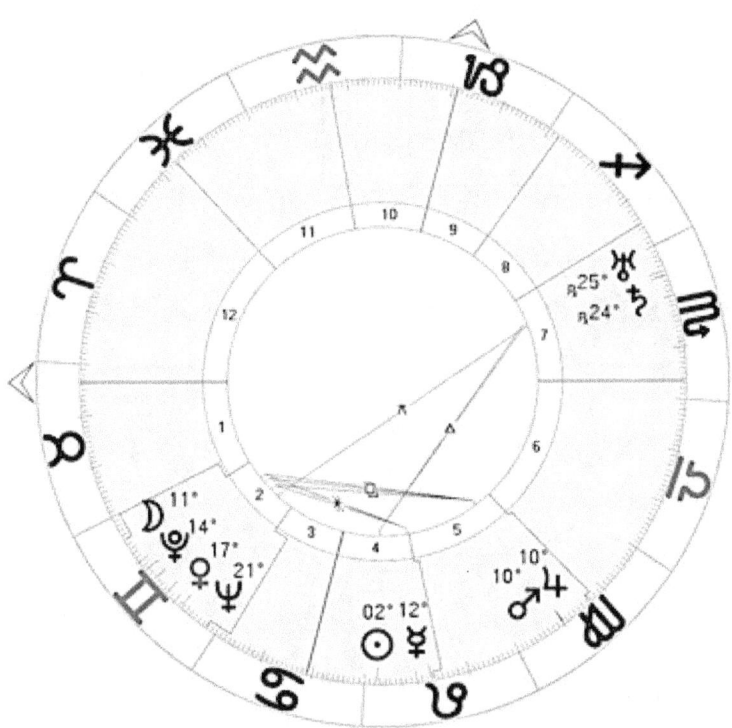

## 1. First the planets in signs – as per their matrix

| Positive | 6 | + 2 (Sun in own sign) +1 (Moon) + 1 (Venus chart ruler) + 1 (Moon, Venus, Neptune and Pluto stellium) | = 11 |
|---|---|---|---|
| Negative | 4 | | = 4 |

Learn to Read Your Birth-chart in 5 Steps 223

| Fire | 2 | + 2 (Sun in own sign) | = 4 |
| Earth | 2 | | = 2 |
| Air | 4 | + 1 (Moon) + 1 (Venus chart ruler) + 1 (Moon, Venus, Neptune and Pluto stellium) | = 7 |
| Water | 2 | | = 2 |

| Cardinal | 0 | | = 0 |
| Fixed | 4 | + 2 (Sun in own sign) | = 6 |
| Mutable | 6 | + 1 (Moon) + 1 (Venus chart ruler) + 1 (Moon, Venus, Neptune and Pluto stellium) | = 9 |

## 2. Secondly the planets, angles & houses

- Sun: *Leo 4<sup>th</sup>*
- Moon: *Gemini 2<sup>nd</sup>*
- Ascendant is: *Taurus*
- Midheaven is: *Capricorn*
- Ruling Planet: *Venus Gemini 2<sup>nd</sup>*
- Rising Planet - if any: *None*
- Further angular planets: *None*
- Planet/s in their own sign: *Sun in Leo 4<sup>th</sup>*
- Stellium/s: *Gemini 2<sup>nd</sup>*
- Any remaining planets: *Mercury in Leo 4<sup>th</sup> House, Mars and Jupiter in Virgo 5<sup>th</sup> House, Saturn and Uranus in Scorpio 7<sup>th</sup> House, Neptune and Pluto in Gemini 2<sup>nd</sup> House*

## 3. Third major aspects and/or aspect patterns

*Sun trine Saturn/Uranus conjunction | Squares = tension Mars/Jupiter to stellium Moon/Pluto/Venus*

# Bruce Lee

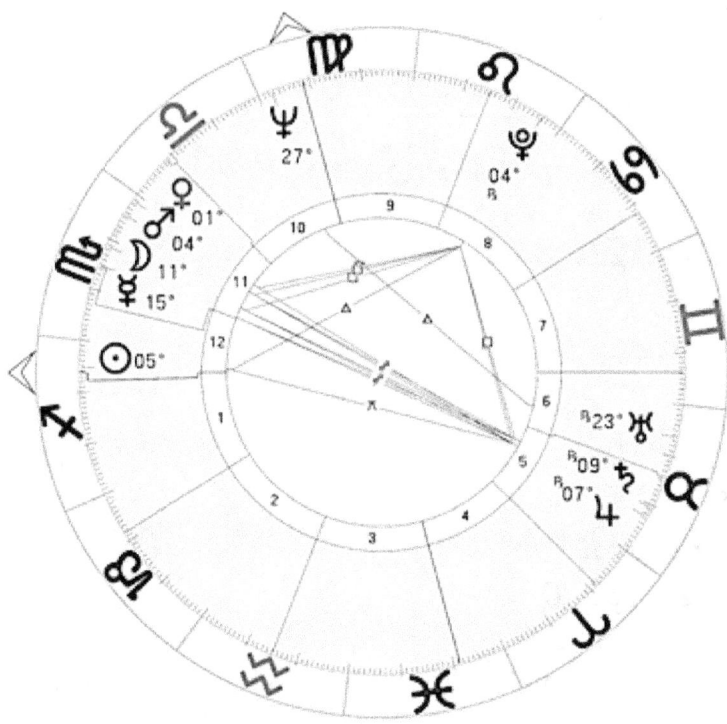

## 1. First the planets in signs – as per their matrix

| Positive | 2 | + 2 (Sun and on Asc Angle) | = 4 |
|---|---|---|---|
| Negative | 8 | + 1 (Moon) + 1 (Mars own sign) + 1 (Moon, Mercury, Venus, Mars stellium) + 1 (Neptune on MC Angle) + 1 (Jupiter chart ruler) +1 (Jupiter, Saturn, Uranus stellium) | = 14 |

| Fire | 2 | + 2 (Sun and on Asc Angle) | = 4 |
|---|---|---|---|
| Earth | 4 | + 1 (Neptune on MC Angle) + 1 (Jupiter chart ruler) +1 (Jupiter, Saturn, Uranus stellium) | = 7 |
| Air | 0 | | = 0 |
| Water | 4 | + 1 (Moon) + 1 (Mars own sign) + 1 (Moon, Mercury, Venus, Mars stellium) | = 7 |

Learn to Read Your Birth-chart in 5 Steps

| Cardinal | 0 | | = 0 |
|---|---|---|---|
| Fixed | 8 | + 1 (Moon) + 1 (Mars own sign) + 1 (Moon, Mercury, Venus, Mars stellium) + 1 (Neptune on MC Angle) + 1 (Jupiter chart ruler) +1 (Jupiter, Saturn, Uranus stellium) | = 14 |
| Mutable | 2 | + 2 (Sun and on Asc Angle) | = 4 |

## 2. Secondly the planets, angles & houses

- Sun: *Sagittarius 12th*
- Moon: *Scorpio 11th*
- Ascendant is: *Sagittarius*
- Midheaven is: *Virgo*
- Ruling Planet: *Jupiter Taurus 5th*
- Rising Planet - if any: *Sun Sagittarius 12th*
- Further angular planets: *Neptune Virgo 10th*
- Planet/s in their own sign: *Mars Scorpio 11th*
- Stellium/s: *Moon/Mercury/Venus/Mars in Scorpio | Jupiter/Saturn/Uranus in Taurus*
- Any remaining planets: *Pluto in Leo 8th*

## 3. Major aspects and/or aspect patterns

Most notable a huge T square involving Moon, Mars and Venus in Scorpio 11th House (also draws in Mercury) on one leg. With Jupiter and Saturn in Taurus 5th House on the opposite leg. And with Pluto in Leo 8th House on the third leg - pulling it all together. A powder keg of a situation. His Sun trine Pluto was key to keeping it (possible rage) under control.

# Amy Winehouse

## 1. First the planets in signs – as per their matrix

| Positive | 6 | +1 (Jupiter own sign) | = 7 |
|---|---|---|---|
| Negative | 4 | + 1 (Sun) + 1 (Moon) + 2 (Mercury ruler and in own sign) + 1 (Jupiter, Uranus, Neptune stellium) | = 9 |

| Fire | 5 | + 1 (Jupiter own sign) + 1 (Jupiter, Uranus, Neptune stellium) | = 7 |
|---|---|---|---|
| Earth | 3 | + 1 (Sun) + 1 (Moon) +2 (Mercury chart ruler & own sign) | = 7 |
| Air | 1 | | = 1 |
| Water | 1 | | = 1 |

Learn to Read Your Birth-chart in 5 Steps

| Cardinal | 2 | + 1 (Moon) | = 3 |
|---|---|---|---|
| Fixed | 3 | | = 3 |
| Mutable | 5 | + 1 (Sun) +2 (Mercury chart ruler & own sign) + 1 (Jupiter own sign) + 1 (Jupiter, Uranus, Neptune stellium) | = 10 |

## 2. Secondly the planets, angles & houses

- Sun: *Virgo 5th*
- Moon: *Capricorn 7th*
- Ascendant: *Gemini*
- Midheaven: *Aquarius*
- Ruling Planet: *Mercury Virgo 5th*
- Rising Planet - if any: *None*
- Further angular planets: *Mars Leo 4th (wide) | Neptune Sagittarius 7th (wide)*
- Planet/s in own sign: *Mercury Virgo 5th | Jupiter Sagittarius 6th*
- Stellium/s: *Jupiter/Uranus/Neptune in Sagittarius*
- Any remaining planets: *Venus/Mars in Leo 4th | Saturn Scorpio 6th | Pluto Libra 6th*

## 3. Major aspects and/or aspect patterns

*Harmonious triangle: Moon/Neptune trine Venus/Mars & sextile Saturn/Pluto with Venus sextile Pluto - artistic and musical. Challenging: Sun/Mercury square Moon/Neptune - could be hard on herself; drank (Moon/Neptune) to deal with the situation; a lost soul.*

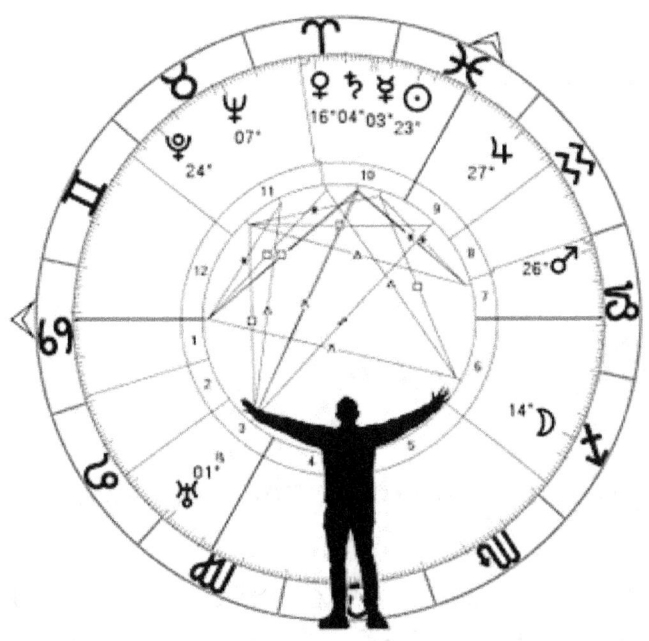

# One Step Further

## The Spiritual Roadmap

# Introduction

## γνῶθι σεαυτὸν

Know Your Self – the inscription over the Temple of Apollo at Delphi.

At the beginning of this book, I asked you, what is the purpose of your life? Why are you here? And, what have you come to experience, to learn or to give?

My belief is that the time and place, you were born in, encapsulates the answer, or answers to these questions. And the best representation you'll find for that event, I suggest, is in your birth-chart. It is then your job to unravel it for the answers to such questions. It is your spiritual roadmap.

What follows are some aids that I can provide to hopefully help you with your enquiries.

## But let me back up a bit to help put things into context as I see it...

My starting point for this excursion is based on the belief that we are souls first and foremost, having human bodies. Not the other way around, by the way, as is commonly portrayed.

I hope you'll agree with me that the human body could be described as a beautiful organic vehicle, but a vehicle that cannot operate properly without that vital component, a soul enmeshed within it. It's a soul and body symbiosis.

Ensoulment is the term for the moment the soul – one of us - takes up this symbiosis with a human body. This won't be any old body but a body that is fitting the soul's current endeavours and needs. Just when this happens in the development from the foetus to a child, is a matter of belief, conjecture and debate...

> In the time of Aristotle, it was widely believed that the human soul entered the forming body at 40 days (male embryos) or 90 days (female embryos), and quickening was an indication of the presence of a soul. Other religious views are that ensoulment happens at the moment of conception; or when the child takes the first breath after being born; at the formation of the nervous system and brain; at the first detectable sign of brain activity; or when the foetus is able to survive independently of the uterus (viability).[1]

As you'll gather, there are a number of possible moments when ensoulment could occur – and this varies across cultures and religions. However, such detail need not really concern us in this quest. It is enough to accept it happens during the process of our coming into the world.

> If you want to find the secrets of the Universe, think in terms of energy, frequency and vibration.
>
> Nikola Tesla

What is important to bear in mind is that, no matter how things appear here we are dealing with energy. The vibrational level and frequency we come to exist in here, on the Earth (vibrating at a frequency of 7.83hz), is lower, much lower than our natural soul energy. It is the reason we have need of a physical body, in order for us to fully interact and participate within the physical environment we find ourselves in.

So, consider your physical body as your earthsuit, for the time you are here visiting, learning, relating and experiencing on the planet.

The physical body and the planet provide testing boundaries, limitations that, by comparison with our normal soul state, means, being here and lowering our vibration, it is a bit like walking through treacle. We meet resistance – that can come in all kinds of forms.

# But why here?

One might ask, if, being souls, and made of pure light, what is the point of getting ensnared in this lower vibrational level – the physical world? It's a challenging question and I'm going to attempt to answer it.

I would suggest two obvious reasons:

1. One answer is that, it is easy to experience and express love in comfortable circumstances (at higher energy levels) but <u>can</u> we still experience and express love when faced with the resistance of lower levels? Testing it is good for the soul. This is part of the answer. We have a soul reason, a purpose for being here – and being here at this time (you might look into the article, **How Astrology Works**, in the Bonus Pack, in reference to "this time"). This reason or purpose is always tied up with our spiritual development, with our learning, awakening, becoming conscious, becoming a more loving being.

   Once we enter into the lower energy levels of Time, we become more noticeably involved in working with what we call karma. Out of the resistance what we believe, think and create then determines what happens next – that's karma for you. And we can get trapped in it; spending lives (rebirthing) in and out of what we've wittingly or unwittingly, created. And this won't change until we begin to awaken to our situation and take back conscious control of our destiny.

2. We also have a collective purpose for being here. I discuss this in the book, **Love's Story of Why We Are Here**. I won't go into it here except to say that this is the idea that everything around us is also seeking, nay needing to awaken and get back to the pure light or higher vibration. It/we are all part of the same stuff.

The situation, each of us is in, is unique. We may share common ground with other souls but our perspective and experience will be unique to ourself.

Coming to identify with the human body, we have taken on, happens at the same time as we are disconnecting from our soul's normal vibration, past memories or past lives, to settling into the new situation. It takes time, probably around six or seven years.

It is more or less complete when we are not only familiar with our parents, our siblings, identifying with our name, with our gender, and enough of our language, but also when we are familiar with where we live, our friends, our school, our neighbourhood generally. We are then gradually becoming the person we are to become for this life experience.

What has also happened in this process is that we, well most of us, will have lost the link to our original plan or intention; our reason for coming here. This is the risk we take in coming into Time.

The thing to also bear in mind is that, from the off, our potential will be operating – whether we are conscious of it or not. Our energy setup will be attracting certain experiences towards us – while it will be ignoring or repelling others. And this continues through our physical life. It is important we therefore become awake to it, and begin to work on it to improve and refine it.

This is how our birth-chart can help us: To get to know what we are working with. By that, get to know our Self, and by that, piece together our original intention/s behind our visit. And which, I believe, may naturally fall into place by better integrating our energies as represented in our chart.

# Not everyone's cup of tea

It has to be said that probably most of us pass through life while not really becoming awake to what we are attracting or repelling, let alone being aware of any spiritual intentions for the life we are in.

It is fair to say that in our cultural condition (I speak to being in the West) we are not ordinarily encouraged to look into such (often deemed "fringe") matters. Instead, as children, we are inducted into what is seen as the acceptable wisdom, and worldview, as our compass for going out into the world.

When our parents encourage us to focus on our life ahead, they are most probably concerned for what we are planning around our work, education, relationships, home and family. And, where belief is concerned, they will probably want us to follow a more conventional path – whether religious or otherwise – as they probably did themselves.

It is all in the hope of our achieving a good life. And of course, there is nothing intrinsically wrong with that. It is good; indeed, we need to be grounded in every which way we pursue life.[2]

But what is left to one side, or more commonly left out, is any concern for us to uncover our spiritual purpose for being here at this time.

We will, of course, make spiritual progress in our lives, if our intention is to become more joyful and loving beings – it is not that complicated. It is a step in the right direction. Yet, in all innocence we will still be on the merry-go-round – also known as the Wheel of Samsara. We can spend life after life tethered to the Earth, until we eventually awake to the reality, indeed the bubble of illusion, we have created and are in. And at that point we truly can begin our personal journey back to our natural state.

If you are going to make sense of your current life situation, and direction of travel, you need to explore and study ancient and esoteric knowledge, and importantly have a map, your birth-chart to help guide you.

And, importantly, alongside this study, take note of where you are in your life, your intentions, your current work, where you live, and the people you live with, your friends and neighbours. Especially take note of your family background. Treat it all as symbolical and look to where it is reflected in your chart. Your external world will, of course, provide remarkable insight into your spiritual situation.

> Looking at things, even through basic astrology, can also flag up interesting group patterns that can provide further insight into links with the people you are with. For example, simply looking at Sun-signs in my core family group, consisting of my parents, sisters and myself (six people), the pattern involved my father (a Leo) and my mother (an Aquarian), a further Leo sister and also an Aquarian sister – therefore four people born on the … Leo/Aquarius axis. One other sister is a Gemini and myself a Libra – which in turn means there were two Fire signs and four Air signs in the original grouping.
>
> On a broad, positive, sweep, a group theme of friendliness, being sunny, witty and communicative, while encouraging optimism, detachment and independence, was prominent in my childhood home. This core pattern can also be seen to have developed out later around a Leo direction, with all four sibling relationships having a Leo involved. My Leo sister married a Scorpio. My Aquarian and Gemini sisters each married Leos, and my partner is also a Leo (with, by the way, Aquarius rising – that Leo/Aquarius axis again). Talk about being with a pride of lions, or in the lions' den – dangerous methinks. All of this is meaningful and a resource to be understood.
>
> You might see what you can find by checking out your own family birthdates just on Sun-signs alone. If you … wish to go deeper look for other themes – definitely check

out their Moon, Saturn and Venus signs too, as these will help to provide insight into the nature of your relationship/s.[3]

The Parts that follow are by way of adding to the Five Steps, and to this discussion...

# Part 1
# Contemplating the Orchestra

In Step One, and elsewhere, I've made comment about liking the birth-chart to an orchestra.

If we can accept that our chart is a mirror for our Self, then getting to know each of the players is going to help us get closer to knowing who we are – what we are dealing with.

The planets' link to music is not a new idea. Pythagoras, the Greek mathematician and astronomer, is said to have coined it the "Music of The Spheres." He discovered a mathematical relationship in the frequencies of the seven natural musical tones of the chromatic scale. And he argued similar for the seven known planets of the time – the Sun out to Saturn.

The astrologer/astronomer, Johannes Kepler (1571-1630), also subscribed to this musical idea. He believed that the planets in their movements, and relationship to each other, make music, that only the soul can hear – and is influenced by it. It stands as a theory as to how the planets may influence each of us.

Visit https://en.wikipedia.org/wiki/Musica_universalis if you wish to find out more on Kepler's ideas…

Personally, I subscribe to another theory as to how it all works – see the article; **How Astrology Works** in the Bonus Pack.

But with my orchestra comment I was thinking of something much simpler... That is seeing the orchestra as an analogy for the situation your birth-chart represents. Bringing together all the planets in your life, as a path to self-awareness, self-integration.

In brief it is viewing the planets as the players of your orchestra where, importantly, you (soul-you that is, as I would see it) are the conductor. Conducting a situation that is ultimately transitory, embedded in Time.

In this scenario you will be seeking to play pieces that draw on all the players, playing at their best – in harmony.

So, to take it a step further, here are those players you've met before. This time with comments about them in the part they are inclined to play in your life. See if it is useful to you, as you go about learning to read your birth-chart.

# Beginning with the Sun...

### Sun ☉
This represents your heart, your core, your vitality. It has a direct link to soul you - it's where the light of your soul shines through your current life. It's your natural centre, your inner foundation, your essence, the centre around which all else in your life, revolves. But just to reaffirm, it is not you, the conductor. Call it the lead player.

### Moon ☽
This is your stomach, gut feelings, your instincts, your moods, your link to the natural world. It's your need for rhythm, routine. It's your habits, your behaviour, your subconscious mind. It is where you'll ebb and flow, it's your need for security, need for familiarity. Along with your Sun, your Moon helps set your circadian rhythm, the beat to your life. It could be worthwhile considering that what you believe about yourself is coming from you and not what you have been taught to believe by your upbringing.

## Mercury ☿

How you get around, how you communicate, how you learn, what grabs your interest, how you search/scout for information, how you share what you know. It's the urge to know and inform. It's where you can be sharp, quick witted and possibly a bit of a trickster too.

## Venus ♀

It's how you feel morally, how you are moved, touched. Your version of the Mores. It's how you put value on, and appreciate, your world of people and things (your taste in things). How you are inclined to relate to others, how you discriminate – what/who you may love or hate. It's your (worldly) artistic inclinations.

## Mars ♂

It's your energy, your drive, your force, giving expression to your passion. It's how you are inclined to aggress your world. It's how you take the initiative or act on decisions. It's how you may lead from the front. It's your survival instinct and the warrior within you.

## Jupiter ♃

It's your level of optimism, faith and trust in life. It's where/how you seek to explore and expand on your personal boundaries. It is where you'll seek joy and indulge in your passions. It links to belief in yourself, where your glass is half-full.

## Saturn ♄

It represents your boundaries, your ring-pass-not, where you can feel limited, restricted, hampered or tested. It's where your glass is half-empty. It's knowing your limits, having the wisdom to pace yourself. It's where you'll need to learn patience and work with Time. It's what stops you from getting too big for your boots, what teaches you humility.

## Uranus ⛢

It's where/how you break with tradition and convention. Where/how you can break through mental and social barriers, where you seek/need stimulation, excitement, something new. It's where or how you'll seek independence, break social boundaries, where you may act off a higher cause, where/how you embrace "change" in your life. It offers a breakthrough, lightening insight, revelation.

## Neptune ♆

It's where you'll seek refinement, seek inspiration, seek the ideal. It links to spiritual direction, inspiration, healing and transformation. It is where/how you appreciate/express fine arts. It's also where you may be woolly, where structures you rely on can dissolve into mirages. Where you can be all at sea with yourself and your direction of travel. Where you may be vulnerable, manipulated by others.

## Pluto ♇

This is where you face your truth, where you may have developed fears or phobias – undercurrents you may not be fully aware of, or that you fully acknowledge. Where there is a need for purification, where certain beliefs/constructs you have about yourself and life may need to be revised to make way for a renewal. It represents your hidden power to transform what serves no spiritual purpose into something valuable/wonderful in your life.

# Part 2

# The Running Order of the Signs

Alongside the signs matrix (discussed in Step One), the signs are in the order we find them in, not just because their arrangement is beautifully cohesive but because they also form a cyclic process of development, of entry and exit.

On a human level they broadly fall into three categories of development: that is the personal, the social and the transpersonal (Fig.66).

Within these three broad categories, lies a story of twelve steps, having a beginning and an ending, from the personal towards the transpersonal - in their highest archetypal form of expression.

So, this is a cycle which begins in Aries and ends in Pisces - before returning to a new cycle. Each sign in the cycle forms

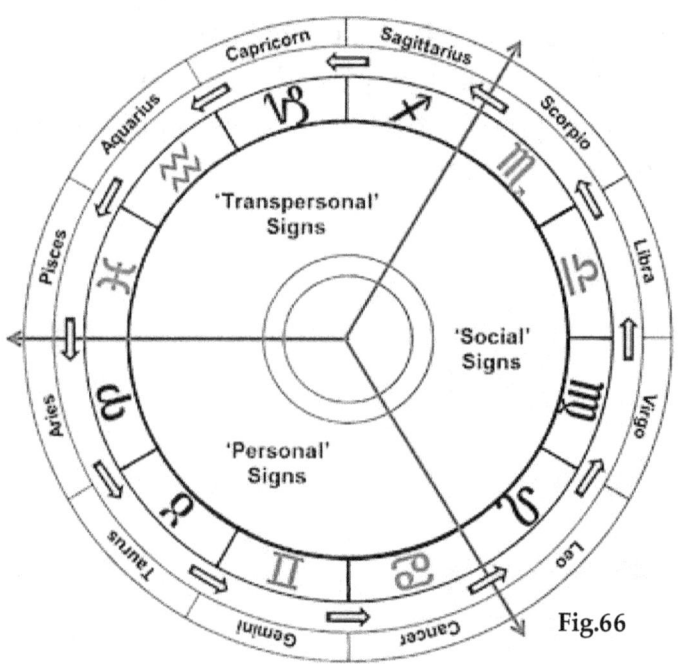

Fig.66

part of the narrative of the cycle and thereby represents a theme, or step, in the order, process and flow of the cycle.

Bear in mind, this is an archetypal journey through the twelve signs. It fits well into the Spiritual Roadmap and I'm hoping it will help you, at very least, to look deeper into the twelve steps of the zodiac itself.

## The Traveller comments

Alongside the description for each sign, I've also added the Traveller comments. This is the archetypal traveller entering and leaving the cycle.

The Traveller comments follow the cyclic procession of the signs and represent spiritual unfoldment in context with the symbolism of the signs. They are intended to be considered as twelve stages of growth and movement on our spiritual life journey. We move from the invisible to the visible and back to the invisible. Each time we do this we have something to learn, and give, from our experience.

Leaving our spiritual homeland to come this Space Time universe, there is risk involved: In our forgetting why we came and what we planned to learn/experience. In our forgetting that we can also go backwards as well as forwards in our spiritual learning and development. Thus, as mentioned, we can become, or remain, trapped on the Wheel of Samsara. To get off the wheel we not only need our map but also to apply it, which takes effort.

# The Personal (or private) segment

*Aries to Cancer - have a "personal" agenda – they have a "me and mine" preoccupation about them.*

## Aries phase – getting our involvement started

**The Traveller** leaves their spiritual homeland and starts out on a new phase or cycle of their journey.

Here we are like The Fool of the tarot cards. We are starting out, naïve and innocent. This is the phase of involution; the decision and act of entering a new beginning, to become a new arrival in the physical. It's the moment of leaving the security of the womb and being born into the world. But hey, this is not a time for reflection on the dangers or on what we may have left behind. It entails risk and the determination to emerge. The focus is on getting the job done. Going out into the world and beginning our adventure.

## Taurus phase - landing

**The Traveller** arrives in the physical, becomes awake to the physical body and physical world.

And like a paratrooper, we successfully land in our new situation. First things first before we go further. Here we are now earthing ourself in the physical world and our new physical body. Do we have all of the basics in place, all the resources we need to be nourished - oxygen, water, food, shelter, someone to look after us – before going forward. All boxes ticked we can go to the next phase.

## Gemini phase – where are we?

**The Traveller** is being inducted into their immediate environment. Identification with their new life begins.

So, where are we? It's one thing to plan what might be, and another to be there on the spot and doing it. We may be one of twins (as in Gemini) but for most of us this phase entails exploring by ourselves, under our own steam. We need now to explore; discover; be curious, embrace; find out what's going on; mentally know and form a picture of where we are, and identify who we are with. It involves developing a means of communication, letting others know we are here, and what we need. We need this interaction with our immediate environment. Here's a driver for knowledge and developing mental wellbeing/security.

## Cancer phase – home is where the heart is

**The Traveller** gains familiarity, is becoming 'at home' within their physical body and immediate world. Correspondingly the forgetting and disconnection with their spiritual homeland is underway.

And, following Gemini, we also need to feel at-home. Here we are developing emotional familiarity/attachment with where we are. This is where we belong; where we are nurtured; linking up with family, with parents (especially whoever is mother), with siblings, with relatives. The *house* in Taurus, becomes the *home* in Cancer. Here we are building our roots that will influence how we face and fair in the world. It is identifying with our own personal base camp – in context with the Capricorn (inner) mountain we will seek to climb.

# The Social segment

*Leo to Scorpio have a "social" agenda – or relating to others from a personal baseline. They have a "you and me" or "others and me" about them.*

## Leo phase – letting others know who we are

**The Traveller**, now identifying with their current life, projects forward into the world that lies outside the immediate familial home. Still a child, they begin to meet and pitch who they are within the world of other travellers. This point represents a high point of joy and expression of being in the physical, and becoming aware of separateness. By contrast the Traveller is heading towards the furthest distance from their homeland. Between here and Scorpio the traveller is learning, growing and maturing in the physical world, populated by other travellers.

But we weren't the only paratrooper to land and find a safe shelter at the time. We are one of a generation. And this is our next big challenge. Armed with the love and security (or possible lack, if things have been tough) our family have provided for us, we begin the next phase of our journey. That is, meeting up with others of our generation.

We are going out, playing, going to school, learning, preparing ourselves for adult life ahead – as our culture wishes us to see it and experience it. We were naturally made-ready for this adventure, building a sense of our own identity, in context with our peers, building our persona in context with our competitors; forming friends and possible foes. We look for heroes (or perhaps villains) to guide us through this phase. We need to make a show of what we are made of.

Here we participate in gameplay, competitions, being measured. We are getting the measure of ourself against others. All leading to gaining confidence and skills to help us take on and succeed in the world.

## Virgo phase – cleaning up our act

**The Traveller**, in context with other travellers, moves on to establish their place in the culture and community they are in. Now the traveller needs to stand on their own feet, take care of needs and be able to offer something; for something in return.

We now move into a phase where we quieten down and clean up our act. We are maturing and internalising what we learnt through the Leo phase. We can't stay a child forever and we are transitioning towards adulthood. We need now to participate within our community in a more mature way.

We need to begin taking on responsibility for nourishing and looking after our interests. Seeking or developing a means for making a living in the world, standing on our own two feet. Negotiating on our worth; offering a service in exchange for income and to maintain our well-being. Looking after our health; pursuing further education; being responsible and efficient with our resources.

Here we are seeking to establish a continuity that will eventually (if not already) be based outside the security offered by our familial home circumstances.

## Libra phase – linking up with others

**The Traveller** becomes attracted to others, is meeting up with travel companion/s or soul mate/s, and building on relationships into partnerships. The traveller is now at the balance point of their journey.

We've arrived at the balance point on our journey into maturity. Our focus now shifts to forming close relationships. We are dealing in likes, attraction, appearances and ideals. Building on our ability to attract, and the attraction others have over us. Socialising; making close ties; meeting and forming more mature friendships with the view of forming strong and intimate bonds and partnerships.

We are finding love in the world; sowing the seeds of a new life with a special person – or persons. This becomes another milestone in our moving on from childhood ties. We are cutting the umbilical cord with our familial basecamp and moving to a hopefully secure and settled long-term relationship.

## Scorpio phase – the truth will out but will I see it?

**The Traveller** in intense involvement with life awakens to some of the realities of physical life and also death. He or she begins to awaken to the light and darkness within; the soul is emerging as the operator in the physical. He or she now begins seeing through some of the accepted norms and conventions of human life, and facing the truth. Here begins the undoing and struggle to reawaken, to regain one's soul mission – and to start the return journey, or possibly not, if caught up at this crossroads – it's a phase of danger and heightened awareness. This is potentially the dark night of the soul, of struggles, tests and trials.

Appearances can be skin deep. This is where the gloss can start to come off on any of our ideals, fantasies or projections we may have developed up and through our Libra phase.

Partnerships built on shaky ground will now be tested and could be found wanting. Here, we meet some of the physical realities and commitments of the world we have moved into; an awakening to the process of change and depth of feeling in exchanges with life and relationships. It includes the assumptions and/or projections we make around our self-image, sexuality, intimate exchanges with others; and bringing children into the world.

Now we may begin to call ourselves parents – and we may notice how what goes around has come around. This phase calls in legal and binding agreements. It may involve close calls with authorities that remind us of the darker, or more vulnerable aspects of human life. This is where "truth" may out or be at a premium; where we meet with the polarities of the birth and death ends of life. If we hadn't sensed it before, this phase will bring us to sense our own mortality.

# Transpersonal segment

*Sagittarius to Pisces have a "transpersonal" agenda - or looking beyond our personal and social relationships, into a wider public, collective, global, spiritual context. They have a "the world and me" or an "us" (as in "all of us in this together" broader sense) about them.*

## Sagittarius phase – beginning the return part of our journey

**The Traveller** having come through the darkness begins to gain a renewed faith, hears the call to broaden out their understanding, to broaden their belief and vision of place in the physical world as they have so far understood it to be. Now, in growing context to finding one's true homeland – or what is perceived as one's true homeland – the search is on for something more.

Here we begin our global or transpersonal phase. In the ideal – if Scorpio gave us the wake-up call needed – this is where we embark on an endeavour (odyssey even) to broaden our horizons and look deeper into our lives. We need answers to such questions as: Why are we here? What is the point of it all? Is there a higher force looking out for us?

Depending on where we are at, or what we are becoming, this phase may be to explore having more fun or recreation in our lives. It could be more adventure, holidays abroad, a wanting to see the world, learning a new topic of interest, a language, new skills, a new job. It could be moving abroad. Or it could be the beginning of a search for higher meaning – our own holy grail.

At this point we will be found wanting to stretch ourselves in some way, bring more light into our lives. If we have gone through challenging times and/or brought children into the world, this in itself can spark such a search for meaning. That said, it may be our children's education, or our work, that sparks a decision to move house. Or we may have had a religious upbringing and now seek to pursue it with greater fervour.

Discovering ourselves through the stories and experience of others; finding shelter in faith and belief about life; settling on what is good and wholesome. All help to mark this potentially emancipating phase.

## Capricorn phase – the mountain before us

**The Traveller** gaining wisdom through the acceptance of personal boundaries and limitations of matter and time, now needs to go it alone. Finding peace, they now seek to achieve and complete their spiritual quest for this journey, within what are now known and accepted physical constraints.

We are heading to the top of our game. The mountain that we have been seeking for much of our lives, or possibly has evaded us – because we've had difficulty knowing who we are, or what we wanted to do with our life – is now in front of us. Time and tide wait for no one comes the call. We have a finite amount of time to climb our own mountain of success – no matter how big or small. What has gone before us now supports or even hinders our reaching what we see as our summit.

Now we begin to take stock of our achievements, or not. If not, it's where regrets may mount and have their price. We can now see more clearly what needs (or is needed) to be done – the work still to do and goals to be achieved, for ourselves and possibly for others. But now we are becoming more aware of the time left to do things, our physical limitations perhaps. We are beginning to acknowledge old age, the limitations of the body. Our own mortality is not only being acknowledged but is also being accepted as real. And as time calls on us to write our Will, or revisit our Will, we may now also be called grandparents, senior citizens or pensioners.

If we have achieved climbing our desired mountain, we have arrived and probably feel a sense of inner satisfaction, inner security and maturity. We are wiser now. We can look back on our adventure and smile at all the good times, the testing times, at all the love we have received and shared. We can now know and accept our boundaries, our personal limitations. We can now know and accept ourself more easily - warts and all. We are becoming a sage of our personal journey – with wonderful stories to tell about it.

# Aquarius phase – renewal!

**The Traveller** is now open to a break-through in their understanding and consciousness. Their soul now begins to peer through the constructs and constraints of physical life, take it for what it is - illusion. The Traveller now seeks emancipation, freedom for their self and for fellow travellers. There's a growing desire to reconnect with one's true home and true nature. An acceptance of detaching from the physical body and the world of separation, has begun.

The Aquarius phase is what arrives after we come down off that personal mountain on the other side. Often the mountain relates to the position we acquired through our work and lifestyle. And through the prism of ordinary or conventional life this phase is us being in retirement. We may buy into this as meaning we are on our way out. This may be true, and for a lot of us we may stop dreaming at this point, and fit in with the norm to literally retire from life. But in fact, this phase may afford us a wonderful opportunity to nourish ourself creatively, spiritually, and to take up new adventures that help us to find we were always more than the roles we took on in our working life. Our job title, or say our home title of "mum" or "dad," and all the constructs, and labels, that have gone before can now fall away.

Now we can get down to finding our truer self. A need may stir within us for something new; sharing our time and wisdom with others; finding common ground with humanity at large; taking up a new hobby, a new study; planning our *forever-home* by the sea. This phase provides a glimmer (or more) of what is missing, something remarkable and revolutionary, something much different to what our life adventures had shown us up to this point. It can be a very exciting and emancipating time – that helps us prepare to move on. Here is opportunity to begin getting all our spiritual "ducks in a row." To start taking care of loose ends.

# Pisces phase – the letting go and return

**The Traveller** discovers he or she was, after-all, a traveller, a visitor. A visitor who came here to learn, to serve, to make a contribution, and leave the physical world, hopefully, a better place than it was – and to especially complete on their pre-life plan. Now there is self-acceptance, he or she can joyfully participate in the world knowing they will be returning back to their true homeland. Going home conjures powerful feelings. It turns out it was all so simple, beautifully clear and complete from the start – well, it seems that way, for now.

Pisces is often associated with death rather than a letting go and return. What is often missed by our human condition and upbringing in our developing stages of life is that it is at the Scorpio phase where we begin to die. Dying is a physical, emotional thing. Pisces is about returning home, not dying. Some of us don't get past the dying phase into the transpersonal. We stop the adventure at Scorpio – too fearful to carry on or too blind to see there was further to go on the journey.

Pisces in the ordinary sense is the place of dreams, of escapes, of solitude and isolation. And also, it is a place of confusion and uncertainty – especially if one hasn't prepared for it. It is the ocean of dreams. It is the final phase in our current adventure. We may approach the coming transformation with sadness, with fear or with joy. Many of us, of course, may enter this phase living in a care home or receiving end of life palliative care. Usually this is accompanied by our body getting into increasingly poor shape and needing more attention. That said, it can be a remarkably peaceful experience (especially with receiving end of life care) that allows us time to reflect on where we have been and where we might be going to next.

For some of us this will be an easy letting go and surrendering to the ending of our current adventure. We have discovered the illusion of life and death; and everything is becoming as it should be. We surrender and embrace the experience. Leaving the world, we are going beyond the conditions of Time and Space, and returning home.

But so much depends upon what we have come to believe about death in how we handle this phase. We have to trust in what we discovered as greater than ourselves. If, on the contrary, we believe this is it, this is my swan song and death is final; this viewpoint may have been comparatively easy to subscribe to when we were in our prime, and our journey ahead looked to be a long one. Now it could be more challenging to face our demise while holding to this view of death.

## Shades of Pascal's Wager

For most of us, we live in a land of belief regarding the matter of life after death. I say most of us because there are some of us who would claim to have had direct experience of death and returned to physical life – and who don't buy their experience as being simply the outcome of chemicals or a dying brain.

So, given for most of us this wisdom is based upon what we believe, I argue it is better to believe in there being life after death, than to believe death is final.

In my book, **Life and Death: Making Sense of It**[4] (under Shades of Pascal's Wager in reference to the philosopher Blaise Pascal and his wager on believing in God) I made a logical argument for belief in the afterlife being better than not believing in it – and I discussed it as follows:

*To help lay out the logic of what we know, don't know, and/or believe, in this dialogue, I'm going to use two people:* Person A is a disbeliever in the afterlife. Person B is a believer in the afterlife. From what both sides of this debate can anticipate, or agree on, the following arguments can be made:

- **Physical death**: Both Person A and Person B will go through physical death regardless of what they believe.
- **What they believe going into death**: Person A will go to their death believing there is nothing on the other side. Life ends at that point. Person B, on the other hand, will go to their death believing that there is an afterlife; that something transformative will happen to them. Person A believes death is the end of everything and that by deduction life ultimately has no meaning, other than what meaning they give to it, through being alive. Person B meanwhile believes in something that is ongoing. Person B sees life as meaningful and spiritual in essence.
- **Consequences of their beliefs**: No matter who is right, one outcome of this scenario is that Person B's belief gives cause for them to be less fearful and less stressed over their eventual death than Person A. Person A can only view his/her life as finite – what's left in physical years from where they are now – whereas Person B is less restricted and can choose to view their life as ongoing and indeed infinite.
- **In actuality**: In the actuality of the event, if there is nothing on the other side of death then the beliefs of either party are of little consequence, as neither Person A or Person B will be in a position to comment or care about it. If, on the other hand, there is an afterlife, Person B is likely to be better prepared to accept they have passed out of their physical body and are now in new circumstances – the circumstances they believed would happen. By comparison, Person A is now experiencing something they didn't expect. It could be a nice surprise but given they have carried their disbelief with them, they will probably be in denial that they have actually died, and therefore are now in danger of becoming stuck in a confusing limbo situation with no immediate resolve.

*Given this scenario, one is now asked to consider which of the two options it is better to believe in. Which subscribes to the more optimistic or favourable belief about life and death, and which the more pessimistic? Indeed, placing the eventuality of death in context, which belief best supports one having a joyful and a happier life in the here and now? Is it Person A or Person B? To my mind this is a no-brainer...*

And besides, this is a cycle, and going through the phase of Pisces can only lead back to Aries... So, do we eventually return for our next adventure? I believe we do, unless we are done with the need for it, or decide to go elsewhere.

## Aries phase – new cycle:

Here we are like The Fool of the tarot cards. We are starting out, naïve and innocent. This is the phase of involution; the decision and act of entering a new beginning, to become a new arrival.

# Part 3

# Self-reflection/self-development

Something else to think on... Contemplate these twelve areas (drawn from the houses of astrology) to focus on; to help you form and ask questions of yourself; and work from the answers you give:

1. Your persona | identity | your authentic self.
   How you like/love yourself?

2. Your attitude to security | material things | money.
   Are you able to attract what you need?

3. Your education | interests | contacts.
   How are these a reflection of yourself?

4. Your family background | parents/siblings/other relatives | moral compass | cultural influences.
   How have these influenced the value/s you put on yourself.

5. Your pleasures/fun and challenges – where/how you compete with others | your talents, what you are good at – or desire to be good at.

How have these further influenced and confirmed the value/s you put on yourself.

6. Your health, fitness, work, business | how you serve your community. How are you at looking after yourself and keeping well?

7. Your relationships outside of immediate family | friends and lovers | the people you surround yourself with.
   What are they telling you about yourself and where you are heading?

8. How do you look on/deal with difficult life experience, setbacks, loss, death (of those around you)? What does your own mortality mean to you? How are you?

9. Where are you at with your dreams and desires, experience of travel abroad, with languages and further education? What is it all leading you towards? What are your worldly/cultural interests? What is your system of belief, your religion?

10. Your (business) ambitions and life goals, what are these and where do you want to be in x years? What are your political motivations and interests? What is your relationship with Time?

11. Your involvement in humanitarian issues | society | social networks | clubs | groups | movements.
    What do you accept or reject of your culture?

12. What is your spiritual purpose? Do you follow any spiritual practices? What kind of arts and music do you enjoy? Where do you go to be by yourself, to get away from it all? What are you doing to refine yourself?

# Part 4

# The Nodes of the Moon

What they are and what they mean in your birth-chart...

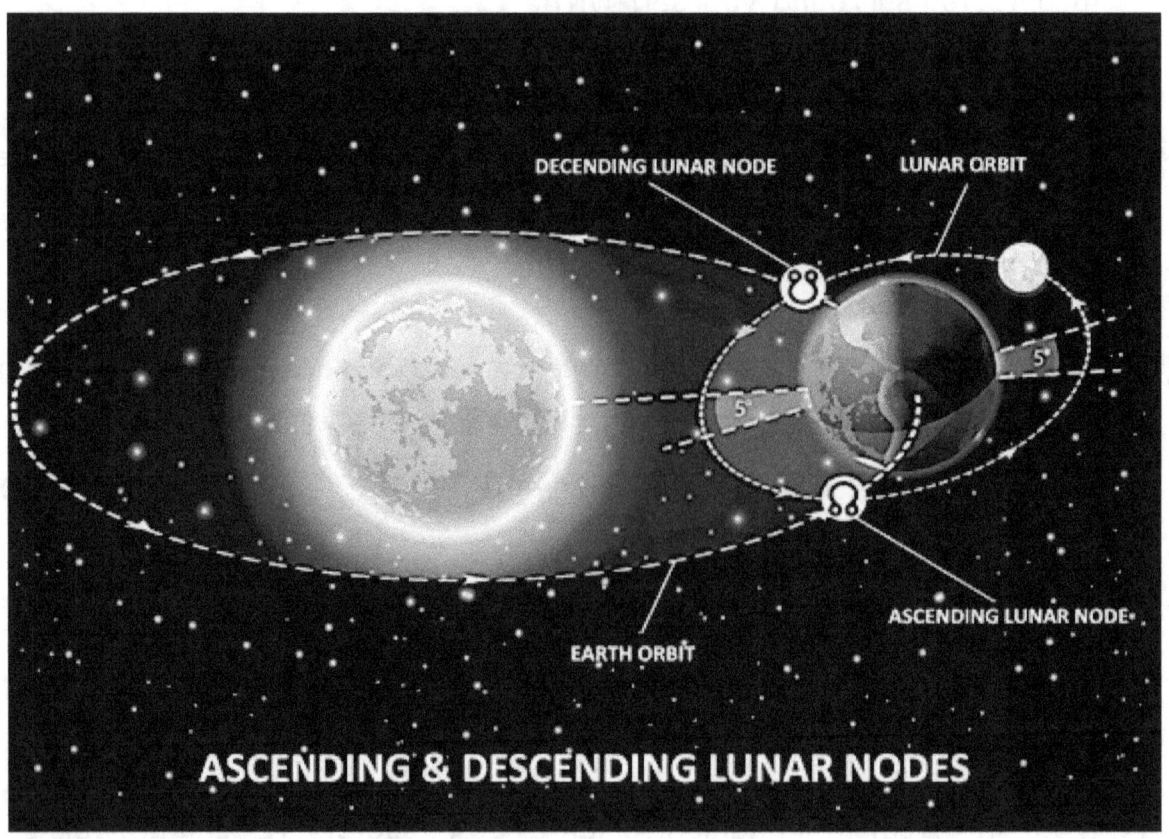

Fig.67

## Astronomically

Astronomically, all planets cross the ecliptic, the path the Earth takes around the Sun. They create nodal points when crossing south or north.

The Moon's prominence with its proximity to the Earth makes its nodes of particular interest to astrologers.

The nodes of the Moon (Fig.67) are thus created as the Moon crosses the ecliptic, in its path around the Earth. The Moon is inclined to the ecliptic by a few degrees – just under 5 degrees.

The north (ascending) node ☊ represents the Moon crossing the ecliptic from south to north. The south (descending) node ☋ meanwhile, represents the opposite – where the Moon crosses the ecliptic heading south.

The crossing points themselves are also moving along the ecliptic. They move slowly, mostly in a retrograde motion; that is, going backwards along the ecliptic, and thereby through each of the zodiac signs clockwise. One whole Moon node cycle takes just under 19 years to complete.

# Astrologically

In astrology the Moon nodes will be found opposite one another in the birth-chart. That said, often the south node will be left out of the chart – but its position easily worked out from the north node.

The Moon nodes are used in both Western and Vedic astrology. In Western astrology the north node represents the dragons head – and opposite the tail. In Vedic astrology the nodes are treated as like planets – Rahu (north) and Ketu (south)

> The traditional view in both Western and Oriental astrology is that the north node is benefic; and the south node malefic, although in modern Hindu astrology the tendency is to regard both nodes as malefic.[5]

In Western astrology the nodes have become linked to associations, alliances, and relationships whether beneficial or not so.

I'm one of many astrologers who, looking for a more profound insight into the nodes, took nourishment from the work of Martin Schulman – with his Karmic Astrology book;

*The Moon's Nodes and Reincarnation.*[6] You might find it helpful to get a copy of this book.

In essence this perspective holds that the south node links to our past experience, past live/s, our karmic baggage. It's a direction that can be very appealing to us, in this life, because we have been there and done it before – in previous existence/s. It's where we can feel comfortable, where we could happily spend our current life too – and where a lot of us most probably do or endeavour to do so, and fairly, we do so unconsciously.

The north node represents the way forward to new experience and learning – that we now need. It is arguably, our way out of the karmic situation we are in – helping us get us off the Wheel of Samsara, in theory at least.

What is important to make clear in this is that, like any planet in your chart, the node positions should not be read in isolation. You need to consider it like this:

You are working with your whole chart, learning to move your energies in the direction of your north node.

In the example here (Fig.68); for Abraham Lincoln, it is what the Moon node in Scorpio 8th house represented; in context with his whole chart.

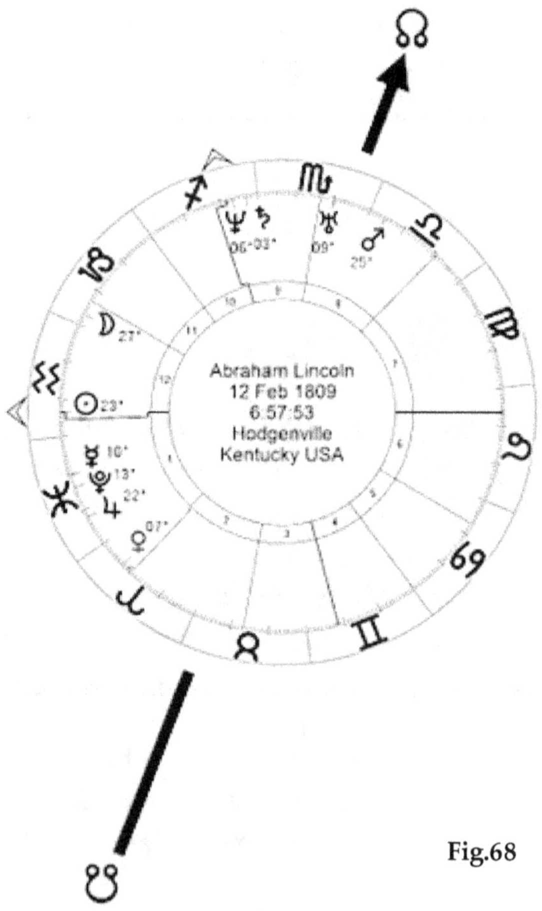

> I am not bound to win, but I am bound to be true. I am not bound to succeed, but I am bound to live by the light that I have. I must stand with anybody that stands right, and stand with him while he is right, and part with him when he goes wrong.   Abraham Lincoln

Fig.68

This also means that the simple cookbook descriptions that follow can only be used as a guide to how you need to work with your Moon nodes.

# Moon nodes through the Signs and Houses

From a spiritual learning perspective...

## North node in Aries and/or 1st House
## South node in Libra and/or 7th House

**Past**: South node in Libra and/or 7th house, suggests a strong tendency in your past to be tied up in your relationships – harmonious or otherwise. How you got on with people was important to you and to this end you were inclined to compromise your own needs for the sake of being liked by others.

You became dependent on others for their opinion and guidance. This influenced how you saw yourself and the decisions you made in your direction in life. It suggests you had a tendency to sit on the fence a bit too much while letting others take the lead on your behalf. Following, in this way, meant you could stay in your comfort zone and avoid responsibility for when things didn't work out.

**Now**: Your learning now requires you to strike out for yourself. To live by your own decisions and mistakes. The focus is on becoming self-reliant, self-sufficient, discovering yourself, building up your ego, being decisive and cutting your own path through life. Your relationships will blossom through balancing your personal needs with having consideration for others. But now you are required to take more of a leadership role in such exchanges – at least be equal – or indeed be independent and go it alone.

Drifting back into your old ways of letting others direct your life is likely to lead you into more difficulty. Until you get this right, you may indeed find difficulty in forming relationships, still finding dominating partners attempting to force your hand.

# North node in Taurus and/or 2nd House
# South node in Scorpio and/or 8th House

**Past**: With your South node in Scorpio, and/or 8th house, it suggests you have been involved in, or experienced, some of the more intense elements of life, challenging and deeply emotional times, possibly living in difficult circumstances, testing relationships. Perhaps you lived in fear of losing control over your life; or fear of getting hurt (perhaps you did get hurt); or you were the one doing the hurting in some form or another – involved in criminal behaviour. This represents a strong theme around putting the darkness behind you and wanting to be back in control of your situation.

**Now**: Your way forward now involves finding peace through building stability and grounding yourself. It involves leading a simpler and quieter life, than you have led up to now. It involves cultivating a sense of self-worth. It is possible that you were financially poor in your previous experience and now need to be comfortable with the resources you have.

You'll need to find peaceful solutions in any personal power struggles, or emotionally intense circumstances – in which you will probably still find yourself attracting and getting embroiled with. It is what you are likely to be used to. It can provide you with an odd sense of familiarity and comfort – so be careful regarding where it might lead.

# North node in Gemini and/or 3rd House
# South node in Sagittarius and/or 9th House

**Past**: Your south node in Sagittarius, and/or 9th house, suggests you were a risk-taker, you loved your freedom and you gained much experience from travel and exploration of other cultures. You expanded your horizons, developed a world view, probably held strong beliefs. You probably took a self-righteous moral high ground in your interactions with others – you knew best. Your beliefs were probably not always based on evidence or facts. And whether reliable or not, you kept a lot of the experience and wisdom you gained to yourself – never giving a thought of how you may help others through the experience and knowledge you gained.

**Now**: In this life your tendency is to follow a similar path. A yearning for exploration, and going off on distant travels, whether physically, intellectually or metaphysically. And you can, if you have time; curiosity is encouraged.

The difference is that now you are required to communicate/share what you know, share your experience and knowledge. And to do this you need your knowledge to be sound. You also need to learn to listen to the needs of others; find ways of helping others to understand what it is that you want them to know. Heading into delivering education, in one form or another, is now an obvious direction for your travels.

## North node in Cancer and/or 4th House
## South node in Capricorn and/or 10th House

**Past**: With your south node in Capricorn, and/or 10th house, you probably were a self-disciplined, organised and controlling person. You were focused in on your responsibilities and ambitions. Managing your affairs well and being successful was a priority. You needed to be in control, an authority on matters. Your business was probably more important to you than anything else. In doing so you became out of touch with your feelings, out of touch with any sense of belonging and the needs of others who were close to you, under you, or, in some way, in your care. You were no fun to be with.

**Now**: Now you need to bring your discipline and sobriety into a more caring atmosphere. You need to round off some of the sharp intellectual edges and be in touch with how you feel.

You need now to focus on your emotional security; to be at-home in yourself, and with others around you. You need to allow yourself to be vulnerable and dependent on others. It can be cold up there climbing mountains by yourself. Ambition needs to be tempered and balanced with a sense of belonging, with roots and family. Taking this journey will provide an enormous boost to your confidence and well-being.

# North node in Leo and/or 5th House
# South node in Aquarius and/or 11th House

**Past**: With your south node in Aquarius, and/or 11th house, the suggestion is that in your past you were a groupie. Well, no, not necessarily, but collective involvement in movement/s or group/s; being absorbed in societal matters and concerns that you felt strongly about, are likely to have been an important part of your life. This nodal position also suggests you were independent and radical in your thinking.

But you were more a follower than a leader – happy to keep a low profile as one of the gang let's say. Probably your relationships were friendly less personal, and they or you suffered as a result.

**Now**: Now you are being encouraged to bring your experiences forward, lift your confidence and optimism; and express yourself, strike out as an individual – and worry less about what others think of you – as long as they think you are a winner.

You need now to be more creative, more adventurous, more competitive, more noticeable, more of a risk-taker, and somewhat more conventional and personal in expression. You need to make your mark. It is not always fun being just a team player, no matter how radical and rebellious the activities are. Consider that it's time to learn to be a child at heart again – and get noticed when you achieve something.

# North node in Virgo and/or 6th House
# South node in Pisces and/or 12th House

**Past**: Having your south node in Pisces, and/or 12th house, would imply that in your past you were a dreamer. You probably sought solitude and escape from some of the harsh realities of life. You probably avoided dealing with the messy details of life. But then, you were probably involved in finding yourself through spiritual practice that helped you to refine your lifestyle, wants and desires. And this probably took you to the point of self-sacrifice, self-abnegation.

This is fine as long as you are not being hoodwinked into giving too much of yourself to others - who may not have valued or deserved your sacrifice. Chances are you became a bit of a lost soul, living a life of disappointment and possible loneliness.

**Now**: Now you need to retain a spiritual direction, compassion and sense of service, but seek refinement through the better nourishing and earthing of yourself – you need to retain good health to make progress. You are now dealing with the nuts and bolts of life and need to become more streetwise in your endeavours and goals.

It is important to learn to be more practical, orderly and organised. Particularly, you need to become more discerning, and knowing where your boundaries are. You must learn to develop a more all-round healthy and earthy lifestyle, perhaps be involved in some kind of community service, but meanwhile become no-one's fool. Then, being earthed, pursue your dreams or quest, from a more organised and stable position.

## North node in Libra and/or 7th House
## South node in Aries and/or 1st House

**Past**: Aries, and/or 1st house, south node suggests a past where you did your own thing, took the initiative and worked independently. You were probably a bit of a hot-head, impatient, controlling, argumentative, insensitive to others, inclined to be restless, impulsive and self-centred – probably riding roughshod over anyone in your way.

Your impulsiveness probably led you into making all sorts of mistakes and errors that you then had to redo and fix – and maybe some were too big to fix.

**Now**: "No one is island" is the lesson you need to learn to achieve balance. You need to bring all that optimism, energy and drive into your relationships – where others count in your life in equal partnership/s. Now compromise is a keynote.

You need to learn to get on with people, be friendly and kind. If we liken your situation to driving a motorcycle or car; you can no longer simply drive solo but now you have your passenger/s to consider in any decision going forward. So, temper your fire and haste, and learn to generate harmonious accord with those around you. Be able to put yourself in the position of the other person's shoes, and learn to be cooperative. This is what is now needed for success.

## North node in Scorpio and/or 8th House
## South node in Taurus and/or 2nd House

**Past**: Your south node in Taurus, and/or 2nd house, suggests you were good at nourishing yourself and having all the material things you needed to make your life comfortable.

But you were also too preoccupied with accumulating your own physical wants and needs, with looking after your own security, to notice how selfish you had become, and set-in-your-ways, ploughing your own furrow. You were too stubborn and entrenched in what had become an over-simplistic and narrow view of the world, to take stock of the needs (and difficulties) others were facing around you; with your partner/s and friends, indeed with the world at large.

There is an "I'm alright Jack" theme to this, that you could still find very attractive.

**Now**: There is more to life than the accumulation of wealth or material things. Investing in the physical world has its limitations. You need to move on, gain a clearer picture of who you are and what you are involved in. This is your opportunity to burn bridges, deal with truths about yourself, exorcise some of the demons you are carrying, and experience the cathartic cleansing power of being in touch with how you feel.

Be true to yourself. You need to deal with what you may have suppressed, and dramatically so - in love, in pain, in joy and anger, and in loss. This is a kind of death, a tough node to deal with, but if you can weather the storm, you will come out of it refreshed, more alive and at peace within – and ready to move on.

# North node in Sagittarius and/or 9th House
# South node in Gemini and/or 3rd House

**Past**: Your south node in Gemini, and/or 3rd house, suggests that in your past you were full of facts, a sharing soul but probably restless, opinionated, superficial, a bit of a flutter-by. You probably had a lot to say though much of it could be gossip, tittle-tattle or information that wasn't always complete, thought through, nor the consequences of sharing it considered properly.

The tendency was for you to stay in your local area, with what we could generally call local knowledge. You didn't look into matters too deeply. You probably didn't travel any great distance and/or rarely, if ever, did you consider any bigger picture to what grabbed your interest.

**Now**: Now, your north node implies that you need to bring your enthusiasm for being-in-the-know to dig deeper and expand your life experience much wider. You need to broaden your mind in other words, to become more philosophical with your ideas and come to know deeply what you believe to be true. To be more worldly-wise. You achieve this through activities such as reading, writing, study and travel to distance places.

Now you are expected to round out any subject that is dear to you – not just be skipping over the surface of it; and being happy with a few facts that you can gossip about. All this contributes to you now developing faith in yourself – and respect from others.

# North node in Capricorn and/or 10th House
# South node in Cancer and/or 4th House

**Past**: This south node in Cancer, and/or 4th house, suggests that, in your past, you were a homely sort of person who focused more on your family (whatever your role in it) than your own development and ambitions. You probably held a low profile, passive and sentimental view of life; indulging in the past and childhood. You sought a quiet and secure life with no great expectations of yourself – or if you did have dreams, that might bear fruit, it was for, or through others, than for yourself.

**Now**: Now you are encouraged to come out of your shell. Hold onto your caring nature but be responsible and ambitious with it. You need to plan ahead; build up your confidence, bring more structure and security into your life – invest in your talents, in who you are. Now you need to take a lead, and seek out long term goals.

It is a mountain that you need now to climb – in whatever that means for you – but make it a mountain worth climbing; and make it a goal that you give something back to those who have helped you to climb it.

# North node in Aquarius and/or 11<sup>th</sup> House
# South node in Leo and/or 5<sup>th</sup> House

**Past**: Your Leo, and/or 5<sup>th</sup> house, south node suggests that you were all about you. You were a proud and egocentric person. You were likely very competitive and had to win – probably at all costs. You saw the world as revolving around you, with your wants and needs. You were probably seen as childish and a bit of a narcissist by those who knew you. You sought the limelight a bit more than you should. That said you were also a creative and optimistic person who could be fun and generous.

**Now**: Now you need to bring your strength, optimism, competitive leadership qualities and prowess to bear on the needs of others – to be the bigger person in a kindly way. You need to build on relationships that are based upon true friendships, freedom and equality. You need to be confident enough, in yourself, to take a lower profile in your dealings with your world. You will probably be encouraged to get involved in society in some radical and emancipating way – in a way that helps to bring about social change.

Now your support of such a cause, or causes, will help to lift the lives of people, that in turn helps to contribute to lifting of the human spirit. It is an honourable direction of travel.

# North node in Pisces and/or 12th House
# South node in Virgo and/or 6th House

**Past**: Your Virgo, and/or 6th house, south node suggests you were concerned with your welfare and keeping the wheels of your ordinary day-to-day existence turning efficiently. Your security depended upon it. You were probably a worrier and a perfectionist to boot, who enjoyed routine and focusing in on the detail and small things in life. This is how you kept in control over your life.

But you were also overly narrow and materialistic in your worldview. You probably looked after your health and well-being but had little time for entertaining a more spiritual perspective on life – or for that matter, a spiritual practice.

**Now**: Now you are faced with needing to explore these bigger concerns. This is about the healing of your inner self. You need to learn to go with the flow, love yourself and trust in your higher self to know the way. The focus now is on refining your spiritual situation most probably through a spiritual practice/s. You are learning to be more compassionate and to link with a greater understanding and the greater collective.

And more; this Pisces north node (and/or 12th house) suggests at some level your learning probably involves some form of service in the healing of others.

## References

[1] Wikipedia on Ensoulment. https://en.wikipedia.org/wiki/Ensoulment [Accessed 15/10/2023]

[2] This parental encouragement wasn't entirely true for myself. I was the only (and eldest) boy in a family of four children. My father was a merchant seaman, away for long chunks of time, and my mother worked hard to make ends meet at home. She made sure we were all cared for. She worked her socks off. Our parents certainly loved us and wanted the best for us. Even so I only ever had passing conversations with my mother, regarding where I was taking my life. And away for long stretches, my father didn't really feature in the discussion. I nearly followed in his footsteps. But I left school at 15, on a Friday and began work, in a small engineering factory, on the following Monday. Thus began my life as an adult. It was only later that I pursued my education proper. That I walked away from my Catholic faith, in my early teens, was probably a bigger concern for my family (certainly my father)

than where I was heading. But every cloud has a silver lining and, looking back, I consider their leaving me, effectively, to my own devices was a part of what I now know as my potential energy, represented in my chart, being given expression – or what I was attracting. Yes, it is working whether we are conscious of it or not. It was natural that I had to find my own way, that eventually, after many turns, took me to exploring the "fringes," astrology and spirituality.

[3] O'Neill F. (2016) Life and Death: Making Sense of It; Some Inspiration Publications.

[4] Ibid.

[5] Brau JL, Weaver H, Edmands A (1977) Larousse Encyclopedia of Astrology, P204, McGraw-Hill Book Company.

[6] Schulman M. (1978) The Moon's Nodes and Reincarnation. Samuel Weiser Inc.

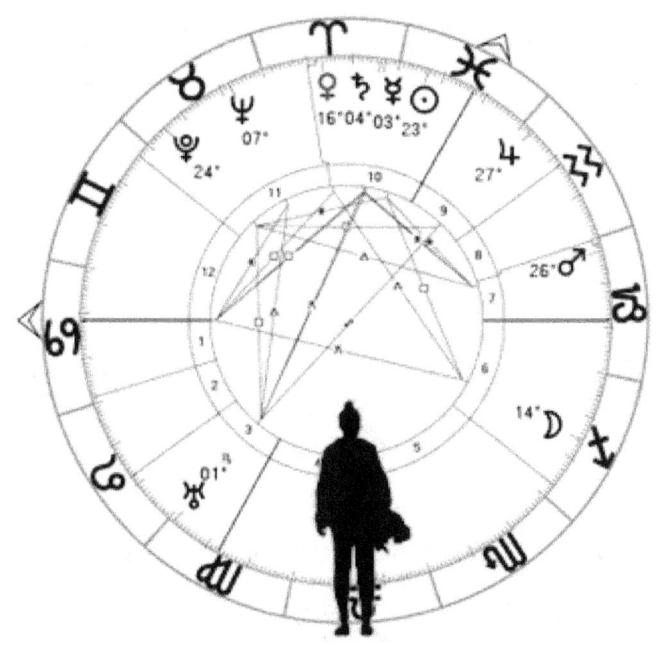

# The Resources

# The Zodiac Signs Resource

**The Zodiac Signs Resource is linked to Step Two of the course.**

I'm trusting you'll find the following resource – self-explanatory. Each sign is listed with its matrix, a brief description, its theme, what it links with, additional keywords and symbol.

The whole is to help you gain insider knowledge of what each sign stands for. More importantly, to help you to develop your own impression and interpretation, especially in how each may apply especially to you.

## Aries ♈ – The Ram

Cardinal | Fire | Positive

Aries in our birth-chart is where we seek to initiate new experience objectively, urgently.

### Its theme is:

Beginnings, initiating something new, starting a new and vital round of experience.

# Links with:

Starting a new cycle; Spring being sprung; the beginning of things; that first onrush of energy; the inauguration of personal action; direct experiencing of one's environment; the emergence of life upon a new cycle of Earth existence; being born; going head first into things; projecting out; taking the plunge into the unknown; optimism going forward based upon naivety, inexperience; attracting "beginner's luck;" the instinctual, the fiery, the urgent, charging ahead; action with force, instinct and innocence.

# Some keywords linked to Aries

Get-there-first-ness, get it done-ness, urgency, energetic action, haste, initiative, spontaneity, pioneering-ness, love of adventure, the spirit of enterprise, courage, risk-taking, self-sufficiency, doing things head first, wanting quick results, self-assertive, doesn't bear a grudge.

**Or**: Impatience, impulsiveness, me-first, selfish action, aggression, hot tempered, forcing issues, "I want it now," argumentative, insensitive to others, pushy, acting without thinking, too quick to be thorough, restless.

# Symbol

Note: The following images representing the zodiac signs are taken from a German Mediaeval Woodcut. The original block of images is courtesy of Wikimedia. The shorthand icon for each sign is what is normally used.

This sign is symbolised by the ram. It has a tendency to head-butt anything in its path. Being head-first, head-strong is aptly associated with Aries. This is the energy required to move forward, to be born into the world.

# Taurus ♉ – The Bull

## Fixed | Earth | Negative

Taurus in our birth-chart is where we seek to structure and stabilise experience - be productive, be secure and enduring.

## Its theme is:

Settling, founding, becoming manifest, tangible and structured. Being earthed.

## Links with:

Nature, natural order, rhythm, pace, cycles; the creation of things and form; beauty and sensuality; stabilising, strengthening and preserving what one has; being peaceful and slow moving, a browsing approach; being resistant to change; becoming anchored, grounded, stable and secure; owning, maintenance and conservation of resources; being robust, steady and powerful; being nourished and natural; seeking the quiet life; giving stability to personal life experience through a structuring and resting on secure, practical and reliable foundations - earthing oneself; establishing material and fundamental needs.

## Some keywords linked to Taurus

Perseverance, consolidation, self-maintenance, resourcefulness, robustness, vigour, strength, endurance, being industrious, conservation, gathering-together-ness, construction, assembly, reliable, sure, stable, earthy, earthing oneself, being sensual, creative, careful, unmovable, "Making things simple uncomplicated," actualising in physical reality, the physical body, the builder.

**Or:** obstinate, resisting change, slow, sluggish, inclined to hoard, inflexible, sticks rigidly to routines, possessive.

## Symbol

Like the bull that symbolises this sign, the Taurean is peace loving and will like to take their time. They do not easily lose their temper, but watch out if they are driven to do so!

# Gemini ♊ – The Twins

Mutable | Air | Positive

Gemini in our birth-chart is where we seek to "know" and share through direct experience or acquired information.

## Its theme is:

Finding out, exploring, gathering, knowing and communicating what is known.

## Links with:

Making connections, contacts, studying, discovering and communicating; developing a mental picture of one's place in the world; becoming adaptive and versatile; making quick mental adjustments through experience; building local knowledge; getting around, knowing one's immediate circumstances through curiosity and travel; the excitement of finding something out; the security that comes through being "in the know;" sharing one's knowledge with others; the immediate and external as a mirror of oneself;

## Some keywords linked to Gemini

Mobility, versatility, curiosity, inquisitiveness, transference; adaptability, being communicative, eloquent, being changeable, sprightly, nimble, informative, go-between, retrieving information, obliging manner.

**Or:** "fingers in every pie," restlessness, talkative, gossipy, superficial, shallow, skips over the surface of things, the trickster, being "two faced," spreading oneself too thinly.

## Symbol

This sign is associated with the twins - one of three humanised signs in the zodiac. This indicates both the humanity and (asexual) duality of the Gemini nature. It may also symbolise a kind of telepathic knowing, that identical twins often share - or a nose for sensing things.

# Cancer ♋ – The Crab

Cardinal | Water | Negative

Cancer in our birth-chart is where we seek to familiarise and be "at-home" within our experience.

## Its theme is:

Becoming at-home within the familiar - being emotionally rooted, in touch with the rhythm of life/nature.

# Links with:

Seeking, establishing and defending one's emotional security; establishing one's roots, one's base, one's home – being emotionally rooted; nurturing emotional ties with one's environment, home, family, relatives, things; being and feeling "at-home" with oneself and environment; developing a sense of belonging (at a gut level); forming links with the past, one's history and hereditary background; seeking familiarity with the immediate environment as an extension of oneself.

# Some keywords linked to Cancer:

Protectiveness, caring, devotion, nurturing, containing-ness, need for familiarity, parental home, concern for background, heritage, roots, nostalgia, (old) memories, habit patterns, vulnerability, sensitivity, receptivity, the inner world of childhood/parenthood, family and cultural codes of conduct, where one feels safe, established traditions, customs, rituals, institutions, "home is where the heart is."

**Or:** clinginess, withdrawal, turning inward-ness, sentimental longing for the past, overly sensitive, defensive, clannishness, timidity.

# Symbol

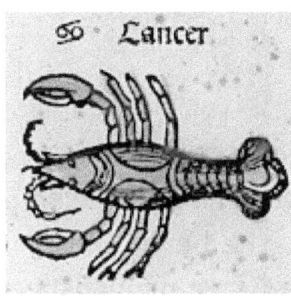

The crab is associated with this water sign for a number of reasons: The crab is territorial, as is the Cancerian. Its hard outer shell helps to protect its inner softness or vulnerability. If the crab is challenged it moves sideways, rather than face things directly. If threatened the crab will of course defend itself – and if it gets its claws into you, you will know about it.

# Leo ♌ – The Lion

## Fixed | Fire | Positive

Leo in our birth-chart is where we seek to express ourself powerfully within and through life experience.

## Its theme is:

Expressing (childlike) trust, confidence and power, through challenges and display of prowess.

## Links with:

Embracing the world outside one's parental home and how we measure up to it; developing and maintaining a childlike trust in one's own prowess to tackle challenges; the world of heroes, heroines, play and adventures; becoming a worthy competitor and champion; self-abundance, self-involvement; being a roaring lion, king of the jungle, regal, proud, powerful, dangerous, competitive; the promotion of oneself; the desire to be noticed, appreciated and applauded; self-display, self-confidence, enthusiasm; the sustained expression of creative potential.

## Some keywords linked to Leo

Generosity, magnanimity, displays big-hearted-ness, grandiosity, big gestures, life as a game, fun, play, adventure, drama, "centre of stage," performance, assuming leadership, natural magnetism, charisma, pride, self-confidence, self-reliance, the hero, chivalry, energetic, enthusiastic, assertive, powerful, competitive, outspoken, love of pleasure.

**Or:** limelight seeker, exhibitionist, vane, domineering, autocratic, conceited, ostentatious, inclined to be arrogant.

## Symbol

The lion, of course, the king of the jungle, is associated with Leo. This big cat literally eats other animals for breakfast. It is equally an attractive loveable animal with enormous strength. It has a regal air about it and assumes a position of power. We know not to mess with the lion...

# Virgo ♍ – The Virgin

Mutable | Earth | Negative

Virgo in our birth-chart is where, or how, we seek to prepare and participate within our community.

## Its theme is:

Adjusting to a growing interdependence and need for exchange with and within one's community.

## Links with:

Adjusting to the needs of others; the desire to be of service, to make a contribution, within one's community and be integrated as an interdependent part of that whole – adapting to a work ethic; recognising and empathising with the vulnerabilities and needs of others; purity, nourishment and cleanliness combined; service and rewards for hard work; seeking an ordering of body, mind and motive; concerns with duty, health and efficiency; a shift in one's maturing process to becoming a community member – involving versatility, study, hard work and attention to detail.

## Some keywords linked to Virgo

Diligence, care, domesticity, tidiness, health and hygiene concerns, systematic, methodical, analytical, cautious, prudent, pure, critical, discerning, comparing information, concern for "nuts and bolts" of life, "taking care of the pennies (the small things) so the pounds (the bigger things) look after themselves," watchful, concern for detail, humble, efficient, liking routine, practical, measures life by facts and logic, precision-oriented, reserved, conventional, fastidious, diet-conscious.

**Or:** worrying, servile, overly modest, overly critical, cynical, fussy, fears around health.

## Symbol

This sign is represented by the virgin usually holding an ear of wheat – representing the harvest. This is the maiden, perfection itself, beautiful, untouched, pure at heart and fertile. It is an ideal state prior to forming more intimate relationships – as indicated in Libra and Scorpio.

# Libra ♎ – The Scales

## Cardinal | Air | Positive

Libra in our birth-chart is where we communicate through attraction towards our world, others and ourselves; where we seek to establish balance and harmony in relation to others and our world.

## Its theme is:

Balancing, levelling up, evaluating, attraction and equality in relating to others and world.

## Links with:

Falling in love; going beyond parental/sibling/family level of familiarity in relationships; bringing balance to relationships; weighing things, judging, getting things into proportion; decisions being made on consideration and compromise; establishing equality, fairness, and co-operation with others; attraction, communications and social interaction as a basis for forming close ties with others (and/or environment); developing a balanced, appreciative and harmonious relationship between self, others and the external world; seeing life from another's viewpoint – being able to be in another person's shoes; appreciating and idealising form and beauty.

## Some keywords linked to Libra

Diplomacy, being tactful, sociable, kind, friendly, evaluating others, negotiating, seeking fair play, "seeing both sides of the coin," compromise, the peacemaker, public spirited, communal sense, being romantic, likes and dislikes, ever seeking "peace and harmony," charming, idealistic.

**Or:** indecision, "sitting on the fence," too easy-going, lazy, preoccupation with being nice not rocking the boat, being judgemental, overly concerned with appearances, the superficial and one's personal image, vanity.

## Symbol

This sign is represented by the scales, keeping things in measured balance, bringing things back to balance. This typifies the Libran tendency to be seeking balance, but also their tendency to move out of balance from one extreme to the other; and then to endeavour to centre things again – back to balance. Note this sign is the balance-point between the north the subjective and personal and the south the objective and transpersonal signs – hence the scales.

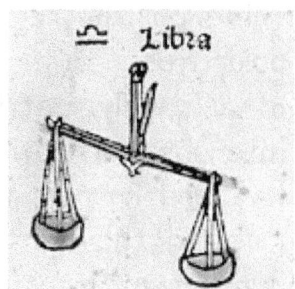

# Scorpio ♏ – The Scorpion & the Eagle

## Fixed | Water | Negative

Scorpio in our birth-chart is where we experience and face up to hidden realities behind the gloss. We face some truths about life – such as everything ages and passes away, such as nothing and no one prepared us for this... Life is darker and deeper than the bed of roses of Libra. Here we are dealing with powerful emotions, that can be dark.

## Its theme is:

Intimate partnerships, emotional and sexual entanglement; the baggage we carry; facing shadows – such as worries about the past, present and future.

## Links with:

Intimate partnerships, emotional entanglement and baggage; facing the shadows of one's past; struggle between the pull of the emotional/instinctual and physical, and the pull of the spiritual; which way to go, the scorpion or the eagle, the lows and highs of this sign; the rejuvenating forces of nature – rebirth; dealing with paradoxes and polarities – with life and death and renewal; all things shadowy, undercurrent, otherworldly; getting to the bottom of things, driving towards the truth; emotional intensity, unification or entanglements in relating; passions, strong likes and dislikes, love and hatred; intense, deep emotional and raw sexual involvement with others; meeting the light and darkness both within and external to oneself; crime and punishment; meeting with crises, awareness of, and facing death and destruction head on; benefits derived from hidden sources.

## Some keywords linked to Scorpio

Intensity in moods and relating, deep commitments, self-sacrifice, penetrating, passionate, tenacious, cool persistence, "getting to the bottom of things," detection, research, cutting, eliminating, ejection, destroying, "burning bridges," catharsis, "the shadow," undercurrents, possession, secretiveness, combative, discipline, centred in emotions.

**Or:** ruthless, rejection, destructive, violence, the underworld, jealousy, possessiveness, vendettas, resentments, fear, taboos, phobias, hatred, hidden danger, decay, self-conviction.

## Symbol

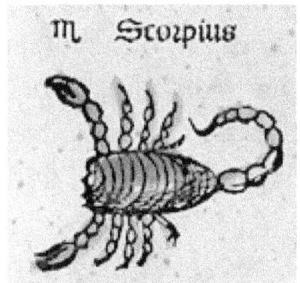

The duality aspect of the Scorpio nature can probably be best explained by the creatures (the scorpion and the less well-known eagle) that are associated with the sign. The scorpion is a predator creature that is earth-bound. It crawls around the ground, feeds on other insects, and other scorpions. As we know it has a venomous sting in its tail – a sting that comes from behind, like a knife in the back. The other creature, the eagle, is also a predator but not earth-bound, a creature of the air. It happily lives in remote mountainous areas. It soars to lofty heights. It has amazing eyesight for spotting its prey. Both creatures are dangerous but whereas one creature creeps and crawls the other uses its abilities to seek the (spiritual) heights, and has a clear vision of its territory.

# Sagittarius ♐ – The Centaur/Archer

## Mutable | Fire | Positive

Sagittarius in our birth-chart is where we seek to expand experience and rediscover our enthusiasm for life – in context with knowing more, and after facing the (maybe harsh) realities of Scorpio. Where we seek to express and renew our faith in the bounty of life.

## Its theme is:

Desire to expand on one's understanding, a development/broadening of belief and perspectives in relating to others and the world.

# Links with:

Freedom of the spirit to roam; targeting distant horizons and trusting in one's aim and direction being true; optimism in going forward; expanding one's experience and understanding through travel and higher learning; the search for deeper meaning to one's existence; a broadening out of belief and perspectives in relation to other people and world; seeking the bigger picture overall; developing belief and trust in benevolent forces greater than oneself; seeing oneself in context with the multiplicity and diversity of life forms - becoming part of a greater unifying whole; structuring, and giving intellectual voice to, a deeper philosophical or religious relationship with life; living by a moral compass derived from a perceived higher source.

# Some keywords linked to Sagittarius

Aspiration, travelling (external and internal), learning other cultures, philosophy, being philosophical, expansive, optimistic, frank, sincere, "straight and true," distance-oriented, reaching-out-ness, risk taking, speculative, free ranging, seeker of freedom, careful, projection, future oriented, "light at the end of the tunnel," religious fervour, jovial, benevolent, opportunity, versatile.

**Or:** opportunist, over-confidence, playboy, exaggerative, extravagant, boastful, brash, moralising, judgemental, dogmatism.

# Symbol

The centaur is the symbol adopted for this sign – and very apt too for insight into its meaning. Centaurs were believed to have existed at one time, but regardless they have a place in Greek mythology. This creature is part human and part horse. It carries a bow and arrow. The symbol suggests a being with intelligence and intention, built for speed that can move apace, across all kinds of terrain, and is directed towards a goal of its own creation. The centaur fires its arrow at a distant target, and then gallops in chase of the arrow. From finding the arrow it fires again, at a new distant target – and so the journey of discovery continues...

# Capricorn ♑ – The (Sea) Goat

## Cardinal | Earth | Negative

Capricorn in our birth-chart is where we face our mountain and achieve self-acceptance. Where we are challenged and experience resistance (particularly bounded by time) in gaining success in our world; in gaining our wisdom, freedom and maturity.

## Its theme is:

Reaching for, and achieving one's aims/goals within the limitations, and time constraints, of the physical and mental world.

## Links with:

The goat for its determination and climbing ability, or the sea-goat, a mythical creature, that is both at home on the mountains and in the sea – a creature that seeks to achieve the heights or can plumb the depths; knowing worldly boundaries through experience; seeing oneself in context with levels/hierarchical structures and systems; ambition and a "never give up" tenacity to succeed; establishing one's position, one's status in the world at large; increasing awareness of the limiting conditions of Earth life; the wheel of karma; awareness of the inner (soul) and outer (physical) mountain one climbs in conquering one's circumstances towards freedom; coming to terms with one's own limitations and boundaries; achieving self-acceptance and self-fulfilment; reaching maturity, patience, humility, wisdom.

## Some keywords linked to Capricorn

Responsibility, duty, self-discipline, serious attitude toward life, effort, hardship, ambition, aspiring, seeking perfection, achievement, reaching the summit, control, solidarity, construction, management, leadership, solitude, an untiring struggle for preservation, perseverance, toil, methodical, patience, humility, industrious, enduring, status-oriented, sober, reflective, strict adherence to rules, authoritative, establishment, rational, cautious, methodical.

**Or:** pride, status quo, controlling, authoritarian, unforgiving, frustrating, frustration, limitations, deliberate, severe, pessimism, anxiety over limits/personal prestige, aloofness, obstacles we create for ourselves that are blocking our path.

## Symbol

The symbol for Capricorn, the mountain goat, allows us insight into the extremes of Capricorn. The Capricorn theme suggests a mountain to climb. This should give us all the insight we need to anticipate why the ideal Capricorn will tend to be good at planning and organising around what they have to do. However, the ideal Capricorn will also tend to "set the bar" for themselves; or in other words they decide how steep or dangerous their mountain is. They can set their goals high and be very comfortable in the climb and in their achievements. Alternatively, they can be over-ambitious and fall short on their expectations – and the disappointment that follows can be especially hard for them to deal with.

Another (mythical) creature associated with Capricorn is the sea-goat – a goat with a fishtail. Here we are reminded that Capricorn is opposite Cancer, a water sign, with all the innermost feelings, mood and emotion that that can stir up. Symbolically a tree has its roots in Cancer and it blossoms with its highest branches in Capricorn. The two go hand in hand.

But Cancer also represents the past, a past we humans cannot really go back to. Here the sea-goat represents a need to transform from living in the sea to climbing out and living on dry land. The need is to disconnect from the past. We, as adults, the parent, the grandparent, are obliged to leave behind childhood (home, or womb), treat as a distant memory and enter into a bigger worldly arena involving responsibility, making mature decisions and succeeding – even in the knowledge of one's own mortality.

# Aquarius ♒ – The Water Bearer

## Fixed | Air | Positive

Aquarius in our birth-chart is where coming down off the mountain we have gained wisdom and a new sense of freedom. We seek something new, emancipating, innovative, that helps move us on from convention, tradition, old habits where they are outworn methods of operating and hindering progress. The focus now is also on helping others move on in some way. We seek to share our knowledge with the young at heart.

## Its theme is:

Going beyond limiting boundaries via new perspectives, new visions and creations. Gaining freedom from the past through innovation and social emancipation.

## Links with:

No longer animal but conscious being; change and freedom from the old, and moving into the new; radical reformation, the creative process; new technologies, new social movements, new breakthroughs, new boundaries created through arts and drama, human invention, holistic inventions; ideas/communications concerned with the emancipation of humanity from limiting structures, or established patterns that inhibit the creative expression of humanity; establishing an inner detachment from the limiting/conditioning factors of the world and self; revolutionising self to focus on one's community/world at large; regaining the inner child; developing a love for, and the emancipation of humanity.

## Some keywords linked to Aquarius

Innovatory, inventive, originality, sociable-ness, friends, egalitarian, humanitarianism, brotherhood, sisterhood, sciences, revolutionary freedom fighter, reform, the unusual, what is new, social media, intellectual, telepathy, powers of reasoning, independent, unconventional, eccentric, uniqueness, being different, non-conformist, impersonal, progressive, one in search of a cause, one with a mission, a visionary, adapting to new trends.

**Or:** liberation-at-all-costs, fanatical, reactionary, rebelliousness, extremist, shocking, dramatic, tactless, erratic, unpredictable, impractical, undervaluing personal friendships.

## Symbol

The symbol associated with Aquarius is the water bearer. It is one of three signs directly associated with humanity – the others being the twins of Gemini and the virgin of Virgo (both ruled by Mercury). The water bearer quenches the thirst of all-comers, without exception. Water is associated with the divine, with inspiration, with the transference of means to higher consciousness. Here the water bearer is helping to quench the human thirst for knowledge and understanding – helping move humanity ever forward towards consciousness, awakening.

# Pisces ♓ – The Fishes

## Mutable | Water | Negative

Pisces in our birth-chart is where we refine, where we seek or express unconditional love and compassion, where we seek perfection; where we need to let go of our human indoctrination, preconceived notions, constructs and conditioning; and even our physical form. We return to nature, to the ocean of dreams. This is where we may experience surrender to something greater than ourselves. The sign links to feet, and the need to keep a good foothold even when climbing inner mountains.

## Its theme is:

Transforming, completing, releasing, letting go, service and sacrifice.

# Links with:

Dreams and ideals – seeking perfection; expression through the arts – such music, theatre, painting – and healing arts; refining, completing, releasing, letting go, service and sacrifice; the giving up or surrendering of oneself in sacrifice and service to others or a greater whole or transcending ideal - identity with the whole of life, selflessness; emotionally volatile, intuitive, sensitive, psychic qualities; swimming in opposite directions – uncertainty in decision making, finding which way to go; highly adaptable, fluid, impressionable, transformational; unconditional love and compassion; returning to one's source, one's original mind; ridding the illusion of duality; now knowing/understanding the illusion; the dissolution of matter; dissolution before the beginning of a new cycle.

# Some further keywords linked to Pisces

Receptive, sensitive, impressionable, intuitive, other-worldly, transformative, subtle, fine, wispy, dreamy, illusion, fantasy, romantic, escapist, isolation, solitude, open spaces, the dissolution of barriers, being at-one, peace, images, ideals, meditation, psychic, mediumistic, visions, cosmic receiver, poetic.

Or: delusion, uncertainty, confusion, lacking confidence, victim, procrastination, lost soul, sorrows.

# Symbol

The symbol of Pisces is represented by two fishes, linked together by a cord, and swimming in opposite directions. It symbolises the watery, changeableness and uncertainty of the situation and direction that the typical Pisces is likely to experience. It is imperative that decisions are made and direction found – for personal protection as much as anything. This symbol, the fishes, is also linked to the story of Jesus. His life story, as handed down to us, is representative of the highest form of Piscean expression – with compassion and forgiveness being at its heart.

**Ends.**

# The Planets by Sign Resource

The Planets by Sign Resource is linked to Step Two and Step Three.

## The Inner Personal Planets

### ☉ Sun – Rules Leo

#### Represents

The power of self-integration; self-expression; one's essence, will and vitality; one's creative centre; the heart; the point from where one gives out and shines; where the light of the soul is focused; where one will tend to radiate from; the power source for this life.

#### By sign

> **Aries**: Assertive, enthusiastic, personal; likes to pioneer, take risks, be courageous, spark off ventures and do things one's "own way;" or can be inclined to be combative, forceful, selfish.
>
> **Taurus**: Practical, earthy and resourceful; wants to build things to last; keeps things simple at a steady structured pace; or can be possessive, stubborn, preoccupied with own interests.

**Gemini**: Detached, adaptable, versatile and communicative; seeks easily digestible information and ideas; hunter/gatherer and sharer; or can be inclined to spread oneself too thinly, be shallow, superficial, inconstant.

**Cancer**: Resourceful, contemplative, protective and sensitive; inclined to be reserved, territorial and traditional; open to mood swings; strong ties to the past; or can be inclined to be over-sensitive, overly-protective, shy and retiring.

**Leo (Ruler)**: Enthusiastic, playful, projecting self-assuredness; prefers to be at the centre of things or lead from the front; seeks challenges and to build up confidence; or can be overly proud, boastful and preoccupied with own self-importance.

**Virgo**: Efficient, methodical, moderate, adaptable, analytical, critical and prudent; keen on detail; often strong work/service ethic; or can be overly fussy, fastidious and inclined to worry.

**Libra**: Easy going, diplomatic, sociable and peace loving by nature; seeks to strike equality/balance in relationships and in the exchange of ideas – relative and idealistic; or can be over-idealistic; indecisive and lacking confidence.

**Scorpio**: Tenacious, analytical, critical, emotionally charged, intense and passionate; desire to reveal what is hidden – even the taboo; or can be inclined to brood on matters, be vindictive, hold vendettas.

**Sagittarius**: Free ranging, optimistic, pushes back boundaries, enlarges the picture, deepens experience; enjoys interaction and adventure; or can be inclined to be extravagant and rebellious in nature.

**Capricorn**: Practical, reserved, responsible and serious; a realist, aware of limits; sets sights on achievable goals; needs recognition but can tend to avoid being in the limelight; or can, alternatively, be inhibited, lacking confidence, inclined to be depressed or to worry.

**Aquarius**: Freedom and independence; seeks to express the new, the radical, the idealistic and unconventional; an emancipator at heart; or can be rebellious, erratic, extreme.

**Pisces**: Impressionable, reserved and receptive, but also highly adaptable, changeable and artistic; seeks perfection for self and others; seeks to inspire, and be inspired; or inclined to be impractical, insecure, uncertain about life.

# ☽ Moon – Rules Cancer

## Represents

Maternal/feminine impulse; the Moon's position indicates instinctual and emotional responses; natural (body) rhythms, receptivity, reflectivity; one's habit patterns and conditional responses; gut behaviour; one's moods – where we wax and wane; links with the subconscious; also, a sense of belongingness, family, familiarity, security; association with the past, with memories.

## By sign

**Aries**: Instinctually feels comfortable acting on impulse; will be driven by a sense of urgency; prefers being able to do one's own thing; needs personal involvement; or can be inclined to mood swings and impatience.

**Taurus**: Needs to take time, slow to change and reserved; prefers peaceful, solid, reliable, steady and productive circumstances; enjoys routine habitual circumstances; or can be inclined to be stubborn, a stick in the mud.

**Gemini**: Busy, chatty, witty and variable in temperament; prefers to give and receive information in short headline bursts; likes short regular journeys; or can, alternatively, be dualistic in nature, and inclined to be restless and to worry.

**Cancer (Ruler)**: Works off gut feelings; sensitive and receptive; needs to feel "at home" protected – happiness depends upon it; domesticated, family oriented; or can alternatively be retiring, moody, emotionally unstable.

**Leo**: Responds to circumstances that test/challenge abilities; will love competition, adventure, fun and games; needs to feel appreciated above all else – confidence depends upon it; or can be over-confident, ostentatious, up and down.

**Virgo**: Inclined to be conventional, orderly, clean, and industrious; at home in duty oriented and protective environments; professional mother/carer; or can be overly critical, fussy, timid.

**Libra**: Responsive and sensitive in love; needs harmonious, sociable (and often attractive, idealistic) environs to function well in; strong need to be liked and comfortable with people; or can be elusive and fickle in feelings.

**Scorpio**: Attracted to emotionally charged circumstances; likes atmosphere of intrigue and controversy, an element of danger; passions and mood can run high; or can be resentful, controlling, moody, spiteful.

**Sagittarius**: Optimistic, speculative, philosophical and frank; will enjoy travel and broadening horizons; inclined to like exotic learning environments, and other cultures; or can be inclined to be restless, thoughtless, overly extravagant.

**Capricorn**: Seeks stability within conventional, hierarchical structures; needs clear orderly objectives in life; probably at home in circumstances having clearly marked boundaries; or can be inclined to become overly authoritarian, pessimistic, discontented.

**Aquarius**: Socially open, emancipating, enjoys living in unconventional environs; naturally inclined towards circumstances that break with traditions, are new or shocking; or equally can be unpredictable or erratic in behaviour.

**Pisces**: Easy going, imaginative and adaptable; but also very sensitive to atmospheres and people – psychic abilities likely; seeks refinement in environment and in one's self; or can be indecisive, restless, vulnerable and inclined towards escapism.

# ☿ Mercury – Rules Gemini and Virgo

## Represents

Alertness of mind; mental and nervous activity; the urge to know and inform; communications, linking, contacting, co-ordinating information; the power of knowledge; converting experience into ideas; knowledge of self and environment; indicates how one will tend to gain knowledge, form ideas and communicate ideas.

# By sign

**Aries**: Mentally alert, competitive, grasps things quickly; able to make quick decisions and capable of leading from the front; can be challenging in communications; entertains courageous and bold ideas; or can be quarrelsome, seeking to get one over.

**Taurus**: Conservative/pragmatic in thought and ideas – sticks with the tried and tested; needs time to think things through; has reluctance to change one's mind; interest in music and the arts generally; or inclined to be mentally sluggish, narrow-minded.

**Gemini (Ruler)**: A quick, inquisitive and agile mind; versatile in thought and communications; knowledgeable across a wide range of subjects; or can skip over the surface of things, gathering superficial or trivial knowledge; a bit of a trickster/hustler.

**Cancer**: A retentive memory; what is felt is what is remembered; intellect and thinking processes influenced by feelings; highly intuitive and perceptive; thoughts and ideas often focused on home/family; or can be irrational, narrow minded.

**Leo**: Mentally creative and competitive; confidence/self-assurance in communications; needs ideas/knowledge to be appreciated; entertains strong convictions and opinions; good orator, persuasive; or can be prejudiced, conceited, likes the sound of own voice.

**Virgo (Ruler)**: An analytical, tidy and logical mind; thinking that is methodical and practical; naturally studious, inclined to acquire specialised knowledge, following conventional pathway; or can be over-critical, small-minded and pedantic; inclined to worry.

**Libra**: Mentally quick with a reasoning and balanced mind; expresses diplomacy and refinement in all forms of communications; weighs up opposing ideas/views before reaching decisions; or can be inclined to procrastinate, be indecisive, over-idealistic.

**Scorpio**: Inclined to have an intense, instinctive and perceptive mind; capable of profound thinking; good at keeping secrets, or detective work bringing the hidden to light; a probing and investigative mind; good at selling; or inclined to be sarcastic/vindictive in communications.

**Sagittarius**: Inclined to be philosophical, seeker of knowledge, broadening experience and horizons; interested in higher education, travel, other cultures and languages; open and frank in communications; or can also be blunt, tactless, and even dishonest.

**Capricorn**: Serious minded pragmatist; takes a cautious and practical outlook on matters; inclined towards having a business mentality; mentally strong with powers of concentration; or can be narrow-minded, inclined to be negative in one's thoughts and ideas.

**Aquarius**: A quick, intuitive and creative mind, an "ideas" person; inclined to be original, inventive, offbeat and radical in thinking; mentally stimulating and inquisitive; or can also be eccentric, extreme, impersonal and fixed in opinion.

**Pisces**: An imaginative, receptive, impressionable and creative mind; tunes-in and communicates by feel; inclined to form ideas by instinct than by logic; attraction to the visual and healing arts; or can be prone to woolly thinking, indecision and escapism.

# ♀ Venus – Rules Taurus and Libra

## Represents

The urge to relate and unify with others through sympathy, feelings and evaluation; the urge to be attractive or to the attraction of others; sensual, social and artistic pleasures; the mores and the arts; earthy idealism, earthy love, feminine attraction; the interdependence of spirit and nature; the urge towards harmony in relating to self, others and environment; indicates how/where one will tend to place one's values and appreciation for what one has in life.

# By sign

**Aries**: Passionate and demonstrative in relating – in expression of love and sexuality; will prefer to initiate romantic encounters; naïve in affairs of the heart; independence crucially important; or can be self-centred/selfish in relating.

**Taurus (Ruler)**: Strong personal powers of attraction and desires; constancy, loyalty and stability important in relationships; artistic appreciation and talent likely; inclined to over-indulge in sensual pleasures; or can be sensually greedy, over-possessive/grasping.

**Gemini**: Witty and charming nature; will enjoy variety in love life and social life; attracted towards mentally stimulating people; or can be fickle, superficial and flirtatious – which can lead to issues in forming lasting bonds/friendships/relationships.

**Cancer**: Deep and sincere feelings of love; caring and protective towards loved ones; romantic, needs to feel loved and secure, have affection demonstrated; home focal point for social activities; or can be over-sensitive, easily hurt.

**Leo**: Romantic, expressive, creative and competitive; desire for adventure/fun/drama in love-life; generous/warm-hearted; attraction towards others with kudos/popularity; or can be patronising, too proud, possessive or jealous.

**Virgo**: Artistic and creative (often with fine handiwork), cautious, modest, reserved in forming relations on intimate level; seeks perfection in partner/s; dedicated in commitment; or overly fussy, idealistic and critical expectations can lower spontaneity and make for missed opportunities in love.

**Libra (Ruler)**: Artistic, an appreciation for beauty, the arts and refinement; in relating needs to feel part of a union of minds; seeks balance, harmony and equality in partnerships; or can be over-idealistic, or trying to please everyone.

**Scorpio**: Emotional, passionate and sexually intense in love; magnetic sexual attraction; tendency towards "all or nothing" when it comes to love; seeks authenticity in partners; or can be inclined towards extremes – power struggles, manipulation, secretiveness, jealousy.

**Sagittarius**: Friendly, fun-loving, positive, romantic and optimistic attitude in love; will retain independence; seeks honesty, truthfulness in partnerships; possible long-distance relationships; or can be overly flirtatious, inconsiderate.

**Capricorn**: Inclined to form conventional, dependable partnership/s; will seek mature, experienced partners; can be wide-age difference; holds feelings under control; or can be inhibited, controlling, cold, finds difficulty in expressing affection.

**Aquarius**: Friendly - inclined to base close ties around friendship and communication; will like variety and probably hold contemporary views on relationships; enjoys being independent, or can be detaching, touchy, uncompromising.

**Pisces**: Romantic, deeply sensitive, idealistic and artistic – likely love for music and the visual arts; capacity for great giving and sacrifice in love; or in relating can be overly sentimental, impressionable and vulnerable to deception.

# ♂ Mars – Rules Aries and (shares) Scorpio

## Represents

Physical activity, drive, force, directness, aggression, decisiveness; heat and activation; emotional charge; masculine energy; combat with the forces of nature and/or the resistance of matter, urgent action, do or die; penetration, regeneration, one's sexual power/prowess/impulse; indicates how/where we tend to aggress, assert and project ourself onto our environment, our world and direct ourself forward in life.

## By sign

**Aries (Ruler)**: An action person, head-strong, direct, a "do it now" urgency combined with enterprise, courage and self-motivation; strongly independent; or can be impulsive, impatient, reckless, inclined to act without thinking and to force one's own way on others.

**Taurus**: Practical, pragmatic, industrious and enterprising – sets realistic achievable goals; likely strong powers of determination, perseverance and endurance; focus likely on material wealth/security; or can be obstinate, difficult, defensive.

**Gemini**: Mentally alert and active, with a quick intellect; strong and forceful communicator/orator; likely to be quick to respond; will enjoy lively discussion, debate; or can fritter energies, be highly strung, overly-argumentative – must have the last word.

**Cancer**: Highly charged emotional life – reacts according to feelings; ambitious; powerfully protective towards home and loved ones; arguments in the home and with family members likely; or can be moody, defensive, irritable, quarrelsome.

**Leo**: Competitive with gamesmanship and leadership qualities; self-assurance and self-confidence; demonstrative, dramatic, pioneering; inclined to assume authority; or can be melodramatic and domineering towards others.

**Virgo**: Industrious; will apply energies towards activities and goals that have practical and useful outcomes; cautious and economical use of energy; methodical, precise and exacting; or inclined to be a workaholic, stressed, emotionally frustrated.

**Libra**: Strong urge to be socially active/ intimate with others; passionate in one's affections; active communicator; inclined to be a peace-maker; or inclined to be frustrated through indecision; may force peace and harmony at any cost.

**Scorpio (older Ruler)**: Strength of will; fearless and determined; stands one's ground in conflict; sexual power; power struggles commonplace; light/dark moods within oneself; secret/hidden activities; or can be moody, revengeful, and aggressive; a danger of turning aggression against oneself.

**Sagittarius**: Enthusiastic and optimistic; spirited, independent; love of adventure; strong focus on broadening horizons through enterprise, education, or travel; or can be extravagant and inclined to lose sight of goals.

**Capricorn**: Industrious, enterprising, courageous; ambitious with the capability to plan and reach objectives through application and continued effort and activity; ability for leadership role/s; or can be overly duty-bound and a workaholic.

**Aquarius**: Strongly independent and progressive; inclined to follow own way of doing things; energetic and socially interactive; will fight for worthy cause/s; innovates solutions to problems; can be rebellious, perverse, impatient.

**Pisces**: Emotionally sensitive and changeable in reactions; difficulty focusing one's energies in one direction; avoids personal confrontation but likely to attract such; will sacrifice self for others; or inclined to be confused, unstable, indecisive, with too many irons in the fire.

# The Intermediate Planets

## ♃ Jupiter – Rules Sagittarius and shares Pisces

### Represents

Expansion, growth, new horizons to aim for; "can do" optimism and natural belief in self; the urge to self-improvement and a deepening of one's participation in life; the urge to find joy and meaning to one's life; opening to a higher power, a higher good; setting moral standards; embracing a broadening world view and beliefs; travel to distant lands in experience and learning; developing belief and philosophical perspectives; Jupiter's position indicates how one will tend to broaden out and make sense of life.

### By sign

**Aries**: Self-sufficient; generosity of spirit; has honesty; takes life head on; leadership qualities; pioneering spirit; seeks new horizons; or lacks balance, has a tendency to be overly-optimistic, impulsive and have inflated self-importance.

**Taurus**: Sound judgement, generous; love of the good things in life; inclined towards financial and business interests; strong opinion on social, political and religious matters; or tends to over-indulge, be wasteful, experience of illness through excess.

**Gemini**: Broad-minded, versatile, inquisitive and philosophical; a strong urge to explore and to gather facts and information; likely to have talents in communications/marketing; or is crafty, insincere, inclined towards superficiality and taking advantage.

**Cancer**: Forms strong attachments to home/family; enjoys a secure and comfortable home; charitable; educational, moral and religious outlooks established in early life; good business sense; or can be overly-touchy, impressionable.

**Leo**: Confident, expressive and dramatic; leadership qualities; big hearted, speculative, inspirational; strong need to impress, do things on a grand style; likes having an audience; or can tend to exaggerate, be arrogant and extravagant.

**Virgo**: Conscientious; strong moral values; dedication to one's art, work or service; organising abilities; attraction to research/education/teaching; or gets submerged in detail, is overly critical, tends to make mountains out of molehills.

**Libra**: Social influencer; easy-going; attracts many friends and connections; has a strong appreciation for the arts; strong sense of justice/fair play; seeks equality in partnerships; or can be conceited, lazy or overly dependent on others.

**Scorpio**: An optimistic attitude to life; passionate and intense sexual drive; shrewd with keen judgement; deep feelings; positive dealings with light/dark moods within oneself; or over-rates oneself, is aggressive, conceited.

**Sagittarius (Ruler)**: Strongly optimistic, ethical, philosophical, liberal-minded, love of justice; seeks to broaden knowledge and horizons; love of travel, distant lands, cultures and languages; or extravagant, boastful, given to hyperbole, non-committal, seeks freedom at any price.

**Capricorn**: Resourceful, trustworthy, sense of duty, responsible, leadership qualities; hard worker; optimism and wisdom combined – with realistic sense of what's possible; or hypocritical, sceptical, cynical, distrustful.

**Aquarius**: Broad-minded; creative; radical/philosophical thinker, humanitarian, environmental interests; strong sense of freedom and justice for all; qualities as orator/communicator; or inclined to be tactless, intolerant, obdurate, wilful.

**Pisces (older Ruler)**: Compassionate, altruistic, benevolent nature; idealistic, unconditional, humorous, intuitive and imaginative; interest in metaphysical/spiritual matters; or escapist, self-deceptive, over-imaginative, addictive tendencies.

# ♄ Saturn – Rules Capricorn and shares Aquarius

## Represents

Awareness of limits or where one feels limited, restricted; the urge to control, condition and organise one's life; the urge towards self-acceptance, having position, status, responsibility, maturity, seriousness, discipline, perseverance, patience and humility; awareness of time, the ageing process; tests and trials; becoming wise through experience; the ring-pass-not of matter; Saturn's position indicates our relationship with time; how one will tend to deal with boundaries, limitations, obstacles and tests for this life.

## By sign

**Aries**: Self-reliance, self-discipline and self-restraint; ambitious; takes responsibility for actions; takes calculated risks rather than on impulse; inclined to go it alone; or is autocratic, irresponsible, inclined to make jerky start/stop progress – a case of driving with the brakes on.

**Taurus**: Material and financial security is a focal point; inherently constructive, practical, economical, reliable and methodical – seeks to endure; or can be controlling, intransigent, overly-conservative, inhibited and/or apathetic.

**Gemini**: Disciplined and logical thinking process; intellectual and impartial; urge to gain knowledge having practical application; serious/reserved in communications and social interactions; or closed/rigid mind, insecure in expression.

**Cancer**: Inclined to be ambitious, reserved, business-like and shrewd; home/family a focal point but also likely cause for difficulties; territorial in behaviour; or overly-controlling, sensitive to criticism, emotionally insecure, overly-defensive.

**Leo**: Competitive, authoritative, reliable with leadership abilities; self-confidence/self-worth built up over time through testing experience; strong need for respect/recognition – that probably comes from within as may not come from outside; or inhibited, feelings of resentment/personal restriction, sense of being blocked on one's life-path.

**Virgo**: Serious, analytical and organised mind; meticulous care/attention to detail; strong sense of duty/work ethic; needs things to run efficiently; concerns with (others – possibly elderly) health and hygiene; or pedantic, over-critical, mistrustful.

**Libra**: Seeks secure, reliable partnerships; will be cautious and formal in communications/socialising; will be tactful, impartial with strong sense of responsibility towards others; or is lonely, controlling, austere, impractical, discontented. Note Saturn in Libra or 7th House often seen as an indicator for a secure marriage.

**Scorpio**: Inclined to be private, secretive, ambitious and determined; has a serious, purposeful and realistic outlook on life; delves deeply into difficult/challenging life matters; endures hardship; or sceptical, melancholic, resentful, even cruel.

**Sagittarius**: Trustworthy, prudent, authoritative and dignified; seeker of freedom/justice; higher education and academic interests – humanities, philosophy, religion, sciences, politics; lives/works abroad; or tactless, has intellectual pride, is lacking wisdom, is insincere.

**Capricorn (Ruler)**: Self-contained, conventional, responsible, methodical, disciplined, industrious and ambitious with strong will to achieve personal status and goals; having the patience of a saint; or self-critical, controlling, cold-hearted, pessimistic, isolated.

**Aquarius (older Ruler)**: Reasoning, reliable, individualistic, studious with scientific mind; serious communicator; socially just and fair, having a liberating attitude towards others; good organiser/delegator; or dogmatic, standoffish, isolationist.

**Pisces**: Compassionate, innately modest, reserved; propensity towards service and sacrifice for others; tendency to seek solitude and nourishment in natural surroundings; or inclined to isolation, self-pity, depression or despondency.

# The Outer Transpersonal Planets

## ♅ Uranus – Rules Aquarius

### Represents

The urge to freedom/detachment beyond established conventions, limitations, boundaries of self or environment; the urge to radically alter imposed constructs; the emancipation of one's community; the emancipation of humanity; the urge towards invention, innovation, originality, revolution, break-through, crisis, revelation, awakening, higher (transpersonal) forms of communication, intuitive awareness; shocking, electric, vivid, the unexpected, the surprising, the explosive, change for change sake; Uranus' position indicates how one will tend to transcend limitations and boundaries, enter new pathways, open new doorways, be original and creative.

### By sign

**Aries**: Deep need for freedom and independence, to do one's own thing; urge for radical reform or be more courageous/adventurous; or sudden bursts of energy, inclined to start new things on a whim without bringing things to any conclusion.

**Taurus**: Use of unconventional ways of dealing with practical matters; resources notably inclined to wax and wane through one's life; or instability between (Taurus) need for stability, and (Uranus) need for change.

**Gemini**: Quick, intuitive, inventive and versatile mind; scientific aspirations; an organised original thinker and convincing orator; or, inclined to be restless (to worry unduly), be eccentric and obscure.

**Cancer**: A changeful, creative and stimulating home environment; urge to uproot and move home - to other lands/cultures; eccentric/individualistic ways of caring for others; or emotionally cold and unsettled; shocking disruptions in the home or family.

**Leo**: Spirit of enterprise; love of adventure; need for creative and playful expression; seeks individual freedom; inclined to rebel against authority; or can be wasteful, stubborn, wilful or uncompromising.

**Virgo**: Analytical, quick and adaptable mind; likely interest in technology and/or alternative medicine; disruptive changes in one's vocation or health; or inclined to be faddy in interests, and over-critical of others.

**Libra**: Artistic and creative talents; changeful eccentric relationships; inclined towards unconventional and progressive views on relating; seeks freedom and independence, equality in partnerships; or lacking in harmony; inclined towards being out of balance, a trouble maker.

**Scorpio**: Independent and radical, with strength of feeling; energetic and forceful character; courageous and fearless; urge to bring new things into being; or cold and calculated, inclined to lead others into danger.

**Sagittarius**: Eccentric and free thinker; love of adventure; urge to explore beyond cultural boundaries; motivated towards innovation/reform in social, educational, religious or political areas; or fanatical, restless, rebellious.

**Capricorn**: Scientific interests; innovative use of one's resources; urge to electrify and change established order; extraordinary aims in life, with wilfulness to achieve; or fanatical about one's status and achieving certain goals.

**Aquarius (Ruler)**: Original/radical and intuitive thinker – a contemporary and progressive mind; likely humanitarian interests – seeking change through collective and cooperative work; or extreme in behaviour, awkward in social contact.

**Pisces**: Highly intuitive, inspired, sensitive, receptive and responsive to change; interest in the human condition as seen via the unconscious, spirituality, the arts (music, dance) and nature; or being at the mercy of changing emotions, sudden disappointment.

# ♆ Neptune – Rules Pisces

## Represents

The power of the imagination; seeking the ideal; developing an emotional sense of unity with all life; selfless compassion and sacrifice; atonement; unconditional love; the urge to let go; the urge to dissolve the material and transcend to finer energies/realms/spiritual existence; the place of dreams; the ocean; merging with the intangible, the utterly beautiful; all things nebulous; the arts, notably music and composition; Neptune's position indicates how well we will tend to see through illusion and deception, how well we can transform, become more refined, become at one with our higher self or soul.

## By sign

**Aries**: Inspired, pioneering and selfless action; a care for humanity; following a spiritual path; or confusion in direction, uncertainty in taking action on worldly matters; disappointment and loss.

**Taurus**: Strong imagination and flair for art or creative design; love of music and the arts in general; aesthetically refined lifestyle; or inclined to over-indulge, be addicted; have disappointment and uncertainty regarding ownership and material security.

**Gemini**: Intuitive, imaginative and receptive; inspired communications, artistic, poetic or automatic writing; seeks to broaden knowledge/experience; or having a dual nature, confused imagination, developing woolly ideas.

**Cancer**: Highly instinctive, sensitive, receptive; a deeply caring nature; self-sacrificing, treats all-comers as family; has psychic abilities; idealistic regarding home and homeland; or hyper-sensitive, melancholic, carrying a deep sense of loss.

**Leo**: Flair for the dramatic, ability to act; appreciation of beauty, music and art; dreams and wishes; romantic identification with heroes, heroines, leaders or celebrities; or tendency to exaggerate, be wasteful, self-delusional.

**Virgo**: Intuitive and sensitive understanding of others; likelihood of healing abilities; charitable work; provides service to a higher cause within one's community; or over-idealistic, puritanical, overly critical, uncertainty over one's vocation and community value.

**Libra**: Idealistic/romantic view of life/love; refined appreciation of beauty and art; artistic abilities; appreciation for etiquette and manners; seeking the ideal in partnerships; unconditional love and service in relationship/s; a leaning towards Platonic love; or unrealistic expectations of others, being over-impressionable; attracting disappointment in love-life.

**Scorpio**: Highly intense and sensitive to impressions; psychic ability; attraction to the spiritual/mysterious and paranormal; unconventional approach to sexuality/morality; or inclined to depression, addictive tendencies, danger of becoming a victim; can be cruel and hurtful towards others.

**Sagittarius**: Strongly religious/philosophical/devoted approach to life; dreams big; seeks refinement in education and knowledge; a longing for faraway inspiring places; or an overactive imagination, self-deception, lacking discrimination.

**Capricorn**: Idealistic or strange views on worldly success/achievement; dreams brought down into reality; living a meditative ascetic lifestyle; or lacking a sense of reality; a dreamer lacking confidence to succeed; achievement through deception.

**Aquarius**: Intuitive, innovative and artistic; gifted in arts/music; interest in global and environmental matters; a seeker of social change, based upon higher humanitarian ideals; or peculiar notion of independence and freedom; easily yields to temptation.

**Pisces (Ruler)**: Highly sensitive, receptive and artistic – notably music; abilities as a psychic or medium; interest in metaphysics; seeks refinement, higher ideals through living a pure life; a person of service; or tendency to escapism, pessimism, susceptible to drugs/alcohol, danger of becoming a victim.

# ♇ Pluto (or ♇) – Rules Scorpio

## Represents

Purification; removing that which contaminates and holds us back; return, rebirth, endings; the urge to bring to light what is hidden; renewal, regeneration, transformation through eradication; trial by fire; meeting the repressed parts of the self; destruction of inner darkness, compulsions and desires; Pluto's position indicates how one will tend to eradicate baggage, cleanse oneself of one's past, heal woundings and clear the path to one's soul – or fail to do so, or attempt to avoid doing so.

## By sign

**Aries**: Extraordinary determination and courage in the face of challenges; ability to see things through; leadership qualities; or the craving for power, attraction of others with power, inclined to be unnecessarily forceful and dictatorial.

**Taurus**: Obsessional preoccupation with security and material possessions; or gains and losses through over-indulgence or via manipulation by external powers/control/s.

**Gemini**: Powerful communicator, ability in intellectual/scientific research, and discourse; reformer in areas such as psychology, IT, education or transport; or manipulative of the media, ruthless in exposing truths/untruths.

**Cancer**: Forms deep emotional bonds with the past, one's hereditary, one's home and family; inclined to experience deep insights into people; or a tyrant in the home, living a solitary existence, sadness/upheavals in one's home-life.

**Leo**: Powerful need to make an impression on others/world; extraordinary achievements likely; air of authority/leader; or uncompromising and dictatorial in position of power.

**Virgo**: Organised, inquisitive and penetrating mind; the pursuit of scientific objectives; reformer in areas of health and work; service in the community; healer; or a workaholic, pessimistic outlook on life; obsessed with hygiene.

**Libra**: Strong ability to counsel/influence others in improving relationships, and transforming public perceptions; powerful diplomat/orator/communicator; or extreme views on relationships, mistrust and the need to control others.

**Scorpio (Ruler)**: Emotionally intense and charismatic; secretive, hidden, undercover; powerful influence on others; achievement through tenacity and endurance; deep-seated passion and sexual drive; or prone to power struggles, fanaticism, dark moods, paranoia.

**Sagittarius**: Passionate and pioneering in areas of education, travel, religion, philosophy and justice; deep desire for knowledge and urge to explore the depths of life; or fanatical regarding needing one's freedom to roam.

**Capricorn**: Power of persuasion/determination; urge to transform established structures/poor working practices; successful realisation of business/economic/political goals; or ruthlessness, depression, isolation, position of danger.

**Aquarius**: Urge to reform; applies scientific, technological, humanitarian knowledge, research; strongly independent, passionately involved with emancipation/change; or exaggerated plans, extreme views, taking extreme actions.

**Pisces**: Healing abilities, able to cleanse physical and psychological woundings; need for seclusion, meditation and contemplation; interest in metaphysical realms; work in secrecy; or deep sense of loss, depression, spiritual torment.

**Ends.**

# The Planetary Aspects Resource

**The Planetary Aspects Resource is linked to Step Three.**

For interpretation purposes each of the following aspects (and their respective keywords), are split into two parts: the more positive expression – often represented by flowing aspects such as the trine – followed by the "Or" encompassing some of the more challenging considerations of the given aspect. It will depend upon the planets involved but the latter can often be indicated by the square, opposition or quincunx.

The hope here is that you can absorb and get past the keywords to a sense of a theme operating that is represented by the aspect.

For instance, with the Sun and Moon we have the dynamic of the shining Sun (Yang) need to express with warmth and creatively, and the reflective Moon (Yin) need to feel good, feel "at home" emotionally secure. Whether the aspect between the two is naturally conducive to the best of this or not gives rise to the keywords.

Remember, all aspects can be expressed positively where there is conscious intention. So, while the flowing aspects tend to work out easily, the more challenging aspects require (conscious) effort on our part to be expressed out positively.

Also keep in mind that, as with the chart components themselves, interpretation of an aspect cannot be done solely in isolation. Chart interpretation is always about relationship. The relationship between each of the planetary components, and in context with their relationships to the signs and houses involved.

# ☉ Sun

Self-expression; one's essence; will; vitality; one's creative centre; the heart.

## Sun/Moon

Inclined to be strongly self-motivated, self-contained, independent, self-reliant and self-integrated; inclined towards an inner harmony – objective and subjective sides working together; will have a natural well-being, with good stamina and recuperative powers; likes to be in control; is sensual; has bouts of creativity; enjoys new beginnings, new enterprises, sowing creative seeds; seeks recognition; likely to form a strong identification with mother; forms long lasting relations with others – friends, partners, family; encouraged by one's childhood/parents to be self-expressive, to do one's own thing, find one's own niche, without too much interference from others; creative abilities often supported through close family ties.

Or: inner tension or conflict; a moody disposition – deeply emotional; deep discontent; inclined to be one-sided and subjective, unaffected by other people leading to misunderstandings; lacks empathy for others; self-confidence is inclined to wax and wane; inclination towards indecision, insecurity and uncertainty – fluctuating energy; a likely disconnect between conscious intentions and subconscious emotional needs; difficulty in feeling "at home" in oneself or with others - likely stemming from one's childhood; discord between parents; challenging relations with others; an inclination to be selfish; inclined to be authoritarian in the home; achieving inner harmony requiring conscious effort and discipline to bring about balance.

## Sun/Mercury

Mentally active, alert, inquisitive, has a healthy intellect, a clear mind; seeks knowledge; versatile, adaptable, thinker; quick witted and powerful in argument; has likely interest in, and knowledge on, a broad range of topics – good at quizzes; involved in varied forms of learning and communications; ideas person capable of making effective connections between different disciplines; likes to be mobile; enjoys change of scenery; a busy occupation.

**Or**: an overly busy mind, inclined to fidget; lacks clarity; a worrier, nervous, unsettled, restless; inclined to be a "know it all;" not a good listener; may need to be less self-centred.

## Sun/Venus

Natural charm others find attractive; implies kindness, contagious warmth and affection that people find endearing; has strong desires, powerful feelings; sexually potent; seeks romance and intimacy; very creative, having artistic flair, a strong aesthetic sense, strong sense of values; has an appreciation of beauty in all forms; a love of pleasure; clothes tend to play an important role in how one feels; passionate over living a comfortable and ideal lifestyle – in luxurious surroundings.

**Or**: overly idealistic; in danger of being too nice for one's own good – inviting disappointment; needs affection, needs to feel loved – and inclined to do so at any price.

## Sun/Mars

Bags of energy; strong willpower, confident, quick reactions, a fighting spirit, courageous, self-motivated, actively ambitious, naturally assertive with a love of friendly competition; winning combination of initiative, self-esteem and self-confidence; thrives on adventure; drives to achieve whatever is important; sets clear objectives; has an active lifestyle; sexually active; will take on leadership role/s; won't suffer fools gladly; inclined towards robust health - need of physical exercise or sports to help channel excess energy in a healthy way; advancement in life likely to be based on personal efforts and determination – a self-made person.

**Or**: "more haste less speed" – having to redo or start again on projects; can be impatient, reckless, headfirst, inclined to taking unnecessary risks; careless and moody; fiery temper; over-reactive, argumentative, aggressive; inclined to enjoy picking fights no matter how small, and going head-to-head in combat; can be selfish, "me-first," authoritarian; accident prone; danger of stress and burnout from an over-active lifestyle – needs periodic breaks from activity; needs to develop patience and self-control.

## Sun/Jupiter

An optimist, self-confident and cheerful; has faith in self, and is honest, kind and sincere; a positive and optimistic outlook on life; inclined towards positive experience; propensity to attract material wealth and abundance – described as "lucky;" feelings of being protected by life, attracts what is needed from life without too much hardship; likely to see life as theatre – enjoys drama; naturally enthusiastic, gregarious and generous towards others; big-hearted wins many friends; a popular and fun person to be around; has leadership qualities; aspires towards success in life – motivated by a strong urge to expand life experience, to broaden personal horizons through travel, education, ideas, awareness and developing belief; strong desire to improve one's position in the world.

Or: lacks moderation, is ostentatious, wasteful, extravagant, a pleasure seeker; inclined to overdo things seeking to live the good life; displays false pride and blows things out of proportion; does not always have the wherewithal to succeed; inclined not to complete on what is begun; reckless and careless with money; inclined to be restless, discontent with responsibilities and limitations in life; life experienced as a struggle; one's faith being tested – never loses hope however; needs to work towards success through conscious self-improvement and control – avoiding self-indulgence and by being entirely honest with oneself.

## Sun/Saturn

A practical, methodical, mature and serious person; a pragmatist, a realist, a responsible person; has self-control and is well organised – has a dislike of clutter or waste; very conscientious in fulfilling duties; good at focusing on the job in hand; inclined to take a sober and sombre outlook on life; good powers of perseverance and patience; achieves objectives through sacrifice and exercising self-discipline; ambitions are well-grounded; considers nothing is achieved without effort and industry; makes advances in life at a steady but sure pace; likes to be in control; capable of being in authority; otherwise can be shy, very modest and reserved – a certain shyness and reserve that can put others at ease.

Or: withdrawn, pessimistic, somewhat cold and aloof; viewed by others as selfish and uncaring, even ruthless; expects to be facing obstacles and frustrations in life – and gets them; likely fear of authority; feelings of personal inadequacy, self-doubt; inclined towards bouts of depression, inhibition and despondency; inclined to be judgemental, hard on oneself and others; a tendency towards separation and loneliness; will be prone to poor vitality and health issues generally, as the result of stress, being hard on oneself; important to stop judging oneself and others too harshly; likely will need to lighten up, to achieve self-acceptance and find genuine love for oneself.

## Sun/Uranus

Innovative, intuitive, unusual, creative, progressive and eccentric; an original thinker; will be strongly independent and liberating; likely strong-willed and individualistic – will march to their own tune; not afraid of change; seeks excitement and adventure; keenly intuitive, can have an uncanny sense for the "next big thing;" can come up with the most original and unique solutions to problems; open to the odd, paranormal and unusual perspectives on the world; interest in cutting edge developments in technology or science; electronics, computers, motorcycles or astrology likely to interest; will go to great lengths to achieve personal goals and objectives; will be radical, provocative, unpredictable, dramatic and contradictory; will hate being told what to do and when to do it; won't easily adapt to other people's needs or wishes; expects the unexpected, a sudden shift, often in a good way.

Or: pride, selfishness, alienation from others, erratic temperament, hysteria, a lack of self-control and self-discipline; refuses to be bound by any convention; over self-confident, inconsistent, lacking perseverance – inclined to start things and lose interest inclination to be perverse, disruptive and unpredictable in behaviour; needs to listen to the ideas of others before making decisions; experiences sudden changes, setbacks and potential accidents – likely due to own rashness, impatience and carelessness.

## Sun/Neptune

Inclined to be idealistic, highly sensitive, imaginative, impressionable and inspired; inclined to have a gentle manner; inclined towards mind, body and spiritual refinement; will love the colourful, the beautiful; attracted to artistic and creative pursuits – such as music, painting, photography or drama and theatre (ability as an actor); can be fascinated by metaphysical or esoteric topics; inner life is very active and psychic experiences are likely; will tend to soak up surrounding vibrations – for good or ill; inclined to have vivid, even lucid dreams, visions and yearnings; likely to have great compassion and the ability to feel and understand the needs of others, have sympathy and empathy with others; inclined to be in the service of helping people in need; a healer or involved in the healing arts; strange and mysterious things can happen that defies reason; love of nature and solitary walks an attraction; likely to travel far and wide in life; an empathic connection with the sea likely.

**Or**: sentimental and impressionable; susceptible to fantasising, over-idealism, self-deception; may be easily swayed by others to follow their dreams or ideals instead of one's own; puts on an air of confidence when not at all sure of oneself; escapist tendencies – and need to be careful around drugs or alcohol; inclined towards depression, neurosis and becoming disillusioned with life; needs to avoid influences that can lead to disappointment and loss; there may be a need to say "No," to stand one's ground than be drawn into questionable schemes.

## Sun/Pluto

An intense, very confident, powerful, magnetic and dynamic personality; has a strong will combined with a wealth of creative power and energy; will have a presence about them; one who feels driven by a deep, inner sense of destiny, great faith and trust in own abilities, and who can accomplish what he or she sets their mind to; will expect to conquer any obstacle, problem or setback; a strong desire to achieve personal goals and gain personal recognition; will want to be the world's best at something – and that idea spurs on efforts; will possess natural leadership qualities, organisational qualities and executive skills; has the wherewithal to persuade others to follow their lead; will be inclined to be secretive and to love working behind the scenes; indicates an ability to transform circumstances and to re-invent oneself where necessary.

**Or**: stubborn, inclined to be wilful, zealous, even fanatical, compulsive and manipulative – a tendency to dominate or manipulate others; can provoke strong likes and dislikes in response from other people; can be sometimes arrogant with it; such intensity of feelings, personal motives and desires may be kept under wraps, hidden, for much of the time; often this will be subtle with probably little intention or room for compromise at the end of it; alternatively can carry self-doubt and a degree of paranoia; personality clashes and power struggles likely to be experienced, and could be almost on a daily basis; here we can say that what happens externally is a mirror for the dialogue that is going on within; there is a need to be conscious of inclination towards taking advantage of others, and to learn to be there as much for their needs as one's own; self-reform required.

# ☽ Moon

One's moods, need for security; instinctual/habit patterns and emotional/conditional responses; the subconscious; the ego; where we wax and wane.

## Moon/Mercury

Feelings, emotions and interests are powerfully combined – a fertile mind; can fluctuate between rational and/or very emotional; has a good memory; loves change and variety; thoughts are influenced by feelings and vice versa; witty, clever, a fine sense of humour; highly perceptive and able to tune into what others are feeling; a sympathetic/compassionate listener; others likely to seek person's advice - to be their sounding board; loves to (possibly endlessly) discuss one's own experiences and feelings; interest in the past, families ties, cultural roots; likely talent for foreign languages; interests driven by one's feelings/emotions, what one identifies with; habits formed around one's need for mental stimulus – need to write, keep a diary, tell stories or teach for instance; feelings, personal life and problems of others a driving force behind direction in life.

**Or**: lacks persistence and depth in thought and action; inclined to be indecisive; thoughts and communications heavily influenced by how one feels, what mood one is in; sudden changes in mood; arguments and serious falling outs with family member/s likely; overly concerned with personal security and safety; memory is not always that reliable; issues with communications – how one speaks, writes or gets around is frustrated in some way; inclined to engage in gossip; will criticise others and stretch the truth to suit own purposes; inclined towards developing nervous habits; there's a likely need to be understood and loved.

## Moon/Venus

Warm-hearted, affectionate, compassionate and sympathetic; good sense of rhythm and balance; refined nature; an appreciation of the finer things in life including the arts and culture; likes to be in the fashion; home tastefully decorated and artistically arranged; needs a comfortable home; very hospitable; charming with an instinct for the subtleties of social interaction; affection for one's mother; needs to feel the family around; needs friends around; has a sense of fun and a liking for parties; relationship with the female sex is generally easy and harmonious; inclined to be romantic and sentimental; desire for affection and tenderness; tenderness in love, needs to feel emotionally connected to partner; women feel at ease in company; courteous when dealing with the public; will love the good life; has artistic potential; painting, photography or music; loves beauty; has a good fashion sense.

**Or**: potential for over-indulgence and extravagance; money could come and go; unhappiness through affairs; difficulty expressing feelings; gets very jealous; needs to be assured that all is well; great need for security; inconstant in friendships; popularity comes and goes; periodic bouts of self-indulgence and self-pity; lazy in the home.

## Moon/Mars

Independent and enterprising spirit; a great deal of emotional energy; has vitality, is resourceful; will be bold and courageous; energetic and swift in response; good self-control; passions quickly aroused; feelings and actions in sync with each other; naturally bold and forthright; not afraid to take risks; one's actions are determined by feelings; can be astonishingly frank; speaks one's mind; direct in confrontational situations; Will "lay cards on the table;" others know where they stand; in love, usually honest about feelings; enjoys keeping busy and initiating new projects and enterprises; competitive or aggressive situations brings out the fighter; resists restriction and being ordered around – prefers to work "with" others than "for" others; has capacity for leadership and often motivated to take charge of situations.

**Or**: develops powerful likes and dislikes; indiscreet, intolerant; is restless, impatient; has turbulent moods; volatile temper; can be very brusque; instinctively aggressive; tendency to bully; tends to act without thinking; actions often lack consideration for others; tends to rule the roost at home; gets involved in family arguments; has a stormy home life; marital quarrels likely; can expect setbacks in life caused by impulsiveness or impatience; needs to learn how to channel energy into constructive endeavours, and how to compromise with others – forgive mistakes too.

# Moon/Jupiter

Self-expansive disposition; optimistic about future; upright, moral, will have a well-defined sense of ethics; sincerely modest; praiseworthy, self-sacrificing; generosity of spirit; open-minded; kind-hearted; responsive; sympathetic and compassionate; obliging manner; ability to laugh at oneself and/or see humour in difficult circumstances; financial well-being; an excellent mother or a good and successful relationship with one's mother; often member of a large family; socially aware, sociable, protective, tolerant, forgiving, always ready to overlook other people's mistakes; expects the best from others and capable of drawing the best from them; has a knack for making others comfortable and happy; has many friends; often benefits in life with or through others; sensitive to needs and feelings of others; a good listener; desire to help others in need; the ability to feel what others feel; non-judgmental; advice is trusted; emotional honesty and good humour make popular and appreciated by others; immensely romantic and sentimental; Relations with women are usually positive and often personally advantageous; enjoys having a good time; an emotional approach to belief/religion; an excellent cook; travel and overseas connections; international business contacts.

**Or**: exaggerated behaviour; extravagant, careless, unstable emotions; tendency to laziness and over-indulgence in pleasure-seeking activities; suffers from over-eating; use of food for security blanket; a need to avoid overdoing it physically or emotionally; excessive protection of others; personal conflicts over matters of outlook and spiritual beliefs.

## Moon/Saturn

Considerate, self-disciplined, self-control, cool, reserved, responsible; a common sense/practical outlook on life; good at organising; expresses care and attention; will like things orderly and tidy; a private person; instinctively cautious; emotionally self-contained; usually at ease with one's own company; enjoys occasional periods in seclusion; conserves resources, careful with money; will have a strong sense of duty and responsibility to others; particularly strong feelings linked with one's family and past; family duty; a caring for the elderly; instinctively kind to the elderly and the young; not romantic or sentimental; shy (with women especially); inclined to keep an emotional distance from others; difficulty in making and keeping friends; does not find it easy to express feelings towards others outside of family or those who are trusted.

**Or**: a difficult childhood; deep-rooted unhelpful habits; emotionally inhibited – cold in response; very self-conscious; becomes anxious in a crowd; anxious about what others think; can fear being exposed; has an aversion to change; worries a lot; inclined toward unhappiness and depression – dark moods; feels overwhelmed and exhausted by family responsibilities; relationship with a parent is distant or emotionally unfulfilling; inclined towards recycling old feelings of anxiety and worry. Inclined towards having low self-esteem, a sense of inferiority; bleak self-limiting outlook on life.

## Moon/Uranus

Strongly individualistic, strong self-will, independent, self-reliant; excitable, attentive, ambitious, instinctual, strives for a goal or objective, determined; responds in an original way; sharp intuition, can be uncannily perceptive about people and situations; emotionally detached; tendency to rebel against restrictions on freedom and independence; capable of sacrificing emotional and family relationships for the attainment of personal objectives; instincts and intuition can be quite pronounced; changeable, restless, highly-strung, emotionally-charged, purposeful, progressive; can have sudden changes of direction; unusual and original forms of expression; interest in the metaphysical and sciences.

**Or**: has difficulty empathising with others; has anxiety and nervous tension; inclination to stress; unrest or restlessness; stubbornness, fanaticism, independence at any price; tendency to exaggerate; excessive self-will; subject to sudden emotional outbursts;

many upheavals or changes in family life or home; breakages in the home, paranormal experiences in the home.

## Moon/Neptune

Refined; idealistic; spiritually and religiously inclined; emotionally sensitive; subtle responses; sympathetic; has inner vision; inspired; psychic; imaginative; artistic; vivid dreams; highly perceptive and sensitive to influences around and able to pick up on the feelings of others and environment; ability to heal; can be content to just go with the flow; has empathic manner that others find attractive; can get caught up in romantic idealism and inclined to be easily infatuated with potential partners; sometimes entertains illusions concerning one's mother or wife; ability to tap into a wide range of creative talents, including music, writing and visual arts; seeks to be of service to others; expresses unconditional love.

**Or**: extreme emotional sensitivity; unstable emotions; can be confused, uncertain, insecure; inclined to be neurotic and escapist in behaviour; can be obsessional and deceitful; liable to be untidy at home; tendencies to experience family dramas, family scandals; likely to suffer losses; needs to be alert to deceptive influences or undermining emotional currents in one's life.

## Moon/Pluto

Deep intense, impersonal moods and feelings; sensitive to otherwise hidden emotional nature; psychic qualities; interest in the occult; interest in death or afterlife; instinctive unconscious response to outside stimuli; a complex emotional life; craves deep experiences; changes in life derive from unconscious drives; deep (possibly karmic) links associated with mother or family member; one inclined to be controlled by what is felt inside but otherwise hidden; personal relationships very emotional; passionate and often stormy; can usually sense emerging difficulties in associations and deal with them; hard and dedicated worker; indicates endurance, inner strength and stamina; ability to analyse other people's problems; effective psychotherapist or counsellor; strong force of will.

**Or**: a driven person; shocking and intense reactions; volatile like a volcano; emotionally fanatical; torn between a fanatical striving for the attainment of desired objectives and a soft-hearted sentimentality; obsessed with particular objectives and obtaining them; inclined to do things often against one's better judgment; tendency to be subtly very manipulative and controlling; feelings of jealousy and possessiveness; offended vanity or conceit, personal insults; compulsive or obsessive behaviour; sudden emotional upheavals; upheaval in home and family life; power struggles in the home or with dominant women; personal relationships can be intricate and often strained; fluctuating circumstances to do with money; needs to learn not to force feelings and emotions on others.

# ☿ Mercury

The urge to know and inform; how one will tend to gain knowledge, form ideas and communicate with others.

## Mercury/Venus

Considerable charm, grace, eloquence and gentleness; has a sense of fun and humour; jocular; intellect influenced strongly by feelings; literary interest, able to put thoughts on paper; harmonious disposition; light-hearted living; need to share ideas and affections with those who are close; pleasant manner, easily interacts with others; enjoys social activity and good company; tactful, diplomatic; thoughts often on love and relationships; likely to be good at marketing/advertising; does well in interviews; has creative flair, an eye for beauty, artistic design; talent as speaker or writer.

Or: vane or conceited; changeable in affections; can be somewhat gossipy, insincere; tendency to be indiscreet; thought and feelings get mixed up; can be a charming liar; flatters people to get what is desired; has difficulty learning; inclined to be lazy; can lack power to achieve goal/s.

## Mercury/Mars

An alert and agile mind; thrives on mental stimulation; ability to think quickly and decisively – a penetrative and determined thinker; passionate; direct in communications; impressive speaker; talks fast and is eager to persuade; has a debating mind; likes arguing; instigates or participates in (heated) discussions; knows how to press a point; quickness at repartee - able to retaliate in the right manner; produces controversial ideas; has ability to put own ideas into action; likes a challenge; ability to judge; practical disposition, skill or dexterity; benefits from "hands on" skills.

**Or**: can be very irritable; hot-headed, impatient; lacks tact; acts before thinking; very restless; excessive nervous reactions; verbally aggressive, cutting and judgemental; has a somewhat barbed wit; potential to incite or enter into arguments and disputes; resorts to sarcasm and swearing; takes rash actions; minor accidents - cuts and bruises likely, mostly through tendency to impatience; insomnia through inability to turn off the mind.

## Mercury/Jupiter

An optimist; expresses positive and confident outlook on life; good judgement, thoughtful, philosophical, liberal, constructive intellect; good communicator/orator; has a wealth of ideas; can express ideas easily and lucidly; has good sense of humour, wit and generous nature; enjoys talking; successful speaker or writer; understands things well; exercises intelligent reasoning and tolerance of other's ideas and perspectives; interest in literature; desire to broaden knowledge; well-read and erudite; appreciates value and benefits sound education; successful linguist; others frequently seek this person's counsel and advice; can be devoted in the service of others; socially popular person; sometimes comes into contact with the law; likely to travel, correspond abroad, have higher education or business interests overseas; often successful in business; good at selling things.

**Or**: frivolous, mischievous, unreliable; inclined to be intellectually arrogant; has a tendency to exaggerate, be verbose, be a phoney; tendency to be absent-minded; inclined to overlook important details; has a tendency to gossip; be careless, particularly when nervous; likely problems with investments, contracts or legal documents.

## Mercury/Saturn

Realistic, conservative, disciplined, methodical, tidy; intellectual, a logical and critical thinker with good powers of concentration; has ability to come straight to the point and be precise in speech; also taciturn; serious, realistic and conservative; a deep thinker, both academically and philosophically; ability to organise; ambitious, industrious, works hard consistently to achieve educational or practical objectives; reasoning powers and problem-solving abilities (mathematical gifts); powers of concentration to succeed with academic study or research work; age and experience bring wisdom and good judgement.

**Or**: lacks versatility; unable to adapt to changing circumstances; difficulties in communications – often through hesitation; does not interview well; security minded; poor memory; is narrow minded; not free with information; limited in ideas; has restricted education or educational achievements; prone to bouts of self-doubt; can be shy, inhibited or lacking self-confidence; can put others down; cynical, cold and calculated; given to brooding; inclined to melancholy, depression and pessimism.

## Mercury/Uranus

Independently minded and flexible; modern and contemporary outlook on life, revolutionary; original thinker; a mind that's open to new ideas (an "ideas" person), very inventive; able to think laterally and progressively; receptive to change; has intellectual curiosity; highly strung, dramatic, sharp and astute; comprehends things quickly; has a talent for speaking; has reformatory views; always prepared to challenge convention or the status quo; often holds bizarre opinions; curious sense of humour; can be a practical joker; intuition is acute and reliable; the fields of science, mathematics or technology of great interest; has ability to find solutions to awkward problems.

**Or**: impatient, easily bored; tendency to eccentricity for the sake of it; can be a busybody with too many irons in the fire; can be tactless and/or brutally frank; inclined to be contradictory; holding views that are radical to the extreme; a sarcastic wit; interrupts in conversation; socially isolating; proneness to bouts of nervous tension, anxiety and mental stress.

## Mercury/Neptune

A sensitive highly intuitive, idealistic and perceptive person; naturally inclined to understand and sympathise with others, be compassionate; instinctively knows what others may be thinking; an active imagination and strong powers of visualisation; a creative person, flowing with ideas; a talent for music, the arts, films or literature; an imaginative use of language; metaphysical and spiritual subjects interest; meditation and forms of mental relaxation also likely important; prone to experience spiritual or psychic phenomena; telepathic, able to tune into those who are close and pick up on their thoughts; inclined to use thought in seeking spiritual and physical well-being.

**Or**: tendency to daydream; lacks clarity; absent-minded; gullible; prone to self-deception in thinking process; inclined to avoid facing uncomfortable realities; thinking sometimes results in confusion; communications can be obscure; relies on intuitive jumps in exchanges that are sometimes difficult to follow; issues making important judgements and decisions; can be deceitful; can carry vague fears and imaginings; becomes nervous/anxious when chaotic conditions prevail; inclined to think the worst and worry a lot.

## Mercury/Pluto

A very persuasive, dynamic and powerful communicator; intellect is sharp and penetrating – a probing mind; ability to get to the bottom of things; an able conversationalist; enjoys debate, argument; has ability in impressing ideas onto others; ability in selling – possible gift of the gab; a powerful writer; good powers of observation and psychological insight into others; keenly aware and able to assess situations quickly and accurately; well-suited to investigative and research work; sudden urges to travel; has a talent for learning.

**Or**: over-estimation of self; opinionated; piercingly critical; cynical; overbearing or intellectually arrogant; premature action or hastiness; tendency towards explosive moods; can be obsessive; scheming; sly; unable to make compromises; relations with others can be strained; can be restless; stressed for no rational reason; worries a great deal.

# ♀ Venus

The urge to relate to others; to unify with others through empathy, feelings and evaluation. The urge to be attractive to others. The urge towards harmony in relating to oneself, others and environment.

## Venus/Mars

Friendly, warm-hearted, charming; an enthusiastic, sensual and passionate nature; demonstrative, a lively and outgoing personality; inclined to be very amorous and romantic; strong need for emotional and physical experiences; active, impulsive; quickly forms ties of affection; enjoys social activity; generally relaxed in company; inclined to have strong sexual needs; enjoys controversy; quickly forms ties of affection; inclined to form unions based solely on physical attraction; the thrill of the chase may often be more exciting than the outcome; works hard and plays hard; actively pursues luxury; artistic talent likely, particularly involving body movement such as dance, drama, or hands-on such as ceramics or sculpture.

**Or**: short-lived enthusiasms; inclined to be discontent, self-indulgent with bouts of aggression; blows hot and cold; inclined to be superficial; inclined to be permissive; has difficulty in controlling passions; very erotic impulses; difficulties in love through flirtations or infidelity; shallow connections; unhappy emotional relationships.

## Venus/Jupiter

A charming, generous, warm-hearted, tactful, optimistic and expansive nature; pleasant, affectionate and sociable; has a good sense of humour; embraces life wholeheartedly; exceptionally good sense of form, of values, beauty and harmony; artistically successful; knows how to enjoy life; has good taste; love of luxury and pleasure; desires prestige and respect; ability to make oneself popular – people find attractive and appealing; ability to feel at ease in social situations; excellent host or hostess; likes entertaining; good manners; a devoted friend; fortunate connections with people; worldly benefits via social contacts; romantic encounters generally positive and happy; numerous love affairs likely.

**Or**: extravagant; over-generous; somewhat ostentatious and self-conceited; prone to indulging in sensuality and trivia; vulgar tastes; negligent and wasteful; inclination toward laziness; lacks drive or ambition; easy come, easy go; tendency to take things for granted; false conduct in relationship/s; restless need for company – avoiding being alone.

# Venus/Saturn

A responsible, earnest, reserved, loyal and deep person; has strict values and sense of duty; has a strong sense of reality; thrifty, sober, economical, self-controlled; dislikes glamour and ostentation; can be embarrassed by compliments or gratitude; duty takes precedence over desires; enjoys time alone and being content with own company; limited or disciplined in feelings; coolly affectionate; views relationships seriously and values stability and fidelity in love; trust needs to be earned but once established very loyal and steadfast, a faithful friend; likely attraction to older, more mature persons, friends or partners; in love, inclined to put practical considerations before romantic desires – can be at the expense of emotional satisfaction and spontaneity; marriage may often prove long lasting if difficult.

**Or**: conflict between duty and pleasure; displaying selfish, exacting feelings; is emotionally indifferent or inhibited in affections; can lack self-confidence; can dislike being touched; can be sexually frigid; disappointments in love or delays in marriage likely; can indicate estrangements and separations from loved ones; being unsatisfied in life; tendency to be careless in appearance; developing a hard-heartedness; inclined towards self-torment; tendency to become alone or lonely.

# Venus/Uranus

Impulsive, adventurous; thrives on change and variety; independent, romantic; unconventional attitude and values; artistic talent (modern, original, unusual, new trends); magnetic charm; unusual tastes; sudden strange desires; demonstrative, expressive and spontaneous in feelings and affections; quickly aroused; a stepping up of sensations and feelings; fun to be with and open to experimentation; enjoys informed gatherings; desire for new and novel friendships; quick in setting up friendships; tends to prefer younger or lively people; believes in sexual freedom; expressions of love tend to range between sentimentality and eccentricity; choosy in love; attracted to exotic and unusual partners; will not allow freedom and independence to be compromised; rebels against commitment and/or emotional pressure to meet expectations from others.

**Or**: self-willed and obstinate; dislike of routine, easily bored; flirtatious behaviour; perverse feelings; repressed emotional desires; sexual deviations; inclined to be promiscuous; tendency towards loose morals; tendency short-lived enthusiasms; will try anything once; tendency to quick and broken love affairs, separations; sarcastic about others; bouts of insecurity; moodiness, sensitiveness, nervousness; proneness to anxiety, stress and unpredictability.

## Venus/Neptune

Idealistic, compassionate, sentimental and sympathetic; refined delicate feelings; great sense of harmony, keen sense of beauty; very inquisitive; has a creative imagination; good taste, refinement and artistic appreciation or talent – talent for music, poetry and visual arts; highly romantic and inclined to be a dreamer; strong feeling for the mystical and magical; always finds the mysterious pleasurable; enjoys sleeping; desires to see beautiful visions; seeks refinement; inclined to accept suffering to achieve a more refined level of being; the wish for a perfect love; sensitiveness in love.

**Or**: indecision, self-deception, confusion and uncertainty; emotional blindness; poorly developed sense of reality; unobtainable ideals; a tendency to hide behind a cloak of fantasy; can be susceptible to seducing influences; disillusionment and disappointment through misplaced affections; a danger of poor judgement in love; erotic aberrations; risk of scandal through unreliable associates.

## Venus/Pluto

Powerful urges; strong desires arise from the unconscious; adaptability with determination; strong aesthetic sense; artistic power and creative talent; likely desire to want to transform oneself; capable of powerful and sustained efforts; normal release of undesired pent-up feelings; agreeable and obliging nature through maturing process; very amorous and passionate; no room for middle ground in love life, gives and expects total commitment; can enter into unions that seem destined or fated; tends to feel that they and partner are meant for each other – soulmates.

**Or**: a disagreeable nature; little endeavour to oblige others; lacks adaptability; problems can occur in relationships through power struggles; a tendency to explosive feelings, inclined to being secretive, jealous, possessive, violent, ruthless; powerful sexual drives that can lead to immorality – with a willingness to pay for what one wants; the erotic can often dominate other aspects of one's personality; a tendency to take the law into one's own hands.

# ♂ Mars

How/where we aggress, assert and project ourselves onto our environment; how we will tend to direct ourself forward in life; penetration, regeneration, one's sexual power, prowess, impulse.

## Mars/Jupiter

Assertive, productive, energetic and resourceful person; strong passions and emotions; self-expansive; generous; great enthusiasm for life and ability to actively enjoy life; enterprising, adventurous, courageous, athletic, sporty and competitive; does things in a cheerful way; able to use higher education to good ends; ambitious for personal success; one who makes own "luck;" rarely backs down from challenges and achieves whatever sets out to accomplish – quitting not an option; able to make decisions quickly; has a good sense of timing; knack for being in the right place at the right time; frank; has religious ideals; sense of honour; an urge for freedom; organising talent; can successfully lead others.

**Or**: prone to exaggeration; inclined to be restless, discontent, wasteful, boastful; inclined to rudeness and lack of consideration for others; rebels against rules and regulations; inclined to bully others; can be pushy doesn't know when to stop; needs to be aware of potential for coming across as arrogant; judgement impaired due to impatience; financial dealings can be perilous; a spendthrift; potential to be hooked on gambling; attracts clashes over one's beliefs.

## Mars/Saturn

A hard worker; very practical; self-assertive; self-reliant; disciplined; controlled emotion; practical, materialistic, severe and ambitious; exacting, demanding; inclined to "stick with it;" careful; doesn't like interruptions; has considerable powers of endurance; hard-earned progress; has executive ability; concentrated energy; dealing with constructive or destructive energy; progress that is painfully slow; attainment of goals through sustained effort, determination and perseverance; often celibate; good self-control; in stressful or challenging situations, can be counted on to keep a clear and cool head; good at physical and manual work, or activities requiring self-discipline and stamina; likely interest in sports, in machines, in agriculture and buildings.

**Or**: up against the clock; obstructive and restraining tendencies; enthusiasm and need for action and adventure in conflict with need for restraint; tendency to drive with the brakes on; too much caution loses opportunities; can easily become irritable and frustrated with oneself; tendency to turn anger in on oneself; can vary between the melancholic and the impulsive; can be bitter and resentful about the past; carrying (and in combat with) feelings of inferiority; inclined to be preoccupied with own needs, interests, be selfish and unscrupulous; can be cruel and aggressive in exchanges; tendency to hardness and self-willed obstinacy; in extremes, a tendency to put oneself in the line of fire and get hurt or injured.

## Mars/Uranus

An assertive, energetic, enterprising, impulsive, courageous and original person; unconventional in interests or activities; likes to produce controversial ideas; live by own rules; freedom and independence go with the territory; will rebel against anyone who attempts to restrict them; an adventurous spirit; a risk taker, unafraid of challenging or potentially dangerous situations; dares to try out new and different things; at best when faced with challenging situations and the pressure of deadlines; quick reflexes; acts in spurts with speed and precision; unconventional lover; can be an unpredictable and challenging person to live with; being provocative and wilful can lead to conflicts and heated arguments with others.

**Or**: reckless, headstrong, disruptive; obstinate, intolerant, impatient; highly strung – strong emotional tensions; can have an explosive temper; eager to fight; aggressively independent; erratic self-will; restless, impulsive, fanatical or too eccentric; inclined to force ideas onto others; inclined towards sexual infidelity; careless accidents; needs to take care to avoid injuries and accidents.

## Mars/Neptune

Energetic, sensitive, a seeking to self-refine oneself; strong desire to help others – be of service; a missionary, a visionary; active dreams; one's imagination is emotionally driven, strong and assertive; one who is inclined to be impulsive, mysterious; a tendency towards religious fervour; develops interest in metaphysical subjects; one who directs their energies towards a higher good; can effectively direct energies into spiritual pursuits; is abstemious; practices self-denial or control of feelings or passions through meditation, mental or spiritual aspiration; the ability to succeed in activities that involve creative and imaginative powers – potential talent in music, drama, visual arts or fashion; physical movement that helps refine the body such as yoga, martial arts or swimming likely to appeal; tendency to sexual sensation-seeking.

**Or**: misguided; moody; irritable; discontented; feelings of inferiority; mental and emotional confusion; confusion over direction in life, one's ambitions and goals; the state of being unsatisfied; holds irrational fears; works on feeling without clear plan of action; sensationalist; prone to self-deception; can suffer from an excess of fantasy (sexual fantasy) or disturbing obsessions; sometimes pretends to be bolder than one actually is; may exaggerate in order to deceive others as well as self; inclined to force beliefs on others or lead them astray; can be target of scandal; inclined towards misuse of drugs and narcotic poisons; lacks energy; is susceptible to infections and viruses; needs to learn to channel energies most effectively.

## Mars/Pluto

Great self-confidence, will-power and ambition; a reformer; a natural detective; not afraid to voice opinion; emotionally charged focussed and concentrated energy; intense passion, force and vigour; power and stamina; the power to make things happen; extraordinary staying power; tireless worker, will see any task through to a successful conclusion; never say die attitude; sudden bursts of illumination and creativity; desire to get to the bottom of things – get to the truth behind appearances, behind the unknown; power to express energy positively or negatively; emotional struggles within – dark moods to spiritually enlightened moments; challenging, confrontational; desire to transform level and use of energy; strong need for sexual expression or can head towards complete denial; interest in matters of life and death; secretive, plays cards close to their chest.

**Or**: volcanic; compulsive, obsessive behaviour; can be erratic; sudden bursts of violence; a tendency to be reckless; emotionally reactive and vengeful; controlling; inclination to dominate or manipulate others – that often backfires; confrontations and power struggles likely; tendency to take the law into own hands; self-injuries possible; needs to learn humility and modesty, to live in harmony with others.

# ♃ Jupiter

The urge to self-improve and deepen one's participation in life; the urge to find joy and meaning to one's existence; opening up to a higher power, a higher good; optimism and belief in oneself; where we attract opportunity and opening doors.

## Jupiter/Saturn

Has common sense, responsibility, perseverance and self-discipline; philosophical, conscientious, patient, industrial; has a sincere sense of duty; conservative in judgements; somewhat conventional in outlook; believes in law and order; even-tempered, reliable and fair when making decisions or judgements; self-confidence built on awareness of own limitations; has a respect for formal discipline; optimistic in the face of difficulties; a tenacious pursuit of one's plans; life can alternate between periods of optimism and pessimism; experiences times of abundance and/or hardship; personal successes are hard won; has need to renew one's faith in life periodically; steady growth and hard work results in well-earned progress; has a good head for business; stubborn in business; understands the cycles of expansion and consolidation; good sense of timing; frugal with money; the growth of consciousness through response to religious, materialistic, scientific, philosophical influences; maturity and experience gained as a result of previous difficulties and learning to accept own limitations.

**Or**: emotional tensions and inhibitions; frustration; quick irritability; discontent; a lack of self-confidence; losses and/or inconstant success; financial anxieties; feelings of dissatisfaction with one's lot in life; challenged to find a middle path between enjoyment and restriction; the necessity to suppress pessimism and self-destructive thoughts; dissatisfaction with oneself and others.

## Jupiter/Uranus

Optimistic, intuitive, self-expansive and far-sighted; progressive; modernising, humanitarian and scientific; urge for freedom and independence; unpredictable; inclined to be extravagant; enjoys change; deviates from convention in thought and ideas; quite happy doing own thing; delights in own originality and uniqueness; finds clever ways of improvising; liberal in judgement of others; spontaneously magnanimous; desires deep (possibly esoteric) knowledge; philosophical interests; has good intuition; quick grasp of a situation; the ability to have fortunate ideas and to realise them; has lucky hunches; an exceptional sense of timing; sudden windfalls; could bring a blissful realisation to self or others; has considerable commercial ingenuity; an eye for good opportunities; has faith in own abilities; trusts in the future and optimistic about own success.

**Or**: fanatical religious zeal; extremist tendencies; inconstancy and tactlessness; can be contradictory and self-opinionated; tendency to magnify or exaggerate things; inclined to have a hurtful sense of humour; inclined to be imprudent and anti-social in compensation for personal inadequacies; loyalty is sometimes brought into question; subject to sudden events that can change life dramatically; handling of financial matters erratic; too sudden expansion followed by loss; worries about prosperity.

## Jupiter/Neptune

A selfless, compassionate, altruistic and emotionally sensitive idealist; inclined to be refined, creative, imaginative, philosophical, intuitive and perceptive; possibly possesses psychic or mediumistic skills/ability; likely to develop keen interest in metaphysical and spiritual matters; seeks to broaden-out understanding and horizons through mind, body, spirit techniques – such as meditation or yoga; may have an enthusiasm for taking risks; likely to have a talent for music, theatre, dance, film or painting; a love of the sea and distant shores; philanthropic, inclined to be receptive to the needs of others; likely to be involved in helping others, being of some kind of service to others – possibly through religious movement or health and healing; a great love of humanity; the ability to give love to those who are in need of it.

**Or**: inclined to look at the world through rose-tinted glasses; can have an over-active imagination; be a dreamer; tendency to be scatter-brained, impressionable, pretends to be more successful than actually is; is an escapist; can be over-optimistic and overgenerous with one's resources; inclined to lead oneself into chaotic situations; inclined to be a do-gooder; a tendency to suffer fools gladly; could suffer from religious delusions; can be excessively dramatic; often has a confused attitude to money; inclined to be involved in doubtful commercial ventures; an inclination towards speculation and wastefulness; susceptible to becoming addicted to gambling, drugs or whatever provides an escape from what is experienced as the harsh realities of life.

## Jupiter/Pluto

A frank, sincere and candid person; a person of vision; an entrepreneur; an excellent organiser whose judgements are keen and fair; ambition and self-motivation is pronounced; will pursue goals in life with passion and intensity; strong desire to make a mark on the world, to accomplish something of significance; a striving for power in either the spiritual, mental or physical spheres of life; a born leader; likely to be known for organising abilities, and taking charge of situations; can wield considerable influence and patronage leading to the success of endeavours; not averse to using compulsion to achieving fruitful outcomes; motivated by the desire to improve the conditions of those around; ability to breathe new life into worn out organisations or structures; a successful marketer or propagandist; popular and greatly respected; handles money well; ability to attract wealth.

**Or**: ruthless; arrogant; a possible megalomaniac; inclined to manipulate and turn others against them; the making of enemies; tendency to make others the scapegoat for one's own responsibilities or inadequacies; tendency to provoke higher authorities than oneself – and suffer consequences; need to not to let power go to one's head – and to lead by example.

# ♄ Saturn

The urge to control, condition and organise one's life; the urge towards self-acceptance, having position, status, responsibility, maturity, seriousness, discipline, perseverance, patience and humility.

## Saturn/Uranus

Ambitious, determined, self-willed, independent and practical; innovative; mechanically-minded; intellectual; suggests good self-control, self-discipline, tenaciousness and toughness; embraces structural change; change seen as a force for good; understands that nothing in life remains the same forever and will give way to the new; radical and modern, yet likewise conservative and traditional in outlook; possible interest in anything "retro" combining the best of both old and new; dialogue arises between the urge to conform and the urge to assert oneself individuality; considerable determination and self-will brought to bear once decisions and a course of action are made; has a rebellious streak; doesn't like own freedom being restricted; desires to be free yet also feeling duty-bound; inclined to be able to detach from feelings; needs periodic isolation from others; talent for scientific work requiring patience, original thought and application; ability to cope in demanding situations, with power to pull through and endure.

**Or**: rebellious; irritable; obstinate; provocative in conduct; tends to be inconsistent; inclined to want to buck the system by any means; the urge for freedom at any price; spasmodic feelings of inferiority; abnormal anxieties; nervously-tensed moods; emotional tensions or strains leading to stress or conflicts, or acts of violence; sudden periods of fatigue; inclined to become manic depressive; needs to find a balance point between conflicting urges.

## Saturn/Neptune

Practical idealism; self-restrained, cautious, devotional, self-sacrificing person, an ascetic with foresight; creativity/art that is directed into given form and purpose – as in classical piano music; able to materialise one's visions and dreams; spiritual values often more important than material success; periodic struggles likely between pursuing spiritual inclinations and meeting the demands of the material world; or between idealistic and materialistic tendencies; ability to make sincere sacrifices and help others in need; can suffer a great deal and experience much disappointment in life; a renunciation of worldly interests; a love of open (isolated or lonely) places where the land meets the sea.

**Or**: loss due to confused impractical thinking; has frequent change of mood; distrust, insecurity, feelings of vulnerability, dissatisfaction; suffers from frustration with life; inclined to disappointment with life; a readiness for sacrifice; inhibition of creative potential; can lack genuine sympathy for others; can be deceitful; prone to bouts of low energy and illness; acute emotional frustration; deep neuroses; be indrawn, introspective; inclined to worry a lot; a likely conflict between idealism and materialism – there may be a need to generate inner harmony through balancing spiritual needs with physical realities.

## Saturn/Pluto

Self-disciplined, tenacious, tough, enduring, modest, determined; inclined to be private, disliking self-revelation; but not afraid to be upfront, even "warts and all," if it serves a purpose; hard-worker, struggles hard for success; has the ability to perform the most difficult work with extreme self-discipline; believes nothing of lasting value comes without hard work and some sacrifice; the capability to make record efforts of the highest possible order; does not let subconscious urges take over; has the power to perform at the highest level, but only after time served learning from the ground up; a likely keen interest in history, archaeology and ancient buildings; seeks to establish certain truths about life; authority and expertise in subject area is acknowledged and respected by others.

**Or**: a hard and unfeeling disposition; cold-heartedness; a tendency to seclusion from others; loner; uncomfortable participating in teamwork; can suffer from feelings of doom and gloom; frustration with life leading to deep-rooted obsessional tendencies; inclined towards paranoia, sometimes dominated by a fear of the future; likely fear of unconscious forces; can be a martyr to the cause; must needs learn to let go as emotional pressures mount; learn to trust in the bounty of life, that one is loved.

# ♅ Uranus

How we will tend to transcend limitations and boundaries, enter new pathways, open doorways, be original and creative; the urge to freedom/detachment beyond established conventions/boundaries of self or environment.

## Uranus/Neptune

Highly intuitive, highly imaginative, idealistic, inspired, mystical and original; a visionary; combines idealism with innovation; a person with an aura about them; ability to tune into prevailing conditions in most circumstances; mediumistic or psychically gifted; inclined to have sudden unusual experiences and visionary dreams; carries much emotional and mental sensitivity, and nervous tension; seeks inner vision; inner illumination and enlightenment; has interest in spiritual and religious matters; an interest in mysticism, art, music, breakthroughs in technologies that help to emancipate the world; seeks the dissolution of boundaries.

Or: unstable, unpredictable; lacking emotional balance; a nervous sensitiveness; holding fanciful or plain wrong ideas; tendency to self-deception, one-sidedness; sudden uncontrollable states of consciousness; sudden bouts of lethargy and weakness; attraction towards risky stimulants or mind-altering substances; one life crisis tending to follow another in rapid succession; can become disastrously infatuated with a movement, with people or particular person.

## Uranus/Pluto

Potentially dynamic creativeness; a pioneer and powerful reformer; ability to lead; able to summon untiring effort and endurance in endeavours; a strong awareness of purpose and of objective; the fight for the establishment of innovations and reforms; can suddenly summon up sufficient inner power to create a new situation; ability to transform people, a situation, or an organisation, using new/original methods; will challenge accepted standards of society; resists conforming to others' values if this means compromising their own; can sometimes be autocratic in endeavours; can be ruthless where, when change is necessary; change is seen as a force for good, even if it precipitated by crisis.

**Or**: restless activity; precipitates action not planned or thought through; can place great stress on one's health and on the health of others; has difficulty admitting dependence on others; inclined to be one-sided, an extremist; exposure to volatility and forces beyond personal control; tendency to attract violent destructiveness; can be manic about means of destruction; power that needs to be used for social reform and personal transformation – otherwise could lead to ruin.

# ♆ Neptune

Developing an emotional sense of unity with all life; at-one-ness; selfless compassion and sacrifice; how we see through illusion and transform; how we become more refined; how we become at one with our higher self or soul.

## Neptune/Pluto

Person with high degree of sensitivity; has a great imagination, vivid fantasies that they can be taken for invention; can make things powerfully dramatic; concern for one's spiritual awareness and development; inclination towards self-refinement through an intensified and purified soul-life supported by disciplined spiritual practice – such as meditation, dance or martial arts; inclined to experience clairvoyant visions; interest in the metaphysical, paranormal and psychical; actively seeks to delve into such unusual phenomena; encourages new forms of spiritual awareness being brought slowly but surely to the surface; a powerful creator of images through artistic form – such as through music, theatre, visual arts or mediumistic demonstrations; often unconscious of the (potentially hypnotic) image one is projecting onto others; seeks to be of service to the world in some way.

**Or**: Inclined towards confusion; subject to daydreaming or a dangerous disconnect from reality; can hold with a confused and hazy interpretation of experience; will be subject to ignoring or treading on acceptable patterns of behaviour; can be obsessional; can have a ruthless streak; prone to outbursts of violence, or a victim thereof; inclination to trick others through "smoke and mirrors;" inclined to be fraudulent; attracts disappointment and loss – or lost souls.

# ♇ Pluto

The urge to bring to light what is hidden; how we will tend to eradicate baggage, cleanse ourself of our past, heal woundings and clear the path to one's soul; renewal, regeneration, transformation through eradication.

Aspects to Pluto are covered by the other planets.

**Ends.**

# The Angles Resource

**The Angles Resource is linked to Step Four of the course.**

Check out the ascending (Rising) and culminating (Midheaven) signs of your birth-chart (and/or someone else's) through the following resource...

The resource provides key ideas and keywords for each sign.

Always bear in mind that understanding your birth-chart is about the relationship between components. While it is necessary to view components in isolation, to aid our understanding, it is also important, once understood, that they are must-needs brought back into context with the other components of your chart. This is in order to have access to a fuller picture of your Self.

But, on a personality level, some components do tend to jut out more than others, and the rising sign, plus the sign on the Midheaven, are two of them.

## Ascending or Rising Signs

## ♈ Aries Rising

Projects a warm, dynamic, active, urgent and self-motivated persona; is a self-starter, self-sufficient, assertive, spontaneous, competitive and wilful; inclined to be fiery and impulsive; open to taking risks; needs to be always busy.

Can otherwise be impatient, quick-tempered, aggressive, tending to act without thinking; can overlook details and often has to undo and redo on actions taken.

Further insight into Aries rising can be gleaned from looking into Mars, the ruler of Aries, by sign, house and aspect.

## ♉ Taurus Rising

Projects a slow-moving, peaceful, practical, resourceful, sensual and down-to-earth conventional persona; will like to think things through; will be patient; prefers to be secure and comfortable, enjoying the simple life; will like to have beautiful things around them.

Can otherwise be lazy, stubborn, uncompromising, possessive and fixed in their routine.

Further insight into Taurus rising can be gleaned from looking into Venus, the ruler of Taurus, by sign, house and aspect.

## ♊ Gemini Rising

Projects a friendly, in good humour, communicative, mentally quick, agile, inquisitive, enthusiastic, informed and versatile persona; inclined to be talkative, changeable, sprightly and nimble; will enjoy variety, have fingers in many pies of interest.

Can otherwise be restless, mentally over-active; be given to being nervous, overly talkative and superficial.

Further insight into Gemini rising can be gleaned from looking into Mercury, the ruler of Gemini, by sign, house and aspect.

# ♋ Cancer Rising

Projects a homely (or home-builder), domesticated, sensitive, impressionable, caring and nurturing persona; inclined to be receptive to the needs and care of others; family oriented; will tend to follow established conventions, traditions, institutions, family and cultural codes of conduct.

Can otherwise be over-sensitive, moody, petulant, on the defensive and easily hurt.

Further insight into Cancer rising can be gleaned from looking into the Moon, the ruler of Cancer, by sign, house and aspect.

# ♌ Leo Rising

Projects a warm, sunny, self-assured, optimistic, outgoing, sociable and self-confident persona; will be the life and soul of the party, will want to be seen and appreciated; inclined to be protective of others and generous by nature; will enjoy having fun, taking up challenges, taking up sports, being on an adventure, or in a drama.

Can otherwise have a sensitive ego, a lot of pride and inclined to be somewhat arrogant and stubborn.

Further insight into Leo rising can be gleaned from looking into the Sun, the ruler of Leo, by sign, house and aspect.

# ♍ Virgo Rising

Projects a gentle, modest, reserved, prudent, intelligent and quiet persona; inclined to be diligent, careful, tidy, systematic, methodical and analytical in their approach to life; inclined to be helpful to others, especially animals and those who are ill or vulnerable; inclined to be a perfectionist, seeking high standards, particularly in their work, their health and hygiene.

Can otherwise be over-critical, fussy, inclined to find fault and to nag.

Further insight into Virgo rising can be gleaned from looking into Mercury, the ruler of Virgo, by sign, house and aspect.

# ♎ Libra Rising

Projects a communicative, engaging, outgoing, diplomatic, tactful, sociable, kind and friendly persona; will seek to keep things in balance and harmony; inclined to be the peace-maker in exchanges; will probably be attractive and refined in appearance and personality; will have an appreciation for style, beauty and the arts.

Can otherwise be over-idealistic, indecisive, preoccupied with the cosmetics of life.

Further insight into Libra rising can be gleaned from looking into Venus, the ruler of Libra, by sign, house and aspect.

# ♏ Scorpio Rising

Projects a strong-willed, emotionally intense, introspective, passionate, sexy, subtle, assertive, reserved and private persona; inclined towards deep and meaningful conversations; capable of generating a fascination over others; detective-like mentality, driven to get to the bottom of things; seeks emotional security.

Can otherwise be defensive, unfeeling, cold, and sometimes ruthless, inclined to be nosey and mistrusting of others.

Further insight into Scorpio rising can be gleaned from looking into Pluto and Mars, the joint rulers of Scorpio, by sign, house and aspect.

# ♐ Sagittarius Rising

Projects an open-minded, philosophical, benevolent, optimistic, versatile, adaptable, adventurous and a risk-taker persona; inclined to be honest and direct in exchanges; will seek to broaden horizons and belief likely through travel and forms of further or higher education; inclined to love nature and enjoy outdoor activities; will likely be searching for meaning to life.

Can otherwise be wasteful, a "gold digger," opinionated, blunt and tactless.

Further insight into Sagittarius rising can be gleaned from looking into Jupiter, the ruler of Sagittarius, by sign, house and aspect.

# ♑ Capricorn Rising

Projects a practical, cautious, often shy, patient, self-controlled and mature persona; inclined to be serious (but can have a dry sense of humour with it), industrious, tenacious, goal-setting and ambitious; seeks to improve status and material success through honest achievements; inclined to hold one's looks into old age.

Can otherwise be too controlled, lack spontaneity and be hard on oneself and dreams.

Further insight into Capricorn rising can be gleaned from looking into Saturn, the ruler of Capricorn, by sign, house and aspect.

# ♒ Aquarius Rising

Projects an intuitive, inventive, mentally quick and sharp intellect, communicative, individualistic, friendly and sociable persona; inclined to have enthusiasm for what is new, contemporary, original and innovative; motivated by a sense of justice, fairness and emancipation for others as a primary motivation; an independent and original personality.

Can otherwise be a bit too "off the wall," eccentric, unpredictable and different in appearance – just to be different.

Further insight into Aquarius rising can be gleaned from looking into Uranus, the ruler of Aquarius, by sign, house and aspect.

## ♓ Pisces Rising

Projects a sensitive, emotional, impressionable, dreamy, romantic and peace-loving persona; will tend to feel things intensely; needs emotional security; possible psychic and/or healing abilities; seeks refinement in lifestyle; appreciation of the arts, notably video/film, poetry and music; spiritual endeavours and retreats – needs time in seclusion.

This sign can otherwise be attracted to intoxicants, stimulants and means of escaping from, or avoiding, life.

Further insight into Pisces rising can be gleaned from looking into Neptune, the ruler of Pisces, by sign, house and aspect.

# Midheaven Signs

Remember, the theme of your midheaven sign is linked to how you are likely to go about making something of yourself in your world. The same "fuller picture..." advice as for each of the rising signs, also applies here. Consider the following...

# ♈ Aries Midheaven

Life goals or aspirations likely to include: being self-motivated, becoming independent, self-reliant and taking a lead role; success through action and having the courage to take risks and achieve one's goals; being the proverbial, "I did it my way" person.

# ♉ Taurus Midheaven

Life goals or aspirations likely to include: building financial and material security into one's life through persistent effort and industry; having all the trappings of worldly goods and sensual experience one can afford; devoting oneself to creating a lasting and pleasurable outcome from one's efforts.

# ♊ Gemini Midheaven

Life goals or aspirations likely to include: having a variety of experiences; pursuing many interests; being informed; being knowledgeable on a range of topics/subjects; having a lot to communicate; being the go-to person for certain information - such as a tour-guide or teacher.

# ♋ Cancer Midheaven

Life goals or aspirations likely to include: putting down roots and being emotionally secure; being "at home" in oneself and in one's life; having a beautiful home and nurturing a beautiful family; building recognisable traditions and links with the past.

# ♌ Leo Midheaven

Life goals or aspirations likely to include: gaining recognition and personal status through one's achievements; winning at the game of life, in whatever that means for the individual, will be what is important for self-confidence and self-esteem; the need to feel appreciated and valued by others – or one's audience.

## ♍ Virgo Midheaven

Life goals or aspirations likely to include: having a regular vocation or career that makes a valid contribution; being healthy in body and mind; having an ordered and clean home environment; having detailed knowledge on specific topics; having a simple uncomplicated lifestyle.

## ♎ Libra Midheaven

Life goals or aspirations likely to include: achieving harmony in one's work and home-life balance, between activity and relaxation, between social interaction and spending time alone; having harmonious relations with people and environment; living in beautiful surroundings; being surrounded by art, music and the finer things in life; helping others achieve same.

## ♏ Scorpio Midheaven

Life goals or aspirations likely to include: being able to fully express one's power and control over one's circumstances; achieving emotional security; finding solutions to deep personal matters; having empathy with others; feeling loved; being involved in analysis, research, investigation.

## ♐ Sagittarius Midheaven

Life goals or aspirations likely to include: acquiring knowledge and success through higher education; freedom to roam, to explore, to travel; speaking other languages;

gaining wisdom and developing one's own deep beliefs about life; financial and material success; a home in another part of the world.

# ♑ Capricorn Midheaven

Life goals or aspirations likely to include: conquering the mountain, the peaks one has set for oneself; achieving material and financial security; succeeding through being in it for the long game and not cutting corners; achieving endorsement, status and respect from others in one's profession; being an authority or leader.

# ♒ Aquarius Midheaven

Life goals or aspirations likely to include: obtaining one's freedom, complete independence; following a radical and new lifestyle; being a (founding) member of a progressive society or group that breaks with convention/tradition; emancipating others through a cause one supports; access to the latest gizmos; inventing something new and revolutionary.

# ♓ Pisces Midheaven

Life goals or aspirations likely to include: mind, body and spiritual refinement; developing one's intuition and receptiveness; being a practitioner in holistic or healing arts; being a person of service such as a medium, a nurse or a nun; going on escapes or retreats; visiting wild places; journeys overseas; caring for other creatures, a career in music.

**Ends.**

# The Twelve Houses Resource

The Twelve Houses Resource is linked to Step Four of the course.

## 1st House and Ascendant (Asc)

Personal matters or self-centred interests. Being linked to the Ascendant too (the persona) this house tends to be expressed outwardly in a highly personal or private manner.

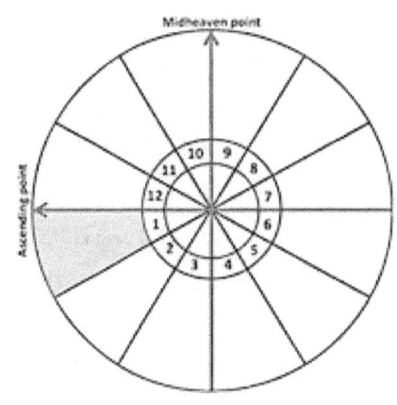

This is where we put a personal touch on matters, how we project out to others. It's a "me first" approach but not necessarily implying selfishness, rather individuality, going it alone; or just as importantly how others may perceive us, or how we want them to perceive us.

Has affinity with Aries and Mars. This is the shop window on oneself.

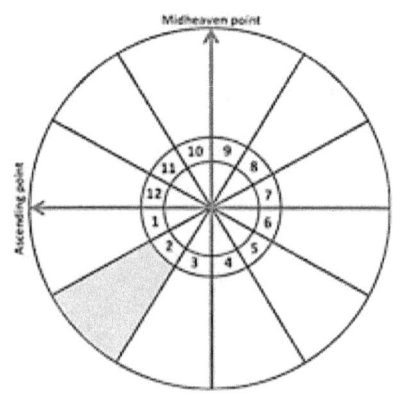

# 2nd House

Relates to having possessions, resources we have or need, and security. The focus here is largely on acquisition, having or how we acquire things, essential things (or what we consider essential) like a house, car, the trappings of modern life, and notably money in order to be secure in ourselves - being "earthed."

It is equally about being nourished, or how we are nourished - having enough of anything and everything.

Has affinity with Taurus and Venus.

# 3rd House

Personal relationship to environment - learning, finding out, communications, interests, local journeys. This is all about "knowing" where we are and being personally secure through knowledge and communications.

It is also linked to the means of communication - speaking, writing, sharing ideas, the media, computers, means of getting around etc., and local environment. Stuff we need to know in order to negotiate our world - and mostly our immediate local world.

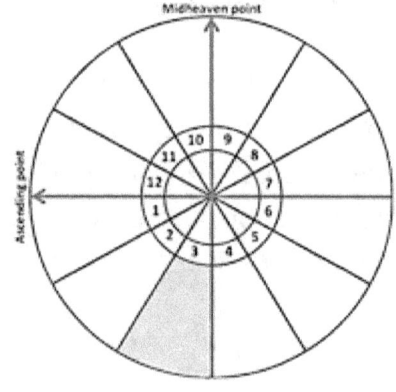

Has affinity with Gemini and Mercury.

# 4th House and Imum Coeli (IC)

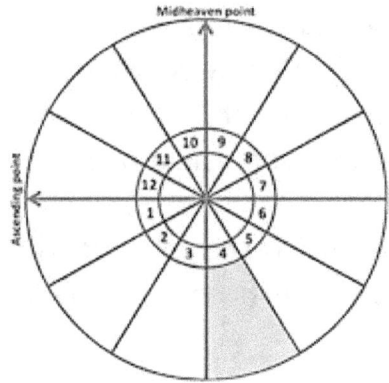

It's home, home life, relatives, links to the past, one's roots. This is about the bricks and mortar of emotional security so how/where we grew up; our home and family matters; being amongst kinfolk, having a sense of belonging; digging into one's heritage.

It is identifying emotionally with one's family, environment, or one's country and culture - patriotism.

Has affinity with Cancer and the Moon.

# 5th House

Recreation, creativity, adventure, competition, sports. This house is about childhood and areas of activity that allow us to express our prowess and creativity.

It is the means by which we show others what we are made of – hence association with play, school, challenges, taking gambles and sports.

Has affinity with Leo and the Sun.

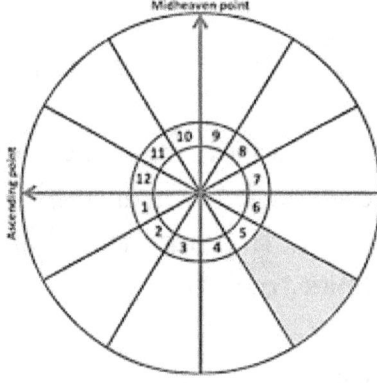

# 6th House

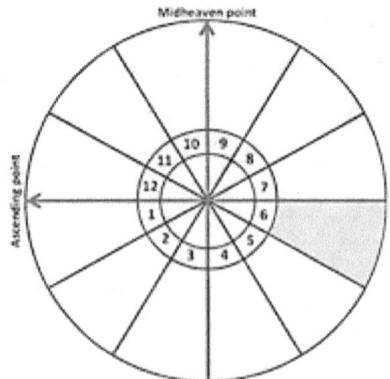

This house relates to health, work and service within one's community. It links to participating in one's community on an exchange basis so hence the emphasis on "work" – to do something with or for others and get something back.

It also has strong links to conventional forms of education, routine activities, maintenance of health and efficiency, being clean and pure.

Has affinity with Virgo and Mercury.

# 7th House and Descendant (Dsc)

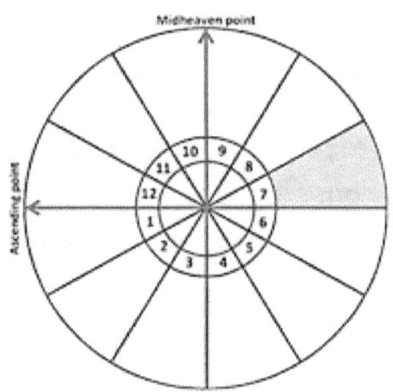

It's about relating, others, partners, love matches, agreements, marriage, the trappings of attraction or attracting partners, harmonious environments. This house links to all things to do with relating and relationships.

Being in opposition to the 1st house which is about "me," this house is about the "other" or "us."

Has affinity with Libra and Venus.

# 8th House

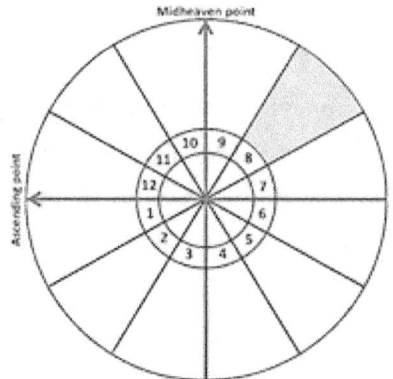

This house links with legal matters, undercurrents, issues that are hidden. Being opposite the 2nd house, this house links to possessions but here gained through others (such as through a will or dowry), shared resources with others.

Mixed up with the 8th house are passions, powerful feelings, undercover activities, crime, taboos. In any relationship there is a point when the gloss comes off and truer feelings and intentions, or hidden (known or unknown) agendas, are revealed – and it depends then whether we can live with that. This house links with death – something has to die in order to be transformed – and things that go bump in the night.

Has affinity with Scorpio and Mars/Pluto.

# 9th House

This house links with travel and explorations, the bigger picture, expanding to new horizons. Seeking higher education, higher knowledge, distant lands, far-reaching worldly goals. This house is really about those things that aid and abet the stretching of oneself; taking gambles, investment, religion or philosophical speculation and orthodox belief systems.

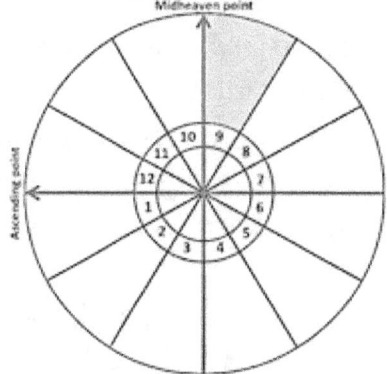

Being opposite the 3rd house there are links with writing, publishing and worldly exploration.

Has affinity with Sagittarius and Jupiter.

Learn to Read Your Birth-chart in 5 Steps

# 10th House and Midheaven (Medium Coeli - MC)

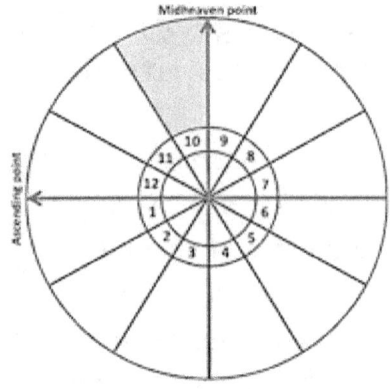

This house links with social status, position, responsibilities and necessities. This house also links to the Midheaven – the worldly highpoint of our success. We can say that all the internal love, homeliness and nurturing of the 4th house here comes seeking external fruition.

This house links to how we express ourselves in the outer-world and achieve outer trappings of success – our goals, status, job, career, public, political position and reputation.

Has affinity with Capricorn and Saturn.

# 11th House

The 11th house has an identification with groups, social activities, social networks, collective objectives, innovations, inventions that help to emancipate free or release others. This house, opposite to the 5th house, has much to do with the means by which we become part of something bigger, a team, a group or movement can be bigger than the sum of its parts.

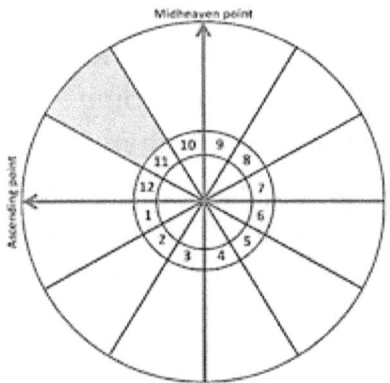

This is the house of social objectives, humanity, of unions, all for one and one for all. The competition of the 5th House gives way to the appreciation and recognition of the contribution of others, and, at best, from whichever side they are on.

Has affinity with Aquarius and Uranus/Saturn.

# 12th House

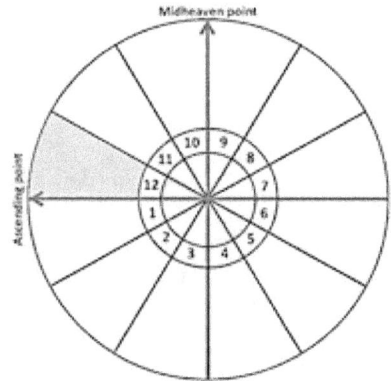

This links to self-abnegation in service for others; or self-disintegration, escapism, confinement. Much of what this house represents is concerned with structures transforming or losing their boundaries, becoming less rigid and more fluid – hence it has links with water, gases, clouds, dreams and the effect of drugs.

Being opposite to the 6th house it also has links to health, work and duty but to higher causes – or importantly what are perceived as higher causes – such as being in-service, healing, spiritual quests – unconditional service to humanity in some way or other. It is also known as the house of disappointment – a reminder not to get too carried away on our hopes and dreams.

Has affinity with Pisces and Neptune/Jupiter.

**Ends.**

# The Planets by House Resource

**The Planets by House Resource is linked to Step Three and Step Four of the course.**

A planet's occupation of a given house can throw up some real tangible insight into likely experience/s and outcomes in a person's birth-chart. On a mundane or worldly level this can be more so than a planet's position by sign.

This is notably going to be true for outcomes associated with the slow-moving outer planets (of Uranus, Neptune and Pluto), that by zodiac sign can be linked with generations, by house their association is likely to be a lot more up-front and personal.

## Empty houses

Not all of your houses will be occupied by planet/s (we are covering), but they <u>will</u> be occupied by signs. To gain insight into an unoccupied house what you can do is check out the sign on the cusp of the given house and also consider the position of the ruling planet for that same sign.

So, if your 5th house (Fig.61) was unoccupied and its cusp was in the sign of Aries, you would consider Aries and also look to the position of Mars for insight into it. On the face of it, it suggests a young at heart pioneering spirit.

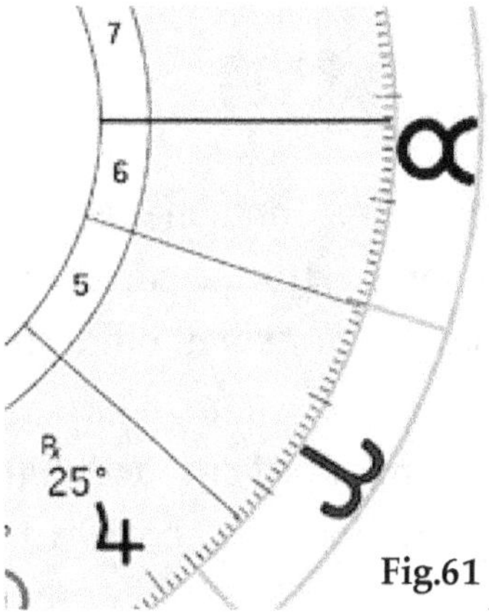

Fig.62

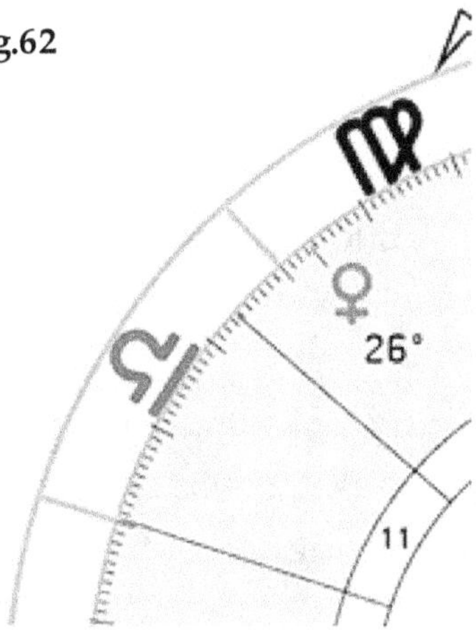

If it was say, your 11th house (Fig.62) that was unoccupied, with its cusp in Libra, you would look to Venus (which, in this instance, happens to be next door in Virgo and 10th house) for insight into it.

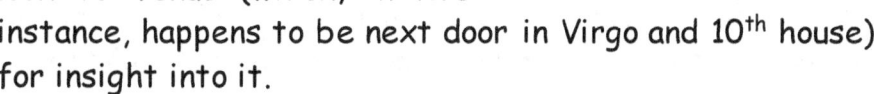

Fig.61

In some way you would be inclined to enjoy friendly relationships more than intimate relationships; probably have a circle of friends of like mind or interests. Probably be artistic, creative, theatrical and radical in some way; and apply it in your career (10th house) objectives.

If it was an unoccupied house with its cusp in say, Aquarius, you would look to the position of Uranus for insight into it. With this example though you would also look into the position of Saturn as the old ruler.

This area is also discussed under **Compensatory behaviour** of Step 1 Part 2.

# Get the idea...

What follows are keywords associated with each of the planets by house. To repeat here; always try to get the idea, or feel of what theme is underlying the keywords – so that you can learn to apply your own take on the matter.

# ☉ Sun

01: Focus on oneself, one's individuality; self-confident, assertive, enthusiastic, personal; takes care of health; inclined to lead, take initiative, take risks; works towards personal ambitions; can appear self-centred.

02: Interest in acquiring money, possessions, resources; building things to last; expression of creative talent; talent for owning things.

03: Self-expression through mental pursuits, study, acquiring information; a good student; interest in communications, writing or teaching; seeks connections with neighbours; close ties with brothers and sisters; being a go-between.

04: Home and family important interest; love of houses; ties with the past; could indicate late development; reclusive tendencies.

05: Creative expression; games, sports and adventures; avenues for building self-confidence and expressing one's power; love of pleasure; theatre, and children.

06: Concentration on work; keen on detail; tidy environment; interest in health and diet, service or healing profession, possibility of overwork; need of holidays.

07: Interest in other people, need for partner, need of audience; focus on building relationships; marriage; expression of power through others.

08: Ability to handle other people's resources; legacies; healing ability; magician – now you see me, now you don't; expresses strength in a crisis; interest in the occult; intense experiences; sexual prowess.

09: Interest in higher education and spiritual growth; love of travel and learning other languages; time spent abroad; professional success, strong sense of values.

10: Achieving fame or recognition in chosen vocation or profession; the architect of one's own worldly success; leadership roles; corporate person; dealing with authority; political power, ambition.

11: Creative thinker; leader in group activities; many friends in societies or on social media; links with people in high places; likely interest in causes, the future, in technology, environmental matters.

12: Works behind the scenes; identification with schools, hospitals or other institutions; devoted to a cause; interest in the arts, in research, in retreats; reclusive tendencies.

# ☽ Moon

01: Strongly receptive, changeable, seen to act on impulse; needs personal involvement; expresses powers of imagination; good appetite; identification with mother, emotionally charged.

02: Seeks security based on having financial and material resources in place, and being well-nourished; changeable or unstable finances, resources; artistic ability; business interests; need to feel earthed in peaceful, solid, reliable, steady and productive circumstances.

03: Enjoys reading; needs fuel for imagination; story teller, literary ability; loves to chat; likes short regular "round and about" journeys; need for variety; emotional communicator.

04: Strong interest in home, family and mother or motherhood; rich inner life; possible interest in roots, ancestry and borders; reclusive tendencies; many changes of residence likely.

05: Dramatic personality – makes a good entrance; love of competitions – such as quizzes, card games; love of adventures and fun with women and children; enjoys getting out and about; many love affairs.

06: Concerns with health and diet, weight-watching; frequent changes of employment; protective environments; professional carer, emotional need to help others, to serve.

07: Need for relationships (with women) for own security; easily forms emotional attachments to people; vulnerable to changes in partnerships; seeks a beautiful, harmonious home.

08: Intensive emotional life; critical experiences; strong and passionate sexual activity, conscious of death; benefits received through others such legacies; likely interest in the paranormal.

09: Strong religious convictions; desire for continuing education; love of travel – but enjoys coming home more than anything; inclined towards taking risks to provide emotional security.

10: Need for public recognition, emotional attachment to the father; need for orderly conventional procedures; changes in life goals and/or profession.

11: Lives in an unconventional environ; breaks with tradition; enjoys going retro; enjoys radical and independent thinkers; turnover of friends; emotional need to be part of groups or societies; attraction to technology and the means of bringing about change.

12: Love of solitude, quiet places, seas and rivers; heightened sensitivity and imagination; rich dream life; seeks to be "at home" in oneself through mind body & spirit activities or retreats; psychic ability.

# ☿ Mercury

01: Mental alertness; quick decisive ideas; strong urge to communicate and/or move; direct and/or hasty in communications – gets to the point; likes to talk about oneself, keep oneself in the frame.

02: Good business sense; interest gaining money or possessions through negotiation, ideas and communications – e.g., buyer, seller, firm's representative; seeks reliable conventional profession that draws on knowledge; lives by wits, gift of the gab.

03: Gift for communication; good student; writing or teaching ability; knowledgeable across a wide range of subjects; much moving around in local environment; much contact with siblings.

04: Knowledgeable and talkative family background, sharing ideas with relatives; the home the focus for most communications; mental occupations carried out in home – may work from home; interest in family background, history, or politics; changes in life but likely to stay local.

05: Story teller; abilities in drama and theatre; competitive writer or talker; good communication with children; speculative investments; academic mixed with social pleasures.

06: Interested in the discipline of writing/communications; can converse on matters of health and hygiene or work-related matters; literary or academic profession; analysis and report writing; danger over-doing mental activity.

07: Refinement in communications; literary interests; relationships as an interest – match-maker; eloquent, witty and diplomatic speaker, considerable communications with people, business partnership/s.

08: A legal-eagle; investigative mind; interested in death, sex, psychology, "fringe" matters, e.g., astrology and the paranormal; quietly reserved, taciturn; skill in handling other people's resources.

09: Eternal student; avid traveller; orator; lecturer; writer; worldly ideas; evangelical streak; seeks professional status.

10: Professional or business writer; business mentality; serious communicator; academic professional, financial and worldly/political interests.

11: Bringing inventive ideas into reality; interest in technology and gadgets; participation in social media friends and groups; new forms of communication, e.g., interest in ESP.

12: Hidden communications, taciturn, loner; distance healing abilities; creative visualisation; practices hypnosis; active dream life; mediumistic/psychic; teaching yoga or meditation, communes with nature; explores mind enhancing drugs.

# ♀ Venus

01: Inclined to have good looks, be attractive and charming; can be occupied with one's appearance; sociable, is passionate and demonstrative in relating, likes to take the lead; naïve in affairs of the heart; love of pleasure, given to overindulgence.

02: Love and appreciation of material things; love of luxury; musical and/or artistic talent/abilities; attracts financial success through pleasant ways of doing it; inclined to over-indulge in sensual pleasures; can be sensually greedy, over-possessive/grasping.

03: Talent for writing – writer of romantic novels; a love for learning; inclined to love reading and studying only what is liked or enjoyed; good education, intellectual tastes; artistic; charming, eloquent and witty in communications.

04: Likes a comfortable, clutter-free, harmonious home; needs to feel loved and secure in the home – need for affection; a love of entertaining; home focal point for social activities; possibility of inherited wealth.

05: Love of children, fun and adventure; creative and competitive ability; romantic personality; needs love affairs; love of drama, parties and pleasure.

06: Seeks the body beautiful; enjoys good health; enjoys participating in work activities; good at getting others to work harmoniously; vocation involving some form of art or beauty; social life and work life inclined to be inseparable; strong likes and dislikes.

07: Social skills; popular personality; equality in partnerships; successful relationships; likely happy marriage; lives harmoniously with others; a social butterfly; an appreciation for beauty, the arts and refinement;

08: Seeks authenticity in partnerships; financial gain or inheritance through partnerships; ability as a priest, counsellor or therapist; enjoys harmonious sexual experience; interest in occult matters; an easy death.

09: Inclined to retain independence; long distance relationships; marriage abroad; links with friends or business partners in foreign countries; love of travel, religion, study and philosophy; high ideals; talent for publishing.

10: Forms conventional, dependable partnership/s likely with mature, experienced partners; financial success; good public professional presentation; success in the arts or the entertainment world; talent for gaining publicity; could be famous for beauty or wealth.

11: Popular independent person; many friends, artistic friends; happy amongst like-minded friends; good fortune through involvement in groups or social networks; high ideals.

12: A love of solitude being secluded; shyness; secret relationships; love of story and mysteries; mediumistic tendencies; has social conscience; love of arts – notably dance and music; impressionable, vulnerable to deception.

# ♂ Mars

01: Pioneering; independent action; displays urgency combined with energy, enterprise, courage and self-motivation; physical strength, action, aggression; good at starting own enterprise.

02: Industrious and enterprising; drive and energy focussed on making a living, gaining material security; likely challenged at saving money; runs own business; tendency to work on the land; good energy and good health.

03: Forceful in communications; enjoys lively discussion/debate; active in immediate environment – always on the go; desire/need to round-out education; affairs of brothers and sisters a focus of interest.

04: Strong attachment to home, inclined to be protective towards home and loved ones; active around the home; dominant in the home; arguments in the home; identifies with roots; work from home; unconscious anger.

05: Participates in games and competitions; expresses courage and self-confidence; inclined to assume authority or leadership role; passionate in love-making; love of pleasure; love of children and/or desire for children.

06: Industrious activity; cautious, efficient and economical use of energy, or inclined to be a workaholic; practical, precision and methodical work; desire to serve, possible health problems through stress.

07: Energy devoted to building relationships; forceful and passionate in one's affections; sexually active partner/s; quarrels with partner/s; possibility of lawsuits.

08: Dealing with finance or financial transactions for others; powerful sex drive; secret/hidden activities; links with surgery; possibility of accidents; interest in psychology and occult matters; desire for offspring.

09: Love of travel involving enterprise, challenge and pioneering adventure; love of sport; continuing education; seeks self-improvement, a broadening of horizons; likes to take a gamble.

10: Industrious, enterprising, courageous; plans and reaches objectives; ambitious goals; leads organisation; career as athlete, soldier, surgeon, butcher, blacksmith; tendency to be a workaholic.

11: Enterprising, innovative; keen to help free others; fights worthy causes; strikes out for own cause or for the underdog; attracts many friends; also quarrels with friends; socio-political work or activities.

12: activity behind the scenes; secret love affairs; will sacrifice self for others; difficulty expressing anger; possibility of chronic health problems; accident prone; victim of unexpected disappointment.

# ♃ Jupiter

01: Confidence in one's own abilities; self-important; leads from the front; optimistic about life; jovial; generous towards others; creates opportunities; theatrical; looks to distant horizons.

02: Talent for handling money; prosperous; inclined towards financial and business interests; financial success; tendency to over-indulge, in danger of excess.

03: Likely has a good education; love of study; involved in education; philosophical interests; talents in communications/marketing; company rep; good public speaker; pleasant relationship with siblings.

04: Good relations with parents; secure and comfortable home; happy home-life; good business sense; optimistic moral and religious upbringing.

05: Love of theatre, drama, literature, film, the arts in general; pleasure seeking; competitive; gambling and sports interests; orator – plays to the audience; many love affairs, love and understanding of children.

06: Good health; involved in medical or charitable work; organiser; strong desire to be of service to others; work is lucrative; attraction to research/education/teaching; possibility of over-work.

07: Outgoing personality; attracts many friends and connections; good business or professional associates; attracts fortunate relationships/marriage; strong appreciation for the arts.

08: Attracts inheritance; prosperity/wealth through marriage partner; many sexual contacts; philosophical over matters of life and death; interest in exploring the psychic and paranormal events.

09: Love of learning and exploration (notably morality, religion, philosophy, law) and travel; qualities as orator/communicator/lecturer; love of freedom; takes gambles; seeks self-improvement and spiritual growth.

10: Hard worker; leadership qualities; attracts professional success and honours; prefers comfortable circumstances, ease of accomplishment.

11: Attracts many friends and professional contacts, high ideals; humanitarian; environmental interests; qualities as orator/communicator;

12: Charity or social worker; success with matters of the sea, success with businesses linked to gas and oil, to the arts, music and dance; activity behind the scenes; interest in metaphysical/spiritual matters; inclined towards psychic/spiritual experiences.

# ♄ Saturn

01: Austere and serious persona; sense of personal authority and responsibility; sense of limitation or inadequacy; takes calculated risks rather than on impulse; puts in effort; faces obstacles, delays; inclined to go it alone; inclined to pessimism.

**02:** Careful and controlling with money and resources; economical; works hard to build structure; or can be subject to testing financial problems; feelings of deprivation; fear of poverty.

**03:** Mentally disciplined; conscientious student; reserved in communications; talent for writing or teaching; sense of responsibility for siblings; responsibilities around neighbourhood; possibility of limited education and sense of inadequacy in mental activities.

**04:** Home and family, or one's background a concern; takes on family responsibilities; emphasis on strict parental discipline; comes from difficult family background or lacks proper home; sense of isolation in one's home, insecure over one's identity.

**05:** Artistic ambition; love for older people; self-confidence/self-worth built up over time - often through testing experience; strong need for respect/recognition; competitive but afraid of losing - brings difficulty enjoying sports, games and competitions; responsibilities involving children or there is a lack of children; sense of being blocked in self-expression.

**06:** Industrious, serious, analytical and organised mind; work in areas such as science, technology or medicine; concerns with (others - possibly elderly) health and hygiene; tendency to having health problems from overwork, or stressful worry and inhibition.

**07:** Seeks secure, reliable partnerships; needs stability in relationships; marriage to older person or authority figure; marriage delayed; challenging business partnerships; undemonstrative; many responsibilities to other people; tends to be celibate; tends to be lonely, alone or feel alone.

**08:** Remains cool and a strength in a crisis; endures hardships; takes responsibilities for other people's money or resources; legal-eagle; hard-nosed; sexually repressed; can have morbid fear of death; inclined to be cynical about life.

**09:** Focus on continuing education; academic interests; spiritual aspiration; questions faith and belief; political interests; professional ambition; business interests abroad; lack of travel or difficulties expected in foreign places; risk averse.

10: Industrious, ambitious; achieves recognition as a result of hard work and effort; leadership, authority abilities; reversals of fortune; sense of inadequacy; pessimism over future or success.

11: Scientific mind, serious communicator; deep sense of responsibility to society; liberating attitude towards others; long-lasting but not close friendships; contacts who are older and wiser; isolation from contacts.

12: Compassionate and reserved; responsibility behind the scenes; sorrows born in secret; a person of service; scientific research; work for institutions; isolation and low in spirits; potential for depression or despondency – and illness resulting from it.

# ⛢ Uranus

01: Projects conspicuous individuality; eccentric, clever, original; strong need for freedom/independence; love of change; unusual appearance or mannerisms; interests in science and technology.

02: Unconventional values; sudden changes in financial affairs; unusual talent; unconventional ways of dealing with practical matters; technical skills; money earned in unusual ways.

03: Intuitive, original thinker; thought, speech, and writing unusual; erratic education; disconnect from siblings likely; odd and interesting happenings while going from one place to another; talent for writing, teaching or science; interest in unusual subject matter.

04: Unconventional family and/or background; many changes of residence; disrupted or broken home; emotional instability; unsettling life experience.

05: Love of adventure; need for creative and playful expression – can be creatively brilliant; unusual or gifted children; original in interests or hobbies; little regard for convention; bizarre romances.

06: Need for independence in employment; many changes of employment; unusual type of work; inventive in one's work; unusual diet, interest in alternative medicine; potential health problems.

07: Attracted to unusual people; offbeat relationships; strong need for independence in relationships equality in partnerships; intuitive communications; possibility of divorce or separation.

08: Creative, urge to bring new things into being; healing ability; strong attraction to fringe and/or paranormal matters; unconventional ideas about sex, life and death; money from others received in unusual ways; risk-taker; propensity for attracting unexpected crises.

09: Unorthodox social, educational, religious or philosophical ideas; original thinker and teacher; much adventurous travel – will tend to go alone; spiritual consciousness; sudden change in objectives.

10: Unusual profession; technical or scientific work/interests; urge to electrify and change established order; reputation for being unorthodox and bringing in change; interest in holistic arts and craft; sudden changes of fortune.

11: Utopian and revolutionary ideas; humanitarian interests; interest in the future and technological innovations; unusual friends; creative stimulation from friends and groups.

12: Highly intuitive, inspired, sensitive, receptive and responsive to change; psychic experiences; involvement in the arts (music, dance) and love of nature; brilliant researcher; creative in solitude; possibility of mental health issues through unresolved conflicts within oneself.

# ♆ Neptune

01: Projects a dreamy persona; inclined to be strongly intuitive, sensitive and very impressionable; powerful imagination; has acting ability, musical or mathematical talent; will go off on a whim; lives in a dream, is otherworldly; poor sense of time.

02: Talent for music, dance, poetry, creative design or mathematics; earns living through creative art/s or psychic activities; somewhat laisse affaire over finances and resources; uncertainty regarding ownership and material security; tendency to dissipate one's resources.

03: Dreamy reclusive nature; powerful (or confused) imagination; mediumistic gifts; inspired communications, artistic, poetic or automatic writing; tendency to daydream.

04: Rich dream life; psychic abilities; idealistic regarding parents, home and homeland; musical home/background; possibility of broken home or uncertainty about where one's home is; emotional instability.

05: Creative/artistic ability, love of the theatre and drama, love of adventures; escapism through characters stories; romantic identification with heroes, heroines, leaders or celebrities; romanticism, creative inspiration, uncertainty in love affairs; disappointment with or through children.

06: Desire to serve humanity; vocation in holistic health; likelihood of healing abilities; lack of ego gratification in work; uncertainty over one's vocation and community value; mysterious and undiagnosable health problems.

07: Refined appreciation of beauty and art; seeking the ideal in partnerships; artistic, musical, poetic, or mathematical partner; ill or alcoholic partner; dissolving relationships; confusion, deception, or self-sacrifice in relationships; Platonic love; unconditional love and service in relationship/s.

08: Mediumistic/psychic ability; attraction to the spiritual/mysterious and paranormal; unusual or strange sexual patterns; possible celibacy or renunciation of sex; financial matters need care; danger of becoming a victim.

09: Intuitive; dreams big; publisher interests; strongly religious/philosophical/devoted approach to life; interest in mysticism; a longing for faraway inspiring places; links with the sea; given to idealism, evangelism, fanaticism.

10: Dreams brought down into reality; a dreamer with (or lacking) confidence to succeed; profession involving charity, health, psychology, music, acting, or the arts; spiritual leadership; investment in ocean, oil or gas; achievement through deception – possibility of public disgrace, ruin or martyrdom.

11: Intuitive, innovative and artistic; gifted in arts/music; inspired by hunches that are reliable; idealism; humanitarian causes, interest in global and environmental matters; unusual contacts; possibility of loss of friends.

12: Spiritual endeavours; person of service; highly sensitive, receptive and artistic – notably excels in dance and music; abilities as a psychic or medium; interest in metaphysics; reclusive tendencies, sensitivity to other planes, rich inner life, active dream life, tendency to various forms of escapism – e.g., drugs or alcohol; danger of becoming a victim.

# ♇ Pluto (or ♇)

01: Powerful personality; extraordinary determination and courage in the face of challenges; leadership qualities; investigative abilities; psychic or healing ability; potential for self-transformation; strong sexual orientation; hidden or reclusive tendencies.

02: Resourceful; drive to acquire material things; obsessional preoccupation with security and material possessions; transformation of values, talent as healer or psychic.

03: Penetrating mind, psychological insight, powerful communicator, or intense in communications; difficult or lonely childhood; probing of early experiences; reformer in areas such as psychology, IT, education; media or transport.

04: Strong attachment to home, family, one's hereditary mother and the land; difficult relations with others in the home - tendency to be dictatorial; deep unconscious drives, potential for radical self-transformation, possibility or much repression and sadness/upheavals in one's home-life.

05: Powerful need to make an impression on others/world; air of authority/leader; compulsion to create, powerful bonds with children, intense sexuality, great capacity for pleasure; extraordinary achievements likely or uncompromising and dictatorial in position of power.

06: Organised, inquisitive and penetrating mind; the pursuit of scientific objectives; service in the community; reformer in areas of health and work; compulsive worker; vocation as healer, obsession with health, diet, or cleanliness; inclined to be a workaholic; can have pessimistic outlook on life;

07: Charismatic; strong ability to counsel/influence others in improving relationships; possibility of influencing large numbers of people; attraction to powerful people, tendency to be dominated in relationships; or extreme views on relationships, mistrust and the need to control others.

08: Powerful personality; emotionally intense and charismatic; secretive, hidden, undercover; strong influence on others; interest in the occult and paranormal; healing powers, strong sexuality, intense experience, strength in crisis, interest in, and understanding of, death.

09: Drive to learn, travel or teach; passionate and pioneering in areas of education, travel, religion, philosophy and justice; intellectual leadership; spiritual transformation, religious fanaticism.

10: Strong public image, charismatic and ambitious; successful realisation of business, economic or political goals; power of persuasion/determination; urge to transform established structures/poor working practices; dominating father; crisis in career and/or spectacular comebacks; authoritarian tendencies; tendency towards depression and isolation.

11: Drive to transform oneself and society; seeks the emancipation of others; tendency to dominate friends and groups; interested in or applies scientific, psychological, technological, humanitarian knowledge or research; attraction to communal living; or exaggerated plans, extreme views, taking extreme actions.

12: Healing and psychic abilities; able to cleanse physical and psychological woundings; intense inner life, interest in the metaphysical realms and application of therapy; work in secrecy, in service; power behind the scenes; reclusive tendencies; inclined to celibacy or secret affairs; deep sense of loss/depression/spiritual torment.

**Ends.**

# Books & Where to Next

## Books

If you are contemplating getting further books on Western natal astrology, here are a sample of the authors and books I'd recommend you look into:

| Alan Oken | Astrology: Evolution and Revolution – a path to higher consciousness |
|---|---|
| Alexander Ruperti | Cycles of Becoming – Planetary Patterns of Growth |
| Charles & Suzy Harvey | The Principles of Astrology |
| Christina Rose | Astrological Counselling |
| Dane Rudhyar | Astrology and Modern Psyche |
| Donna Cunningham | An Astrological Guide to Self-Awareness |
| Erroll Weiner | Transpersonal Astrology – Finding the Souls Person |
| Howard Sasportas | The Gods of Change |
| Katharine Merlin | Character and Fate – The Psychology of the Birthchart |
| Liz Green & Howard Sasportas | The Development of the Personality |
| Noel Tyl | Synthesis and Counselling in Astrology |
| Robert Hand | Essays in Astrology |
| Roy Alexander | The Astrology of Choice – A Counselling Approach |
| Stephen Arroyo | Astrology, Psychology, and the Four Elements |

Some of these books have been around for a number of years – some of the best were written back to the 1970s – in my opinion of course.

I'd also recommend you get hold of an ephemeris; such as the Neil F. Michelsen & Rique Pottenger – The American Ephemeris for the 21st Century.

# Where to Next

If you want to get further involved in astrology, for study or interest, check out the following organisations.

These are in the UK or USA, but you can explore and study online these days so it shouldn't be an issue where you are, as long as it suits your language. You may also get help via these links to find organisation/s closer to your home should you need:

## Learning establishments:

The Faculty of Astrological Studies – https://www.astrology.org.uk/

The Mayo School of Astrology – https://www.mayoastrology.com

Astrological Psychology Association – https://www.astrologicalpsychology.org

Kepler College - https://www.keplercollege.org/

ISAR (International Society for Astrological Research) - https://www.isarastrology.com/

## Also check out:

The Astrological Association of Great Britain – https://www.astrologicalassociation.com

American Federation of Astrologers – https://www.astrologers.com/

## For research into astrology:

ISAR (see above)
Urania Trust – http://www.uranian-institute.org/xresearch.htm
Correlation Journal of Research in Astrology - https://correlationjournal.com/

# Glossary of Terms

The list here is intended to help provide a quick explanation of some of the terms occurring across this workbook – and in some cases related to items not mentioned in the book, or are mentioned in the Bonus Pack.

| Acausal | Doesn't cause any effects. Astrology is said to be acausal when it is argued the planets do not cause events. |
|---|---|
| Acausal Time Template | My own philosophical description for a birth-chart. The birth-chart is a template for capturing the (acausal) planetary positions for a moment in time and place. See, Article 1 in the Bonus Pack |
| Age of Aquarius | This expectation of a coming (or already arrived) Age, is based upon the backward movement of the Spring Equinox through the constellations of stars. As it goes into and through a new constellation it is given the title of an Age – by astrologers. Depending upon how you view it we are either still in the constellation (and Age) of Pisces, at the border of Aquarius (the new age) or we are already in Aquarius. Discussed in Article 3 of the Bonus Pack. |
| Anecdotal | Based on personal experience or account – subjective. See Article 7 in the Bonus Pack. |
| (The) Angles | The four cardinal points where the horizon plane and the meridian plane intersect the ecliptic. These are known as the Ascendant, Midheaven, Descendant and Imum Coeli. See Step 4 for more information. |
| Ascending sign | The sign on the ascendant. Any of the 12 signs that could be rising in a 24-hour period. |
| Astrological houses | The 12 houses of astrology. Often seen as a mundane zodiac linking to 12 life areas – such as money (House 2) health (House 6) or relationships (House 7). See Step 4 for more information. |
| Astrology | The art that draws on data provided by astronomy. It uses this to help calculate and represent moments of time, in context with locations on the Earth. The art of the astrologer is in interpreting the symbolism, the meaning from the resulting birth-chart pattern. |
| Astronomy | The science that studies all non-Earthly phenomena, including the sun, moon, planets, comets, stars, galaxies, dust and gases etc. |
| Autumn equinox | The equinox in autumn, on or about 22/3 September in the northern hemisphere and 21 March in the southern hemisphere. It is when day and night are equal length, as the sun crosses the celestial equator in a southerly direction. |

| Birth-chart | Also, birth chart or natal chart. An astrology chart usually composed of the planets of our solar system, 12 signs and 12 houses constructed for the time, date and place of birth of a person. |
|---|---|
| Birth-chart report | A report produced from a birth-chart reading. |
| Cardinal signs | Aries, Cancer, Libra and Capricorn. Directive/activating energy. |
| Chart ruler | Planet associated with the ascending or rising sign. See Step 3 for more information. |
| Chinese astrology | Chinese astrology is based on 12 animal signs in a repeating 12-year cycle – so the signs are linked to years rather than constellations or seasons. It identifies 5 elements: fire, earth, metal, water, and wood (instead of 4 of Western astrology). Each element is linked to a motivating force in a person's life. Because the animals are on 12-year cycles and there are 5 elements, the Chinese zodiac-element cycle lasts for 60 years before repeating. |
| Classical astrology | Astrology handed down by the Greeks. It is otherwise known as Hellenistic astrology or traditional astrology. |
| Correlation | In astrology, the modern view that the planets don't cause/influence outcomes but synchronise in their cycles with the cycles/events on the Earth. See Article 1 in the Bonus Pack. |
| Demise of astrology | 17th into 18th centuries in Europe. Corresponds with the rise of empirical sciences. Re-emerged as modern psychological astrology at the turn of the 20th century. See Article 2 of Bonus Pack. |
| Ecliptic circle | The path the Earth takes in its orbit around the Sun. On a broader level it applies to all planets and asteroids orbiting the Sun. |
| Energy patterns | All matter is energy (Einstein) and astrological charts are viewed as representing the dynamic and vibrant energy pattern of people or situations. |
| Ephemeris | A table carrying the positions of the planets (by geocentric/tropical zodiac signs) for a given period. As a book will often contain tables for a period of 1 to 50 or more years. See Step 3 for more information. |
| Fertile Crescent | Ancient area of the modern Middle East. Covered the area of Egypt, Syria and Iraq and included Egypt, Phoenicia, Assyria, Mesopotamia and Sumeria. See Article 2 in the Bonus Pack. |
| Fixed signs | Taurus, Leo, Scorpio and Aquarius. Static/holding energy. See Step 2 for more information. |
| Four Elements | The four elements of Western astrology are: Fire, Earth, Air and Water. See Step 2 for more information. |
| Geocentric | Earth-centred. As viewed from (the position of) the Earth. |
| Grand cross | Where four or more planets are in the pattern of a cross involving 4 squares and 2 opposition aspects. See Step 3 for more information. |

| Grand trine | Where three or more planets are in triangular relationship with each other – involving 3 trines in the pattern. See Step 3 for more information. |
|---|---|
| Heliocentric system/model | Sun-centred system. All the planets orbit the Sun (rather than the Earth as was believed up to mediaeval times). The system/model was devised by Nicolaus Copernicus and published in 1543. See Article 4 of the Bonus Pack for more information. |
| Hemisphere emphasis | In the birth-chart; where planets are counted above or below the Asc/Dsc angle; or east or west of the Mc/Ic angle. And the emphasis that places on interpretation. See Resource 3 of the Bonus Pack for more information. |
| Horoscope | An astrological forecast of a person's future. Or an antiquated name for a birth-chart. Not used so much in modern astrology, but popular in newspaper versions. |
| House systems | Each house system will have 12 segments. However how these segments are sized depends upon which house system is used. There are at least 16 house systems in use. A most popular one is Placidus or another is Equal House. See Step 4 to learn more about these systems. |
| Inner planets | In astrology the inner planets are Sun, Moon, Mercury, Venus and Mars. See Step 3 for more on inner planets. |
| Intermediate planets | What I am calling the "intermediate planets" are Jupiter and Saturn. See Step 3 for more information. |
| Major aspects | Conjunction, sextile, square, trine and opposition. I also include the quincunx. These are considered most important in the birth-chart. See Step 3 for more information. |
| Mesolithic | Middle Stone Age – around 12,000 plus years ago. Possible starting point for astrology. |
| Midheaven sign | Any one of the 12 signs on the midheaven (Mc) point at the time and place of birth. See Step 4 for more information. |
| Minor aspects | Generally given less importance in astrology. Examples are: semi-sextile, semi-square, sesquiquadrate, quintile, biquintile and decile. See Step 3 for more information. |
| Mutable signs | Gemini, Virgo, Sagittarius and Pisces. Mutable, changeable energy. See Step 2 for more information. |
| Natal astrology | Or Western natal astrology. Applying astrology to people. |
| New age | A broad movement offering alternative approaches to traditional Western culture. Areas of interest include spirituality, mysticism, astrology, holism, meditation, instrumental music, and environmental matters. See Article 2 in the Bonus Pack. |
| Nicolaus Copernicus | 1473-1543 Nicolaus Copernicus was a Renaissance a mathematician, astronomer, and Catholic canon, who formulated a model of the universe |

| | |
|---|---|
| | that placed the Sun, rather than Earth, at its centre. Discussed in Articles 4 and 5 in the Bonus Pack |
| Nodes | Refers to any pair of points that mark the intersection of two primary orbits, especially the orbit of the Earth and that of another planet or the Moon. The nodes of the Moon crossing the ecliptic are commonly used in astrology. See One Step Further for more on Moon nodes. |
| Northern Hemisphere | Half of the earth lying between the North Pole and the equator. |
| Ophiuchus Constellation | Known as the "thirteenth constellation." It crosses the ecliptic between Scorpio and Sagittarius. Used as an argument to discredit astrology, but astrology is built around the number 12 not constellations. |
| Outer planets | In astrology, Uranus, Neptune and Pluto. Jupiter and Saturn will commonly also be included. See Step 3 for more information. |
| Personal signs | Aries through to Cancer. See Step 2 for more information. |
| Planetary aspects | In astrology the relationship between planets (from the Earth's vantage point). See Major Aspects and Minor Aspects in Step 3. |
| Planetary exaltations | In traditional astrology planets are said to be exalted, or strengthened, in certain signs. For instance, Venus in Pisces or Mars in Capricorn. Arguably this has gone out of use in modern natal astrology. |
| Planetary patterns | These patterns refer to Marc Edmund Jones 7 patterns of broad planet configurations in birth-charts. See Resource 2 in the Bonus Pack. |
| Polarities in signs | Starting with Aries, signs run positive then negative, then positive and so on. See Step 2 for more information. |
| Precession of the Equinoxes | Due to gravitational pull of the Sun and Moon, the Earth wobbles, as it spins. As a result, the spring equinox (the start of the tropical zodiac) occurs a little earlier each year, when measured against the background stars. See Article 3 of the Bonus Pack. |
| Quadruplicities in signs | Starting from Aries the signs run cardinal, fixed and mutable – and repeat… Modes of energy. See Step 2 for more information. |
| Reading the birth-chart | Interpreting what is in a birth-chart. See Step 5 for more information. |
| Sign rulership | Planets are said to rule or be at home in certain signs. For instance, Mercury rules Gemini and Virgo, the Moon rules Cancer. See Step 3 for more information. |
| Signs Matrix | The component building blocks of the signs, i.e., polarities, triplicities and quadruplicities. These conditions also mean that each sign is unique in its matrix. See Step 2 for more information. |
| Social signs | Leo through to Scorpio. See Step 2 for more information. |
| Spring equinox | Opposite to the autumn equinox. The equinox in spring, on about 21 March in the northern hemisphere and 22 September in the southern hemisphere. It is when day and night are equal length, as the sun crosses the celestial equator in a northerly direction. See Step 2 for more information. |

| Star Constellations | In reference to astrology the 12 (or 13) star constellations of the zodiac belt (around the ecliptic). Star constellations are visual made-up patterns identified from ancient times. |
|---|---|
| Stellium | Three or more planets in the same sign – or (I'd argue) in the same house. See Step 5 for more information. |
| Summer solstice | The longest day – around the 21$^{st}$ June in northern hemisphere and the 21$^{st}$ December in the southern hemisphere. |
| Synchronicity | The simultaneous occurrence of events which appear significantly related but have no discernible causal connection. See Article 1 of the Bonus Pack. |
| T square | In planetary aspects three or more planets involving two (or more) in opposition aspect with a third (or more) square to the opposition. See Step 3 for more information. |
| The Angles | The Ascendant (Asc), Midheaven Mc), Descendant (Dsc) and Imum Coeli (Ic). The angles of an accurate birth-chart. See Step 4 for more information. |
| The Big Four | Name I've given to the Sun, Moon, Ascendant and Midheaven when being applied in a quick or broad reading of a birth-chart. See Step 5 for more information. |
| The Mars Effect | The Mars Effect is the statistical correlation between athletic eminence and the position of the planet Mars relative to the horizon at time and place of birth. It has also become the umbrella name for the huge research work (involving other planets) carried out by Michel and Francoise Gauquelin. It was first reported in *The Influence of the Stars* (1955) by Michel Gauquelin. Find out more about this research in Article 6 of the Bonus Pack. |
| Theosophist | Theosophy teaches that the purpose of human life is spiritual emancipation and claims that the human soul undergoes reincarnation upon bodily death according to a process of karma. Theosophist, a follower of the movement founded in 1875 as the Theosophical Society by Helena Blavatsky and Henry Steel Olcott. Relates to Alan Leo in Article 2 of the Bonus Pack. |
| Transpersonal signs | Sagittarius through to Pisces. See Step 2 for more information. |
| Triplicities | In astrology, groups of three signs belonging to the same element of Fire, Earth, Air or Water. See Step 2 for more information. |
| Tropical zodiac | Zodiac of 12 (symbolical) signs that are built on the Earth/Sun relationship. It ties in with the seasons and is most used in Western astrology. The other, sidereal zodiac, links with the star constellations in the zodiac belt. |
| Typical signs | In interpretation, a person may be described as "typical" where their Sun sign and at least one other major component, supporting the Sun |

| | |
|---|---|
| | sign, is also present to make it "typical." It may be the Moon is in the same sign as the Sun, or the Ascending sign is the same as the Sun sign. |
| Vedic astrology | Another name for Hindu or Indian astrology. The obvious difference between Vedic and Western astrology is that Vedic astrology draws on the sidereal zodiac – which is out by 24 degrees with the tropical zodiac – and the belief that the stars and planets do influence our lives and set our destiny. Vedic astrology does not include the trans-Saturn planets. |
| Weighting | In doing a chart reading; using the counting of components to decide where the emphasis lies for interpretation. For instance, if a person has a count of 8 in Negative Signs and a count of 12 in Positive Signs the emphasis leans towards, they having an outgoing extraverted personality – more so than introverted. See Step 5 for more information. |
| Western astrology | Astrology popularly used in the West. Greek design, based upon the tropical zodiac. Incorporates the planets of the solar system, 12 signs, and 12 houses. |
| Western zodiac | See Tropical zodiac and Zodiac. |
| Wheel of Samsara | In Eastern religions the continual cycle of life: birth, death, rebirth, death, rebirth etc. The Wheel represents what we are trapped in and need to break free of, move out of through awakening and creating wholesome karma. It is mentioned in Article 1 of the Bonus Pack |
| Winter solstice | The shortest day. Around 21$^{st}$ December in the northern hemisphere and around the 21$^{st}$ June in the southern hemisphere. |
| Yod pattern | Triangular aspect pattern involving at 3 (or more) planets. Planets A and B are forming quincunxes to planet C, and a sextile between themselves. Planet C becomes the main focal or stress point – also known as the Finger of God. Read more about this pattern in Step 3. |
| Zodiac | In Western astrology the (tropical) zodiac comprises of 12 signs each 30 degrees in length, beginning from the 1$^{st}$ Point of Aries – 21$^{st}$ March. See Step 2 for more information. |
| Zodiac belt | A belt around the heavens extending 9° on either side of the ecliptic (see Ecliptic circle). The orbits of the Moon and planets (except Pluto) also lie within this belt. |

# Index

About Western astrology.........................1
Air Signs..............................................69
Albert Einstein birth-chart...................173
Amelia Earhart Birth-chart..................214
Amy Winehouse birth-chart................220
Angles and Houses.................................6
Angles tree illustration........................139
Ascendant key ideas............................136
Aspects...................................................5
Aspects - common combinations.........116
Astrological progressions......................97
Astrological transits..............................96
Astrological Trends...............................95
Astrology - Polarities............................68
Astrology - Quadruplicities...................70
Astrology - the aspects........................110
Astrology - Triplicities..........................69
Astrology before software....................12
Astrology holistic & symbolical system...2
Astrology Software...............................13
Astrology used for..................................2
Astrology with software........................12
Atypical Aries.......................................44
Big four..............................................160
Bill Lomas birth-chart.............84, 123, 188
Billie Holiday birth-chart....................102
Birth moment........................................2
Birth-chart............................................7
Birth-chart - important document..........7
Birth-chart DFI....................................10
Birth-chart DIY....................................11
Birth-chart incorporates.......................32
Birth-chart needs.................................10
Birth-chart orchestra analogy.............236
Bonus Pack...........................................9
Born on the cusp.................................42

Bruce Lee Birth-chart.........................217
Cardinal Signs......................................70
Chart analysis counting system...........183
Chart analysis example.....35, 164, 169, 173
Chart analysis example................178, 188
Chart analysis running order...............184
Chart Ruler.................................101, 160
Coco Chanel birth-chart.....................103
Compensatory behaviour......................75
Course aims...........................................7
Course offers.........................................8
Course provides.....................................8
Course resources...................................9
Course schedule....................................8
Descendant key ideas..........................136
Earth Signs...........................................69
Elisabeth Kübler-Ross birth-chart..43, 151
Elizabeth Taylor birth-chart................169
Empty houses.....................................350
Ensoulment........................................231
Ephemeris - what it is..........................94
Equal house systems...........................146
Ernest Hemingway birth-chart..............11
Exampling Janus software....................14
Exampling Planetdance software..........19
Fire Signs.............................................69
Fixed Signs..........................................71
Four Elements in signs.........................69
Four House Systems with same chart..146
Grand Cross.......................................117
Grand Trine.......................................116
Handy House reference......................142
Higher purpose......................................6
House Systems...................................143
Houses as mundane zodiac.................134
How much data we need......................29

| | |
|---|---|
| Imum Coeli key ideas | 138 |
| Intermediate Planets | 106 |
| James Randy birth-chart | 2 |
| Jane Austen birth-chart | 121 |
| Janus software | 14 |
| Jimi Hendrix birth-chart | 158, 164 |
| Johannes Kepler | 236 |
| Key to Symbols | 24 |
| Know Your Self | 230 |
| Love unconditional | 81, 108, 284, 285, 301, 332 |
| Love for humanity | 283 |
| Main forms of astrology | 1 |
| Major Aspects | 112 |
| Marilyn Monroe birth-chart | 124 |
| Mary Baker Eddy birth-chart | 177 |
| Midheaven key ideas | 137 |
| Minor Aspects | 116 |
| Modern Western astrology | 1 |
| Moon nodes | 254 |
| Moon nodes astrologically | 255 |
| Moon nodes astronomically | 254 |
| Moon nodes in Signs and Houses | 257 |
| Mozart's birth-chart | 35 |
| Mutable Signs | 71 |
| Natal astrology | 1 |
| Negative Signs | 68 |
| Personal Planets | 105 |
| Personal signs | 73 |
| Planets | 5 |
| Pop astrology | 1 |
| Around since 1930s | 2 |
| Positive Negative signs | 68 |
| Positive Signs | 68 |
| Practice homework | 129 |
| Precession of the Equinoxes | 66 |
| Predictions | 98 |
| Pythagoras | 236 |
| Quadrant house system | 146 |
| Retrograde Planets | 25 |
| Roadmap for finding your Self | 7 |
| Ruling planets | 100 |
| Running Order of Signs | 72 |
| Shades of Pascal's Wager | 249 |
| Sidereal zodiac | 4 |
| Signs and Modes of Change | 70 |
| Signs Matrix | 66 |
| Signs order - Personal segment | 241 |
| Signs order - Social segment | 243 |
| Signs order - Transpersonal segment | 246 |
| Signs running order | 240 |
| Social signs | 74 |
| Software for Free | 18 |
| Software to buy | 13 |
| Solar Fire software | 14 |
| Solar System essential data | 92 |
| Soul and tests | 245 |
| Southern Hemisphere | 3 |
| Stars and asteroids | 3 |
| Stellium explained | 162 |
| T Square | 117 |
| The Angles | 135 |
| Transpersonal Planets | 107 |
| Transpersonal Signs | 74 |
| Traveller comments | 241 |
| Tropical zodiac | 4 |
| Tropical Zodiac | 65 |
| Two zodiacs | 4 |
| Typical Cancerian | 43 |
| Typical or atypical Sun sign | 41 |
| Typical Sign descriptions | 46 |
| Unaspected planets | 116 |
| Vincent van Gogh birth-chart | 44 |
| Water Signs | 69 |
| We know where we are | 28 |
| Weighting the planets | 182 |
| Western astrology defining | 2 |
| What astrology offers | 7 |
| Why many house systems | 144 |
| Why souls are here | 232 |
| Yod aspect | 118 |

Zodiac ............................................................ 3     Zodiac themes ........................................... 77

# Figs

1. Birth-chart of the magician James Randi p2
2. Astrological angles and houses p6
3. Birth-chart done for you example (Ernest Hemingway chart) p11
4. Janus 5.3 Opening screen p15
5. Janus 5.3 Setting up a birth-chart p16
6. Janus 5.3 The chart is cast p17
7. Planetdance Opening screen p19
8. Planetdance Setting up a birth-chart p20
9. Planetdance The birth-chart of Bill Lomas is cast p21
10. Key to astrological symbols used in the course p24
11. Example of too little information in the birth-chart …p29
12. Example of too much information in the birth-chart …p30
13. Example of enough information in the birth-chart …p31
14. All twelve zodiac signs illustrated p32
15. Ten or more planets illustrated p33
16. Twelve houses illustrated p33
17. The aspects illustrated p34
18. Mozart's birth-chart p35
19. Mozart's birth-chart with Moon in Sagittarius p36
20. Mozart's birth-chart with Gemini on the MC p38
21. Mozart's birth-chart with Sun, Mercury, Saturn and Neptune highlighted p39
22. Tropical Sun Sign dates of the year p42
23. Elisabeth Kubler-Ross birth-chart p43
24. Vincent Van Gogh birth-chart p44
25. The Tropical Zodiac - indicating seasons of the year …p65
26. Precession of the Equinoxes p66
27. Signs split into Positive and Negative p68
28. Signs split into their four elements p69
29. Signs split into their modes of change p70
30. All together signs matrix p72
31. The cyclic running order of the signs p73
32. Anne Frank's birth-chart p75
33. Solar system some essential data p93
34. Ephemeris example p94
35. George Michael birth-chart and transits for 25/12/2016 p97
36. Planet rulership of signs p100
37. Traditional conditions or Dignities p101
38. Billie Holiday birth-chart p102
39. Coco Chanel birth-chart p103
40. Andy Warhol birth-chart – aspects p110
41. Conjunction aspect p112
42. Square aspect p113
43. Sextile aspect p113
44. Trine aspect p114
45. Quincunx aspect p114
46. Opposition aspect p115
47. Grand Trine aspect p117
48. T square aspect p117
49. Grand Cross aspect p118
50. Yod aspect p118
51. Houses and meaning - hand-drawn p134
52. The Angles p135
53. Tree analogy for understanding the Angles p139
54. Angles and Houses p141
55. The Celestial Sphere p145
56. Examples of four House Systems p147
57. Jimi Hendrix birth-chart p158
58. Jimi Hendrix birth-chart - with aspect lines p164
59. Elizabeth Taylor birth-chart p169
60. Albert Einstein birth-chart p173
61. Mary Baker Eddy birth-chart p177
62. Bill Lomas birth-chart p188
63. Positive-Negative signs count for Bill Lomas p189
64. Element signs count for Bill Lomas p190
65. Mode signs count for Bill Lomas p192
66. The running order of the signs p240
67. The Moon's nodes astronomically p254
68. Moon nodes direction of travel in the chart p256

# About the author

Francis O'Neill writes on after-life, mind body & spirit, and astrology topics that he is passionate about.

As well as being a practicing astrologer, he has spent a good deal of his life in field archaeology, in the UK, and also as a lecturer in adult education.

He lives in the Cotswolds (UK) with his partner, the song writer and musician, Annie Locke.

His book, **Learn How to Read Your Birth-chart in 5 Steps** is a follow-on from the **Discover Proper Astrology** series.

> *Discover Proper Astrology is a series of six bitesize self-help books on discovering and applying Western astrology. The series is intended to redress the balance, and aid improving one's knowledge of modern Western astrology.*

# Find out more...

You can find out more about the writer's books, and his spiritual interests, by visiting the publisher website, SomeInspiration.com, where, like other online, and bricks & mortar stores, you can also buy a copy of these titles. The website also offers his books in less expensive PDF format.

### Reminder: Please leave a review ☺ **Thank you**

If you have found this book of interest and helpful, please leave a review at wherever you got it from. It could encourage others to read it, and it will certainly encourage the author to keep writing. All reviews are read and very much appreciated. Thank you for your support.

www.ingramcontent.com/pod-product-compliance
Lightning Source LLC
Chambersburg PA
CBHW081718100526
44591CB00016B/2410